**PEARSON**  ALWAYS LEARNING

# The Wayne Writer

Custom Edition for Wayne State University

Taken from:
*Scenes of Writing: Strategies for Composing
with Genres*
by Amy Devitt, Mary Jo Reiff, and Anis Bawarshi

*A Little Argument*, Second Edition
by Lester Faigley and Jack Selzer

*Having Your Say: Reading and Writing
Public Arguments*
by Davida H. Charney and Christine M. Neuwirth
with David S. Kaufer and Cheryl Geisler

Cover Art: Courtesy of Wayne State University

Taken from:

*Scenes of Writing: Strategies for Composing with Genres*
by Amy Devitt, Mary Jo Reiff, and Anis Bawarshi
Copyright © 2004 by Pearson Education, Inc.
Published by Longman
New York, New York 10036

*A Little Argument*, Second Edition
by Lester Faigley and Jack Selzer
Copyright © 2013, 2010 by Pearson Education, Inc.
Upper Saddle River, New Jersey 07458

*Having Your Say: Reading and Writing Public Arguments*
by Davida H. Charney and Chrsitine M. Neuwirth, with David S. Kaufer and
Cheryl Geisler
Copyright © 2006 by Pearson Education, Inc.
Published by Longman

Pearson Learning Solutions, 501 Boylston Street, Suite 900, Boston, MA 02116
A Pearson Education Company
www.pearsoned.com

Printed in the United States of America

5 6 7 8 9 10 V092 16 15 14


000200010271751863

MM

ISBN 10: 1-269-44110-8
ISBN 13: 978-1-269-44110-0

# Detailed Contents

# Introduction

Joe Paszek, Thomas Trimble, and Nicole Varty

> *Well, I don't have as much time to write as I used to,*
> *but in my life, writing has been an important exercise*
> *to clarify what I believe, what I see, what I care about,*
> *what my deepest values are [...] the process of convert-*
> *ing a jumble of thoughts into coherent sentences makes*
> *you ask tougher questions*
>
> —President Barack Obama

President Barack Obama's reflections on the importance of writing in his own life point to some of the core beliefs of writing teachers. While writing is often used to inform readers and present knowledge, writing also plays a fundamental role in the creation of knowledge through the use of writing to dialogue with others and in our questioning of what we know about ourselves and the world around us.

Wayne State's undergraduate composition sequence, which includes Basic Writing (ENG 1010), Introduction to College Writing (ENG 1020), and Intermediate Writing (ENG 3010), is designed to provide students with a toolbox of writing skills they will need to use in their lives as both scholars and citizens.

This textbook, which is designed to function as a common text for all three courses in the composition sequence, is based on a number of core assumptions about college-level writing and the best ways to teach and learn how to write.

### 1. There are many forms of writing.

This statement may seem obvious, but too often, both instructors and students have assumed that there is one definition of "good"

Courtesy of Wayne State University.

writing that applies to all situations. That assumption falls apart, however, when we consider the range of writing we use and come into contact with everyday. Just as the kind of language we use when emailing or texting friends is different than the language we use when communicating with a parent or employer, different situations and different disciplines within the university require very different styles and formats of writing. With that variety in mind, no single writing course can prepare students for all the different kinds of writing you will encounter at college. What a writing course can do, however, is provide you with a broad set of tools you can use to adapt their writing to the range of writing situations they will encounter in their courses.

### 2. Writing can be taught and learned.

It is not uncommon to hear people talk about writing as if it were a natural born talent that you either have or you don't. Years of writing studies research, however, has established that everyone has the capacity to write and that effective instruction can play a significant role in helping students become better writers. Just as importantly, research that has examined successful writing classrooms has established a broad set of best practices that can help you learn to write more effectively.

### 3. Learning is successful when students can take what they have learned and adapt those skills to new and unfamiliar situations.

The ability to take what you learn in one situation and adapt and apply that learning to a new situation is called *transfer*. Research on learning has established that students' ability to transfer knowledge is best achieved when they have a working knowledge of key writing studies concepts (*discourse community*, *genre*, and *rhetorical situation*) and are able to carefully *reflect* on these concepts in order to adapt previously learned skills and knowledge for a new writing task.

# The Wayne State Composition Sequence
## ENG 1010-BASIC WRITING

ENG 1010 provides you with extensive practice in the fundamentals of college writing and reading in preparation for ENG 1020.

## ENG 1020-INTRODUCTION TO COLLEGE WRITING

ENG 1020 fulfills the University's Basic Composition (BC) general education requirement. This course is designed to provide you with practice in a set of specific writing and reading skills you'll use in courses.

## ENG 3010-INTERMEDIATE WRITING

ENG 3010 is one of several courses that fulfills the University's Intermediate Composition (IC) general education requirement. The course is designed to provide you with opportunities to research the use of writing in your major.

# Some Key Terms

There are several key terms that inform our work in the composition sequence and build on our assumptions about writing and the teaching of writing. They are *discourse community, genre, rhetorical situation,* and *reflection.*

## DISCOURSE COMMUNITY

You'll notice that we use the term "discourse community" frequently in the composition course sequence. This term shows up in many disciplines, including linguistics, sociology and rhetoric and composition studies. Because it is multi-faceted and used across disciplines, "discourse community" is a complex term that can be tricky to define.

As you talk and read about discourse communities, you will see that we draw from a few key writing studies theorists for our working definition of the term, including John Swales, James Gee, Ann Johns and Ann Beaufort. Beaufort points to discourse communities as one of the key knowledge domains that students should understand in order to transfer knowledge effectively. In his article "The Concept of a Discourse Community," John Swales outlines six characteristics that define what a discourse community is, and how it differs from a speech community. James Gee, however, raises several complications in how we think about discourse communities, such as how an individual's first discourse community relates to those encountered later, and how one can truly belong in a discourse community.

Ann Johns further adds to the conversation by discussing conflict in and around discourse communities, noting that there can be tensions between an individual's identity and the "price of membership" within a discourse community. She argues that one must assess and understand member roles, goals and how genres work in a discourse community to effect change within that community. You'll develop a working definition from these writing studies theorists, and you'll notice that our attention to discourse communities grows sharper as it progresses from ENG 1010, to 1020, to 3010.

In ENG 1010, you'll tackle the basic knowledge of this key term and start to hone your awareness of discourse communities. Discourse communities are all around us. They function in all areas of life and lay the foundation for communication. In the assignments you'll complete in 1010, this awareness will take shape as you identify how authors write in and for discourse communities.

In ENG 1020, you'll work to identify personal, leisure and civic discourse communities that you are a part of, and you'll begin exploring those discourse communities, forming arguments for, in and about them. You'll integrate this growing knowledge into assignments by writing about discourse communities, using appropriate research methods to learn about them, and writing about your findings.

In ENG 3010, you'll turn your attention to professional and academic discourse communities rooted in the discipline you choose to pursue as someone majoring in that field and, later, as a professional. You'll do so by learning to understand and practice methods from either writing studies or your disciplinary community, which you'll use to develop a focused and sustained research project that investigates your professional and/or academic discourse community.

## GENRE

Genre is a term that many of you might have heard or used before when talking to your friends about movies, music, or novels. Often when we use *genre*, we refer to specific formula or characteristics that must be satisfied in order for a text to "fit" into that category. For instance, when we talk about a "horror" film we call to mind a movie genre that usually consists of scenes intended to frighten the viewer, often involving suspense and/or violence; supernatural threats of some kind (vampires, ghosts, preternatural beings—think Michael Meyers or Jason Voorhies); various music cues to heighten emotional response; and the list goes on.

In your ENG 1010, 1020, and 3010 courses, we talk about genres in a slightly different way. According to writing studies scholar Carolyn Miller (1984), genres can be seen as "'typified rhetorical actions' that respond to recurring situations and become instantiated in groups' behaviors" (158 qtd in Wardle 767). Or, to put it in more straightforward terms: genres are forms of writing for engaging in community activities. By understanding these social actions, we are able to participate more fully in those communities. Thus, in your classes, rather than focusing on only the content or the form of a piece of writing (as we would when discussing movie genres), we focus on the ways in which that piece of writing functions within a community and helps its members to achieve the goals, objectives, and actions of that community.

In ENG 1010, you will be introduced to some building blocks of genre, namely the idea that writing is intended to *do something*. For instance, when you write an email to your professor and when you send a text to one of your friends, you are writing to very different audiences, for very different purposes. By the end of ENG 1010, you should be aware that genres like these are intended to convey information to a specific person/community/group of people but use different strategies to do so.

In ENG 1020, you will begin by reading and writing familiar genres such as film reviews and persuasive essays to explore how different genres enact distinct social functions shaped by writers' rhetorical situations and discourse communities. From there, you will begin to read and write academic genres such as the argumentative essay and to experiment with adapting genres to achieve your own goals as writers and researchers.

In ENG 3010, you will move from thinking about communities where you have a certain amount of expertise (e.g., home and social communities) and focus on disciplinary and professional communities where you are new members. Being able to identify and analyze unfamiliar genres (written forms of social action that will help you to achieve the goals of your professional lives) is a vital skill that will help you develop expertise in your major courses and in workplace settings after college.

## RHETORICAL SITUATION

Writing Studies scholars use the term *rhetorical situation* to describe the interactions between persons, places, and things when people communicate. Describing the rhetorical situation of an interaction that involves written communication helps explain the creation, production, and use of a particular piece of writing. Elements of a text's rhetorical situation include the author, the audience, the text's purpose, and the events that inspired creation of the text (what some rhetorical scholars call the *exigence*). Understanding the rhetorical situation of any speech or writing event is not only important for readers. Writers must also understand the rhetorical situation in which they are working—including who they are writing for, what other texts or events readers will be thinking about about when they encounter their writing, and what special challenges they face as they engage difficult or controversial topics. As such, rhetorical situation provides an important set of tools and strategies for both readers and writers and is critical to the way we approach the teaching of writing at Wayne State.

In ENG 1010, you'll use the concept of rhetorical situation to read and study a variety of college-level texts, looking for authors' purposes and writers' use of language to communicate with their intended audiences. In your own writing, you'll use the concept of rhetorical situations to create awareness and to plan for writing as on ongoing conversation between you and your readers.

In ENG 1020, you'll use the concept of rhetorical situation to explore the relationship between situation and the language choices you make in your writing as you articulate claims and to try to prompt readers to take particular actions. By the end of ENG 1020, you'll use your understanding of rhetorical situation to plan and conduct research using academic sources in the construction of your own written arguments.

In ENG 3010, you'll use the concept of rhetorical situation to examine how writing is used in your major. You'll use rhetorical situation, together with the other key concepts in the course sequence, to consider the range of topics, audiences, goals, and ways of creating knowledge that are embedded in the specialized discourse communities of your major.

## REFLECTION/METACOGNITION

Reflection and metacognition are intertwined processes that together form a vibrant tool for writers. While reflection is often described as a skill or set of skills to practice, or "moves" to make, metacognition refers to the thinking that happens in and around those moves. Educational Researcher Gregory Schraw highlights the effect of metacognition on learning in this way, "metacognition is essential to successful learning because it enables individuals to better manage their cognitive skills, and to determine weaknesses that can be corrected by constructing new cognitive skills" (Schraw 123). Sandra Giles expands on this more specifically in regard to reflection's influence on understanding of the rhetorical situation, composition and revision processes in her article "Reflective Writing and the Revision Process: What Were You Thinking?":

> Reflection helps you to develop your intentions (purpose), figure out your relation to your audience, uncover possible problems with your individual writing process, set goals for revision, make decisions about language and style, and the list goes on (193).

In your ENG 1010, 1020 and 3010 courses, you will engage with reflection and metacognition in many different assignments, at various points in your writing process, and with slightly different purposes each time. Throughout your time practicing reflection, however, you will likely encounter three major types of reflection, drawn from writing studies scholar Kathleen Blake Yancey's 1998 book, *Reflection in the Writing Classroom*. Yancey presents reflection-in-action, constructive reflection and reflection-in-presentation as three main ways to conceive of reflection, and you may recognize all three as you encounter the Wayne State composition sequence.

Reflection-in-action is a mid-stride kind of reflection that asks you to take stock of your writing process as it's happening. You have the opportunity in this type of reflection to ask yourself "what's going on" and articulate that to yourself and your instructor (Yancey 42). Sandra Giles also talks about this kind of reflection as a tool you can use to gain distance from your own writing, to enable more critical thinking about your draft and to enable more effective revision. Reflection-in-action also enables the kind of metacognition that Negretti describes as "student writers' metacognitive awareness of how to adapt their strategies to achieve determinate rhetorical purposes and their ability to monitor and evaluate the successfulness of their texts" (Negretti 146). This type of reflection usually occurs in the midst of a single writing task, and assignments that ask you to engage in this type of reflection might be writer's logs, journals, draft letters, reader review or peer review letters, blogs or all of the above.

Constructive reflection is a type of reflection that Yancey describes as happening "between and among drafts" (51). In other words, you might be asked to look back over an entire unit or writing project that occurs over a chunk of time, and reflect on multiple writing tasks that built together to form the project or unit. This might translate into assignments like project reflection letters, course learning outcome reflections, or mid-term reflections.

Reflection-in-presentation is the final type of reflection Yancey outlines, and this takes a specific form in our ENG 1010, 1020 and 3010 courses. Yancey is describing a form of reflection that would help construct a final course portfolio, and here she aligns with Edward White, another writing studies scholar, who advocates portfolio grading in writing classes. Both Yancey and White support this kind of reflection for its ability to help students provide their own collection of and context for a semester of writing work. In a final portfolio you might write for one of your composition courses, you could be asked to provide a collection of your work from over the course of the semester, selecting examples that demonstrate your learning in particular areas. You will be asked to compose a reflective argument that describes the relationships between your selected pieces and the learning you think they represent.

# Closing Remarks

In the chapters that follow, you will see *discourse community, genre, rhetorical situation* and *reflection/metacognition* reappear in various forms. Your instructors in ENG 1010, 1020 and 3010 will be leading you through assignments designed to help you practice wielding these tools in your writing, so that you, too, can clarify what you believe, care about, and value in the academy and beyond.

## WORKS CITED

Beaufort, Anne. *College Writing and Beyond: A New Framework for College Writing Instruction.* Logan, UT: Utah State UP, 2007.

Gee, James Paul. "Literacy, Discourse, and Linguistics: Introduction." *Journal of Education.* 17.1 (1989): 5–17. (also in Downs and Wardle's *Writing about Writing: A College Reader,* 481–95)

Giles, Sandra L. "Reflective Writing and the Revision Process: What Were You Thinking?" *Writing Spaces: Reading on Writing,* Vol. 1. Eds. Charles Lowe & Pavel Zemliansky. West Lafayette, IN: Parlor Press, 2010. 191–204. Print.

Johns, Ann M. "Discourse Communities and Communities of Practice: Membership, Conflict, and Diversity." *Text, Role, and Context: Developing Academic Literacies.* Cambridge, New York: Cambridge UP, 1997. 51–70. (also in Downs and Wardle's *Writing about Writing: A College Reader,* 498–518)

Miller, Carolyn. "Genre as Social Action." *Quarterly Journal of Speech* 70 (1984): 151–67.

Negretti, Raffaella. "Metacognition in Student Academic Writing: A Longitudinal Study of Metacognitive Awareness and Its Relation to Task Perception, Self-Regulation, and Evaluation of Performance." *Written Communication* 29:142 (2012).

Schraw, Gregory. "Promoting Metacognitive Awareness." *Instructional Science* 26 (1998): 113–25.

Swales, John. "The Concept of Discourse Community." *Genre Analysis: English in Academic and Research Settings.* Boston: Cambridge UP, 1990. 21–32. (also in Downs and Wardle's *Writing About Writing: A College Reader,* 466–80)

Wardle, Elizabeth. "'Mutt Genres' and the Goal of FYC: Can We Help Students Write the Genres of the University?" *CCC* 60.4 (2009): 765–789.

White, Edward. "The Scoring of Writing Portfolios: Phase 2." *CCC* 56.4 (2005): 581–600.

Yancey, Kathleen Blake. *Reflection in the Writing Classroom.* Logan, UT: Utah State UP, 1998.

# Basic Writing: An ENG 1010 Overview
## Gwen Gorzelsky and Amy Metcalf

One important way to write more effectively is to understand what type of writing you need to do for a particular situation or assignment. There are several types of writing used in nearly all professions and academic majors and also used in real-life situations like job search cover letters, internship applications, a proposal to start a new student organization or serve as a professor's research assistant, complaint letters and business reports. Although each type of writing can look different depending on the purpose for which you're using it, certain types have a central purpose that cuts across many writing situations. Further, some of them can be combined. For instance, writers often build on a summary to draft a response, on a response to draft an analysis, and on all three to draft an argument. Here are some of the most important types that span many writing situations:

**Summary** explains information, plans, and others' ideas or arguments concisely. Summaries are used in cover letters and complaint letters, all kinds of applications and proposals, and all academic majors. (Please see the chapter on summary for a fuller explanation of what summary is and how to write it.)

**Response** provides the writer's position on information, proposals, and others' ideas or arguments, usually so the writer can enter a larger conversation about the topic discussed in the text to which he or she is responding. Responses appear in business letters responding to a request or complaint, letters to the editor, and academic majors in the social sciences and humanities. (Please see the chapter on response for a fuller explanation of what response is and how to write it.)

**Analysis** examines an argument or set of information by looking closely at each piece and how the pieces fit together, usually to evaluate the entire argument or set of information. Arguments appear in evaluations of business proposals; businesses' materials for clients (like market analyses); and all academic majors. (Please see the chapter on analysis for a fuller explanation of what analysis is and how to write it.)

**Argument** often combines each of the other types of writing to persuade readers to do something. Argument is used in all kinds of proposals, many kinds of applications, cover letters and complaint letters, letters to the editor, and all academic majors. (Please see the chapter on ENG 1020 for more explanation of argument.)

ENG 1010 will help you make your writing more effective by guiding you through a set of writing projects in which you'll practice these types of writing. To complete these projects, you'll begin working with the key concepts and practices described in the introduction to this book: **discourse community**, **genre**, **rhetorical situation**, and metacognitive **reflection** on your own thinking and learning strategies. (Please see the introduction for definition of each concept.)

One important component of this work is developing effective reading and annotation strategies that will help you to write more effectively. Reading the types of texts (or genres) used to accomplish people's goals in a particular setting (or discourse community) is a crucial means of learning about the values, attitudes, beliefs, and perspectives common in that community. You'll need to understand those aspects of any discourse community in which you're writing, whether you're writing a post for a blog on professional ice hockey, drafting a letter to apply for an internship, or writing an argument paper for a philosophy course. While there are many discourse communities within a university (usually at least one for each discipline or academic major), there are certain features many academic discourse communities have in common, such as an emphasis on accurate representations of known facts, the various positions on a given issue, and other writers' arguments.

In ENG 1010, you'll learn about these common features so you're prepared to succeed in your next general education writing course. That course is ENG 1020, often known as freshman writing, and it builds on ENG 1010. But ENG 1010 prepares you for your other college courses as well. You'll begin learning to analyze the rhetorical situation that shapes specific writing tasks. You'll consider what different kinds of writing choices you'll need to make when writing different types of texts for different purposes and audiences. For instance, a sociology professor may ask you to read and summarize several articles on the possible causes of teen pregnancy. Your professor would expect you to write one type of summary as part of an argument paper for the course. She would expect you to write a different type if she asked you to use the same articles to develop a brochure advising teens on how to avoid an unwanted pregnancy. To develop a stronger understanding of how well your writing choices and writing process are working, you'll write reflections. Your reflections will discuss both the projects you write in ENG 1010 and the process of reading, thinking, and writing you used to draft these projects.

As you complete your assignments for the course, you'll learn about each key concept and how it functions in academic texts -- including your own. Here are some of the primary kinds of work you'll do:

- recognize examples of each genre, or type of writing;
- identify the key concepts related to it;
- learn how other writers use the key concepts;
- start learning to use the key concepts in your own writing.

All of this work will prepare you to succeed in ENG 1020, which focuses on writing arguments in discourse communities both in and outside academia, especially public discourse communities like those that discuss political life, culture, and local issues. Because ENG 1020 requires you to write each of the genres covered in ENG 1010, your work with those genres in this course will help you succeed in 1020.

# Introductory College Writing: An ENG 1020 Overview
## JEFF PRUCHNIC

In ENG 1020 you'll apply the Wayne State writing curriculum's core emphases of **discourse community, genre, rhetorical situation,** and **metcognition/reflection** to written and multimedia works focused on specific audiences, such as your classmates, academic and professional audiences of various types, or civic communities you might belong to or wish to influence in a particular way. (Please see the introduction for definitions of *discourse community, genre, rhetorical situation,* and *metacognition/ reflection.)* While, as with all of the courses in the Wayne State required writing sequence, mechanical correctness and appropriate academic writing styles are a key concern, in ENG 1020 you'll also concentrate specifically on rhetoric (or persuasion) and argument as major objective of many important kinds of writing you may be asked to produce. By focusing on rhetoric and on audience, assignments in ENG 1020 will require you do two major types of work. In one type, you'll analyze a particular piece of argumentative discourse to determine how it succeeds (or fails) to appropriately impact its audience. In another type, you'll choose a particular issue and a relevant audience for that issue and then argue for a certain point or for a certain action to be taken by that audience.

Work in 1020 often takes place through the following key writing tasks, several of which might serve as long-term projects in your 1020 course:

**Genre and Subgenre Analysis:** Whether we are talking about Internet memes, restaurant menus, or lab reports, there will be elements of a given genre that appear in all examples of it, as well as many that only appear in particular types—or subgenres—within it. Analyzing the subgenres within a particular genre will help you prepare to write in that genre. By doing subgenre analysis, you'll learn what rhetorical and mechanical elements are necessary for the parent genre's audiences, as well as where there is room to innovate within it.

**Genre Critique:** Genres often serve different functions for different audiences. Consider, to anticipate one of the examples used later in this textbook, the evaluation form (or "report card") often used in K-12 classrooms. This genre has highly specific formal features, but these features are used, and affect, differently the various audiences they served (parents, students, teachers, school officials, statewide education assessment organizations). In critiquing genres, you'll learn how single genres serve multiple audiences, as well as the strengths and limitations of common genres as they impact different communities.

**Researched Position Arguments**: There are writing tasks that will require you to research other scholars' and writers' work in order to cite them as authorities, and there are other tasks that will require you to contextualize your own arguments within the viewpoints of others, and to describe, specifically, whether and how you agree or disagree with prominent perspectives on a particular issue. In writing researched position papers, you'll execute both of these tasks by demonstrating your knowledge about the practical matters of a specific issues as well as current arguments and viewpoints surrounding it. By positioning your own arguments among these other viewpoints, you can most effectively convince your audience that your arguments are both fact-based and responsive to the various disagreements surrounding an issue.

**Rhetorical Analysis:** Whether we are talking about a recent editorial on a heated political issue, a contemporary car commercial, or the music video for a new hip hop artist, almost every act of communication can be analyzed as making a particular argument (trying to convince its receives of something) and as focused on moving a specific and identifiable audience. By studying how other authors adapt their argumentative strategies to their specific audiences, you'll learn how you can analyze your own prospective audiences and make the right moves to reach them through written and multimedia discourse.

**Definition Analysis and Argument:** Arguments about definition (what a particular term means, or whether or not a particular object or event is captured or referenced by a specific term) are at the basis of a surprisingly large amount of disagreements in contemporary political and cultural life. For instance, while they may not always immediately appear as such, many long-standing and polarizing debates in current American culture focus on arguments about definition, for instance, defining the meaning of "cruel and unusual punishment" in arguments about the death penalty or whether marijuana should be classified as a narcotic, a medicine, or simply an inebriating substance like liquor. Similarly, important debates and cultural shifts are often signaled by the changing definition of a particular term (such as "feminism" or "patriotism"). Finally, complicated definitions, or terms that require highly specialized explanations, are often problematic when considered from the points of view of multiple audiences. In performing definition analyses and arguments, you'll work toward applying definitions to "hard cases," explaining specialized definitions for less-specialized audiences, and arguing for why one version of a definition is superior to others for a particular purpose.

**Proposal Arguments:** Whether we are discussing marriage proposals, grant applications, or ballots promoting a change in existing local or federal laws, proposals are arguments in which an author attempts to convince an audience to perform a particular action or indicate their support for some course of action as opposed to others. In analyzing and crafting your own proposals in ENG 1020, you'll learn how to appeal to the common ground you share with an audience, as well as the common rhetorical features of proposal as a genre (such as the importance of outlining the positive and negative consequence of undertaking, or not undertaking, an action being proposed). In doing so, you'll master one of the most common genres in argumentative writing as it occurs in academic, civic, and professional realms.

Through effectively executing assignments and major projects based on these rhetorical tasks, you'll develop the following the following core competencies:

- analyzing and adapting your writing style and rhetorical strategies to most effectively influence specific audiences to which you are writing;

- understanding and replicating the key common features of the discourse communities and written genres you have analyzed;

- synthesizing multiple points of view by summarizing others' arguments and demonstrating where, how, and to what degree they complement or contradict each other; and

- making effective use of available research, as well as available communication technologies and media, in crafting persuasive arguments about contemporary issues and controversies.

Your work in 1020 will help prepare you for the wide variety of analyses and arguments you will be asked to produce in your academic courses in fields other than English, as well as the wide variety of writing tasks you might face at your current job or as a member of various civic communities or groups. ENG 1020 also serves as preparation for your next course in the required Wayne State writing curriculum, whether it be ENG 3010 (Intermediate Writing) or ENG 3050 (Technical Communication I). In both of these courses you will be asked to take what you've learned about audience and genre analysis and use those skills to study the discourse communities associated with your chosen career.

# Intermediate Writing: An ENG 3010 Overview
## GWEN GORZELSKY, JOE PASZEK, JULE WALLIS

# "Good" Writing Is Context Specific

One of the challenges of learning to write effectively in various college courses (and other settings) is that what counts as "good writing" differs from one situation to another. There are obvious differences, for instance, the fact that the question, "u @ school?" uses the right tone and conventions for a text message to a friend but not for an email to an instructor, who probably expects a formal opening and closing, correct sentence structure and grammar, and a clear, concisely stated reason for the message. But there are less obvious--and even more significant--examples. Various disciplines, from chemistry to criminal justice, have different standards for scholars' writing. As a result, you need to learn how to meet these varying standards, which can be quite diverse from one discipline to another. While "good writing" tends to have some important similarities across contexts, such as key points expressed clearly and concisely in language accessible to the target audience, what each audience defines as important, clear, and well written varies quite a bit. For example, the articles in a journal that publishes studies by biology researchers look very different from the articles in a journal that publishes scholarly essays by philosophers. Each journal will require different types of thesis statements, evidence, logical reasoning, and rhetorical moves to establish the writer's credentials, or **ethos.** (Please see chapter 25, "Using Genres to Read Scenes of Writing," for further discussion of **ethos**).

Similarly, the writing done by clinical practitioners like occupational or physical therapists or speech/language pathologists is quite different from that done by marketing professionals or accountants. That's why it sometimes seems like teachers' expectations for students' writing are personal preferences. While it's understandable that it might look this way from a student's-eye view, a bird's-eye-view of writing in college, the professions, and other contexts shows that different expectations for writing don't result from instructors' individual differences but instead from differences in academic disciplines (or majors), professional background, and the like.

The different academic, professional, civic, and leisure contexts where writing is done are known as **discourse communities**, and each one has its own set of **genres**, or types of writing; purposes for writing and related activities, like reading and discussion; subject matter knowledge, like drug interaction information for pharmacists or tax laws for accountants; rhetorical knowledge, or understanding of how to motivate readers in this discourse community; and writing process knowledge, or strategies for producing different types of texts. (Please see the introduction for a definition of the terms *discourse community* and *genre*). Discourse communities can be academic disciplines, like history; professions, like nursing; civic groups, like the Lion's Club; or interest, leisure, or religious groups, like antique collectors, gamers, or inter-faith organizations. To make matters even more complicated, each academic discipline and profession requires different genres, or types of writing. A retail manager will probably need to compose personnel evaluations, business plans, and proposals, while a teacher will need to draft lesson plans, student assessments, and curriculum rationales.

Thus the context in which a writer is producing a text and the type of text being composed play a large part in determining what the audience will expect from the text in terms of information, evidence, reasoning, format, and style. But the **rhetorical situation**--the specific purpose, circumstances, and audience for a particular text--determines how the writer must craft each of these features to ensure that the text accomplishes the writer's goal. (Please see the introduction for a definition of the term *rhetorical situation*). For instance, a school principal writing a memo to school district administrators to seek help addressing risks posed by security issues in her building might emphasize objective explanations of relevant circumstances like inadequate locks, choose professional terms for conveying the problem, and take a tone of some urgency. The same principal writing about this issue to parents might emphasize staff commitment to keeping students safe, use language that appeals to positive emotions, and take a reassuring tone. The challenge for college students and others learning to write in diverse academic courses and professional, civic, and other contexts is learning strategies for understanding each new context and how to write effectively in it.

## GOALS OF ENG 3010

To help you develop such strategies for learning to write in varying contexts and for using different types of writing to pursue diverse purposes, ENG 3010 emphasizes some of the key concepts introduced just above (and earlier in this book). You'll learn what a discourse community is and some of the more prominent--and sometimes conflicting--ideas about how discourse communities work. Even more importantly, you'll learn how to analyze a discourse community likely to be significant for you, probably one associated with your academic major or future profession. You'll learn to identify different genres and what they're used to do in your discourse community, as well as how to analyze a specific rhetorical situation.

This work will help you see how others' texts attempt to accomplish particular purposes given their rhetorical situations so you can craft your own texts to achieve your goals no matter what rhetorical situation you face. It will also help you to achieve learning outcome #1 for this course: "Produce writing that demonstrates [your] ability to identify, describe, and analyze various occasions for writing, genres, conventions, and audiences in [your] discipline or profession from a rhetorical perspective." The assignments you complete to accomplish this outcome will build toward a semester project that asks you to show what you've learned about writing in your discourse community, which will help you achieve learning outcome #2: "Produce an extended writing project that uses research methods and research genres to explore a topic applicable to the course and that draws substantively on concepts from primary AND/OR secondary sources."

Just as importantly, you'll learn approaches that will help you identify and fine-tune your own cognitive strategies so you can undertake such writing tasks more effectively. To do that, you'll complete a set of reflective assignments linked to major projects for the course and culminating in a reflective argument that analyzes your own earlier writing to show how you've met course learning outcomes. These reflective assignments will focus not so much on your emotional responses or personal experience but rather on a critical analysis of your reading, thinking, and writing strategies and of your own texts. Writing them will help you achieve learning outcome #4: "Produce writing that shows how you used **reflection** to make choices and changes in your writing and that explains how you would use reflection and the other skills taught in this course to approach a completely new writing task." (Please see the introduction for a definition of *reflection)*.

## Two Approaches: Writing About Writing and Writing Across the Curriculum

Writing Studies scholars believe that writing is a way of knowing and learning. Writing helps you develop critical thinking, analysis, application of ideas, and other higher level thinking skills. Writing Across the Curriculum (WAC), Writing in the Disciplines (WID), and Writing About Writing (WAW) are approaches to writing instruction that can enable you to build on key concepts and ideas from ENG 1020. WAC/WID and WAW assignments give you an opportunity to develop your writing skills for particular contexts, purposes, and audiences.

Eventually, when you move into disciplinary courses in your major, you'll be asked to write for very specific audiences and purposes. Writing Across the Curriculum/Writing In the Discipline and WAW demonstrate how writing is used in varying ways for varying purposes; how writing can help to develop ideas and expand knowledge; and how writing serves social goals and thus changes depending upon the desired outcome, audience, and context for a particular text.

In ENG 3010, you'll learn how stylistic conventions and disciplinary genres work, whether your course takes a WAC/WID or WAW approach. Many WAC/WID and WAW writing assignments are analytical or research-based (for instance, reflections, ethnographies, interview reports, research reports, literature reviews, and research proposals). Many of these assignments ask you to observe some site of writing or literacy to analyze the writing-related practices used there. Reflection is integrated into both WAC/WID and WAW curricula. Reflection encourages transfer of writing skills to various contexts, purposes, genres, and audiences by asking you to consider how to write for such various scenarios. That is, it asks you to explain how you'll be likely to use writing for different writing tasks with different rhetorical situations, especially academic and professional contexts.

The following similarities highlight how both WAC/WID and WAW use writing in the disciplines to help you accomplish the core objectives of ENG 3010. Both approaches will help you do the following:

- explore the writing practices of your major/professional community;
- explore key concepts of discourse community and genre;
- develop strategies for learning to learn and for using metacognitive thinking to write more effectively;

- critique and change a discourse community from an informed, insider position;
- use group work and discussion to better understand similarities and differences between the majors/professions.

Both WAC/WID and WAW ask you to practice the writing process and to use writing for social purposes. In both approaches, you'll draw on your specific disciplinary area (your major) to develop a semester-long research project for the course. To accomplish this goal, you'll develop your existing writing process to meet the needs of this assignment. In doing so, you'll fulfill course learning outcome #3: "produce writing that shows use of a flexible writing process (generating ideas, drafting, substantive revision, and editing) and shows [your] ability to adapt this process for different writing situations and tasks." In both WAC/WID and WAW approaches, each assignment builds on knowledge you've already developed to help you expand and adapt writing strategies for a variety of situations and tasks.

While both approach ask you to learn to write about arguments conducted *in* your major and *for* your major, the WAW approach uses tools from writing studies to help you do this, especially some of its research methods and key concepts. This approach asks you to write for an audience of writing studies readers, while the WAC/WID approach asks you to write for an audience in your major.

## WRITING ACROSS THE CURRICULUM/ WRITING IN THE DISCIPLINES

In the WAC/WID ENG 3010 course, you'll investigate the particular conventions, rules, and genres of the discourse community in your discipline in order to write a research project for an audience in this field. To help you do this, WAC/WID will teach you to analyze genres and practices in your discipline by looking at writing in your own major or profession, as well as writing from other majors and professions. As you become familiar with particular disciplinary terminology and concepts, you'll complete "learn-to-write" assignments in which you'll practice the genres and conventions used in the discourse community of your major or profession.

## Writing About Writing

In the WAW approach, you'll investigate the particular conventions, rules, and genres of the discourse community in your discipline to learn what purposes they serve and how they accomplish these purposes. To help you do this, WAW provides concepts from writing studies. Using these concepts, you'll analyze how writing is done in your major or profession. You'll learn to analyze genres and practices in unfamiliar writing situations, whether in academic courses, professional settings, or other contexts. Like WAC/WID, WAW encourages you to read, write, and research your particular discourse community. However, WAW instructors will not ask you to write for an audience in your discipline. Instead, you'll examine the various genres your discipline uses to learn what goals these genres accomplish and how they do so.

## ENG 3010 in the General Education Curriculum

If you took ENG 1020 at Wayne State, you probably examined writing in civic and leisure discourse communities. For example, you might have investigated a discourse community where you participated often (such as a sports team, a church group, an online gaming community, or a part-time job). Or you might have analyzed and researched civic issues in Detroit as a part of a semester-long writing project. You probably learned about the concepts of discourse communities, genre, rhetorical situations, and reflection in order to conduct rhetorical analysis. By the end of the semester, you'd developed strong skills in rhetorical and genre analysis and honed your writing process, research skills, and use of reflection to critically analyze your own work.

In ENG 3010 you'll extend the rhetorical skills taught in ENG 1020 and apply this knowledge by producing an argument *about* the writing practices of your major or profession. While there is a much greater emphasis on research within ENG 3010, key skills learned in ENG 1020 transfer over to required assignments in ENG 3010. ENG 3010 asks students to do the following work:

- *Analyze writing in your major.* You'll build on academic reading skills introduced in ENG 1020 to accomplish this goal.

- *Recognize key features of the types of writing done in the specific discourse community of your discipline or profession.* To meet this goal, you'll use what you learned from doing genre analysis in ENG 1020.

- *Interview an expert in your field.* Extending research and writing skills acquired in ENG 1020 will allow you to accomplish this objective.

- *Develop an extended research project.* To complete this project, you'll use concepts introduced in ENG 1020, including genre, writing, research, and knowledge conventions for a specific discourse community.

- *Reflect on writing.* You'll build on the reflection done in ENG 1020 to critically assess your texts and writing processes in ENG 3010.

By doing this work, you'll extend the skills taught in ENG 1020 to investigate writing in your major or profession. In doing so, you'll use primary and secondary research, as well as rhetorical analysis, to learn about the genres, conventions, research skills, and rhetorical situations in the discourse community of your discipline or profession.

## WORKS CITED

Bazerman. Charles. *Shaping Written Knowledge: The Genre and Activity of the Experimental Article in Science.* Madison: U of Wisconsin Press, 1998. Print.

Wardle, Elizabeth and Doug Downs. "Reimagining the Nature of FYC: Trends in Writing-about-Writing Pedagogies." *Exploring Composition Studies: Sites, Issues, and Perspectives.* Ed. Kelly Ritter and Paul Kei Matsuda. Logan, UT: Utah State University Press, 2012. 123-44. Print.

McLeod, Susan H., et al. *WAC for the New Millennium: Strategies for Continuing Writing-Across-the-Curriculum Programs.* Urbana: NCTE, 2001. Print.

# Writing Process in the Digital Age
## NICOLE WILSON

## Understanding the Writing Process

Whether we like it or not, writing is a process, and writing takes time. We can tell ourselves that we do our best work under pressure or that in the past we have been able to successfully turn in a first draft, but as we continue on our academic path, the reality is that we must put effort into our writing.

Different teachers and textbooks will break up the writing process differently. Here we will look at the three main stages in the writing process: prewriting, writing, re-writing. It is tempting to skip the first step and just dive into writing, but what you will find is that some form of pre-writing should occur, that the more time you spend on the first stage, the less time you will have to spend on the subsequent stages, and that different steps in the writing process can fit into the various stages.

When writing studies scholars study the writing process in students, they consistently make two main observations. The first is that no two writers follow the exact same process. For example, a search for "authors' writing process" on YouTube or Dailymotion will reveal several nuanced ways of producing writing. These video interviews demonstrate that instead of following a singularly prescribed method, we all need to interpret the writing process for ourselves and discover how we are the most productive as writers. The second is that the more we discover, both about our topics and about ourselves as writers, the more our writing changes. Rather than maintaining a rigid writing process, we must be willing to evaluate regularly how and why we write as well as to realize that as our knowledge base grows, our writing strategies might need to change as well. This change might be a result of feedback we receive from others or from changing academic or professional expectations of our writing. Regardless of why we might want to revisit our writing process, the goal of this chapter is to explore the fluid possibilities of the traditional writing process. This chapter looks at the three main stages of the writing process and labels them as prewriting, writing, and rewriting. However, unlike some linear explanations of the process, this chapter does not limit the order of the steps. Instead, it asks you to consider that sometimes rewriting is occurring simultaneously with writing, as we rewrite sentences before creating new ones, and at other times prewriting is revisited while rewriting because we want to brainstorm ways to flesh out a current section of a paper. The names of these stages follow traditional organizational patterns; however, they do not occur in the same order for most.

# Consider Ways to Personalize the Writing Process

As you think about how to make the writing process work for you, it is important to reflect on how you have been taught to write in the past. You will want to consider both how you have been taught and different papers you have written.

Some things to consider as you revise your writing process are:

- Which steps in the writing process have different instructors emphasized with you?
- Which steps in the process do you enjoy the most?
- Which steps do you dread?
- Which steps help you most in defining your ideas for a paper?

- Which help you most in organizing your papers?
- Which help you most in proofreading and editing effectively?
- Which paper that you have written in the past is the paper you are the most proud of?
- What makes you proud of that paper? Was it the grade? Was it the way you wrote it? Was it the way it all came together?
- What types of steps did you take to write that paper?
- What might you have done to make that paper better?
- Have you ever experienced writer's block? What caused it?
- What did you do to overcome it?

Most writers experience some type of writer's block. It is important to consider when you have gotten blocked in the past so that you can take steps to avoid that or plan around it. For example, if you need pressure to write, create a writing group among peers and give yourselves an earlier deadline to submit drafts of your paper to one another. Or, if you find yourself caught up in fixing mechanical errors, try throwing a towel over your screen so you cannot see what you type. The important thing is to realize that for some, writer's block is part of the process, and we need to be able to plan to work through it rather than be stopped by it.

In your Wayne State courses, you will be expected to **reflect** on your writing and how the learning objectives for that course have helped your further your skills as a writer. (See the introduction for an explanation of *reflection.*) Personalizing your writing process and understanding how you write before you start a new project will help you analyze how your writing evolves from course to course.

# Prewriting

The prewriting stage includes all of the activities a writer might complete before actually starting to write. This includes brainstorming, doing research, and developing an organizational pattern for the essay.

## BRAINSTORMING

Brainstorming can be both formal and informal. We can think about topics while surfing online, driving, or doing mundane tasks around the house. We can also brainstorm with a pad of paper or a word processing program through writing lists or making mind maps as we trace our thoughts from topic to topic. While we brainstorm we want to consider what we know about our topic as well as what we would like to learn about it. It can be helpful to make visual connections about topics as well through clustering.

We often think once we have our topic, we are finished brainstorming, but that is not the case. Brainstorming helps us develop our sense of the **rhetorical situation** (purpose, tone, audience, and content). This is the time we want to think about our audience/**discourse community** and what we will need in order to effectively reach that audience. (See the introduction for fuller explanations of *rhetorical situation* and *discourse community*.) It is also the time we figure out our purpose for writing. Knowing our purpose will also help us to know what types of research we might need. Purpose and audience together help us determine the logos (logic), pathos (emotion), ethos (credibility) ratio that will be needed for an effective paper. (See chapter 2, "Using Genres to Read Scences of Writing," for a fuller explanation of logos, pathos, and ethos.)

This is also where we will consider the **genre** of our paper. (See the introduction for a fuller explanation of genre.) Depending on which course, ENG 1010, 1020, or 3010, different genres will be used. As you pay attention to your audience, you want to pay attention to which genre will be most useful for reaching that audience. You will also want to be aware of how different genres use research. For example, summary papers use only one source; whereas argument papers use multiple sources.

In addition, brainstorming is not simply picking a topic. Brainstorming also involves considering the span and stases of our project. We can begin by asking ourselves a few key questions.

*ENG 1010*

- What is the issue I want to discuss?
- How do I define the issue?
- Why is this issue important to me?
- What problem(s) does this issue cause?
- Is there a solution?

*ENG 1020*

- What is the issue I want to discuss? How can I focus this issue on my community?
- How does a public community define the issue?

- Why is this issue important to my community?
- What problem(s) in my community are caused by this issue?
- How are people working to solve this problem?

*ENG 3010*

- What is the issue I want to discuss? How does this issue affect my academic and/or professional development?
- How do others in my discourse community define this issue?
- Does/Will my academic and/or professional discourse community see this as an important issue?
- What do I perceive as the problems surrounding this issue? What gaps do I see in the conversations others are having?
- Do I think there is a viable solution to this problem? Can I provide a fresh perspective to previously failed solutions?

Once we have answered these questions as well as the questions our instructors want us to consider, we are ready to being to do research, when it is required.

## DOING RESEARCH

Research can be one of the most time-intensive parts of the writing process. It is also one activity that writers often try to shortcut as much as possible. But while doing quality research might take you a little time, it will make for a higher quality paper. If you are unfamiliar with the research process, the WSU library liaison has put together research guides on the library homepage. The guides most suited for English courses (ENG 1010/1020, ENG 3010, ENG 3050/3060) can be found at http://guides.lib.wayne.edu/English. There are also additional guides on the library website for other departments and research interests.

The key to effective research is remembering that it is more than typing a few keywords into a search engine and hoping to get lucky and find reliable information about a particular topic. Initial research involves looking for the answers to the questions we asked in our brainstorming session, and advanced research involves investigating the gaps we find in the discourse community. Because research can be time consuming, it is important to work at it effectively. Therefore, our first responsibility is to pay attention to the requirements for each course and the research that different disciplines require.

As you begin to select and evaluate your research, you will want to determine what is the most appropriate tier of research given your audience and purpose and into which tier your information fits. Tier I research is scholarly sources. These are found in peer-reviewed books and journals. Tier I research is produced by researchers in an academic discipline, and it includes both primary research (studies, surveys, experiments) and secondary research (evaluation and analysis of primary research). Tier I research thoroughly documents sources and provides the kind of evidence and background expected by discourse community members. It has an academic audience and is the most reliable. Tier II research is produced by professionals in the field. This research is well documented and may include both primary and secondary research. The biggest distinctions between Tier I research and Tier II research are audience and reliability. Tier II research is not peer reviewed and seeks to reach a professional audience rather than an academic one. Tier II research includes books and some informational websites by organizations or the government. Tier II research acknowledges its sources and when reliably published is credible. Tier III research is accountable popular press. Tier III research seeks to provide the general public with information. Tier III sources mention research but often do not properly reference those sources. Tier III sources are newspapers, news magazines, and some informational websites. Tier IV sources are opinion based popular press. These sources can provide us with research questions and cultural opinions about a topic, but they are not as reliable as academic sources.

While going through the research process, you may also want to conduct your own primary research. Primary research includes interviewing professionals in your field and administering surveys on your research topic. Different courses and instructors have differing requirements for primary research, so you will want to discuss with your instructor appropriate interview subjects and/or survey parameters.

The research process can be daunting. When you first begin doing academic research, it can be helpful to use tools in outside sources in addition to our textbook. The Purdue Online Writing Lab (owl.english. purdue.edu/owl) offers strategies for selecting, evaluating, analyzing, and organizing your research. It also can be helpful to remember the spiral nature of the writing process. Although you begin doing research to answer your initial questions, research often causes us to ask more questions. We do not want to limit our experiences with research to finding information only. We should use our research to help us define our topic and consider which elements we are interested in exploring further. Research reminds us that the more we learn, the more there is to discover; therefore, as we progress in our academic studies, we can do initial research to help us determine which direction our in-depth research should take.

## DEVELOPING AN ORGANIZATIONAL PATTERN

In the section of this textbook that talks about span and stases (chapter 4, "Critical Reading Process"), we learn that many papers, especially those in the humanities, have an issue, a problem, and a solution, and it is our job to consider how much time we want to spend on each of these categories. It is also important to consider how the information we have best supports each of the categories. We want to make sure our papers follow a logical pattern as we build our argument. Some writers like to do this with a formal outline. Others like to use a graphic organizer, such as a flow chart or a table. If you are having difficulty considering how your ideas might fit together, you can also use presentation software to help you build your format. For example, in PowerPoint, the smart art graphics offer several different organizational patterns that you can use to experiment with your content and decide how it might best flow together.

# Writing
## DRAFT AS NECESSARY

Regardless of how much pre-writing we do, in order to receive a grade for our work, we must put something to paper. Anne Lamott talks about writing "shitty first drafts" as a way of motivating us to get something on paper. For the initial drafting period, that is the only goal that we need to have. We just need to start putting our ideas on paper. If we have spent the time asking good research questions and creating a flow chart for our project, we will be able to add detail to that chart. Those details become our first draft.

# Rewriting

As seen above, the writing stage is the simplest stage of the process. We can maintain its simplicity if we are willing to engage in the rewriting stage which includes revising, proofreading, and editing.

## GLOBAL REVISION - REVISING

After writing first drafts, when we initially revise our paper, we know that there are possibly significant changes that need to take place. We are considering whether the way we present our evidence is effective. We are looking for which pieces of research might need to be taken out and which might need to be added. Revision is concerned with issues of content and organization.

- Does our paper articulate our argument?
- Does it formulate that argument in a way that will be easily understood by our audience?

When we revise we should go back to our research questions and consider whether those questions are being addressed in our paper. We should also confirm that our paper continually reflects our thesis statement.

## FOCUSED REVISION - PROOFREADING

When we proofread our paper we are looking at our tone and presentation. Does our paper flow as well as we would like it to flow? Do we need to add transitions? Will our audience understand how and why we are making the connections we are drawing? Do we make the correct assumptions about the prior knowledge of our audience? Is it clear to our audience what we are asking of them?

## DETAILED REVISION - EDITING

Editing is when we go over the final details of our paper. This is when we are concerned with grammar. We need to comb over our paper for proper mechanics and formatting issues. We recommend saving this step for last because writers are usually less willing to cut something they spent time editing.

# Digital Ways to execute the Writing Process

In our culture, we write frequently. We communicate with our friends using social media, and we send a text message rather than calling someone. Since we use technology to write socially, sometimes it can be more comfortable using technology when writing academically as well. Below are a few tips of ways you can use different websites for various steps in the writing process.

## DIGITAL BRAINSTORMING FOR TOPIC TECHNIQUES

When you have absolutely no idea of a topic idea, use the google "I'm feeling lucky" feature. It will take you to different topics that are either trendy or artistic, and you could then do your research based on the topic found there. Websites like Google and Wikipedia, or even Pinterest or Tumblr, are great places to find ideas. StumbleUpon and reddit are also good choices for gaining knowledge about a topic because of the ways they are sourced and filtered. In ENG 1020 and ENG 3010, it will be important for you to find academic sources to further the ideas that you find through those avenues; however, social media can be a useful way to consider current events or topics of interest to you and your community.

If you have a topic idea, but you are unsure of how to develop that idea, you could also post questions on Facebook or Twitter that invite your community to respond. As you engage in conversation with others, hopefully you will start to shape how you are thinking about your topic. You can ask people if they know about a certain statistic or quote, or you could ask if they find a certain issue problematic or simply normal.

## DIGITAL WAYS TO DO RESEARCH

As you search for topics, create an account at a digital bookmarking site, for example delicious.com, and then as you see articles online that relate to your topic or interests, tag them. Using a social bookmarking site, rather than an individual computer's bookmarks, allows you to continually add bookmarks regardless of which device you use or location where you study. The tags you develop for your bookmarks will also help you categorize your information so you can narrow the focus of your research.

## DIGITAL WAYS TO ORGANIZE YOUR MATERIAL

Once you have some ideas and information, use your Wayne email to create a Prezi account. Prezi, or a similar presentation program, allows you to choose a template the follows a particular graphical organization. These templates can give you a frame for understanding your material. While Prezi is typically used for giving presentations, it can allow you to explore different relationships between ideas. It might help you see how things fit together or build upon one another. The advantage to Prezi over PowerPoint is again it is not tied to a particular computer, and you are not required to have any software.

If you do not want to use a template found in a presentation software, you can also use your own personal blog or wiki to freewrite about your ideas and consider how others might tag certain posts.

## DIGITAL WAYS TO REVISE

Once you have a draft of your paper, it can be helpful to revisit the idea of organization along with flow. One way to check your organization is by using the highlighting feature in a word processor, for example Google Docs. Pick different colors for various topics or subtopics, then highlight the different sub topics in different colors. Once you finish, look at the color pattern to make sure the paper is organized and flows in a logical manner. Also look for sentences that do not fit within the color scheme and consider cutting those. Highlighting your various points in different colors helps ensure that you have a balanced and well organized paper. If you find that most of your paper is one color, you might want to consider how you might subdivide that particular topic to make sure your paper is accomplishing your purpose.

As you are making revisions and potentially reorganizing material, you can also use the track changes feature. Doing this allows you to easily undo changes you might not like. Additionally, you can create a "graveyard" file for each paper. As you cut things out of your paper, open up a second document on your computer where you paste all of the information you cut out. Then, if you later decide that you need a particular piece of information, it will be easily restored.

## EXAMPLE

In English 1010, I am told to write a paper about a current problem. I see someone wearing a t-shirt that says "I am a modern day abolitionist," so I google that phrase and realize it is about human trafficking and decide to research that topic. My research question will revolve around figuring out what human trafficking is and whom it affects.

In talking with people in my community, I might ask if they are familiar with the term "modern day abolitionist," or I might post a statistic about human trafficking. I would want to discover if my friends are aware of human trafficking and if they know what it involves.

In English 1020, I am told to write a proposal about a current problem. Now, my research question will not only consider the who and what of human trafficking, but it will also ask how the community can prevent trafficking.

As I talk to people in my community, I might ask if anyone has ever had a friend who disappeared because of drugs. For my research, I might try to meet with people at Wayne State who are part of the organization Not for Sale and find statistics about trafficking in Detroit.

In English 3010, I need to consider the professional elements of a topic. Now, my research question will investigate how different criminal justice positions might prosecute human trafficking or how medical professionals might recognize trafficking victims among their patients.

I can ask people in my social networking community if they know people who work in law enforcement or the medical field, and if they ever see evidence of trafficking. I can also look at the Michigan trafficking task force and investigate ways that trafficking is being addressed in the legal system.

FURTHER READING

Duckart, Tracy. "Prewriting." *The Cache*. Humboldt State University, Jan 2012. Web. February 2013.

Lamott, Anne. *Bird by Bird*. Harpswell: Anchor, 1995. Print.

Perl, Sondra. "The Composing Process of Unskilled College Writers." 1979. *Writing About Writing*. Ed. Elizabeth Wardle and Doug Downs. Boston: Bedford/St. Martin, 2011. Print.

Rose, Mike. "Rigid Rules, Inflexible Plans, and the Stifling of Language: A Cognitivist Analysis of Writer's Block." *College Composition and Communication* 31.4 (1980): 389-401. JSTOR. Web.

# Summary

NICOLE VARTY, AMY METCALF, JON PLUMB, AND CHRIS SUSAK

# Introduction to Summaries

As a genre, the summary takes information from an original text and condenses it down into only the most important points required to understand the basic "gist" of the original. More specifically, summaries represent a source text's main claim and supporting points without plagiarizing the original author's work. Often, this task is more difficult than it at first appears and may require several revisions to be done just right – especially because the summary will have to include certain key terms and concepts from the original.

While specific uses of summary can vary, the general purpose behind this genre remains the same across the board – to represent a longer, more detailed piece in a shorter, more concise form. Summaries can vary in length from a few sentences to several pages depending on the length and complexity of the original text, as well as the level of detail required for the summary assignment. Regardless of the length or level of detail required, a summary should *never* include the writer's personal opinion, since the objective of this genre is merely to present a condensed version of the original piece.

Because summaries require writers to engage, understand, and then reproduce another author's work in the summary writer's own words, they are foundational to many different types of academic and professional writing. In academic settings, instructors might first ask students to summarize a source as a first step toward completing a larger, more complex project. In this example, the instructor is trying to ensure that students have a basic understanding of a source text and can accurately reproduce its basic argument before using it for more complex tasks. Practically speaking, most university writing assignments will require writers to briefly summarize sources *before* analyzing or using them to support an argument. Without some summary included in the essay as a background, readers will often not be able to clearly understand why a particular resource was chosen, its significance, or how the resource fits in with the rest of a writer's prose. In other words, many different types of assignments build upon, or take for granted, a writer's ability to summarize multiple resources. Thus, mastering this genre will be an important first step in any student's academic career.

## What is a Summary?

In academic writing, there are many instances where we are being asked to summarize, whether this demand is made explicitly—in the assignment description—or is implied as something that the writer should just know to do. College students are often required to summarize reading assignments or to summarize course material in answering essay questions. There will also be the implicit requirement in longer writing assignments that students incorporate effective summary as a part of their own work.

Although doing research and writing might seem like a lonely task, we do not necessarily undertake either of these activities on our own. When we choose to research a given topic we enter into a wider conversation with other writers interested in the same or a similar topic. Some of these writers will present perspectives or arguments that influence our thinking on a topic; some writers will present perspectives and arguments with which we strongly disagree.

Whether writing a paper about race and ethnicity in Shakespeare's plays or writing about how stress affects the immune system, it is important that you position your argument or research in conversation with other writers in the field. Effective summary helps accomplish this implicit requirement.

Reading through essays published in academic journals shows some of the different kinds of summary that occur in academic writing. Often—before the essay, just under the title of the essay and name of the author—we find what is called an abstract. The abstract is a kind of summary assignment.

It is a short summary (typically between 100-200 words) of a completed work that points out the problem the essay is examining, the method used to examine this problem and the essay's results or findings.

Turning to the body of the essay, there will be a number of different kinds of summary dispersed throughout. There is often, early in an essay, a section that will summarize some key texts on the subject. Throughout the paper, the author will return to these key texts and their important points, with the goal of placing his or her essay in conversation with these other writers in the field. From analyzing whole texts, to scrutinizing key passages, these different kinds of summary are crucial to the development and execution of exceptional academic writing.

## Why Write a Summary?

Summary is an important aspect of college-level writing because it is an important part of the kind of thinking expected of college students. The ability to process the ideas of other writers into our own words helps to gain a deeper understanding of the material. An Intro to Psychology student who has done the reading on behaviorism may be able to answer multiple choice questions on the topic, but a student who has summarized the reading will likely feel more confident when faced with a specific essay prompt. Practicing summary throughout the semester also will make it easier to synthesize course material and concepts when you are faced with more arduous tasks later in the semester, such as a research paper or a cumulative final. In addition, by learning to write unbiased summaries, you'll learn to recognize and evaluate bias in texts you read.

Summary is also important because it is a foundational **genre** of writing. (See the introduction for a fuller explanation of *genre*.) In other words, to make other moves in writing, like response or analysis, you need to be able to write effective summary. It would be very difficult for a reader to follow an argument about gender roles in a popular film series minus the information that the films depict the lives of teenage students at a school for witchcraft and wizardry. Practicing effective summary is important not only within individual assignments but also for developing the broader set of skills necessary for college-level writing.

Whether going over class notes with a friend who was absent or presenting a summary of an important reading in front of the class, in academia we summarize for a number of different purposes and for a number of different audiences. Whether the goal is to inform a classmate or to impress a professor, skillful college writers know how to adjust their account of the material to best meet the demands of the given situation. Summary in the form of a series of texts about the lecture on Sigmund Freud would look vastly different than summary in the form of a PowerPoint presentation about the id, the ego and the superego. Though we could differentiate the two summaries based on the kind of language used, or their length and detail, we would also find a great deal of common information between these two summaries. Effective summary, in each instance, depends on meeting the needs of a particular **discourse community,** genre and **rhetorical situation**. (See the introduction for fuller explanations of *discourse community* and *rhetorical situation.)*

## How to Write a Summary

### PREPARATORY WORK

*Reading and annotation:*

To effectively summarize a piece of text, the first step, of course, is to read the piece carefully. As you read, it will also be helpful to annotate the text you are reading. Annotation is defined by Merriam Webster's College Dictionary as "the making of critical or explanatory notes." As you prepare for summarizing, you will not only want to read the text carefully but also annotate the text, meaning, you will want to take a critical stance, asking questions of the text and critiquing it in writing—in the margins, on a separate sheet of paper or in a word processing file.. You will also want to rephrase points in your own words, explaining to yourself the meaning of the text as you go.

Through reading and annotating the text, you will begin to notice how writers move through their pieces. Marking how writers set up their arguments, establish and provide evidence for their claims, and organize the flow of their ideas are all key to navigating the text you're reading. Noting these moves and critiquing them are key to preparing yourself because you'll use your annotations to write your summary.

### Considering the Text's Rhetorical Situation:

After reading and annotating, you are almost ready to begin your summary. But first, you will want to consider the rhetorical situation of this summary. Why are you writing this summary? In other words, what is your purpose? Who is your audience? And what will you communicate about the text you are summarizing? You will also want to consider whether or not the summary will stand alone or be a part of another genre, such as an analysis, synthesis or argument. If the latter is the case, you will need to understand the role summary plays in the genre you are composing, and what summary looks like in this genre. With these considerations in mind, you are now ready to compose your summary.

### Ask yourself: "What do I already know?"

- reflect on what you know about reading and annotation
- make a plan for how you could approach this text using what you know.
- what do you need to know, in addition to what you already do? How can you gather that knowledge?

### Writing the Summary

There are a few key approaches available as you begin to draft your summary. The first is inquiry-based summary. When you use inquiry-based summary, you work through a series of questions, the answers to which form the frame of your summary. Classic questions in inquiry-based summaries include what are sometimes known as "journalistic questions"-- Who? What? Where? When? Why? and How?

A second possible approach to summary is the structure-based summary. Here you use the structure of the text you are summarizing to guide you through your writing, paying careful attention to features such as chapter titles, section headings, bolded or italicized words, and other key transitions that the writer employs to guide readers through the document. The annotations you made while reading will help you take this approach.

Another option for composing a successful summary is known as "getting the gist." We've all probably heard this phrase in casual conversation. When it comes to writing, there are a few tools you can employ to help yourself communicate the gist of a piece of writing clearly and succinctly. One of those tools is to limit the number of words (or even characters, if you're up for a challenge!) you can use to summarize a text. Try limiting yourself to 20 words, for example. It can be tough, and you will likely need to revise this gist a few times before you have shaved off unnecessary words and chosen the most relevant words to summarize the piece. But once those building blocks are in place, you can then expand on your statement of the gist to create a focused summary.

### Approaches to summary:

- Inquiry-based--answering journalistic questions about a text (Who? What? Where? When? Why? How?)
- Structure-based--consider the text's structural features such as:

  ○ chapter headings
  ○ section headings
  ○ bold/italicized words
- Getting the gist--writing summaries within a character/word limit to discover essential terms/features of the text (Twitter, 20 words, etc.)

# Response
## NICOLE VARTY, AMY METCALF, JON PLUMB, AND CHRIS SUSAK

## Introduction to Response

Responding to sources is a complex intellectual task – but it is also an exciting opportunity to develop your own ideas and write meaningful papers about real issues. Joining real conversations on important issues is the core of your university education. The response **genre** differs from work you have done in the past as it asks you to move beyond simply summarizing an author's work – now you will be asked to contribute to the scholarly work by providing your own "take" on a topic. (See the introduction for a fuller explanation of *genre.*) However, this is not just a time to express opinions but rather to join in a larger conversation between other writers/thinkers.

The goal of a response is to learn and use key strategies/concepts that expert writers use to enter into a greater conversation. Writers (like all of us) respond to what has already been said – writers do not create out of nothing. As when we speak and think about others' positions, in writing we listen to what others are saying (or writing), think about it and then respond to it with their own ideas. There are many ways a writer might choose to respond to a text/set of a ideas, including but not limited to the following responses: agreement or disagreement, extending an author's viewpoint, or posing a question to the text. You will learn more about these and other types of responses later in the chapter.

As mentioned above, the response genre asks you to take on the role of active participant in a scholarly conversation. To respond to an author's idea, you will first want to carefully and closely read the material. In other words, you will want to listen to what these authors are saying.

Responses to a text are often thought of as an *informed* opinion – because our thoughts are *informed* by the texts we are reading, we must show that within our writing. We can also think of a response as a reaction to a text that you explain and defend, *using the text as evidence.* As you read the author(s)' work, use the annotation strategies you've learned to develop your own view on the issues being discussed.

This is the conversation cycle: listen to what others are saying about an issue (read), develop your own position on the issues (annotate and elaborate), directly connect your position to the conversation taking place (talk about the ideas that the authors put forth), and use parts of what others have said to support your unique contribution (integrate quotes into your own original ideas).

During the conversation cycle, keep in mind that responses not only need to be original, contributing something that has not already been said, they also need to speak to the authors who have already joined the conversation. The most important part of responding to the ideas of others is your ability to *connect your own ideas to what others have said, showing how you are adding to the conversation and not merely speaking into the air.*

The genre of Response is considered a foundational genre because it is used in many humanities and social science disciplines, and it is likely that you will be asked to respond to sources in other classes/contexts (e.g. sociology, history, philosophy, etc.). Responding to sources allows us to better engage with writers' ideas – more so than simply summarizing their work. Interacting with texts in this way – combining your ideas with those of others – prepares you for future writing assignments and contexts. For example, in ENG 1020 you will be asked to write a range of arguments, and to do so you will need to be comfortable responding to the others' views and seeing yourself as an authority on an issue. This confidence is first developed in our ability to *join the conversation.*

## How to Write a Response

As discussed above, responses begin by briefly summarizing a text's main point or claim. To appropriately participate in a conversation, you must first *listen* to what has already been said. Beginning a response with a summary of the text's main claims demonstrates your ability to accurately listen to and understand what an author is trying to convey. After the author's main claim has been presented, you can move on to consider the specific aspects of the text which prompt your response. However be careful – even these more narrow elements should be summarized or paraphrased throughout your response so you can clearly show readers how you understand an author's position and how your thoughts fit into the larger conversation taking place.

There are many ways to respond to an author's ideas, but all of them involve some sort of *elaboration,* that is, extending your own thoughts in relation to someone else's. In a sense, responses act like funnels – they lead a reader through the overall point or claim of a piece (the widest part of the funnel), narrow the reader's focus, and then hone in on a particular point of interest (the narrow tip of the funnel). Generally speaking, responses that thoroughly address some specific aspect of an author's claim are not only easier to write but also tend to be more substantive and productive. The list below provides some typical strategies for responding to a text. The list is not exhaustive, but it does represent the most common approaches to an academic response. Notice that in each case, the response should go beyond merely taking a position on a text – it should *elaborate* about *why* you have taken that position and *how* your unique take on the text might affect the way we think about/understand an author's ideas.

- **Agree/Disagree** – At first, this seems like the easiest approach to response. However when agreeing or disagreeing with a part of an author's claim, you must also be careful to justify your opinion. Explain *why* you are taking this position and *how* your position might affect the way we think about the topic under discussion.

- **Add to or Extend a Point** – This response strategy takes the author's claims a step beyond what he or she originally discusses. In other words, this response might apply the main claim to a new situation, or it may show how we could add another significant point to the original claim. Regardless, this response should also discuss the implications of adding to or applying the claim in novel ways.

- **Point Out What is Missing** – Students often feel unqualified to point out an author's shortcomings. However, as a participant in a conversation, recognize that you have a right to respectfully show how an author misses some aspect of the situation. Maybe he or she writes too generally and misses some important specifics, fails to ask a pertinent question, or even reaches too far to show a cause/effect relationship. Point out what is missing but also think about why something is missing, and how we can account for the missing pieces in relation to the original claim.

- **Make a Personal Connection** – Some of the most interesting responses are those that apply some aspect of the writer's personal life to the text's claims. Not only can a personal connection help to prove/disprove an author's point, it also provides a real example for readers to think and talk about in relation to the text. Usually it's best to use the personal connection to concretely demonstrate a particular point or conclusion about a text's ideas. Be careful not to wander away from the purpose of a response here. The objective is not to tell your story, but to use a personal experience to enrich our understanding of the text in some way.

- **Ask a Question of the Text** - Sometimes reading a text can produce more questions than answers, particularly when you are interested in the topic. In this case, show how the author's claims have led you down a "thought path," which ends in a question or series of questions. In other words, describe how you formulated your question in relation to the text, and then try your hand at predicting how that question might lead you in other directions.

- **Connect to Other Texts and/or the Class Itself** – Instructors are generally pleased when their students can connect ideas from a text to other texts or ideas from previous class sessions. More importantly, drawing these connections helps you to see how a particular text fits into the larger purpose behind the course and its topics. This strategy can also help you to organize ideas into categories, compare/contrast approaches to similar problems, and to see how conversations develop over time and in relation to others' ideas.

- **Describe What You Learned and How** – A response can be as simple as describing what you learned and how you learned it from the text. Be sure to relate your learning to some aspect of the course or the day's class session. These types of responses might also discuss how you would use the new ideas in future class sessions, assignments, or to think through other problems.

- **Identify a Shift in Perspective** – Lastly, this type of response might discuss how the author started to see or discuss a topic differently throughout the course of a text, or how your own perspective on an issue has changed as a result of reading. Be careful to explore why the perspective has changed and also how the new way of seeing might affect our thinking/action in relation to a topic.

Of course, after working to summarize a text's main claim and converse with it, there is still the problem of concluding the response. In other words, we must think about how to finish our own part of the conversation. Usually, it is best to conclude your response by somehow inviting others to join the conversation and respond to *you*! One way to think about this invitation is to ask yourself "So What?" Now that you have added your own ideas to the conversation, what should others (your class) do with them? Think of your conclusion as a springboard into class discussion. This is a chance to suggest how your response might be useful to think about in relation to the day's topic of discussion. Should your classmates respond by trying to answer questions, agree/disagree with you, offer a new perspective, or even apply your thoughts to a specific test case?

Regardless of the strategy, use your conclusion to engage readers with your ideas and your contribution to the conversation in a meaningful way. Keep in mind that the techniques associated with effective responses will build into other genres of writing such as analysis and argument. In other words, the responses you write for class are meant to help you practice the skills associated with constructing longer, more complex arguments using multiple authors and resources. Thus, learning how to contribute to conversations via scholarly responses is another crucial step toward effective academic writing.

Monwara Rahman
Amy Metcalf
Basic Writing Section 024
March 6, 2013

## Computers vs. Real Life Experiences

In his article *Do They Really Think Differently?* Mark Prensky claims that "Reflection is what enables us, according to many theorists, to generalize, as we create 'mental models' from our experience. It is, in many ways, the process of 'learning from experience'" (Prensky). In the future technology experts are planning to upgrade the way we learn by having computers teach us. Technology will make things faster and maybe certain lessons will be easier for future generations to learn and understand, but that would not allow them to know how it feels to perform and complete a specific task. This generation of children is addicted to computers and most learn better from them, but when it comes to actually performing tasks most do not perform well. A computer gives the ideas and maybe you can create a mental image of something, but with *experience* you can see the results.

When something is learned from experience, people usually remember how to do it. Some learn from a computer and maybe get a program to show how to complete that task but when it comes to completing that task in real life they might freeze, forget, or take too long to complete it. Practicing certain tasks over and over again will help you improve, and learning from a computer does not give one the opportunity to practice. Something can also go wrong with the task and maybe a solution to the problem was not shown in the computer program. Learning something by experience can help one understand any concept better.

For example, the military is training their future soldiers by using computers. They use computers to teach them how to aim and shoot, drive their special vehicles and give them a sense of what they will face in the field. The computer games give the future soldiers an adrenaline rush that helps them finish the game, but that's not what actually happens in the fields. There is not field action every day. They have to wait for something to happen or wait for instructions from their leader to do something. One might go mad out of boredom because no one knows how long it will be till a soldier is called to do something. The computer game does not have you wait like that; you are always on your toes waiting for someone to attack or something to go off.

So what happens when you are new to the field and have your first real life experience? It will not be pretty. War is never pretty, but you cannot run from it. The computer game does not teach you how to deal with the mental horrors of a real life war experience. In some war games if you have enough points you can bring back a dead soldier like a reward for winning or having the most points. However, what does one get when they come back after losing his friends in the war? While a game can be easily beaten, and a computer teaches everything, it does not teach them what to feel and how to deal with it.

Archives are another example where computers make it difficult to truly learn something. Past authors who were magnificent writers have their writings stored in archives in different parts of the world. Now there are digital copies of the writings and one cannot get an actual sense of the environment where the author wrote that piece. When students need the information from these writings for a paper that they have to write, they have to search up the information they need and get to it any way they can.

Before, one had to travel to the archives to see the writings, but now there are digital copies of them on the Internet. Going to the archives where the actual writing is located gives one a better understanding and feel of what the writer is trying to portray. The environment can say a lot and a better paper will likely come out of it than a paper that was written after looking at the digital copies. Some might argue that it is better that there are digital copies: it makes it available to everyone, easier to get a hold of and a lot cheaper. Others argue that the trip is worth it and by going there, the environment and culture can help you see what went through authors' minds while writing and you can get an actual feel and understanding of it.

Gaining experience by visiting actual archives can help present generations connect to the way the older generation learned. And while this is the case, some of the older teachers that learn and believe in learning from experience sometimes have trouble connecting to students of the present generation. Digital immigrants have a hard time teaching and communicating with Digital Natives. The older generations are known as Digital Immigrants and the present and future generations are known as the Digital Natives. Digital Natives as Prensky explains it are "...all "native speakers" of the digital language of computers, video games and the Internet." And Digital Immigrants are "those of us who were not born into the digital world but have, at some later point in our lives, become fascinated by and adopted many or most aspects of the new technology are, and always will be compared to them, Digital Immigrants" (Prensky). Most of the teachers are from an older generation and do not know how to get through to students and make them pay attention. The younger generation, Digital Natives are into more advanced world technology and this sounds like a new language to Digital Immigrants. Digital Natives involve a computer with everything they do, so it will make sense to bring it into the classroom, so the students will pay attention, understand the information and maybe learn faster. For example a game could be invented to help a student learn about history, math, geography and other subjects that can be taught though a computer.

While it does make sense for computers to be brought into the classroom, it might not be the best in all situations. For example if one is learning to do math, they need to learn to do it by hand and not through a computer device. Doing the math problem by hand will help people remember how to do it in the future when they need it and it will keep them from cheating. Computers are one of the easiest ways for students to cheat on a math problem or any other subject. Doing problems by hand will help students remember and the teachers do not have to worry about the students cheating and not learning because computers give you the easy way out and one does not really learn anything.

If everything is taught by computers to students, then what about learning from experience? Again, "Reflection is what enables us, according to many theorists, to generalize, as we create mental models from our experience. It is, in many ways, the process of learning from experience" (Prensky). Technology gives us speed, accuracy, and could make one actually learn something in class without struggling. But is all of this and more worth losing the idea of reflection and learning from all the experiences of life?

# Analysis
## NICOLE VARTY, AMY METCALF, JON PLUMB, AND CHRIS SUSAK

Whereas summary asks you to briefly report, or "shrink-wrap" the main idea of a text, and response asks you to use summary to then respond to a text (or set of texts), analysis asks for something more: additional meaning to be added to the conversation. Going beyond mere response, analysis works to break down a text or argument into its component parts, and then to discuss or describe those parts using a particular perspective, theory, method or lens.

# How to Write an Analysis

As with summary and response, analysis begins with careful and critical reading. You will likely need to summarize the main claim and acknowledge your response to a text as initial steps in your analysis. After carefully annotating and summarizing the material, you're ready to analyze. Keep in mind that your instructor will likely provide specific instruction as to the particular perspective and/or method you'll use to approach your analysis - however, there are basic guidelines to follow when analyzing written texts:

1   Analyses are based on an objective reading of a text. In other words, while responses ask you to incorporate your opinion (to be subjective), an analysis is based on an observation of structural and contextual features of a text. Some structural and contextual features include the following: formatting, style, tone, examples used, arguments made, etc.

2   Analyses should identify two main things:
    a)   What the author is arguing/claiming, and
    b)   How the author is making that argument/claim.

## Analyzing Media
### JARED GROGAN AND LUKE THOMINET

# Introduction

Today, most people interact with new media on a daily basis by reading their favorite blogs, listening to podcasts, watching a digital short, or even playing video games. Over the past decades, teachers of composition and rhetoric have extensively studied the effects of new media on the reading, writing and research practices of student writers, and have subsequently reconfigured the place of new media in the composition classroom. For example, Cynthia Selfe and Gail Hawisher study how literacy has changed in an information age, how "technological literacy" has taken hold among people of different age, gender, ethnic and racial backgrounds, and how this technological literacy is now recognized as a cultural, economic, and political necessity. There are multiple ways to become technologically literate, and composition and rhetoric scholars have played a major role in understanding this "technological literacy" at the college level.

*The purpose of this chapter is to discuss some of the ways that new media has changed how we read, write, and even think about ourselves as readers and writers.*

We focus our discussion on how analysis and analytic writing *change* as we turn our attention to "reading" new media "texts" that include images, video, and interactive multimedia (like video games). We define the third type, "interactive media", as media that may include image and video components, but also include a more extensive role for *user interaction*. Examples include:

- interactive television: where audiences interact via text message, web forums, or phone in the context of a particular program;
- interactive forums: threads or forums that follow videos and create various narratives and discussion threads;
- video games, interactive advertising: online or offline interactive media designed to communicate with consumers to promote products, brands, services, public services, or corporate or political messages; and
- creative forms of digital art, virtual reality and augmented reality.

While these four forms of new media are important to both how we communicate and what we value in popular culture, they also play an important role in professional and academic writing today.

In the movement from images to videos, to interactive media, this chapter discusses interesting similarities and differences in how we read and analyze these digital texts to write about them in meaningful ways. We do so to offer a basic toolkit for analyzing new media as *"multimodal texts,"* a term that defines any text that integrates written words, static or moving images, and sound. As Cynthia Selfe and Pam Takayoshi point out, "whatever profession students hope to enter in the 21st century--game design, archeology, science and engineering, the military, the entertainment industry, and medicine--they can expect to read and be asked to help compose multimodal texts of various kinds" (3). Rhetoric and Composition scholars have worked with multimodal texts in the classroom for over fifty years, and as Jason Palmeri's *Remixing Composition: A History of Multimodal Writing Pedagogy* argues, we now have multiple ways of teaching students a set of processes and concepts for analyzing and composing texts with visual, audio, and video components.

## WAYNE STATE COMPOSITION CLASSES

In ENG 1010, you may be asked to analyze an image in order to help prepare you for analytic thinking and writing. The ability to break down an image based on **genre** conventions, visual features, or rhetorical concepts helps to train you to create strong paragraphs because it requires several criteria that are crucial to strong analytic paragraphs: *focused topic sentences*, a balance of *strong insights into a text*, and *sufficient detail* leveraged from the text as evidence. (See the introduction for a fuller explanation of *genre*.) For example, a paragraph focused on analyzing Obama's Hope poster would need to start with a structure that included a topic sentence that focused the analysis on a particular visual feature or zoomed in on a particular convention or rhetorical concept. Then, the body of the paragraph needs to balance description of what detail you've identified as example, with insight into why that detail is an important convention, or why it is persuasive to viewers of the text. With practice, you will find some confidence in their ability to connect your strong ability to *read* or *analyze* an image and to *write* analytically in paragraphs. In addition to recognizing and identifying already defined genre conventions or rhetorical appeals taught in class, you may also find self-assurance from opportunities to create and name specific ways that images are persuasive to an audience through their own insight into images. As James Paul Gee argues, it is important for you to be able to fill in what you see in an image or text from your own experiences, background or culture. For example, if you saw political ads in Detroit are now promoting politicians' pride in a keeping local jobs, you might name this *the outsource to Detroit ethos*, or the *pathos of Detroit pride,* and make a case for its importance to the text you're analyzing by balancing sufficient detail from the text as evidence, with your own insight into how this works to persuade a specific audience. You may even find that your insights line up with the ideas of others, and that is a great step forward in developing as a writer.

In ENG 1020, you will likely encounter visual analysis as a means to gain sound practice in applying the basic tools and terms of rhetoric. Analyzing visuals can introduce you to many of the key concepts in rhetoric and also give you an opportunity to demonstrate your ability to think and respond to a given **rhetorical situation**. (See the introduction for a fuller explanation of *rhetorical situation.)* For this assignment you may be asked to find an example of a persuasive text in the media, something with multi-modal components that you think holds some significant persuasive power over an audience. Common choices for analysis in ENG 1020 include the genres of advertising, political campaign advertising, advocacy, public relations documents, popular memes, historic propaganda, graffiti or street art, or recent viral videos. Once you've selected a persuasive image to analyze, you may be asked to focus your analytic writing on the *content* of the image/object itself (the rhetorical features that produce the impact on an audience), the rhetorical situation (author, audience, context), the **discourse communities** (defined in introduction) involved, and/or the larger *trends* in the media.

In ENG 3010, you will find that analyzing images helps you understand the increasing role of visuals (particularly graphs and charts) play in professional and academic discourse communities. Here you can expect that you will think through the practicalities of using such images to represent large amounts of data in the sciences, social sciences and humanities, as well as to consider the ethical questions about over-relying on images, or misrepresenting information graphically. You may be asked to consider what types of interdisciplinary partnerships and appropriations are required to make images work in an academic or professional realm. For example, a professional in nursing may need to rely on expertise in graphic design, marketing, and other areas to make an issue of public health persuasive graphically to a public audience.

## Analyzing Images

We can begin with a sharper focus on analyzing static images. It's important first to expand our subject of analysis from photography to static images that literally surround us every day, like movie posters, street art, billboards, magazine covers, maps, graphs, or charts. Images can be analyzed to explore the important role they play in professional and academic writing, or to examine how they reflect or shape ideas, beliefs or attitudes in specific communities or in popular culture. It is important to know how to analyze images no matter what your field of study. Images are regularly used to convey information and knowing how to read them can help you both identify the information being conveyed and recognize when it is being misrepresented. In most cases it is important to perform an analysis by considering three approaches: *genre analysis, visual analysis* and *rhetorical analysis*.

You can typically start by *identifying* the genre (defined in the introduction). As you know, genres are both established categories used to classify texts and something that changes over time, because genres evolve and even change the dynamic between "the needs, motives, and activities of communities" of writers and audiences. In other words, knowing something about genre will help you analyze features of texts, while paying attention to the author's choices, and the evolving rhetorical situations. We study genres as having taken shape over time and as a having established effective conventions for responding to specific situations. This coalescing of "typified rhetorical actions," in turn, has created expectations by reader--the texts are expected to meet (or adapt) these conventions as they deliver their messages (Miller, 156). Thinking about genre also asks you to think about the medium (the materials, technologies, and mode of transmission used to create and deliver a message). Analyzing the genre of an image requires you to ask yourself what genre of image you are analyzing, and then to describe the genre's established conventions or rules in order to help you and your reader understand the visual choices the artist/author made in creating the image. Knowing the established conventions and practices for creating different types of images, photos, graphics, cartoons or charts will help you understand the features of the image in relation to the goals of the author, their specific choices in medium, the choices made in the process of composing the image, and the purposes of the image in relation to the expectations of the audience.

*Visual analysis* generally considers features like arrangement, balance, contrast, emphasis, cropping, size, shape, line, color, and other formal elements of images. Focusing on visual analysis does not mean you are simply focused on "description," as all forms of analysis do require a *thesis*, or a central point to prove that your analytical approach is supported by the image. Visual analysis does, however, allow you to focus on the features of the image itself, which will provide you with much of your evidence for any thesis you may come up with about the image as a rhetorical text, or about the genre you are studying. For instance, when you first approach a visual, you may take ample time to note down all the visual details of its form that you can, and begin to search for connections that suggest a theme or an overall organization of the image. Any thesis you may craft will need to be proven by the content of the image you analyze by citing the visual details of the object which support the thesis. These details may include reference to the *medium, to particular techniques (in photography, graphic design, etc), or to composition* (the arrangement of elements in the work, the focal point, the use of space, repetition, elements of color, line, perspective, scale, etc.).

A *rhetorical analysis* of visuals considers the features mentioned above, but it also focuses on trying to understand what this image *does* to persuade a viewer or reader to think or act differently. As you saw in earlier chapters, we analyze images rhetorically by examining the rhetorical situation of an image or visual, and by thinking about the interactions between an author, their text (the image), and an audience. We then apply rhetorical concepts and principles to try and understand what a text "*does* rather than what it *is*" (Corbett). Like many rhetoricians, Edward P.J. Corbett says that rhetorical analysis helps us to analyze virtually any text or image, from a speech in front of an American flag, to an essay with a series of graphics, to an advertisement, photograph, or web page, by focusing on rhetorical concepts like *purpose* and *audience,* and rhetorical appeals like ethos, logos, and pathos. (See chapter 2, "Using Genres to Read Scenes of Writing" for explanations of logos, pathos, and ethos.) For instance, we can consider how the three appeals (ethos, logos, pathos) are used to explain how an image can prompt viewers to feel emotions or other effects (types of visual pathos); how an image can enhance a logical claim or argument with persuasive visual evidence, how an image can (mis)represent large amounts of data, be potentially deceptive, or create a bias (all types of visual logos); or how an image can represent and or enhance the "character" or guiding beliefs or ideologies of a person, community, or nation (types of visual ethos). We will discuss further approaches for analysis later in the section on interactive media.

# Analyzing Videos

We can analyze videos as texts in similar ways, by beginning with genre, visual and rhetorical analysis. However, most attempts to analyze video will also *layer* one or two new concepts or "tools" that assist in analyzing videos. For instance James Paul Gee applies the tools of *discourse analysis* to multi-modal texts (texts combining multiple modes of communication, including written, audio, and visual modalities) such as videos. Other theorists will start with rhetorical models for analyzing videos and add concepts from psychology, or critical theories like feminism or Marxism.

Analyses of music videos, for example, can draw on genre or visual and rhetorical analysis, and make room for other suitable theoretical frames. Past students also seemed particularly amenable to take on this complex form of analysis with genre of familiar videos which they said was interesting. Take for example Kanye West's *We Were Once a Fairytale* (directed by Spike Jonze), where West shows a distinct awareness of audience, and plays on themes of conflict, race, and celebrity, that have been integral to his own image in the media. The self-deprecating ethos in the video might challenge you to question the merit of this work, the authenticity of his "cocky" persona, and what this does for him in the context of the genre of Hip Hop, and the entertainment industry more generally (credit to Derek and his blog post so far).

Let's take a look at how this type of analysis might look as a process. When constructing such a rhetorical analysis, you might start with a broader trend in video production or with a particular text. When starting with a text, a brief assessment of the rhetorical situation would lead to more thorough questions about each key component: *the author* (which often raises the question of the ethos of an artist, as well as more a complex picture of producers and production companies and their motives), *the text* (the common facets and techniques of music videos, such as the techniques of a short film, the integration a song and imagery, or the promotional qualities or more explicit elements of advertising) and *the audience* (considering such factors as age, race, and economic status, the values and beliefs appealed to, and the attitudes or ideas reinforced). You could then move on to a close reading of the video, often breaking down a video into key segments, stopping frequently at particular frames to think about and/or discuss persuasive facets of imagery, sound, and lyrics, or to think through key rhetorical concepts.

You might also move from this kind of content analysis to do some research into contemporary trends in music video production, with the intent of grounding your findings in the video you've chosen to analyze. This shift from text to trends can support richer analytic work by deepening insights into video, while offering good basic training in research, integrating research into analytic writing, and even grounding research questions.

## Analyzing Interactive Media

In addition to (or instead of) the other forms discussed above, your instructor may ask you to rhetorically analyze a piece of interactive media. But what exactly do we mean by this term? Actually, we are grouping a rather diverse set of items under this title. We are referring to any work whose content is shaped substantially by user interaction. The most obvious example is that of videogames, but other types of interactive media might also be included. For instance, it might benefit you to consider the discussion below when analyzing television shows (like many reality shows) that rely on viewers to vote for an ending (or a winner). You might also consider it in relation to many items on the internet, in that their networked format is rather nonlinear (it requires a user to click on a button to show a page, and each page might be viewed in any order or even skipped entirely).

Before turning to more exact theories that could help inform your reading of interactive media, let's explore the interactive qualities of video games in a little more depth. Hopefully, this will help you begin to identify some of the difficulties you might face in analyzing this type of media. As an initial example, we will consider *Minecraft* (we chose this game as an example for two reasons: first because it is one of the most widely discussed games in recent history, and second because it is primarily a single player game, thereby avoiding further complications of multiple players influencing the game simultaneously). This games is built around the idea of an open world platform, meaning that the players can move their characters about the game as they please. It is also a sandbox game, which means that players have no specific mission and that they can play freely in the game world. When considering the rhetorical intent of such a game, a number of difficulties immediately arise.

First, there is the problem of even identifying precisely what the game is: is it the experience of an individual player or is it the entirety of all possible experiences that the game allows? To make this more concrete, in *Minecraft*, players collect resources and build objects in randomly generated game worlds. One player might start the game in a forest and build a small house and farm. Another player might start in a more mountainous region and build a towering castle. There are also enemies in the game called creepers. The forest dwelling farmer might find himself hounded by enemies at night and therefore go out and tame wolves to serve as protection. On the other hand, the castlebuilder might hide away at night and spend his days building higher and higher until he has an intricate spire of a castle. These are two fundamentally different experiences of the same game. Which one do we use when analyzing the rhetoric of the game? Is either sufficient on its own?

While this might seem to be a silly question, it is one that has to be tackled in any analysis of an interactive work. No single experience of the game is going to encapsulate the entirety of what could happen (especially in some more recent games). In fact, in his book *Extra Lives: Why Video Games Matter,* Tom Bissel says that meaning in video games is comparative rather than interpretive (117). By this he means that debates over the meaning of a game could not be settled simply by citing evidence from a playthrough, but rather by comparing and discussing experiences with other players. So the analysis of interactive media fundamentally considers co-creation of the game experience by players.

We also want to briefly address the inherent question of why analyzing interactive media is important. To do this, we turn to the work of James Paul Gee on learning and literacy. One of the fundamental claims of Gee's work is that video games represent highly effective learning technologies, and that the principles that drive these games can also be extended to non-gaming situations. To tie this back to the analysis of video games directly, he suggests that video games are a form of literacy that teaches us how to interact with themselves. This is fundamentally a rhetorical activity because the games, through their actions are trying to persuade you to perform your interaction with them in a different way. In this way, we might look at video games as representative of important persuasive activities that are both common to our society and at the same time often taken for granted.

It is well beyond our scope in this chapter to provide a full explanation of all of Gee's theories (he develops a list of thirty-six separate learning principles in *What Video Games Have to Teach Us About Learning and Literacy*), but we might explore one of his concepts. For example, in reference to the "Incremental Principle," Gee says, "Learning situations are ordered in the early stages so that earlier cases lead to generalizations that are fruitful for later cases" (225). A clear example of this principle exists in the *Legend of Zelda* game series. In those games, the player is always given a simple set of weapons at the beginning of the game and then introduced to additional weapons and complications as the game continues. Each new weapon, likewise, is introduced in a dungeon that focuses on fairly straightforward uses of the item. Later, the game requires more complex use of multiple weapons to fully explore dungeons and defeat bosses. The lessons that are learned earlier thus transfer to more complex situations where the knowledge is complicated.

This is also a principle often used in composition classes, where lessons often start by focusing on simple writing moves in order to develop towards more complex writing tasks. For example, a professor might first ask you to write a definition essay in order to clearly describe something for a particular audience. Those writing moves might also be used in a subsequent proposal essay where the professor first asks you to clearly define a problem before arguing for a solution. In this way, the use of definition becomes complicated by its subordinate relation to a more complex argument.

Moving forward with Gee's work, you might find it useful to explore the full range of his learning principles. If pressed for time, you might look at Gee's article, "Good Video Games and Good Learning," which was published in the *Phi Kappa Alpha Forum*. In this brief article, Gee reduces his list to fifteen principles and provides a brief explanation of each. If you are using this theory to analyze a game, you might want to consider how the game is setting you up to learn its system. What exactly is it doing to keep you playing? How does it make you better at playing the game?

Finally, before turning to theories that might help make sense of this form of media, we want to take a moment to discuss interactive media analysis in Wayne State composition classes.

- In ENG 1010, you may be asked to analyze a piece of interactive media to develop your critical attention to a variety of texts. Your analysis will have to be an objective interpretation that is supported with evidence from the media itself.

- In ENG 1020, you'll be asked to develop deep critical analyses of nonstandard texts. You will probably be expected to work with the thoughts/theories of others in relation to your analysis of the work. Ultimately, you will be expected to enter into a discourse on this form of media, and, at the very least, demonstrate how that discourse might approach the work you are analyzing.

- In ENG 3010, you may be asked to investigate how interactive media is used in academic settings across the university. Your analysis would therefore focus on particular examples of the media that relate more directly to academic or professional use rather than cultural use.

While each course might ask for different levels of analysis, the tools that one uses remain constant.

# A TOOLBOX FOR INTERACTIVE MEDIA ANALYSIS

What follows is a toolbox of sorts. As in a physical toolbox, each tool has its own use and purpose. No tool is appropriate for every situation. The tools here are a variety of theories that have been used with some success by scholars in the contemplation of interactive media. We are not specifically endorsing any theory listed here but rather providing an introduction to a range of theories so that you might find what works well for you and for the work you are analyzing. The theories covered below include traditional rhetorics, procedural rhetoric, gamic action, and learning principles found in games.

## *Traditional Rhetorics*

First, we need to affirm that traditional, non-digital rhetorics have an important place in the analysis of interactive media. There are a number of theories that might provide some insight into the work being analyzed. For example, Kenneth Burke's theory of rhetoric as identity might be a good place to start. It isn't our intent here to provide a complete overview of Burkean theory (such an overview would require an exceptional amount of space and attention to subtle detail). Rather, we suggest that this non-digital theory can be mapped into interactive media with beneficial results.

Burke, in *A Rhetoric of Motives*, says, "Put identification and division ambiguously together, so that you cannot know for certain just where one ends and the other begins, and you have the characteristic invitation to rhetoric" (1328). Here, Burke discusses rhetoric primarily as a means of identifying communities and building agreement among individuals (through the inclusion or exclusion of others). Extending this to interactive media, we might consider using this rhetorical theory in a number of ways. First, we might consider the context around the game--looking both at how the game came into being (who produced it and why) and how it is used (who plays it and why). In each of these cases, the game might evidence a certain identity of producers or players. For example, consider an indie game produced today with pixelated graphics. We might analyze these graphics as an identity of the indie producers, one that is specifically not like major game publishers. Alternately, we might connect the graphics with an identification by the producers with past "classic" game developments and style from the 1980s and 90s. Second, we might connect identification with the text of the game itself. For example, we might want to ask the question of how the player is or is not meant to identify with the character being played. The level of identification varies greatly between games. In some cases, players might be presented with a blank slate of a character that they can customize however they like. In other cases, a strong character might be presented through which the player must make contact with the content of the game, while never fully being in control of choices. There are even cases (as in several of the GTA games mentioned above) where the character is specifically difficult to identify with for moral or cultural reasons. This too has a strong effect on the rhetoric of the game.

What we hope is that this brief example illustrates why this approach might be fruitful. We must leave it up to you to search out rhetorical theories that interest you. As a starting point, you might want to engage in a discussion with your professor on theories he/she is familiar with. Other possibilities worth exploring might include the following: the classical canons of rhetoric, the rhetorical triangle, and Bitzer's rhetorical situation.

### Procedural Rhetoric

A more recent theory of rhetoric that focuses explicitly on video games is Ian Bogost's concept of procedural rhetoric. In *Persuasive Games,* he defines procedural rhetoric as "the art of persuasion through rule-based representations and interactions rather than the spoken word, writing, images, or moving pictures" (Bogost, ix). To grasp this concept, we need to consider the underlying structure of games. As you are most likely aware, video games (and in fact all computer programs) are built on code. This code works like a set of instructions for the computer—it tells the computer what to do step by step. In the case of video games, the code is telling the computer many different things: what to make appear on the screen, what to do in relation to other internal processes, and, most importantly, what to do when the player interacts with it in some way. For example, if in a game a player were to mouse click on a book, the program might do a number of things: first, it would show the character's hand reaching for the book and picking it up, then it would show the book open in front of the screen so that the player could read it. Once the book is displayed in this way, the program would also include further options for the player—depending on further input, the book might be stored in an inventory, put back down, or a page might be turned. According to Bogost, this rule-based interaction is the basis of digital rhetoric.

In his book, Bogost demonstrates the working of procedural rhetoric through an analysis of *Animal Crossing* (among other games): "Animal Crossing mounts a procedural rhetoric of debt and consumption that successfully simulates the condition of affluenza" (268). Basically, his argument is that the player is encouraged to repeat mundane tasks over and over in order to afford a larger house. In turn, the vast majority of the value from this work goes to increase the wealth of the store owner and real estate agent, Tom Nook. Ultimately, Bogost expects the player to realize the exploitative actions of the game and how those actions reflect modern financial systems.

He also argues that the type of persuasion found in games like this is fundamentally different from other, more traditional attempts at persuasion. By having the player act out the triggers of various processes, the program can strongly reinforce the connection between those actions and the results portrayed by the game. To this end, Bogost doesn't try to claim that every game is a good example of procedural rhetoric. Instead, he primarily focuses on various games with clear persuasive intent: political games, advergames (games that are also advertisements), and educational games.

However, using procedural rhetoric in analyzing games might be a bit tricky. Make sure to read more on Bogost's theory before trying to apply it. A good starting point is his article "The Rhetoric of Video Games." Then in considering this theory in relation to the game you are analyzing, consider the ways that the game is working. Is there any part of the game that seems to be directing you to think of a situation in a particular way? Are there any themes in the game that connect to social or cultural topics outside of the game?

### Gamic Action

While it isn't directly a theory of rhetoric, Alex Galloway's concept of gamic action might be a useful way to start breaking down a game and looking at its component parts. In *Gaming: Essays on Algorithmic Culture,* he first postulates that the fundamental defining aspect of games is that they are actions (2), and then breaks those actions into four different types. These types are built on two sets of binaries: digetic/nondiegetic and operator/machine. So the four resulting actions are: digetic operator acts, nondiegetic operator acts, diegetic machine acts, and nondiegetic machine acts. It isn't our intent here to provide a full description of these four types of actions here. To learn more about this, explore the first chapter of Galloway's book.

It would be valuable, however, to explicate at least the concepts behind the binaries. To start with, diegetic refers to everything that occurs within the narrative world of the game (Galloway 6). In other words, this element represents the characters, their actions, the world, the objects, etc. A diegetic action might involve one character talking to another, a cut scene that drives the plot, or even normal gaming actions like firing guns or driving cars. Nondiegetic elements occur within the game, but outside the narrative (6). Examples of this might include game menus, health bars, inventory screens, or even bugs in the code (malfunctions in the game). They often represent ways that the player interacts with the game, but are objects that would never appear in the actual world of the game. Operator and machine acts, on the other hand, are differentiated by what is initiating the action. Since games are based on a player's interaction with a machine through a program, this differentiation seeks only to point out that some things are within the control of the player and some are not. For example, a game might be programmed to simulate weather effects like rain. Usually, the player has done nothing to instigate this weather. On the other hand, a player can often move a character around a space. This movement was directly controlled by the player and not by the machine.

Hopefully, these differentiations help to point out the different parts of a game. In analyzing a videogame you will want to go beyond simply reciting the plot. Think about how you are able to interact with the game. Consider what is outside of your control. Look closely at the apparatuses that allow you to perform this interaction and don't take their design for granted.

## ANALYZING INTERACTIVE MEDIA

Hopefully, this section, rather than closing down how you approach interactive media has instead opened you to new ways of viewing these objects. While our discussion has focused solely on video games, we want to suggest that many of these principles can be extended to other forms of interactive media. For example, one might easily apply a Burkean rhetoric to interactive forums to discover how, through the technology, rhetorical identity is formed or strengthened. Additionally, one might consider Bogost's procedural rhetoric in relation to interactive advertisements--how does it change the fundamental appeal of the advertisement when manufacturers are able to simulate the functioning of the product or even allow consumers to choose from among multiple advertisements based on theme?

Let's close here with one last look at why this type of analysis is so important. Many forms of media are becoming increasingly interactive in today's networked society. Analyzing these new types of objects must take into account their interactive functioning in order to truly grasp how they work. To ignore this is to be blind to much of the rhetoric in modern society. Not only does analyzing interactive media prepare you for looking at complex texts of all sorts during your academic career, it also prepares you for a world where persuasion is rarely straightforward or passive, where it is far more likely to ask for and expect your active participation.

## WORKS CITED

Bissell, Tom. *Extra Lives: Why Video Games Matter*. New York: Pantheon, 2010. Print.

Bogost, Ian. *Persuasive Games: The Expressive Power of Videogames*. Cambridge, MA: The MIT Press, 2010. Print.

Burke, Kenneth. "From *A Rhetoric of Motives*." *The Rhetorical Tradition: Readings from Classical Times to the Present*. Ed. Bizzell, Patricia, and

Bruce Herzberg. Second Edition. New York: Bedford/St. Martin's, 2000. Print.

Galloway, Alexander R. *Gaming: Essays On Algorithmic Culture.* 1st ed. Minneapolis: Univ Of Minnesota Press, 2006. Print.

Gee, James Paul. *What Video Games Have to Teach Us About Learning and Literacy. Second Edition: Revised and Updated Edition.* New York: Macmillan, 2007. Print.

Selfe, Cynthia, and Pamela Takayoshi. "Thinking about Multimodality." *Multimodal Composition: Resources for Teachers.* Pap/Dvdr. Ed. Cynthia L. Selfe. Hampton Pr, 2007. 1–16. Print.

Selfe, Cynthia L., and Gail E. Hawisher. *Literate Lives in the Information Age: Narratives of Literacy From the United States.* Lawrence Erlbaum Associates, 2004. Print.

# Voice in Academic and Civic Writing
## LaToya Faulk

# Defining Voice and Style

Style consist of both conscious and unconscious decisions writers make about everything from the words we use (diction) and their arrangement in sentences (syntax) to the tone with which we express our point of view and the way we achieve emphasis in a sentence (Butler 1). In other words, voice (or style) supports the overall purpose of the writing in the composing process because it allows writers to make choices about how they will deliver a message to an audience.

Often what distinguishes a writer's voice from others' is how meaning is expressed. We each have a range of voices we put on and take off given the occasion and subject matter. Writing in academic and civic communities demand higher concentration, clear organization of thoughts and ideas, sentence structures that are rich and concise, and a well-thought-out stylistic approach. Style (or voice) is shaped by context, which refers to the conditions and circumstances that determine the existence of a piece of writing. In college writing, stylistic differences are often attributed to the agendas of a discipline, profession or field of study. Disciplines are types of **discourse communities** (as defined in the introduction) where groups of individuals communicate in particular genres to achieve a common goal—whether to persuade, entertain or inform. Although purpose and **genre** conventions largely affect the range of appropriate styles and tones, skilled writers must be able to think critically about their audience and its relationship to style.

(See the introduction for a fuller explanation of *genre.*) This thinking can be achieved by identifying which stylistic approaches best appeal to your audience. You can do so by conducting research that seeks an awareness of the genre conventions widely consumed and valued by a particular group. Then spend time reflecting on the relationship between genre conventions and the ways in which genre conventions impose a stylistic standard.

Various discourse communities have unique literacy practices used to categorize insiders and outsiders or novices and experts. In looking at stylistic differences within discourse communities, we must first understand that discourse communities can be examined and compared in the same way we learn and examine various languages and identities. In an article by James Gee entitled "Literacy, Discourse, and Linguistics: Introduction," Discourse[1] is an identity kit; this kit comes from culturally acquired instructions on how to act, talk and write in ways that others within the community acknowledge and reward. Gee outlines four types of discourse communities: primary, secondary, dominant and non-dominant. Primary discourse communities "constitute our original home-based sense of identity," while secondary—"non-home based social institutions" are communities where we intermingle in the public—for instance, stores, church, schools, community groups, state and national businesses (485). Dominant and non-dominant Discourses make writers aware of how power operates within communities. Although most communities possess a language of insider knowledge crafted through a specific language, style or expression, this knowledge establishes hierarchies or camaraderie among members. However, dominant discourse communities are often seen as empowering because they have the potential to provide access to economic mobility, prestige and status (Wardle and Downs ed. 485). Extending Gee's work, the chart below will help shape an awareness of the variety of stylistic approaches available given the communicative demands of a community. However, keep in mind that there are many different styles and voices that can be found in one single piece of writing within a community. Also, new genres and combinations of genre conventions evolve within various communities. In the evolution of new genres certain stylistic approaches are added, revised, and combined.

---

[1] Discourse (with a capital D) in James Gee's work is distinguished from discourse (with a lower case d). "discourse means connected stretches of language that makes sense", while "Discourses are ways of being in the world; they are forms of life which integrate words, acts, values, beliefs, attitudes, and social identities as well as gestures, glances, body positions, and clothes" (484).

## Style as Identity

Often developing your own unique voice in academic and civic writing comes from evaluating, analyzing and imitating others in the discourse community. This is why rhetorical reading is significant to acquiring a unique voice in academic and civic settings. Like speech acquisition, we acquire our own unique voice by mimicking others and then acquiring a level of confidence in a voice that is often a collage of other voices we admire, respect and consider authentic. Style is twofold—it is a kind of identity and a rhetorical tool used to formalize communication among a group of individuals for easy consumption of ideas. George-Louis Leclerc de Buffon proclaims in *Discourse and Style* that, "writing well consists of thinking, feeling and expressing well, of clarity of mind, soul and taste ... The style is the man himself" (149-154). When we think of 21st century writers like James Baldwin and his essays, we understand his identity as a unique voice penetrating the pages, making his writing unmistakably his own. Baldwin and many other writers who are widely read and published often discuss their unique style as an attribute related to (1) social issues that matter the most to them and, (2) well-known writers who inspire them in ways that push their style and technique forward. For instance, in an interview with the *Paris Review*, when asked about how much he read and how it influenced his own writing Baldwin states, "I read everything. I read my way out of the two libraries in Harlem by the time I was thirteen. One does learn a great deal about writing this way...I'm still learning how to write. I don't know what technique is. All I know is that you have to make the reader *see it*. This I learned from Dostoyevsky, from Balzac" (Baldwin par. 15). Making the reader see it depends upon the genre you've been asked to compose and is determined by word choice and arrangement (understanding the types of historical baggage associated with a word), sentence construction (where you place the subject, verb and object), and often the overall organization of ideas presented in the text.

This leads us to our second understanding of style. As rhetorical tools, stylistic choices are used to conventionalize communication for easy distribution and consumption within a discourse community. In addition to controlling genres, discourse communities share a specific language and style that embed the values and belief systems of that community. Although each member of a community has a personal style and voice, there is also often a shared style or language practice associated with a particular community's norms and habits. These stylistic practices can be explored through observation (*see Exercise 1 below*).

| | INDIVIDUAL (Primary Discourse Community) | SOCIAL/CIVIC (Secondary/Non-dominant) Discourse Community | EDUCATIONAL Dominant Discourse Community | CIVIC/PROFESSIONAL Dominant Discourse Community |
|---|---|---|---|---|
| Range of Expression & Literacy Agendas | Home-based language; Authentic range of true expression, include to share and respond to family, immediate kin and friends | A language that provides a level of emotional and logistical solidarity with a particular social network (e.g. racial, religious, environmental or political group, civic organization, Greek life) | Often standardized, non-home based language where the mastery of a particular or various discourses include obtaining income, status or social goods (liberating or empowering literacies) | Non-home based language; public voice; Although sometimes a personal range of expression is mixed with a certain kind of formalized language practice depending on the setting, writing is formalized in a way that meets a common goal |
| Form | Informal | Formal/Informal | Formal | Formal/Informal/Causal |
| English Usage | Personal freedom and comfort (usage of I), combination of standard and non-standard English, | Structured /Non-structured communication determines when and where standard or non-standard addresses are required. | Personal/Self distance in the writing (impersonal tone), precise language, carefully controlled format or organization | Concrete language, some home-based language mixed with standard English |
| Genres | Facebook posting, Twitter, Email (to friend/family member), text-messaging (to friend/family member), creating a grocery list, journal writing, special interest magazines, personal essay writing, personal Website | Some academic papers, personal essays, some speeches, response papers | Research-based writing or report, persuasive, expository, analytical, professional email, business letter, job application or letter, most academic papers | Political discourse, general-interest writing, causal writing, public speeches on social or political issues that affect the community, newsletter or article |

*Exercise 1: Consider a primary or secondary discourse community you value (e.g. readers and writers of literacy texts, computer engineers, gender studies scholars, Catholics). Find three popular articles or essays written by members of that discourse community whose style you enjoy. Highlight sentences that exemplify why you enjoy the author's style of writing then use those sentences you've highlighted to explain to peers why you enjoy the style of the writing and how you might use this particular style in your own writing.*

Where an understanding of the subject, audience and purpose for speaking are necessary, let us now turn to the matter of using one's primary discourse to employ a unique style in expository and persuasive writing

## Style as home-based identity: primary discourse communities and academic writing

*We affirm the students' right to their own patterns and varieties of language -- the dialects of their nurture or whatever dialects in which they find their own identity and style. Language scholars long ago denied that the myth of a standard American dialect has any validity. The claim that any one dialect is unacceptable amounts to an attempt of one social group to exert its dominance over another. Such a claim leads to false advice for speakers and writers, and immoral advice for humans. A nation proud of its diverse heritage and its cultural and racial variety will preserve its heritage of dialects.*

—Excerpt from the 1972 CCCC Students' Right
to Their Own Language

The above excerpt from the 1972 CCCC Students' Right to Their Own Language (SRTOL) suggests that students have the right to write in the "dialects of their nurture," or the language codes learned in their home-based communities. Although tension remains regarding the extent to which students are allowed to write in the dialects of their nurture without penalty, composition scholars and writing program administrators such as Elaine Richardson, Arnetha Ball, Ted Lardner, Geneva Smitherman, Peter Elbow, Bonnie Williams and Staci M. Perryman-Clark have conducted research that focuses on how SRTOL can affirm students' home-based voices when students engage academic rhetorical situations.

In an article published in 2013 entitled "African American Language, Rhetoric, and Students' Writing: New Direction for SRTOL," Stacie Perryman-Clark conducts a case study with three African American students and investigates the extent to which home-based Englishes, such as AAL (African American Language) or Ebonics can be used in academic writing to affirm SRTOL. Perryman-Clark claims that students should be able to do the following:

1  Make strategic choices and explain how various rhetorical situations allow or discourage the usage of non-traditional academic literacy practices like AAL.

2  Identify and understand certain contexts that require Ebonics or Standard English, but also the way writers actually—and quite deliberately—code-switch in written discourse.

More traditional assignments (e.g. argument, analysis and disciplinary essays with a clear research focus) depend more on abstract writing, active voice, personal distance and more focus on a higher concentration of knowledge. Whether including your home-based language would help address the rhetorical situation of your essay will take some consideration. Understanding your assignment and discussing the genre, your purpose and your audience will provide more information on how to make stylistic choices that appeal to the ethos, pathos and logos of your readers. See exercise 2 below, which gives you an opportunity to discuss your feelings on SRTOL in class, with your instructor or with a peer.

***Exercise 2:*** *Discuss the following questions as a large or small group. How does your instructor view SRTOL? How do you? What types of assignments would put you in a position where it was appropriate to use language practices other than Standard Edited English? How so? How much do you know about the genre that would lead you to believe that other language practices would be appropriate?*

Writing assignments that focus on personal literacy practices or popular culture, where non-traditional academic discourses like AAL are valued, provide opportunities to use or discuss such non-traditional literacy practices. Such assignments may ask you to consider how popular culture and new media use language to persuade specific audiences. For instance, you might analyze the marketing of the 2011 Toyota Sienna minivan more notably recognized as the "swagger wagon."

http://www.youtube.com/watch?v=pUG3Z8Hxa5I

The commercial uses humor and parodies rap lyrics and AAL as a way to appeal to a younger consumer demographic. This stylistic approach leads viewers to believe that the minivan, often a stigma of middle aged suburban white American soccer moms, is cool, fun and perfect for younger new families. The shift in demographic appeal seeks to change the perceptions of the minivan to promote sales among younger car owners. But, how many new young families purchased the "swagger wagon"? Was this commercial effective? Does the style of the commercial succeed in fulfilling the intentions of the composers of the commercial?

*Exercise 3: Watch the video (see link above) and consider how the style and usage of humor support the overall purpose of the commercial. Take time to answer the following questions in groups or as a class. What is the structure of the communication? How is content organized? What devices are used to persuade viewers? What kind of style and tone is used and for what purpose? Does the style speak to the circumstances of the intended audience? Identify key phrases and their location in the commercial which would provide an understanding of the nature of the communication and what it reveals about the culture that produced it?*

# Style as shaped by writing in academic disciplines

Disciplines shape the style of a writing practice all around. Each discipline has a unique identity kit that often characterizes distinct ways of knowing and communicating (Carter 2007). As academic writers, we must understand how and why various disciplines communicate knowledge through writing. As we understand how disciplines create meaning through the writing practices valued in that community, we are also able to understand how style and voice are conceptualized through writing in the discipline. In other words, as decision makers seeking to strengthen our ability to make sound judgments on a stylistic approach, we must understand the "intellectual and social conventions of a disciplinary community" (Herrington, 337). These conventions, according to Herrington and other composition scholars, "vary across disciplinary communities and include the kinds of issues the discipline tries to address, the lines of reasoning used to resolve those issues, the social purpose for communicating and a shared assumption about the audience's role and the writer's ethos" (334). To better understand why disciplinary community analysis is so important, you might consider a research paper in a scientific reasoning course that may require you to have introduction, methods, results, analysis and discussion sections. Early in the composing process, you may need to establish a hypothesis and accumulate evidence related to the hypothesis. These requirements shape the range of style and voice appropriate given the focus of the project. To conclude, genre conventions help shape our stylistic decisions as writers. Therefore it is important to learn all you can about the communicative practices of the professional, civic and academic communities you seek to join or where you already participate. The exercise below gives you the opportunity to explore a disciplinary community at Wayne State. Because outcome statements are public and often announce the goals of a particular community, exploring these statements along with asking an expert questions about the discipline's way of approaching style and voice should provide you with flexibility by giving you a range of choices to consider as you communicate in the discipline.

*Exercise 4: Analyze the outcome statement of your discipline or ask the following questions to a faculty member in your discipline: What are the genres you'll be asked to write? What are the genres' expectations concerning what types of knowledge you'll be asked to create? What ranges of tone, style and voice are available given the content needed to successfully compose in this genre? Has anyone successfully deviated from these expectations? Discuss what you come to learn in a writing **reflection** or with class peer. (See the introduction for a fuller explanation of reflection.)*

## Style/Voice and Tension and Conflict in the Academy

Standard edited English is just one out of several stylistic representations of a linguistic system valued in higher education. It has been my experience that observations and open discussions surrounding style and voice in college often lead writers to questions surrounding who they are and where they might locate a singular authentic style or voice. Identity is multi-layered. We all have multiple forms of language and style, because we are all part of numerous discourse communities that have varying communicative practices. When we feel like a stylistic standard "doesn't fit" or just "isn't us," reluctance to put on a voice that feels inauthentic or fake can force us to resist stylistic rules associated with a particular community. This is quite normal, and one way to negotiate this conflict is to first see association within a discourse community as a choice or a kind of liberation.

As noted earlier in this chapter, certain discourse communities allow us access to social, economic and political goods. These types of communities are seen as liberating because of the human necessity for survival. Second, not being afraid to voice such feelings can lead to experimentation and provocative dialog with your peers and instructor.

When I think of what it means to be a part of several discourse communities, I like to think of it in the same way I think about learning a new language. Do you speak more than one language? Or have you ever tried to learn a new language? For many of us, having to roll new words off of our tongue can feel strange and uncomfortable. You might gain a better insight into the varying ways in which communities shape information if you think of what it takes to learn a new language, like Spanish or French, for example. Exposure and open access to various languages can be seen as an advantage. For instance, a bilingual writer named Ana Menedéz in "Bilingual Imagination," contends that learning two languages opened her up to two different worlds and prepared her for adapting to difference and change (24). What we often learn from our awareness of the varying ways in which communities communicate is that there are infinite ways to interpret things.

We must be very observant and analytical of the multiple ways in which the communities where we communicate are similar and different. Moving in and out of varying communities can prompt metacognition and what many scholars call code-switching. Metacognition is an awareness of how we ourselves make critical rhetorical decisions within various contexts to meet the goals of that community. Code-switching happens when we shift between languages or communicative codes, depending on the context. As writers we must constantly make decisions concerning the effectiveness of our communicative practices. An awareness of where, when and how communicative codes differ is all a part of being a reflective, responsible writer. In this final exercise (adapted from Ann Beaufort's *College Writing and Beyond*), you'll be given a chance to compare how varying discourse communities you interact in differ and shape your identity in various ways.

**Exercise 5:** *Collect ten oral or written genres that you consume and produce regularly for academic and social purposes. Examples might include song lyrics, newspaper articles, email messages, letters etc. Using a table, identify the associated discourse communities that widely utilize the collected genres and briefly outline the purpose of each genre. In groups or as a class, discuss the role the writer and audience plays in each genre, and take time to share the social actions and values represented in each genre. Consider what stylistic choices the writers make, especially those relevant to voice and identity. Why do they make these choices? How do these choices relate to the texts' different purposes? What effects do the choices seem likely to have on the texts' intended audiences?*

## WORKS CITED

Bacon, Nora. *The Well-Crafted Sentence (A Writer's Guide to Style)*. New York: Bedford St. Martin, 2013.

Baldwin, James. Interview by Jordan Elgrably. "The Art of Fiction No. 78." *The Paris Review*. 1984: 91. Web.

Beaufort, Ann. *College Writing and Beyond: A Framework University Writing Instruction*. Utah State University Press, 2007.

Butler, Paul. *Style in Rhetoric and Composition: A Critical Sourcebook*. New York: Bedford St. Martin, 2010.

Carter, Michael. "Ways of Knowing, Doing, and Writing in the Disciplines". *College*

*Composition and Communication*. 58:3. (2007):385-418.

Elbow, Peter. *Vernacular Eloquence: What Speech Can Bring to Writing*. Oxford University Press, 2012.

Gee, James. *Social Linguistics and Literacies: Ideology in Discourse*. Routledge, 2011.

Herrington, Anne. "Writing in Academic Settings: A Study of the Contexts for Writing in Two College Chemical Engineering Courses". *Research in the Teaching of English*. 19:4. (1985): 333-359.

Menedéz, Ann. "The Bilingual Imagination." *Poets & Writers*. January/February, 2011.

Wardle, Elizabeth and Downs, Douglas, eds. *Writing about Writing: A College Reader*. New York: Bedford St. Martin, 2011.

"Students' Right to Their Own Language." *College Composition and Communication*. 25: 25, 1974.

# Understanding Scenes of Writing

1

You are an actor. Each day of your life you play a variety of roles or "parts"—as son/daughter, sibling, friend, student, teammate, employee—and you act out these parts in a variety of scenes, whether at home, in school, in the gym, in the workplace, or in your neighborhoods or communities. As in the scenes of a movie or a play—where actors take their cues from co-actors and directors, the stage and surrounding sets, and the time and place of the action—you take your cues for how to act from the scenes you act within. As students, you constantly negotiate among scenes: from dorm room, apartment, or home to cafeteria, classes, or work; from meetings of clubs or organizations to dinner with friends; from a date on Friday night to a party on the weekend, to the football game on Saturday, and to visits with your extended families on occasion.

Each of these scenes is different; each requires you to play a different role, which involves different strategies for acting and communicating within it. How you dress, how you present yourself, how you interact with others, what you talk about—all these behaviors depend in large part on the scene in which you find yourself. You are constantly coordinating how you act with the scenes in which you act. Within familiar scenes, this coordination becomes so habitual that it seems intuitive and effortless. When you enter new or less familiar scenes, however, you need to make more conscious, less automatic decisions about how to act.

## Entering New Scenes

Think about what you do when you enter the scene, say, of a social get-together at your college or university and you do not already know the people attending. What do you do as you walk into the room? How do you decide where to go in the room and what to do there? In all likelihood, one of the first things you do is look around. As you begin to observe the room, what do you look at? What do you look for? You might pay attention to what people are wearing. Are they dressed formally? Are they dressed to impress? You might also take in the way the room is structured. Are people standing around? Is there space to walk, or is the room set up in such a way that forces people to sit? You almost certainly would focus on how people are interacting with one another. Is the room buzzing with conversation, or are people shyly avoiding one another? You might discover that some are talking in groups while others are engaged in one-to-one conversations.

## READING SCENES

You might notice these things and others as you begin to look around the room. But you don't just passively absorb these images; chances are you also begin to analyze or "read" them to help you decide how to act. That is, you begin to think about what these images tell you about this scene, how people are acting within it, and how you might act. For example, what people are wearing and how they are interacting can tell you whether the scene is formal or informal and whether you will fit in comfortably. (Did you wear the "right" thing? Will you be able to tell raucous jokes or have intellectual discussions?) Drawing from your past experiences with how people present themselves on various occasions and how they interact, you begin to form assumptions about what sort of scene you have entered and how best to position yourself and act within it.

Say, as you make your way around the room, that you decide to join a group conversation. Once again, you probably begin by observing or "reading" the group. You might observe the group dynamic: Is everyone engaged in the conversation or is one person dominating the conversation? Are people interrupting one another or are they taking turns talking? Is it women or men who are interrupted most frequently? You surely also pay attention to the topic of conversation: Is it a topic you know something about? Is it something you are interested in? Is it a topic that must be treated seriously, or is there room for joking and banter? How far along is the conversation? Has it just begun, or has the group already covered much of the topic? Should you listen, or can you contribute something to the discussion? And if you can contribute, when would be the best opportunity to do so?

Timing may not be everything, but it does count quite a bit, as the ancient Greeks understood well. They referred to this notion of rhetorical timing and opportunity in communication as *kairos*. If you want to get people's attention—if you want to persuade them of something, or get them to cooperate with you, or have them identify with you or something you believe in—your timing must be right *given the conditions in which you are operating.* Have you ever known someone whose timing was off, who always made comments a topic behind or leaped ahead to new topics when others were still discussing something introduced and "covered" earlier? In order to get the timing right, you must be able to read the scene effectively.

In addition to paying attention to the group interaction and its topic of conversation, you might also observe *how* the group is handling the topic: What is the style of conversation? Are people having a calm discussion, or is their tone animated? What kind of language are they using to discuss the topic? Is their language elevated or full of jargon and expressions that only they would understand? Are people making declarations, or are they hemming and hawing, qualifying what they say? Are some asking questions? What sorts of things are people using as evidence to support their views in this group: facts, citation of authority, personal experience, gossip, etc.? These are just some of the questions you could, and probably often do, ask unconsciously in order to make effective decisions about how to communicate and behave in an already existing scene.

## Writing Activity 1.1

Describe the scenes you experienced yesterday. What different places were you in, who did you interact with, and what roles did you play?

## Collaborative Activity 1.1

Make a list of all of the different scenes that you participate in at college. Compare your lists in small groups, and select one scene to analyze or read, as in the example of the social get-together we "attended" earlier in this chapter. Describe the various clues to how participants are expected to behave and interact within the scene your group selected. You might consider the kinds of clues we observed in our social get-together:

   How the place or setting of your scene is structured

   Who is participating and how they present themselves

   What style of communicating is common

   What people are communicating about

   How people are timing their contributions

   Any other elements especially important to the particular scene you are analyzing

## MAKING RHETORICAL CHOICES

Observing a scene and reading it by the process described above help you make more effective choices about what to say, how to say it, to whom, and when. Scholars who study the art of communication refer to these choices as rhetorical choices. **Rhetoric** is the use of language to accomplish something, and **rhetorical choices** are the decisions speakers and writers make in order to accomplish something with language. Rhetorical choices include

What sort of tone and language to use;

How to engage and address others;

How to develop, organize, and present one's ideas so that others can relate to them;

What kinds of examples to use when communicating;

When and how to start talking and when and how to stop.

The more appropriate your rhetorical choices, the more likely you are to communicate effectively.

*The scene in which you participate helps determine which choices are appropriate.* Whatever their writing tasks, writers are always making rhetorical choices as they ask themselves questions such as

"What should I write about?"

"How should I organize it?"

"What should I include?"

"How should I begin?"

In fact, "How should I begin?" is perhaps the most significant—and challenging—question a writer can ask himself or herself. Yet answers to this question and others like it do not need to be as mysterious or elusive as they are sometimes imagined to be. Imagine how differently you would answer such questions if you were in your home writing in your diary rather than in a classroom writing an essay examination. You can develop answers to such questions by examining the context of your writing, what we in this book are calling **scenes of writing**.

Just as you make decisions about how to act based on your knowledge of the social scene you are acting in at any given time, so too writers make decisions about how and what to write based on their knowledge of the rhetorical scenes they are writing in. *The more effectively you understand the scene you are writing in, the more effectively you will com-*

*municate. Working from this premise, our goal in this book is to teach you how to make more effective writing choices as you function within and move from one scene of writing to another.*

Begin keeping a list of all the things you write in a day, including such small texts as notes or e-mails as well as longer texts like letters or reports. For each thing you write, describe the writing scene in which it functions—the location or context (workplace, classroom, academic discipline, dorm room, etc.), your role as a writer, your reader(s) and your relationship to them, and your purpose for writing it (what you were trying to accomplish/respond to).

# Defining Scene, Situation, Genre

The four chapters that make up Part I of this book introduce you to the idea of "scenes of writing" and teach you strategies for understanding how to read them and how to write within them. Before we show you how to analyze and then write within different scenes of writing, we begin by defining what we mean by the word *scene* and identify its key components, *situation* and *genre*. These three terms—scene, situation, and genre—figure prominently throughout this book. Indeed, they are the building blocks of all that follows.

Each of these terms receives explanation and examples in what follows, but here are brief definitions of each concept. A *scene* is the overall setting, a place where communication happens among groups of people with some shared objectives. A writing classroom is a scene; so are a restaurant kitchen, a chat room, and an editorial page. A *situation* is the rhetorical interaction happening within a scene. For example, students and teachers discuss readings and respond to each other's writings, cooks and servers discuss food orders, chatters explore topics that interest them, and editorial writers convey their opinions on current issues. A *genre* is a common way of responding rhetorically to a situation, including class discussions and writing prompts, restaurant meal orders, chat room postings, and editorials.

We begin with **scene** because it is the overarching term. *Scene is a place in which communication happens among groups of people with some shared objectives.* Examples of a scene range from a large tax accounting firm to a small business, from a classroom to a sorority house, from a doctor's office to a peace rally, from a baseball game to a bar to a criminal trial—to name but a few. In this book, we will help you explore the way communication happens in a variety of scenes, from academic scenes to workplace scenes to public scenes.

Certainly, not all scenes are so obviously physical as a doctor's office or a ball game. The "place" of a scene can extend across well-defined physical spaces. For example, the college or university you are attending is one scene, a clear physical place. But it also participates in a larger **academic scene**, a "place" of academia that reaches across colleges and universities throughout the world. Within the larger academic scene, there are a number of different disciplinary scenes, such as English, history, geography, and chemistry. These scenes consist of groups of people who have their own bodies of knowledge, facts, and theories; their own research methods; their own ways of communicating with one another—all of which reflect their shared objectives: to advance and convey understanding of a subject matter. You may learn to write case studies in your psychology class, lab reports in your biology class, and profiles in your sociology class. Each piece of writing will reflect its scene and should meet special expectations in terms of use of evidence, special terminologies, special styles and formats.

To illustrate, suppose you are taking a class in architectural history. This class will familiarize you with a specific subject matter: styles of architecture throughout the ages, landmark buildings, and ideas of influential designers like I. M. Pei and Frank Lloyd Wright. You will also gain knowledge of the economic and social forces that have shaped architectural structures—as well as the beliefs and values of architects and others who participate in the larger architectural scene, such as their struggles with the social and ethical issues of preservation. In order to feel comfortable in this scene and function effectively in it, you will need to become familiar with the participants' language—their use of terms such as *rectilinear design* or the distinctions between concepts such as *shingle style* versus *stick style*. Finally, you will need to become familiar with the methods of communicating within this scene—perhaps by writing architectural descriptions of buildings, following guidelines set by the National Register of Historic Places. To participate effectively in this academic scene, you must participate in its **rhetorical practices**—practices which reflect the group's shared objectives.

Like the academic scenes with which they overlap (as students move from architecture classes, for example, to architecture firms), **workplace scenes** are also places where communication happens among groups of people with some shared objectives. Your ability to succeed in the workplace depends on your ability to use the language of the scene in *appropriate ways*, to achieve its shared objectives—whether you are asked to write an e-mail to your coworkers to promote the company picnic or a sales letter to clients to promote a new product.

As in academic scenes, with their specialized disciplines, workplace scenes are also made up of smaller scenes: various departments and social organizations whose specialized ways of communicating reflect their own shared objectives. An engineering firm, for example, represents one workplace scene; its departments (human resources and design, for example) represent smaller scenes. (The profession of engineers represents another, larger scene.) With engineers' emphases on form, precision, and technical detail, an employee in an engineering firm will need to know how to produce an organized and detailed technical report—with title sheet, table of contents, list of figures, definition of the problem, design presentation, letter of transmittal, and closure—and will need to be familiar with the information that should be contained within each section of the report. As we saw with the language of architecture, the shared technical knowledge of engineers is expressed through a shared language. A mechanical engineer is likely to be familiar with a *gear box design,* which may involve terms meaningful to other members of this scene (terms such as *input/output RPM, torque,* and *HP capacity*) but mostly meaningless to those of us outside this scene.

Outside of and often interacting with academic and workplace scenes, groups exist at various levels in civic or **public scenes** to achieve different kinds of shared objectives. If you have ever observed a criminal trial, for example, you would have seen a scene that involves a place (a courtroom) in which communication happens among groups of people (judge, jury, lawyers, defendant(s), plaintiff(s), witnesses, court reporter, bailiffs, and observers) with some shared objectives (most generally, to reach some kind of verdict and, more ideally, to seek justice through a fair trial). The combination of the courtroom, the participants, and the shared objectives is what *constitutes,* in general, the criminal trial as a scene. In other public scenes, political groups, such as the local branch of the Democratic Party, work to elect their candidates and to achieve their agendas by using pamphlets, news releases, fund-raising letters, and other kinds of texts, to spread, in their own language, information about pertinent political issues. Other community action groups, whether created to stop the closing of a local elementary school or to promote the use of the public library, exist in particular scenes and use language in particular ways to achieve their particular objectives. At times, such public scenes can be quite large. City inhabitants may share a common newspaper, with its editorials and letters to the editor addressing local issues, and people may share some regional objectives. Even larger groups like Amnesty International have branches across the nation but still share common objectives and use their newsletters, Web sites, and other ways of communicating to reach their goals.

In this book, we distinguish between academic, workplace, and public scenes in order to help you identify different types of scenes. Actually, these categories may not be clearly distinct. Quite often, scenes overlap. For instance, the trial scene is both a public scene and a workplace scene: a public scene for observers, defendants, plaintiffs, and jurors and a workplace scene for judges, lawyers, court reporters, and bailiffs. Similarly, you likely inhabit multiple academic, workplace, and public scenes, often simultaneously.

## ACTING WITHIN SCENES

We have seen that, just as understanding a scene helps an actor act within it, understanding scenes is an important first step in learning how to write within them. But the writer does not just passively sit by while the scene creates a piece of writing. Instead, the writer actively makes rhetorical decisions. The individual writer acting within a particular scene has a range of choices to make—choices regarding what information to include, how to organize that information, and how best to present it. And to make these decisions well the writer must analyze and interpret the scene. The writer has the very important role of constructing a text that is appropriate in terms of content, organization, format, and style. Writers draw on their knowledge of a scene, especially on how others have responded similarly within that scene, in order to develop strategies for how best to respond.

Imagine, for instance, that you have an item that you would like to sell—a bike, for instance. You might choose to post a flyer at the grocery store, send an e-mail to everyone in your address book, or create a listing for an online auction service like eBay. Another option is to write an ad that will appear in your local newspaper's classifieds section. If you decide to write a classified ad, how will you know what to do? You will have to familiarize yourself with the scene of the classifieds within the newspaper. You might start by defining the groups of people involved in this scene and their shared objectives. One group involved includes the subscribers to the newspaper who come to this place where communication happens (the classifieds section) with the shared objectives of looking for a product/service to buy or sell. Another group of people in this scene is the newspaper's classifieds staff, whose shared objectives are to sell advertisement space and to compile all of the necessary information for selling the product (name, price, contact number) or service while maintaining the newspaper's policy of brevity and space for other ads. The group of those (including you) who *place* ads may even share some objectives with the classifieds staff, such as the objective of brevity, since the cost of advertisements is per word.

Such knowledge of the scene is critical because it helps guide your rhetorical choices regarding content, language, length, and format. For example, knowing that the classified staff needs to pack many ads into a small space and that they charge by the word, you will understand why your ad must be so short. Knowing that some readers come looking for specific items to buy, you will understand how important it is to highlight what kind of thing you are selling. To decide exactly how to achieve your purpose of selling your item, you will likely draw on what you already know about the classifieds from having used them in the past and on the knowledge available in the classifieds section. In the section itself, you would find, first, examples of ads, such as the ones shown here.

**CLASSIFIED ADVERTISING**   WEDNESDAY, DECEMBER 11, 2002

By looking at these examples you can see how people describe their items, the sort of language they use, what information they include and do not include, how they organize the ad, and so on. Observing these features of ads is like observing the kinds of conversations people are having at the party we described earlier. Your second source of information about the scene of classified ads is the explicit guidelines the newspaper staff includes, usually printed at the beginning of the classified section. Looking at the newspaper's policies regarding ads (cost per line, deadlines, and so forth) will tell you how to get your ad placed. By combining your observations about what ads look like and your reading of the newspaper's rules, you can write an ad that effectively participates in this scene—and achieves your goal of selling your bike. So writing a classified ad involves more than just knowing something about the item you are selling; it involves knowing how to develop strategies for presenting that item within the classifieds scene. Such strategies are learned through understanding the scene itself, whatever that particular scene might be.

Of course, even though your knowledge of the scene helps you frame your classified ad, there is still room for individual interpretation and choice—decisions on exactly how much and what information to include, how to balance the item's defects (if any) and its strengths, and how vividly to describe the item. The scene acts on you as an individual writer, but as a participant in that scene you also act on (and within) it.

## Collaborative Activity 1.2

Write a classified ad for an item you wish to sell or can imagine selling. In small groups, share your ads and note similarities and differences in responses. What accounts for the similarities? Speculate also on the reasons for any differences in the ads. To what extent were the content, format, language, and tone influenced by the scene of writing? What part did individual choices and decisions play in the differences among your ads? Explain.

## INTERACTING WITHIN SITUATIONS

When you need to write a classified ad, you encounter not just the large scene of classified ads but also the particular *situation* of writing *your* ad. *Situations, as we define them, are the various rhetorical interactions happening within a scene, involving participants, subjects, settings, and purposes.* In other words, each situation represents a specific rhetorical interaction that involves certain participants who are using language to engage with a certain subject in certain ways for certain purposes. A closer look at the scene of a criminal trial (as described on p. 9) for example, reveals that this scene has many situations in it. A few of the situations—the rhetorical interactions—that together make up the scene of the criminal trial include making opening statements, swearing in witnesses, testifying, cross-examining witnesses, making closing statements, instructing the jury, deliberating, reading the verdict, and sentencing. In each of these situations, a specific group of people is engaged in a specific rhetorical task, which requires them to relate to and communicate with one another in certain ways—to use language to accomplish something specific within the overall scene.

Not every participant within the scene of a criminal trial is or needs to be involved in all its situations, of course. For example, the lawyers, defendants, court reporter, and observers do not participate in the jury deliberations. Only jury members are engaged in the rhetorical interactions of that situation as participants dealing with a specific subject (the facts presented at trial) in a specific setting (behind closed doors at the end of a trial) for specific purposes (to come to a consensus about whether the prosecution has proven guilt beyond a reasonable doubt). In another situation within the scene of a criminal trial—the situation of cross-examining witnesses—a different rhetorical interaction takes place, involving a different group of participants (most immediately, a lawyer and a witness, while judge, jury, and other lawyers observe). In this situation, a lawyer and a witness are usually engaged in a more "aggressive" interaction, with the lawyer perhaps trying to expose or discredit a witness. The situation of cross-examination, then, engages the participants in a specific rhetorical interaction, involving a specific setting (the witness in a chair, the lawyer standing before the court), a specific subject (testimony), and a specific purpose (to test whether the witness's testimony might prove incorrect or unreliable).

Because situation involves rhetorical interaction, it is often referred to by teachers of writing as the **rhetorical situation.** Within a rhetorical situation, how participants communicate about a certain subject will depend on **who** these participants are, what **setting** they are in, and what their **purposes** are in communicating. For example, a writer's purpose (what he or she wishes to accomplish) will influence his or her approach to the **subject,** suggesting what information needs to be included and how the subject might be presented. The writer's understanding of audience and the setting will, likewise, shape how the writer approaches the purpose and subject and will also influence the writer's **tone** (the attitude that comes through the writing) and the writer's **persona** (the image presented, the character of the writer that comes through). *These elements—the participants, subject, setting, and purpose—interact within rhetorical situations.*

Consider the scene you are in while taking this writing course and the rhetorical situations it includes. Within the broader academic scene, you are in the scene of a writing class, and within the classroom you participate in many interactions, from chatting with a fellow student to listening to a lecture to contributing to a class discussion or working on a group task. Even though all these *situations* exist in the same scene of your writing class, they differ in exactly who is participating and in what ways, what subjects they address, and the purposes people have for participating in them. Even the setting varies a bit, with the group work occurring in a small circle of desks rather than the larger classroom of a lecture. Any differences of participants, subjects, settings, or purposes from one situation to another influence how you act within the larger class scene. When listening to a lecture, you probably take some notes for yourself, while in a group activity you might record the group's responses or complete a form for your teacher. You probably use more formal language when contributing to a class discussion than you do when you work with your peers in a group. The persona or image you project when speaking with classmates without the teacher present may differ from that you project when your audience includes your teacher.

## Writing Activity 1.3

One situation in this writing class is responding to the Activities in this textbook. You have already seen in this chapter two other Writing Activities and may have responded to one or both. You have also encountered two Collaborative Activities. Select any one of those four Activities and consider its rhetorical situation. Identify the participants, subject, setting, and purpose in this activity. Explore how each of those elements might affect what you would do in responding to it.

## Writing Activity 1.4

Looking back on the classified ad you wrote for Collaborative Activity 1.2 (p. 12), use the terms you have just learned to describe its rhetorical situation within the scene of the classifieds section: Who are the participants in this situation? What are they interacting about (subject), where (setting), and why (purpose)?

## ANALYZING THE SITUATIONS OF THREE EDITORIALS

The following three editorials, which are on the topic of drilling for oil in the Arctic National Wildlife Refuge (ANWR), exemplify three different scenes and rhetorical situations, each with its own interaction of subject, participants, setting, and purposes. The first editorial is written by the vice president of species conservation at Defenders of Wildlife; the second editorial is written by a student and native Alaskan; the third editorial is written by the chairman of the International Association of Drilling Contractors (IADC).

As you read the editorials, consider the different scenes of writing (a national conservation organization, a university, and a corporation), and try to identify the various elements of the rhetorical situations within these scenes:

- *Who* the participants are, especially writer and readers
- *Where* the interaction is taking place (the setting of the interaction, which in this case has to do with where the editorial appears)
- *What* the subject of the interaction is
- *Why* the writer is presenting the subject in this way (what purposes seem to be driving the interaction)

Notice how, even though the editorials address the same topic, they address it differently based on their rhetorical situations. As you identify elements of each rhetorical situation, pay attention to how they affect how the writers of the editorials present themselves, describe ANWR, and characterize the oil companies.

■ ■ ■

# New Technologies But Still the Same Messy Business

Bob Ferris

*Bob Ferris is the vice president of species conservation at Defenders of Wildlife. This editorial appeared in TomPaine.com, an online journal of progressive opinion.*

Each time an argument for oil drilling in the Arctic National Wildlife Refuge is analyzed and rebutted, a new one emerges. President Bush suggested that drilling would help solve California's energy woes, but that makes as much sense as filling up a car's gas tank because its pistons don't work. Others have argued that ANWR could help us become independent of OPEC, but in the unlikely event that there's enough oil in Alaska to make a difference, trade regulations under the World Trade Organization would prevent keeping all the oil for domestic use.

Now the oil industry is touting advances in technology that would let them drill with minimal environmental impact. They are using this new technology to paint a very pretty, almost clinical picture of petroleum extraction. In recent weeks, a number of media outlets, including the *New York Times* and *60 Minutes* have run stories heralding the new technology.

Yet this pristine view is strongly at odds with experience. Oil extraction, much like open heart surgery, is a very messy business.

Of primary importance is not fancy technology, but whether we should trust oil company claims of cleaner, more ethical behavior. Incredibly, they are projecting this newly sanitary image at the same time they are reporting an oil or chemical spill every eighteen hours on Alaska's North Slope. Then there's the case of BP-Amoco—one of the most likely refuge lessees. The firm must be seriously hoping that their $22 million settlement with EPA for dumping toxic chemicals in Alaska (not to mention the potential congressional investigation of its business practices) will somehow not make it to the public's radar screen before Congress votes on whether to open up the refuge to drilling.

That point aside, while improved technologies can certainly lessen the impact of major surgery or oil drilling, neither is easy on the patient. And the scars—whether on flesh or land—never do disappear. Period.

Conservationists favor technologies that lessen the impact of necessary resource extraction. But all of these technologies have both pros and cons. Using the "targeted drilling" featured in the news reports, drill heads can steer through the rock laterally deep below the earth's surface.

The benefit is indeed a reduced drilling footprint, but the trade-off is a need for dramatically more detailed seismic data, derived by blasting dynamite and by even more intrusive and extensive seismic testing than ever before. This seismic testing is not benign and visitors to the refuge can still see evidence of testing that is nearly two decades old.

The oil industry also boasts of ice roads "harmlessly" made out of water that protect the delicate tundra. They fail to simultaneously mention that the vast volume of unfrozen water they use to make those roads is rare in the arctic. And it is much needed by fish that often get pumped up with the water and become part of these harmless roads.

Drilling and seismic activities comprise just a small percentage of the total extractive insult to land, water and wildlife from oil development. Behind the drillers come the legions of roads, water use, pipelines, garbage dumps, worker housing and a host of associated infrastructure problems that even the most gee-whiz drilling practices cannot eliminate. As the *New York Times* noted in a January 30, 2001 editorial, imposing this industrial sprawl on the pristine coastal plain of the Arctic National Wildlife Refuge is an unconscionable price to pay just to roll the dice on six months worth of oil.

The new technology is promising, but it will never mean that drilling can occur without serious environmental consequences. Defenders of Wildlife would rather see the country's technological elbow grease applied to energy conservation, which would have the same result as drilling, but with less cost to people and the environment.

If we truly need the oil we could extract it from the plugged and abandoned wells that dot our country's mid-section and which contain many billions of barrels. In fact, two areas in north and east Texas contain roughly 7 billion barrels of oil—more than twice the mid-range estimates for the Arctic National Wildlife Refuge. If the president and vice president are so gung-ho to drill why don't they look a little closer to home?

Americans love the promise of having their cake and eating it—the seductive voice that says we can have oil development and an Arctic Wildlife Refuge. We can't, and no amount of oil company advertising will alter the laws of physics and biology to make it so.

## My Opinion: The Shortsightedness and Exploitation of Oil Drilling

Elizabeth Morrison

*Elizabeth Morrison is a senior majoring in general arts and sciences and a* Penn Collegian *columnist. This editorial appeared in the* Penn Collegian *newspaper.*

In a national news magazine recently, I saw an advertisement: "Alaskans support oil drilling." It was an ad picturing smiling (presumably) Alaskan people, grinning in agreement with the oil industry, who (obviously) paid for the ad. I've seen this ad now in the *New York Times, Newsweek* and *Time.* The advertising campaign is an effort to convince the continental United States that because Alaskans support yet more oil exploration, they should also.

I've certainly never polled the 450,000 people who live in Alaska, but I know absolutely that I am not the only Alaskan who is against the opening of the Arctic National Wildlife Refuge for oil drilling.

For those who don't know, there is an ongoing battle between boom and bust oil developers and environmentalists about whether to open up ANWR for oil exploration and drilling, or to keep the land protected.

Situated on Alaska's North Slope, just west of the Canadian border, the 19 million acre refuge is home to several thousand indigenous peoples, grizzly bears, musk oxen, wolves, migratory birds and a herd of 180,000 caribou. But to the oil industry—and those who benefit from it—the refuge is nothing but a potentially profitable lode of black gold.

This battle tipped for a brief period in favor of drilling opponents after the *Exxon Valdez* oil spill. But in the three years since the Persian Gulf War, the political mood has changed drastically. Once purely a state issue, it has now been brought to national attention, and opinions have swung in favor of drilling. Even the change of presidential administration last November did little to stop the tide of opinion. In fact, shortly before the election, the Democratic Party took its opposition to oil drilling in ANWR out of its platform. Since then, a tide of senators and members of Congress have flown in their private jets to the middle of ANWR, looked at the tundra and proclaimed it not worth saving.

Of course, drilling may have seemed logical after the emotionally frenzied aftermath of the Gulf War. Why should we be dependent on foreign oil, politicians asked, when there is oil waiting to be tapped in our own backyard?

I think there are an awful lot of reasons. First, contrary to what developers and oil companies publicly say, there are innumerable variables and guesswork involved in oil drilling—and absolutely no guarantee that oil will actually be found, much less be actually exploitable. Although developers and those opposed to drilling agree that there is indeed oil under the plain, the size of the oil deposit is a mystery.

The U.S. Interior Department's estimates range from 600 million barrels to as much as 9.2 billion barrels. Even the highest estimate, an almost unimaginable amount to most of us, is only the amount of oil the United States uses in just one year. In addition, the department puts the odds of actually finding a commercially exploitable oil field at just one in five. Assuming (and this is a major assumption) an oil field is found, as long as 10 years may be needed to gear up before major production could begin.

Compounding the logical inconsistencies and practical fallibility, opening up the refuge to oil drilling would be a gross intrusion on one of the last untouched wilderness areas in the United States. Politicians and oil men who advocate drilling argue that it would create thousands of jobs and billions of dollars in tax revenues.

In reality, drilling would only be lucrative to certain people, namely those mentioned above. However, those who would not profit and who would be most adversely affected are, ironically (but not surprisingly), those with the least voice in whether the refuge is opened. This includes the indigenous peoples who have lived in what is now ANWR for thousands of years. To advocate drilling is to blatantly disregard the Native Alaskans who bitterly oppose the rape of the land and intrusion on their way of life.

Last summer, at an open forum on this issue, Sarah James, a tribal leader of the Gwich'in Indians said, "This is a simple issue. We have the right to continue our way of life. We are caribou people."

To open the refuge for drilling is also to virtually ignore the environmental effect oil exploration and exploitation has on the animals who live there, and on the land itself. The most-often-cited example is the caribou. The herd that makes its home in the refuge represents the largest migratory pattern in the

United States, and it would be in danger of disruption and displacement, as would other birds and animals.

Oil is a non-renewable energy source; a fact that advocates of drilling conveniently neglect to address. Opening ANWR for oil drilling would only act as a short-term drug for a chronic ailment. It would succeed in putting off, yet again, the urgent need to find alternative energy sources. It would be folly to count on any oil in the refuge to fuel our gas-guzzling lifestyles for long. The contribution to U.S. petroleum needs would be small compared to other means of reducing demand and finding alternative energy sources.

The billions of dollars squandered in oil exploration, oil drilling and oil production is money not spent on potentially more-beneficial activities. Most importantly, it compromises the inherent value of the land, the animals and the people who live there. The proposal to open the ANWR for oil drilling is an attempt at a short-term solution to a problem that requires careful long-term management.

This is no longer a state issue; as I said above, it has long been a national one. We are all dependent on oil, and we all suffer, sooner or later, from the environmental consequences. In our increasingly global economy, the use of one of our greatest natural resources—land—is all of our responsibility.

# Alaska Environmental Bugaboos

Bernie W. Stewart

*From Bernie W. Stewart, chairman of the International Association of Drilling Contractors. This editorial appeared in the IADC corporate magazine,* Drilling Contractor.

As IADC chairman this year, one of my most rewarding activities has been the opportunity to travel to our Chapters and visit with contractors in a variety of markets, both geographical and operational. Most recently, I was the guest of our IADC Alaska Chapter. In addition to participating in a well-attended Chapter meeting, **Doyon Drilling, Nordic-Calista Services** and **Pool Arctic Alaska** graciously hosted me to the North Slope. I was very impressed by how the North Slope drilling contractors and operators conduct their business. Through close cooperation, the industry has developed ingenious adaptations for this very difficult environment.

Speaking of the environment, much is made over the allegedly deleterious effect of drilling on the Alaskan ecology. I'm here to tell you that drilling operations are in no way going to harm the environment in Alaska. Industry's environmental precautions in Alaska deserve tremendous applause.

Technology has been used to great advantage in Alaska. Despite the field's vast area, the Alaskan industry has been miserly when it comes to generating footprints of drilling operations. They have done their utmost to minimize the number of well pads through the canny use of horizontal drilling and offset wells.

The caribou are among the most visible source of nervous anxiety. The fact is that these magnificent animals graze unconcernedly around the drilling rigs. The scene is little different than cows munching pasture around a rig in Texas. One experience was particularly striking. In Alaska, the buildings stand 7 ft off the ground to avoid damaging the permafrost. At one site, a mother caribou stood with her calf in the shade of such a building. So much for our industry's threat to the caribous!

This brings me to the great Alaskan environmental bugaboo— the Alaskan National Wildlife Refuge. The US Congress regularly denies drilling access to ANWR. From the hype, one might conclude that allowing drilling on this frozen wilderness is to invite an environmental disaster on a par with Chernobyl. In all this, one gets the notion that ANWR is a pristine Eden of scenic proportions equal to Yellowstone or Yosemite.

From "A" to "Y," ANWR couldn't be more different from Yellowstone. There are no sweeping forests and grand roiling rivers, all teeming with wildlife unknown in modern society. ANWR is a barren and empty place. It is a land of endless tundra where no vegetation stands taller than 6 in. The principal wildlife is the migratory Porcupine Caribou Herd. Having observed the aplomb with which caribou react to drilling activities elsewhere on the North Slope, I have no doubt that this 150,000-animal herd would be similarly unaffected.

Part of the reason is there's plenty of room in ANWR. Out of the refuge's 19 million acres, 17.5 million acres are permanently off limits to exploration. Development would be confined to only a small fraction of ANWR's coastal plain. Estimates are that this field could reach a peak output equal to 10% of total current US production. Developing ANWR would create jobs, enhance national security and lower consumer costs, all at an extremely remote environmental risk in a forbidding area of the US. In a cost-benefit analysis, it's easy to see the logical solution. ■

## Collaborative Activity 1.3

Working with classmates, select one of the three editorials and describe in as much detail as you can the rhetorical situation to which it is responding. Who are the likely participants in this situation? What purposes seem to be driving these participants? What's the setting in which the editorial appears, including the date of its publication? And how does the interaction between the participants, the purposes, and the setting affect how the subject of the editorial is treated and presented? Describe some of the choices that the writer makes regarding kinds of organization, examples, style, tone, and persona as a result of his or her situation. Then explain how these rhetorical choices were shaped by the situation of writing.

## Writing Activity 1.5

Keeping in mind their different rhetorical situations, compare how the three editorials treat the topic of oil drilling in ANWR. (For example, even though the first two editorials take a similar position on the topic, they differ because of where and when they were published, who wrote them, and who would be reading them.) How do the shared objectives, beliefs, and values of the differing scenes (the national conservation organization, the academic scene, and the corporate scene) affect the rhetorical choices? Look back over the editorials and compare how the writers present themselves in each, the ways they treat ANWR as a place, and how they describe the oil companies. Once you have described the differences, speculate on the effects these differences might have on readers of the editorials.

As the three editorials exemplify, each time we communicate, we act within a rhetorical situation. When we write, we perform a rhetorical action—an action shaped by the situation we are responding to. As you discovered in the previous activities, this action involves all sorts of strategic decisions and choices, choices regarding vocabulary, sentence structure, tone, persona, organization, and supporting evidence. These choices are guided not only by the situation—the participants, subject, setting, and purposes—but by the chosen type of writing (in the case above, an editorial). The type of writing chosen guides decisions about such elements as the use of examples, length (fairly brief for an editorial), tone, and persona (the editorials chosen as examples are informal). The next section will focus further on this key component of scene, the type of writing or genre.

## ACTING WITH GENRES

We know that each of the various situations that make up a scene represents a specific rhetorical interaction taking place within that scene. As participants find themselves in these situations over and over, they develop habits or rituals of interacting within them. In the case of the criminal trial, for example, participants have developed typical rhetorical ways for dealing with such situations as swearing in witnesses, delivering the opening statements, or presenting evidence to the jury. In each of these repeated situations, participants draw on a pattern of action that is already in place, widely accepted by participants in the scene to guide them as they act in that situation. They do not need to invent everything anew. Some of these patterns are more flexible than others (the conventions for the swearing-in of witnesses are more strict than the conventions for opening statements, for example), but all involve certain conventions for using language to accomplish efficiently and effectively certain tasks within the situation. This is where genre comes into play. *Genres are the typical rhetorical ways of responding to a situation that repeatedly occurs within a scene.*

You may already be familiar with the term *genre*, which literally means "type," as in genres of books (mystery, science fiction, autobiography, textbook), genres of music (classical, country, alternative), or genres of movies (action adventures, romantic comedies, "slasher" movies, or thrillers). But genres are more than just categorizations. Genres carry with them certain expectations—expectations that a romantic comedy will end happily or that an action adventure will incorporate high-tech special effects. Where, you might ask, do these expectations come from?

Your expectations of genre are based on your participation in scenes that repeat themselves and your prior experiences with reading, writing, and using genres. For example, how do you know how to respond to the Writing Activities in this textbook? Much of your knowledge comes from having written such classroom activities before, in other classes with other textbooks and teachers. While the details of this particular set of activities and your teacher's use of them probably vary somewhat from your past experience, you know from your past experience what to expect in them and how to respond appropriately, to meet your teacher's expectations.

You might be surprised to realize that most of our spoken and written communication operates within generic conventions. Some of our generic responses, our responses to situations that repeat themselves, are automatic. When the phone rings, you know, without even thinking about it, to answer "Hello" or "Smith residence" or maybe even "Bob [your name] speaking." Any response that varies too much from these typical responses might confuse the caller at the other end. Similarly, when you write a personal letter to a friend, you know to begin by addressing the recipient ("Dear Sue") and greeting him or her (usually with "How are you?" or "How's it going?" or even "What's up?"). How do we automatically know how to act within these situations? We know because these are situations that have been played out many times, and we are familiar with our roles as communicators within these scenes. You are not the first to have answered a phone call or written a personal letter. These generic conventions have arisen in response to a situation that has been repeated. Without these generic responses to situations that repeat themselves, we would have the almost impossible task of inventing new ways of communicating each time we confronted a rhetorical situation.

In the next two chapters, we will teach you how to analyze genres in greater detail so that you can turn your understanding *of* genre into your writing *in* the genre. And then in Parts II and III of the book, you will have the opportunity to apply your genre knowledge to write more effectively in academic, workplace, and public scenes.

## Writing Activity 1.6

To illustrate how genres arise based on rhetorical situations that repeat themselves, consider the genre of the postcard. (If you've never written or received a postcard, answer the following questions for the genre of the greeting card.) What repeated situation does it arise from? What is its purpose? What are the expectations of the readers of postcards? What relationship with readers is established? What are the particular features or textual regularities that make up the postcard? For the next class meeting, bring in a postcard that you or someone you know has received and compare your findings.

## Writing Activity 1.7

Read back over the editorials presented earlier in this chapter. Despite their differences, what do they share in common that defines them as editorials? What makes editorials different, say, from a newspaper article, an advertisement, or even an argument paper you would write in your writing course? What do editorials allow their writers to accomplish that these other genres may not?

# Putting Scene, Situation, and Genre Back Together

Let us summarize the key terms we have been describing and then return to the scene you are now becoming more familiar with, that of the writing course, to show how they work together:

- **Scene:** a place where communication happens among groups of people with some shared objectives. Think of the scene as the overarching site that frames the action.
- **Situation:** the rhetorical interaction happening within a scene, involving participants, subjects, settings, and purposes. Scenes often have multiple situations within them, each with its own specific

participants (who), subjects to deal with (what), settings in which they interact (where and when), and purposes for doing what they do (why). Together, the participants, their subject, setting, and purposes combine to create a specific rhetorical situation.

- **Genre:** the typical rhetorical way of responding to a repeated situation within a scene. As situations within a scene repeat themselves, participants develop rhetorical conventions for interacting and getting things done within them—typical ways of using language to accomplish certain actions in a situation. Genres are these typified rhetorical actions.

The typical writing class, likely similar to the one in which you are currently enrolled, is a scene. It is a place where communication happens among teacher and students who have some shared objectives. These objectives, which are frequently outlined in the course syllabus, vary from institution to institution and teacher to teacher, but, generally, they could include something like "teaching students to write effective academic papers" and "encouraging students to read and write critically."

In this scene, and working to accomplish its shared objectives, are a number of situations, each of which involves teacher and students (who) in specific rhetorical interactions: certain ways of interacting with one another in order to engage in a specific subject (what), in a specific setting (where), for specific purposes (why). Situations in a writing class scene might include peer review workshops involving students, in groups, as they exchange, read, and respond to each other's writing in order to help their writing improve; student-teacher conferences, a different rhetorical situation, as student and teacher meet in the teacher's office to discuss a student's progress on an assignment or in the class in order to help the student make better progress; and class discussion, yet another rhetorical interaction. In each of these situations within the scene of the writing class, students and teachers make different rhetorical choices as they interact with each other on different subjects, in different settings, and for different purposes.

To help them function effectively in these and        other distinct situations, teacher and students use various genres, each of which enables them to respond in typical rhetorical ways to these repeated situations. To respond to the situation of evaluating student writing, for instance, teachers use the genres of margin comments and end comments. To respond to the situation of peer-review workshops, students often use the genre of peer-review sheets as guidelines. To respond to the situation of generating ideas, students use the genres of freewriting, clustering, and brainstorming. To respond to the situation of explaining common concepts, teacher and students use the genre of textbooks. These, as well as other genres such as the syllabus, assignment sheets, class journals, paper outlines, final drafts, and others all help teachers and students function effectively in the various situations of the writing class scene.

## Collaborative Activity 1.4

Working in groups, use our key terms—scene, situation, and genre—to describe your own writing course scene. What makes your writing course a scene (a place where communication happens among groups of people with some shared objectives)? Describe a particular situation or rhetorical interaction within your writing course, and define the subject, the setting, the purpose, and the roles of the participants. What genres are used to interact within this repeated situation? Generate a list of your answers, and compare it with the findings of other groups of your classmates.

# Learning Strategies for Observing and Describing Scenes

Scenes fill our lives. Any given culture is defined by the combination of its many scenes, some of which are more powerful than others. Not all members of a culture, of course, interact within or even are aware of all its scenes. Some scenes require certain credentials from their participants and are therefore more exclusive (such as certain workplace scenes like law firms or social scenes like sororities and fraternities), while others are more public (such as the scene of a peace rally or protest). As we mentioned at the beginning of the chapter, you already interact within numerous scenes and most likely are able to navigate between some of them with more ease than others. You also are just in the process of getting to know some new scenes, scenes such as your academic major and other college or university scenes. And, of course, there are various scenes you probably hope one day to join, including workplace scenes. Observing these less familiar scenes can help you eventually participate in them more fully and more effectively.

If a culture is defined by its numerous scenes, then your role and place in the culture will in part be defined by your participation in these scenes. This is, in fact, one reason sociologists and anthropologists give for why it is important to observe scenes: Observing scenes can tell us things about how a culture works, how people interact, and why people do what they do. By studying the scenes in which we participate, we can learn something about ourselves.

*Ethnography* is the sociological term for studying a scene from an insider's perspective. One gains access to the scene and then conducts field-work by immersion into that scene over a period of time, sometimes lasting years. An ethnographer carefully collects data by observing what happens within a scene: the actions and interactions taking place, the daily routines of people within that scene, who does what, when, and why. He or she col-lects these observations in field notes. The ethnographer also supplements observations by interviewing participants within a scene and collecting arti-facts from the scene, such as written documents used by participants within it. In short, ethnography allows a researcher to observe how individuals interact, behave, and think in specific settings.

Observing scenes is a particularly relevant activity for writers since effective writers are mini-ethnographers of sorts. They observe scenes in order to understand how and why individuals communicate within them. Such observation enables writers to access and begin to identify the various situations and genres contained within these scenes so that they can more effectively participate within them.

You probably already use various strategies for observing scenes. We all constantly observe our worlds in the process of making decisions about how we should act within them, whether we are entering a party or deciding whether to speak up in class. In this section, we will build on this ability so that you can apply it to your acts of writing. We will also help you expand on this ability by guiding you from observation to *analysis* of how and why people do what they do within a scene and the underlying reasons and beliefs that shape people's behaviors and interactions. You will be able to use this knowledge to participate more meaningfully and critically as writers within different scenes.

For example, notice how the following sample ethnography by Stephanie Smith of a greyhound racing track helps to bring the scene to life through close observation and description. Smith's ethnography was writ-ten for an anthropology course and appears in a book called *Field Ethnography: A Manual for Doing Cultural Anthropology.*

The study by itself is interesting for the access and insight it gives into people who participate in this scene. But as you read it, pay specific atten-tion to the scene itself and try to identify some of the situations and genres found within it. From what Smith writes, what do you think makes the grey-hound track a scene? In what ways are the three areas Smith describes smaller scenes that make up a larger scene? What are some of its situations and what are the components of these situations? And what genres do you notice participants using in this scene? Also, as you read, think about how this knowledge of the scene could help you participate within it. What do you learn from the observation, for example, that might help you figure out how to act in this scene?

■ ▨ ▨

# Ethnography of a Greyhound Track: A Study on Social Stratification and Diehards

Stephanie Smith

When I thought about taking on the Rocky Mountain Greyhound Park as the subject for my ethnographic study, I had some preconceived notions about what it would be like. I wanted to study the "type" of person who participated in the dog races. I was assuming there was one type of person I could classify and study, no problem. I imagined this seedy place with lots of middle-aged down-and-out loners, placing bets with money they hocked their TV to get. I was convinced I could construct a model of this type and fit all of my informants into the mold.

Then I went out to the track. My first thought was, "Oh S——!" as I looked around at the crowds of senior citizens, young couples, business types, and even families with four children. A two-second look around at the track will clue in any moron to the fact that the crowd is a diverse mishmash of every type of person. I had a lot of work to do.

Along with the physical and age diversity was the difference in intentions. Not everyone goes out there just to bet. Some go for the entertainment with the kids or the food. Some go for the novelty of betting, picking dogs for their names, or look at the minimum $2 bet. Others are more serious, studying the dogs and placing big bets. The more I studied, the more I began to see an underlying social structure. This structure is determined by the three areas from which the public can watch the races. Although the focus of my study is not the actual greyhound race, that is the reason everyone is there. I think it is important to understand what the races, the park, and wagering, are all about.

## The Common Denominator: The Setting

The Rocky Mountain Greyhound Park opened in 1949, a few months after the first track in Pueblo started. Located in the north-central part of Colorado

Springs, it sits on approximately 25 acres off Nevada Avenue. The elevation is over 6,000 feet, and to this day RMGP remains the highest greyhound park in the world. It is a part of a nationwide system of 57 tracks. Until this year the racing season at RMGP had been three months in the fall. Due to a recent court decision in which the state of Colorado approved tracks to operate live racing six months a year, the season has been changed to April through September. (Although not publicized, gambling or wagering occurs all throughout the year via closed circuit television. People gather at the park and wager on live races broadcast from other parks.)

The RMGP consists of a racing track, spectator stands (indoor and outdoor), an administrative building, and an immense parking lot (see map). Spectators have three areas to choose from: the Grand Stands, the First Turn Tavern, and the Cloud 9 Restaurant. Admission to each area is $1, $2, and $3, respectively. Race programs sell at $1.25. The park and all areas are opened to the public one hour before the program begins. The program is a set of races, usually 13, that take place one or two times a day. Matinees take place at 1 P.M. Wednesday and Saturday; evening performances take place at 7:30 P.M. A typical 13-race program will last three and a half hours. Most of my work was done during the evening programs.

## Procedure of a Race

Many people arrive as the park opens an hour before the first race. I had even seen a small group waiting for the gates to open one Friday evening. I noticed that the majority of people who arrive at the park early come to figure out their bets, study the night's dog selection, and to view the previous night's replays on the many TVs that cover every nook and cranny of the place.

About fifteen minutes before post time the dogs are paraded before the spectators. There are eight dogs per race, each one wearing a numbered blanket and a muzzle. (The muzzles are worn only to determine the outcome in photo finishes.) They come out single file in numerical order led on a leash by official handlers. Each dog is subject to an inspection; the muzzle and blanket are pulled and tugged. The purpose is to show each dog and its statistics up close on the TV screens. The dogs are paraded up and down the length of the track for all the spectators to see. During this time the people can change or confirm their choices and place a bet. When the scoreboard says "0 min to post," the dogs are placed in the gate according to their numbers. At the announcer's last call the handlers leave the gates and the lights are turned out in the spectator areas. An Aldritt mechanical lure they call "Rocky" then pops out of its gate making its way to the dogs' gate. The announcer does a Johnny Carson type "HERERRRRRRRRRR's ROCKYYYYYYYYYYYYYYY!" at the end of which the gate to the dogs is opened, and the dogs are off.

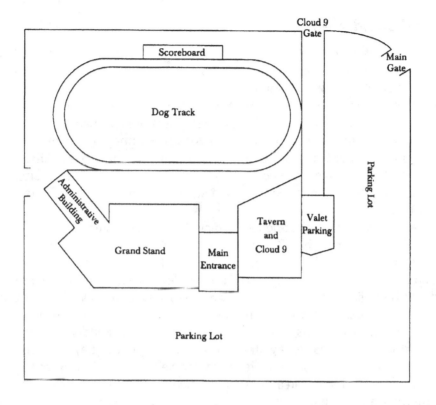

The greyhounds take off from the gate chasing the lure, reaching speeds from 25 to 40 mph. The general speed of the race is determined by the class, "A" being best, "E" and "M" being the lowest ranked. The first turn is usually the deciding factor in the race. The best dog can easily trip or be knocked out on the first turn. After the dogs come out of this turn, the leading two or three dogs are apparent. Of course this can always change, which is what people are literally betting on. When the dogs have gone three-quarters of the track, a light shines on the finish line. The dogs pass the line and a picture is taken. If the 1st, 2nd, and 3rd places are obvious then the paybacks are listed on the scoreboard and TVs right away. If there is any doubt, the picture is analyzed and scores held back until the judges reach a conclusion.

Meanwhile the dogs are stopped by a net farther down the track. The dogs are herded into one area and the handlers scramble to get their dogs back on the leash. The dogs once again are led single file in numerical order back to their respective trainers. The next batch of eight dogs take their place in the lineup to be paraded. This exact procedure is followed for every race I saw. It was pulled off smoothly even in inclement weather and as it says at the bottom of the race programs, "strict post time observed."

## Grand Stand Area

The Grand Stand area holds the largest number of people, 3800, and at $1 is the least expensive to gain entrance to. It is a huge indoor structure with three levels that look out a wall of windows onto the track. The first level is primarily food and betting windows. The entire north wall is dedicated to betting windows (and one information booth), 34 total. There are two bars and concession stands on the south side. The food consists of hot dogs, hamburgers, chips, popcorn, nachos, candy bars, and such. The bars offer beer, wine, and mixed drinks. There are many doors leading to the patio on this side. Scattered all over are TVs. Between the two main stairways are rows of chairs facing large TVs.

The second level is tucked under the main Grand Stand area, above the first level. This is similar to the offerings of the first level. It has 20 windows, one food stand, and one bar. A large-screen floor TV dominates the attention around the tables and rows of chairs. The third level is where most of the seating is. It is just like Grand Stand seating, with reams of seats, one flight next to the other, sloped toward the event. Seating right in front of the window is divided into boxes. It costs $2 to sit in a box seat. Box seats offer a better view of the track, cushioned seats with arm rest/drink holder/ash tray, and separation from the general crowd. The range of people that attend the races, especially in the Grand Stand area, is extremely diverse. The dress is casual—jeans and more jeans, I estimate the percent of whites who attend runs about 60 percent. The other 40 percent consist of mostly black, then Hispanics and Asians. There are couples, families, groups, and "solos." The couples range widely in age and race. The elderly couples usually settle in the box seats close to the window. Usually the man gets up and down, presumably to bet, while the woman sits in her seat. Young couples sit in the Grand Stand area toward the window and bet together. Then there are the buddy couples. Quite a few male duos hang out there, of either the same age or father/son type, I saw very few female duos.

I was surprised to find so many families. The families tend to favor the box seating. Many couples bring their children out to the track, and extended family groups, with grandparents, cousins, and so on, are not uncommon. Children under 18 are not allowed to place bets but they can be in certain areas. The next classification, the solos, were the most interesting to me. This is the type I expected to dominate the scene at the track. The solos are people who hang out at the track alone. My own stereotype for a solo is a 40+ male who hangs out in the upper section of the Grand Stand away from other people. He bets on every race using a system he invented. Since this characterization is a stereotype, I found exceptions to it but not many.

One of my informants who frequents the Grand Stand area is "Flamingo," a 35-year-old black man with a granddaughter. He likes to come to the track by himself, claiming "I'm a loner, I cook for a living. I see [enough] people." He plays the dogs every day the track is open but does not consider himself a "diehard." Diehards are "the ones you can't see. They hang out in the Cloud 9 Room. Instead of work, they are here all the time." Flamingo uses a system of betting that allows him to stay away from the track. He comes up with three numbers and then plays the trifecta (see "wagering") with the same numbers the whole night. He does not know statistics or other information about the dogs like some diehards do; he just plays the numbers. Usually he bets in the future for a whole program. This means he will pick his numbers and place his bets for say a Friday night program on Thursday. This way be does not have to be at the track during the races. "This is not exciting to me! I don't have time for this s——! I look in the paper [the next morning] like a kid at Christmas to see if I won." If he wins he can collect the money the next day.

Flamingo claims to do quite well at the track. He uses the winnings as a supplement to his job income. "I could take a second job, but I take a chance on this." I saw him win with this method. Apparently on one Friday he won $130, Saturday night, $106, and Monday, $480. All of these paybacks were off $2 bets. "I've made about $800 in the last three days out of 48 bucks. I expect more but I settle for this." When Flamingo told me these figures I just kind of nodded my head thinking "yea, RIGHT!" However I saw him win $130 from only $2. Something in his method works.

## First Turn Tavern

The First Turn Tavern is located on the first level in the building west of the Grand Stand area. The tavern has two entrances, one from the main gate and another on the west side of the building. This entrance is exclusively for the tavern and the Cloud 9 Room. Access to the Tavern cost $2 and no one under 18 is allowed. The price includes the use of a table for the duration of the program. The decor of the room is in oak, brass, etched glass, and maroon plastic tabletops.

The Tavern has a capacity of 300. There are four tiered levels of tables and chairs all facing the track. Each table has a small TV that operates for an extra $1.50 and broadcasts network TV as well as the greyhound information. The Tavern offers food and beverages in a bar-type atmosphere. The foods offered are various appetizers, burritos, deli sandwiches, salads, cakes, and ice cream. The bar serves beer, wine, and mixed and blended drinks. The food and drinks are pricier in the Tavern than the Grand Stand, and everything is served to the tables by a waitperson. The only reason to get up from your table is to bet (or go to the bathroom). The Tavern has 17 betting windows.

The first thing I noticed when I walked into the Tavern was a sign that said,

AVOID INCONVENIENCES
BY REFRAINING FROM EXTREMES
IN CASUAL DRESS

I suppose "extremes" is the operative word in that request because the dress of Tavern patrons is quite casual. As in the Grand Stand area, the main trend is jeans. For men, shirts tend to be short-sleeve Izod types, and button-up cotton shirts, a step above the T-shirt. The women are just as casual in printed shirts and blouses.

Another major difference about the Tavern people is their age. The 18-and-over policy no doubt raises the average age. Interestingly there are more young-to-middle-aged people than anything else. The proportion of whites in the Tavern rises to about 80 percent, the other 15 percent black and 5 percent Hispanics and Asians. The ratio of elderly persons seems low in comparison to the Grand Stand area, and there are no families. The majority of types in the Tavern are groups of three to five. There are mostly men, but women are definitely an active part of the Tavern scene. The solos who do hang out in the Tavern either do so in the very front, where no one else can see them, or in the back standing at the counter.

The social atmosphere is similar to that of a bar. The low ceiling imposes an air of intimacy not found in the Grand Stand area or the Cloud 9 Room. Everyone has a drink at their table. The waiters and waitresses socialize with the customers and know a good many of them on a first-name basis. The table seating arrangement causes people to look at each other and interact more than if they were sitting shoulder to shoulder in rows of seats. By the same token people do not walk around to other tables and mingle as often as in the Grand Stand area. The wagering seems to be taken quite seriously. Many tables are crowded with various racing papers. Reams of notes are being taken and lots of bets are made.

Mark jokingly refers to himself as a "degenerate gambler." He says, "True pros will sit in the Grand Stand." But Mark is a pro; I consider him a diehard. He hangs out in the Tavern just about every night the track is open. He is a white male in his late thirties (his age is a guess because he would not tell me), has a mustache, wears glasses and dresses in short-sleeve polo shirts and jeans. "Professionally I'm a U.S. Merchant Marine. On my time off I play the dogs [to support myself] until I run out of money."

Whenever I see him he is always very friendly and willing to talk to me, but 95 percent of the time his eyes are on the TV screen. He carries around a spiral book of notecards, which he constantly writes on. I have seen the cards a few times, but I cannot make any sense out of his diagrams and figures. Like most diehards he has a method for betting but he is not eager to reveal it to me. I am not sure I could even understand it. I can say it is extremely analytical. Unlike Flamingo, Mark is definitely interested in what the dogs look like, their weight, present and past performance, and other statistics. Unfortunately, he would not give me exact figures on his paybacks, and he placed future bets so that I never saw the amount of money he bet with. But I can only assume, given Mark's serious dedication and attention, that his bets average much more than the $2 minimum.

## Cloud 9 Room

The Cloud 9 Room is a restaurant located above the First Turn Tavern. It is structured similarly to the Tavern. The Room has four tiered levels of tables, a full bar and food selection, a capacity of 300, and its own betting windows, 11 total. The decor is dark wood, brass, glass, carpeting, and linen tablecloths and napkins. The ceiling is quite high and every table seems to offer a good view of the track.

The restaurant has its own gate to the park (although it can be easily reached by the main gate) and one entrance to the building. Valet parking is offered at $1 to patrons. Upon entrance to the building you must stop at a hostess booth to pay the $3 cover charge and to confirm your reservation; there is no admittance to the Cloud 9 without one. At the bottom of the escalator that whisks you up to the restaurant is a sign that says,

IMPORTANT NOTICE TO CLOUD NINE PATRONS
Proper attire must be worn for admittance
to the Cloud 9
Body Shirts, frayed jeans, tank tops, shorts
and similar styles are not accepted

At the top of the escalator is another hostess booth. A host in a tuxedo takes your reservation slip, checks it against his records, then leads you to your table. Each table has a number, which is given to you in case you want to request that table again. It is just like the procedure at a fine restaurant. The menu has appetizers, steak, seafood, pasta entrees, ice cream, cheesecake, coffee/tea, and vintage wines. There are many servers around to cater to your needs. The waitpersons are very friendly and attentive. Like the Tavern servers, many of the Cloud 9 servers know their customers by name.

The crowd was about 95 percent Caucasian, 5 percent Asian on the night I went to the Cloud 9 Room. The dress varies from nice casual to dressed up. The standard dress for men is a clean short sleeved polo shirt and slacks. Some wear sport coats, suits, or designer sweat suits. It is similar for the women, who wear mostly slacks and blouses, some dresses and some designer sweat suits. Couples dominate this scene. I took a census at one point and out of 30 occupied tables, all were mixed couples or groups except one. That table had two men.

Socializing is the key theme in the room. It is not the milling and mingling around type of interaction characteristic of the Grand Stand area. Socialization occurs at the tables. It does not take long to figure out it is a highly social atmosphere within the table unit. There is much laughter and conversation in the air. Most people have smiles on their face directed at the person across from them instead of the track below them. There is not a dominant preoccupation with betting that is characteristic of the Tavern and among the Grand Stand diehards.

"This is the only place to be," said Mary, an elderly woman who is a regular with her husband Jim at the Cloud 9 Room. They frequent the dog track circuit, which runs from Pueblo to Denver (Cloverleaf). Although the drive from Canyon City is a pain, Mary and Jim do it every weekend to have dinner and bet on the races. To Mary the Colorado Springs track is her favorite because apparently the other tracks do not offer good dining rooms to hang out in.

Mary does not do any betting; she leaves it up to her husband. "I don't come here for the gambling. . . . I like to watch the dogs run. I'm a ranch girl." Jim has the concentration of a diehard. With pen in hand and eyes on the TV screen, he is constantly scribbling on his program and putting his hand on his forehead to think. He keeps himself much too involved to ever talk to me. I can sense he does not want to tell me anything. Mary is quite happy to converse, since she is just there for the entertainment. When I finally asked Jim about the amount he spent on each bet he muttered, "Oh not much, certainly not much for this room." Then Mary piped in, "Oh pooh. You spend about $20 on each bet; I'd say that was a lot of money." After that Jim told me he usually manages to pay for dinner, traveling expenses—he breaks even.

## Analysis/Interpretation

There are so many intricacies at the dog track it is difficult to define the whole "culture" of the place. What makes the culture of the track is the people. The diversity of people is immense and what keeps them coming back is the entertainment, the social opportunity, and of course the wagering, that "$2 dream." At the risk of sounding like a commercial, it truly has something to offer everyone. Because of this the track draws from every social stratum of the city. I found on any given night that the track has a cross section of society in attendance. But the different social classes are not interacting together. The diverse appeal would not be there if everyone were meant to mingle.

A social hierarchy exists, which is staked out quite clearly by the three rooms. The Grand Stand represents the working class, the Tavern is the middle class, and Cloud 9 is the upper class. This structure is supported and perpetuated mainly by the diehards, who maintain myths and preconceived notions about the different sections.

The administration for the dog track has handled this situation quite shrewdly. The Tavern and Cloud 9 Room did not exist until 25 years ago. Before then both the buildings were Grand Stand areas. Stacie Taylor, head of promotions and publicity, acknowledges that there was a need for the type of services that the Tavern and Cloud 9 offer. She says they have served most successfully as facilities for group parties and fund-raiser benefits.

Whatever the intentions of the administration, the different rooms make it possible to separate oneself from others. This is an idea more appealing to the upper class, so it makes sense that the areas reserved to them have restrictions in dress, high prices, and an emphasis on service. It is also no surprise that whites dominate the scene. It is all a reflection of the social hierarchy that exists in the community.

But the nicer areas are not inaccessible to the everyday Joe. It is not like a club where you have to "belong" and be voted on to gain entry. Admittedly, the signs concerning dress code in front on the Tavern and Cloud 9 do have a deterring effect. Any sign indicating some restriction immediately sets off a signal in a person's head that there is some type of assumption about the customers and the atmosphere. I felt some trepidation when I first walked up the ramp toward the hostess booth at the Tavern. Was I dressed OK? Will I stand out too much? But other than fitting in in a superficial sense, I had no worries. If you have the money, entry to the Tavern or Cloud 9 only takes a little planning ahead.

Interestingly, the diehards all have their theories about one another, according to the room. Flamingo told me that the real hard-core diehards were the "ones you can't see" in the Cloud 9 Room. If I were to believe his theory, Cloud 9 would be a place full of solos in suits calmly smoking cigarettes and placing thousand dollar bets. In reality I found the Cloud 9 Room to be a highly social place, with no solos. In fact the crowd would get extremely rowdy during a race, more so than in the Tavern, yelling for their dog to win. My informant Mary, a little old lady going blind in one eye, even started yelling, "Go baby go!" at one point.

The high-rolling diehards that Flamingo imagines *do* exist in the Cloud 9 Room according to Lissa, my waitress one night. I never had the opportunity to speak to them. They either pretended they didn't know what I was talking about, did not want to talk, or really were not diehards. Lissa told me, "I've worked here two years . . . you see a lotta lotta money. I've talked to a couple people here, asked if they had day jobs and they said no. They just follow a winner around [the circuit] and make their money." When I asked her how much a "lotta" money is she told me about $2,000 to $5,000 a bet. Mark thinks that the pros are really in the Grand Stand. I could never quite get to the bottom of his reasoning for this, but he seemed pretty sure about his opinion.

Jane, a cocktail waitress in the Tavern, told me, "There is a different crowd here than at the Grand Stand. They spend money to come in and sit. [People in the Tavern] are willing to spend money in here, there is nicer dress in here. Plus there are no tabs, so I make more in tips. People come in here holding a lot of money."

Crossovers into different areas happen often; the culture does not demand that you stick to one room. But the social stratification between the rooms is so obvious it is hard not to notice it. The mobility among the rooms exist in a downward direction, much more than upward. Nonetheless, the spectrum of intentions from the little old lady who bet $2 on a dog because of the name, to the diehard 30-year-old with reams of notes placing $2,000 bets to pay the rent, all exist at each level. The ratio of the types in each room varies, but they are all in there. The main difference is appearance and bank account. This is obvious from the similarity of offerings in each area. The basics are the same for every room: food, drinks, bathrooms, a view of the track, a place to sit, betting windows, TVs, and people.

I also believe the track is a great service to the people of the community. There are many benefits for the large number of senior citizen patrons: free admission for 60+ and nighttime escorts to cars. Families may bring their children so they do not have to find a babysitter or stay home. On a more subtle social level, as one informant said, "It's a good place to learn about people—lots of weirdos." Perhaps "weirdos" is pushing it, but I think she was right in her assessment of the situation at the Rocky Mountain Dog Track. It is a good place to learn about people and provides a perfect model of how social stratification works. And hopefully make a buck or two in the process.

## Collaborative Activity 1.5

Working in groups, use our key terms—scene, situation, and genre—to describe the scene of a greyhound track. In what ways is a greyhound track a scene (a place where communication happens among groups of people with some shared objectives)? Are there smaller scenes within this larger scene? If so, what are they? What are some of the situations we find within this scene (rhetorical interactions involving particular participants, subjects, settings, and purposes)? And what genres (the typical ways of interacting within the repeated situations of the scene) are used in this scene? Generate a list of your answers, and compare it with your classmates' findings.

## Writing Activity 1.8

Smith describes the overall scene of the greyhound track as well as three smaller scenes within it (the Grand Station, the Tavern, and the Cloud 9 areas). Based on her observations of this general scene and its constituent scenes, situations, and genres, explain to a newcomer in this scene how he or she might act within its different smaller scenes. What from the observations help you determine how someone might act in these scenes?

You can use ethnographic techniques like the ones Smith employs to observe and describe scenes of writing, including their situations and genres. Such techniques can allow you to find out what sort of "place" the scene is, what sort of communication happens within it, who participates in this communication, and what objectives participants share. In addition, such techniques will help you to discover and describe some of the situations that happen within the scene, including who participates in these situations, what subjects they engage in, the specific settings where they interact, and the purposes for their interacting. Finally, by using such techniques, you can also identify what genres participants use to interact typically within the situations of a scene: Through observations and interviews, you can find out what patterns and rituals participants have developed to interact with one another in the situations that make up a scene.

Before you begin your first observation, you should know a few things about how to observe scenes ethically and responsibly. Scholars conducting ethnographic research submit their research plans to review boards, who check that they are following accepted practices for protecting the people and places they observe. Although your observations will not require such review, you should make sure you follow some of the same practices as you observe a scene:

- If someone is in charge of the site you want to observe, ask his or her permission.
- If observing a private group or a stable group of people, one whose participants you can identify, let them know what you are doing with your observation, what your purposes are, and how you will use what you observe—that you will share findings with your teacher and classmates.
- Ask for their consent to your recording their participation.
- Especially when you are observing a private group, whose interactions would usually not be open to public observation, assure them that you will hold what you observe in strictest confidence except for

those purposes you've told them about. Never reveal what you observe to anyone outside of your original purposes—in this case, those connected to your writing class assignment.

Following such practices will help ensure that you observe a scene without damaging it or its participants.

We will now guide you through some strategies for observing scenes, moving from the scene itself to its situations and genres. Once we have described these strategies, we will list them as guidelines for observing scenes in Box 1.2 (pp. 44–45). By the end of the chapter, you will be able to practice using these strategies to observe, describe, and then reflect on a scene you participate or have participated in. In later chapters, you will be able to use these strategies to gain access to less familiar academic, work-place, and public scenes.

## STRATEGIES FOR DESCRIBING THE SCENE

### Place

One of the first things you can identify, when observing a scene, is what the scene "looks" like. Since a scene is a place where communication happens, ask yourself these questions:

> What sort of place is this?
>
> How is it organized?
>
> What are its parameters?

At this point, rather than observing specific interactions within the scene, you are focused on identifying the larger environment in which these interactions are happening. Once you have described the environment of the scene, you can then start to identify what is generally happening within it.

### The Group's Activities

Here you will be observing what is going on within the scene:

> Who is taking part?
>
> What are they doing?

Keep track of the activities you observe and how groups of people are inter-acting/communicating while performing these activities. Try to separate what you have observed from what you think about what you have observed. One effective way to record your observations involves using a **double-entry notebook**. This type of notebook divides your observation notes into two parts. After drawing a line down the middle of each page of the notebook (or using a notebook with two facing pages), you write on one side your direct observations of the scene as they happen. On the other side you note your questions about and your reactions to what you have observed, either while you are observing the scene or during later reflection.

## Writing Activity 1.9

To begin practicing observing scenes, record and gather observations during a half-hour of an ordinary scene in your day, such as having dinner with your family or friends; chatting in your dorm lounge, coffee house, or restaurant; studying in the library or the student union; or discussing topics at a meeting. Describe both the setting and the participants and their activities in the setting, recording details of place and perhaps even sketching out the space or mapping it. In addition to describing the participants and their activities and interactions, be sure to add your own reflections on anything interesting or unusual about the interactions.

### Shared Objectives

Once you have observed the environment of the scene, its participants, and their activities, you need to try to identify the participants' shared objectives so that you can see how communication, including writing, helps them achieve their objectives. Here, you are trying to get a general sense of *why* people are doing what they are doing in this scene. Try to figure out why people are participating in the scene. Ask yourself these questions:

> What is it that brings people together in this scene?
>
> What overarching objectives do they share?
>
> What are they trying to do or accomplish?

### The Need to Interview

Sometimes the shared objectives might be fairly obvious, but often the objectives go deeper than an observer might be able to see. For example, the objectives of a criminal trial might seem obvious—to come to a judgment about a defendant's guilt—but participants might also have deeper or multiple objectives like securing justice, protecting the public, or even pushing a prosecutor to offer or a defendant to accept a plea bargain. All these objectives will affect how people interact within the scene.

Since you might not be able to observe deeper objectives, you might need to supplement your observations with interviews of people participating in the scene. It might not be evident just through observation what people are doing, but by asking them, you would get an insider's knowledge about what is going on. Since you are looking especially for *shared* objectives, try to ask as many participants as possible so that you can find commonalities among their answers.

To help you conduct interviews, consult the interview guidelines in Box 1.1 below. You might need to refer back to these guidelines in later chapters when you observe academic, workplace, and public scenes.

---

**Box 1.1**  *Interview Guidelines*

1. Contact the interviewee, preferably in advance, by phone or e-mail and set up a day, time, and place for the interview. Be sure to explain the purpose for the interview and how much time it will take. Ask permission to tape record the interview if that becomes necessary. (Test your equipment before going to the interview.)
2. Prepare interview questions in advance, but be willing to remain flexible if the interviewee would like to bring up additional issues that might be of interest.
3. When formulating questions, avoid "closed" questions that can be answered with a short response (like "yes" or "no" questions), and instead frame questions that elicit more detailed responses. For example, instead of asking "Is your purpose to convict the defendant?" (a yes/no question), ask "What do you see as your main purposes in conducting a trial?"
4. During the interview, take notes by hand or recorder. For shorter interviews, note-taking should be sufficient, but you might want to develop a shorthand of sorts—notations that can be made quickly as the person is talking but that you can go back to and decipher later.
5. Thank the interviewee for his or her time, and ask if he or she would like to see the final version of the writing project you are working on.

---

**Writing Activity 1.10**

To practice interviewing, interview a classmate on the topic of what the person hopes to achieve by attending college. Formulate at least five open-ended questions. Then interview the classmate, and write a paragraph that collects and synthesizes your findings. In another paragraph, answer the following questions: What was the most difficult part of the interview and the write-up? Were some questions more effective than others? Why? Did any information come up that you didn't ask about, and how did you handle that? Did you revise any of your questions during the interview or add any questions? Did you encounter any problems with recording and then transcribing the information? In your write-up on the classmate, how did you decide what to include and what to leave out?

## Collaborative Activity 1.6

Compare the results of your interview with those of some of your classmates, and try to discover some shared objectives that people have for attending college. Look for both the most general objectives and the ones some sets of people might share. Prepare to share your discoveries with the class.

## STRATEGIES FOR OBSERVING AND IDENTIFYING SITUATIONS

Observing and identifying the environment of the scene, its participants, and their interactions and shared objectives allow you to sketch the general outline of the scene. But because a scene is also made up of various situations—each with its own specific participants, interactions, subjects, settings, and purposes—observing some of these particular situations will give you a more in-depth understanding of the scene. This section outlines some strategies for observing the situations within a scene.

Situations, remember, are the specific rhetorical interactions happening within a scene. A typical scene will include multiple situations, some more visible than others. For example, the scene of a baseball game includes such visible situations as fans buying food, fans cheering the team in the stands, and the home plate umpire calling balls and strikes. But there are also less visible situations that involve coaches relaying signs to catchers, reporters interviewing players after the game, and players meeting in the locker room. As an observer, you may not have access to all these situations, but you can at least try to identify as many of them as you can by looking for different interactions that are happening within a scene. To identify situations, ask yourself questions such as the following:

What types of interactions can you see happening?

What different groups of people might be interacting?

Are there less visible settings where interactions might be occurring?

Once you have identified the different situations within a scene, you can begin observing some of them more closely. In your notebook, try to describe the following:

Who is participating in the situation?

What are people doing, and how do they seem to be relating to each other?

Where are their interactions taking place, in what specific setting?

What is the nature of their interaction? For example, are they engaged in conversation, or are they placing orders, or are they asking questions? What sort of language are they using? What words do you hear? Is the language formal or informal or somewhere in between? What sort of tone do they use?

What subjects are they interacting about?

What is it that brings them together? What are their purposes for interacting?

Here again, you can supplement your observations with interviews (see guidelines for interviewing in Box 1.1, p. 40). By asking yourself and the participants some of these questions, you can begin to identify some of the situations within a scene and better understand how to act within it.

## STRATEGIES FOR IDENTIFYING GENRES

Earlier in the chapter we discussed how, as situations reoccur, participants develop typical ways of interacting within them. That is, they develop habits of communication that help them interact in these situations in fairly recognized and predictable ways. For example, coaches give umpires lineup cards to announce the starting players. Pitchers and catchers have developed signals for communicating to each other different pitches, pitch outs, and so on. Fans and vendors have developed typical ways of interacting, with vendors calling out "programs, get your programs" and fans signaling their interest and passing money down the aisle. These typical rhetorical ways of interacting in repeated situations are all genres. In a more academic scene, the genres might include essay examinations instead of lineup cards, the syllabus instead of the program, and literature reviews instead of pitching signals. Within the multiple situations of a scene, participants will use a variety of genres, both written and spoken, to help them interact efficiently.

One way to identify genres when observing a scene and its situations is to look for patterns or habits in people's interactions. Look for similarities in how people talk within a situation. Look for any written documents that typically appear in that situation. For example, in an office scene you might notice spoken genres such as the hallway greeting, the work request, the delivery of completed work, or the phone call with a client; and you might notice written genres such as message slips, e-mail announcements, employee time sheets, business letters, memos, budget reports, order forms, newsletters, and so on. Each genre is used in a different recurring situation. To connect a genre to its situation, try to pay attention to who uses the genres in each situation and for what purposes.

Because it may not be clearly visible what genres are used in a situation, especially written genres, another way to identify genres is again by asking participants in that situation—the users of the genres. Since they may not know what the word *genre* means, especially as we use it, ask them what kinds of things they typically write in that situation. Ask them also to describe these kinds of writing and to tell you what they call them. If possible ask if you could have or borrow some examples of the genres. Finally, try to find out why they use these kinds of writing: who uses them, when, where, and why. Be sure to record your findings in your notebook for later reference, when you want to understand better how to act in that situation yourself.

We will discuss genre in much greater detail starting in Chapter 2 and then throughout the book.

## Describing a Scene You Participate In

Now we invite you to practice using the strategies we have discussed above to observe and describe a scene in which you participate. Being able to map a familiar scene and its situations and genres will serve you well when you begin to observe and write in less familiar scenes later. As you perform your observations, consult Box 1.2 (pp. 44–45), in which we compile the strategies that we have discussed so far for observing and describing scenes.

### Writing Activity 1.11

Using the strategies outlined in Box 1.2, observe and describe a scene in which you already participate. Address the following questions: What makes it a scene? Who are its participants? What are their shared objectives? Then identify some of the situations within that scene. What kinds of rhetorical interactions happen within each of these situations? Who participates in these interactions and in what settings? What subjects do they engage in, and for what reasons do they engage in them? Finally, try to identify the genres participants use to respond to these situations. How do these genres help participants act within the situations? Be prepared to share your observations with your teacher and classmates, and be sure to keep a record of your findings because you might need to refer back to them in Writing Project 1.1.

## Box 1.2    *Guidelines for Observing and Describing Scenes*

### 1. Select and Gain Access to a Scene.

Once you have selected a scene, determine how you will gain entry into it. Whenever possible, ask for permission from somebody in that scene with the authority to grant it (the manager of a supermarket or office, for example, or an owner of a small business or a teacher of a classroom). Tell him or her what you are doing and why you are doing it. Ask also if you could get permission to interview participants in the scene (refer to Box 1.1 (p. 40) for interview guidelines).

### 2. Observe the Scene in General.

With a notebook or voice recorder in hand, you are now ready to begin your observations. Begin by describing the scene in general terms. Ask yourself and, whenever possible, ask the participants in the scene the following questions:

- What sort of *place* is this scene?
- What *activities* take place within the scene? *Who* participates in these activities?
- What is it that brings people together in this scene? What are the participants' shared *objectives*?

### 3. Identify the Situations of the Scene.

To identify the situations within a scene, use the following questions:

- What *sorts of interactions* do you see happening in this scene?
- Are different interactions occurring in different *settings*?
- Do different *people* participate within these different interactions?
- Are different *subjects* discussed within these different interactions?

### 4. Observe and Describe the Situations of a Scene.

Once you have identified some of the situations within a scene, you can begin observing some of these situations more closely in order to describe them more fully. In your observation notes, try to describe the participants, setting, subject, and purposes of the interaction for each situation. Keep these questions in mind:

*(continued on next page)*

- *Who* is participating in this situation? How do the participants seem to be *relating* to each other?
- *Where* exactly is their interaction taking place within the scene? *When* does this interaction typically take place?
- *What* are they interacting about? And what is the *nature* of their interaction? What sort of *language* are they using? What sort of *tone* do they use?
- *Why* do they need or want to interact? What is the *purpose* of their interaction?

### 5. Identify the Genres in the Scene.

To identify the genres of a scene, look for patterns or habits in the interaction within a situation. Ask yourself:

- What *patterns* of speaking do you notice in those situations?
- What *written documents* typically appear in and are used repeatedly in those situations?

Because you might not be able to observe all of the genres in action, interview participants in the situation about their genres, and, if possible, collect samples. Try to get responses to the following questions:

- What *kinds* of writing do the participants typically write in that situation?
- What are these texts *called*?
- What do these texts *look* like?
- *Who* uses these texts, *when*, *where*, and *why*?

## Writing Projects

### Writing Project 1.1

Based on your responses to Writing Activity 1.11, write a self-reflective essay (4–6 pages) in which you examine your experiences with writing in a scene you have participated in. You might describe your transition from outsider to insider in this scene, the struggles and rewards of participating in this scene, and your adaptation to language and writing in this scene. You might also reflect on how this scene has shaped and perhaps continues to shape who you are as a writer, including what you have learned about writing as a result of participating in this scene. Use the following questions to guide your reflections:

- How did you feel about the scene in which you wrote? Were you comfortable or uncomfortable interacting within it? How? Why?
- Did the objectives of that scene suit you well? Were you able to achieve those shared objectives? Did you struggle with those objectives?
- What subjects did you write about? Were these subjects easy for you? Why or why not?
- For what reasons did you write? Did you have multiple purposes? Where you able to achieve those purposes?
- In what ways did your participation in the scene shape the way you wrote within it?
- In what ways did your participation in the scene shape the way you write outside the scene?

## Writing Project 1.2

Many scenes—whether academic disciplines or organizations, social organizations, political organizations, professional groups, or even hobby groups—have their own electronic forums for discussing issues of interest to them. These electronic discussion groups are known as **listservs** or **newsgroups**. A listserv is an electronic mailing list in which a computer (called a list server) distributes mail sent to people who subscribe to the list. Messages sent to the list are received by all subscribers and are delivered to their private e-mail boxes. A newsgroup is an electronic discussion group in which messages are collected on a system called a news server, where anyone with access to the Internet can retrieve them. Newsgroups are types of "bulletin boards" where, unlike listservs, individual messages are posted for participants to retrieve rather than stored on their computers. The following directories can help you search for discussion groups that focus on a variety of topics such as business, health, music, science, the arts, computers, humanities, nature, politics and religion.

**Directories of Listserv Lists:**
http://tile.net/lists
http://www.liszt.com/
http://www.nova.edu/Inter-Links/listserv.html
http://n2h2.com/KOVACS/ (a directory of scholarly discussion lists)

**Directories of Newsgroups:**
http://www.dejanews.com
http://sunsite.unc.edu/usenet-i/home.html
http://www.liszt.com/news
http://woodstock.stanford.edu:2000/

Join a newsgroup or subscribe to a listserv group related to a hobby or field of interest. After monitoring their messages for some time, use the guidelines in Box 1.2 (pp. 44–45) to identify and define the scene of the electronic discussion group that you joined: Who are the participants on this list? What seem to be their backgrounds? What shared subject or body of information does the group discuss? What seem to be their shared objectives? What language, style and conventions are used? What opposing theories or conflicts exist within the online group? Drawing from the information you have gathered, write a guide for new participants in the group. What should a new participant know in order to participate effectively in this listserv or newsgroup? Use dialogue or quotations from the discussion list or newsgroup to give a clear sense of the scene, including its members, style of communication, and shared objectives.

## Writing Project 1.3

As we mentioned earlier in the chapter, there are various genres available to help people sell used items, the classified ad being one of them. Other ways include posting a flyer at the grocery store, sending an e-mail to everyone in your address book, or creating a listing for an online auction service like eBay. Select a genre other than the classified ad, and use it to sell the same item you were trying to sell in Collaborative Activity 1.2. (p. 12) In making your decision about what genre to use, think about the scene in which you wish to sell your item. Before you start writing the genre, think about the situation of the genre: the setting in which it is used, the people who read it, the purpose embedded within it. Use your knowledge of the scene, situation, and genre to produce a piece of writing that most effectively presents the item you wish to sell. When you are finished composing, write a cover letter to your instructor explaining the choices you made in writing the genre.

## Writing Project 1.4

In the course of studying this chapter, you have heard about or encountered many different genres. Select any one of those genres that you might enjoy writing, and write your own text within that genre. Be sure to consider the scene and situation in which the genre is to be used, including what subjects are most appropriate for the genre, who reads the genre and why, and what your purposes are for writing the genre. When you are finished composing the genre, write a cover letter to your instructor explaining the choices you made in writing the genre.

## Writing Project 1.5

Visit a scene on your campus where individuals meet to discuss issues or to accomplish some shared objectives. Drawing on the questions in Box 1.2: Guidelines for Observing and Describing Scenes (pp. 44–45), describe this academic scene. Remember to keep a notebook in which you collect your observations and to supplement your observations, if needed, with interviews with participants in the scene. Address the following questions: What brings these people together? What is special about the place? Who is typically involved? What is the nature of their interactions? What rules or conventions (either formal or implicit) govern the interactions? Write 4–6 pages as a detailed description of the scene for your teacher and classmates.

# 2 Using Genres to Read Scenes of Writing

*Reading is not just deciphering words on a page—the typical definition of the activity—but also, in a larger sense, observing and making sense of a scene by examining its language, both oral and written.* Reading and writing are interconnected activities that depend on their scenes, situations, and genres—the concepts Chapter 1 introduces. This chapter begins to explore that interconnection and focuses on the concept of **genre**, which we defined in Chapter 1 as *the typical rhetorical ways of responding to a repeated situation within a scene.* You will learn in this chapter how to read and analyze genres in order to access and understand scenes and situations. You will then practice using that analysis to make informed choices in your writing.

## Reading Scenes, Situations, and Genres

Chapter 1 explored how writing is enmeshed within scenes and the specific situations within them. Reading, too, is enmeshed within situations and scenes. When you pick up a book to read, you usually know already what genre the book is: mystery, romance, biography, or textbook, for example. The same is true for shorter kinds of texts, whether letters from friends, sales letters, application forms, or e-mail messages. Your knowledge of the genre provides you with a mental framework for how to read it; it gives you a set of guidelines, what reading specialist Frank Smith calls "specifications," for how to approach and make sense of a text. Because you know the genre, you are already on your way to knowing how to read the text.

You know a great deal about many scenes and situations as well as about the expectations of the genres involved. If you pick up a sales letter, for example, you know these elements of the scene and situation: The writer is acting as a sales agent, not as a friend or colleague; the subject of the letter will be some product; the writer's primary purpose is to sell you something;

and you are being treated as someone who is in a position to buy the product. Because you know the scene of sales letters, you know that someone thought you would share the writer's interest in the product, but you also suspect that the information in the letter will not necessarily be unbiased or fully accurate.

You probably do not think about this knowledge consciously, but you reflect it in your decisions about how to act in response to the text: You might scan for the nature of the product and, if you do not in fact share the writer's interest in the product, you might throw it away without reading further. Similarly, when you pick up a textbook, you know some things about its scene and situation as you begin to read. The *scene* of an assigned text for a course requires that you at least pretend to share the teacher's interest in the subject and that you read the entire text whether that interest is real or feigned. The *situation* places you as a seeker of knowledge and the textbook author as expert, and you read accordingly, highlighting key points, studying definitions, and accepting the information you find in the textbook as accurate. When you read, then, you act on your knowledge of the genre, situation, and scene of the text. *You not only process the words inscribed on the page; you also read the situation and scene inscribed in the genre.*

People adjust their ways of reading texts to the genres, situations, and scenes that those texts involve. For example, as you have been reading this textbook, you have been acting differently as you read the various genres within it, even though you are probably not aware of those shifting habits. The whole book represents the textbook genre and the scene of a writing class; within it are certain genres of communication which reflect their own scenes and situations. You read the body of this textbook for its information, perhaps highlighting important points or new terms, but you read the Writing Activities differently, perhaps waiting for your teacher to assign them before you consider their content seriously and looking for what you are supposed to do rather than what you are supposed to know. You read the Table of Contents differently again, just seeking page numbers or topics, and you read the Index with yet another approach. *This process of negotiation, of repositioning ourselves from one scene to the next and at times within multiple scenes at once, is not the result of guesswork; it is not a random process. Rather, it involves a complex, active process of reading.*

Sometimes, though, we get it wrong. In Chapter 1 we learned about what the ancient Greeks called *kairos,* the art of timing communication correctly. Imagine someone who always misreads scenes, who is constantly saying the wrong thing at the wrong time, like a character in a *Saturday Night Live* skit whose contributions to a conversation are always two topics behind the rest. When others have moved on from discussing the boss's hairpiece to discussing an upcoming concert, the misreading character chimes in with, "And it doesn't even match his hair's real color!" Misreading a scene leads to gaffes and ineffectiveness (in less extreme ways probably) for each of us. We may make a joke in class that a classmate finds offensive, or we might request something of a boss in a way that gets an immediate denial. Sometimes, we misread a scene on purpose, trying to find a way to get other people's attention or to protest accepted behavior. A protester can shout out during a lecture, or a student can refuse to follow a paper assignment (turning in a collage instead of a history paper). Sometimes, though, we are just so unfamiliar with a scene that we fail to read it accurately or completely. The first time we go to a formal party, we may not know what to expect, how to dress, or what kinds of conversations we will have. Learning how to read formal invitations, though, can give us some clues that will help us prepare. Similarly, the first time we want to join a public discussion about a current issue, we can begin more effectively by learning how to read such public genres as editorials and letters to the editor. In both cases, the genres, as typical ways of communicating and acting in their scenes, contain clues about how we can communicate and act effectively in these scenes. Learning how to analyze genres will help you read unfamiliar scenes as well as to think consciously about familiar scenes so you can choose how to act in them as writers.

## Writing Activity 2.1

List at least 10 different genres you read, including if possible at least one genre that you read on a computer. Remember to include not just formal or school genres and not just literary genres but also the everyday genres you read, like the backs of cereal boxes. Then pick three of these genres and write a paragraph describing how differently you read each of them. How does your reading of a cereal box differ from your reading of textbooks and sales letters, for example?

## Writing Activity 2.2

Think of five different genres you have written, including one you write on a computer. How do you think you learned to write each one? Have you read examples of those genres written by other people? If so, how do you think that influenced your writing of them? If not, how do you think you learned to write a genre without reading it? Do you feel more confident writing some of these genres than you do working with others? If so, do you think that confidence is related to how you have learned them? Write a paragraph or two describing your experiences with at least three of these genres and speculating about how you have learned to write them.

# Reading the Language of a Scene

To see how you can read scenes and situations through genres, you first need to see how language—words, sentence structures, forms—can reveal more than just the content of what people have to say. The language people use can reveal who they are, who they are trying to be, who they are communicating with, and what they are trying to achieve. Just as we can learn something about a scene by "reading" the way people dress and behave in it, we can also learn something about a scene by reading the way people communicate in it. The language of a scene tells us a great deal about the scene, about the people in it, even about their values, goals, and beliefs.

Patterns in the language people use are as visible in scenes as are patterns of social behavior such as certain rituals, habits of interaction, ways of dressing, and so on. But you are probably better at reading social behavior than you are at reading rhetorical behavior because you have had more experience learning to read social behavior. For example, you probably are very good at reading the meaning and effect of a facial gesture (a blush or a wink) or other form of body language, but you may struggle with trying to explain the meaning and effect of, say, a passive sentence, subordinate clause, or a strategically placed sentence fragment. Without necessarily knowing any of these grammatical terms, people *choose* these linguistic forms, just as they choose to wear a certain style of dress or other behaviors. So learning to read people's language choices, though it takes some practice, can help you read people's situations and scenes. You can then use that reading to make effective linguistic choices in your own writing; you will be able to communicate effectively with other participants in your scene of the moment.

## THE SIGNIFICANCE OF WORD CHOICES: *BED* VERSUS *RACK*

Think about the word *bed*. When we say "bed," we usually think about a place where we go to sleep. The **connotation** of the word (what the word implies) suggests something positive: A place to rest, a place of comfort and warmth. The Marines, however, use a different word to refer to the object on which they sleep. Instead of "bed," they say "rack." Is this merely a difference in word choice? Is "rack" just another way of saying "bed"? Not really. Even though the two words refer to the same thing, the word *rack* connotes something different from *bed;* it implies something hard and cold, something on which we store objects such as merchandise.

Why would a Marine use the term *rack?* There are probably many reasons. One reason, though, is very likely that the word *rack* reinforces the toughness Marines are taught to develop. To be an effective soldier, one has to depersonalize oneself to some extent. To fight in battle, a soldier has to become more like a machine than a human with feelings; otherwise, he or she might not be able to perform under the horrible conditions of war. The word *rack* facilitates this process of dehumanization by influencing the way that Marines think of themselves more as objects than as persons. This process of depersonalization is a necessary part of a Marine's socialization into and eventual success within the military scene and its various situations.

For a Marine, learning to say "rack" is very much like learning how to clean a gun or how to navigate a minefield. It is part of a Marine's training. The word is part of the military *script* a person must learn in order to act and communicate as a Marine. By critically reading the language of this scene we, as outsiders, gain insight into both behaviors and values of the participants in the scene. We start becoming aware of the scene's implicit script, which is an important first step in helping us make effective choices about how *we* could behave and communicate within this otherwise unfamiliar scene.

In the following essay, Perri Klass reads the medical community's language in order to reveal something about its underlying script. As you read "Learning the Language," pay attention to the language that doctors and nurses use to communicate, and consider what that language reveals about the medical scene and those who participate in it. Part of what makes this essay interesting is that it is written from Klass's experience. Think about what it meant for Klass to "learn the language."

■ ■ ■

# Learning the Language

Perri Klass

"Mrs. Tolstoy is your basic LOL in NAD, admitted for a soft rule-out MI," the intern announces. I scribble that on my patient list. In other words, Mrs. Tolstoy is a Little Old Lady in No Apparent Distress who is in the hospital to make sure she hasn't had a heart attack (rule out a Myocardial Infarction). And we think it's unlikely that she has had a heart attack (a *soft* rule-out).

If I learned nothing else during my first three months of working in the hospital as a medical student, I learned endless jargon and abbreviations. I started out in a state of primeval innocence, in which I didn't even know that "s̄ CP, SOB, N/V" meant "without chest pain, shortness of breath, or nausea and vomiting." By the end I took the abbreviations so much for granted that I would complain to my mother the English professor, "And can you believe I had to put down *three* NG tubes last night?"

"You'll have to tell me what an NG tube is if you want me to sympathize properly," my mother said. NG, nasogastric—isn't it obvious?

I picked up not only the specific expressions but also the patterns of speech and the grammatical conventions; for example, you never say that a patient's blood pressure fell or that his cardiac enzymes rose. Instead, the patient is always the subject of the verb: "He dropped his pressure." "He bumped his enzymes." This sort of construction probably reflects the profound irritation of the intern when the nurses come in the middle of the night to say that Mr. Dickinson has disturbingly low blood pressure. "Oh, he's gonna hurt me bad tonight," the intern might say, inevitably angry at Mr. Dickinson for dropping his pressure and creating a problem.

When chemotherapy fails to cure Mrs. Bacon's cancer, what we say is, "Mrs. Bacon failed chemotherapy."

"Well, we've already had one hit today, and we're up next, but at least we've got mostly stable players on our team." This means that our team (group of doctors and medical students) has already gotten one new admission today, and it is our turn again, so we'll get whoever is admitted next in emergency, but at least most of the patients we already have are fairly stable, that is, unlikely to drop their pressures or in any other way get suddenly sicker and hurt us bad. Baseball metaphor is pervasive. A no-hitter is a night without any new admissions. A player is always a patient—a nitrate player is a patient on nitrates, a unit player is a patient in the intensive care unit, and so on, until you reach the terminal player.

It is interesting to consider what it means to be winning, or doing well, in this perennial baseball game. When the intern hangs up the phone and announces, "I got a hit," that is not cause for congratulations. The team is not scoring points; rather, it is getting hit, being bombarded with new patients. The object of the game from the point of view of the doctors, considering the players for whom they are already responsible, is to get as few new hits as possible.

This special language contributes to a sense of closeness and professional spirit among people who are under a great deal of stress. As a medical student, I found it exciting to discover that I'd finally cracked the code, that I could understand what doctors said and wrote, and could use the same formulations myself. Some people seem to become enamored of the jargon for its own sake, perhaps because they are so deeply thrilled with the idea of medicine, with the idea of themselves as doctors.

I knew a medical student who was referred to by the interns on the team as Mr. Eponym because he was so infatuated with eponymous terminology, the more obscure the better. He never said "capillary pulsations" if he could say "Quincke's pulses." He would lovingly tell over the multi-named syndromes—Wolff-Parkinson-White, Lown-Ganong-Levine, Schönlein-Henoch—until the temptation to suggest Schleswig-Holstein or Stevenson-Kefauver or Baskin-Robbins became irresistible to his less reverent colleagues.

And there is the jargon that you don't ever want to hear yourself using. You know that your training is changing you, but there are certain changes you think would be going a little too far.

The resident was describing a man with devastating terminal pancreatic cancer. "Basically he's CTD," the resident concluded. I reminded myself that I had resolved not to be shy about asking when I didn't understand things. "CTD?" I asked timidly.

The resident smirked at me. "Circling The Drain."

The images are vivid and terrible. "What happened to Mrs. Melville?"

"Oh, she boxed last night." To box is to die, of course.

Then there are the more pompous locutions that can make the beginning medical student nervous about the effects of medical training. A friend of mine was told by his resident, "A pregnant woman with sickle-cell represents a failure of genetic counseling."

Mr. Eponym, who tried hard to talk like the doctors, once explained to me, "An infant is basically a brainstem preparation." The term "brainstem preparation," as used in neurological research, refers to an animal whose higher brain functions have been destroyed so that only the most primitive reflexes remain, like the sucking reflex, the startle reflex, and the rooting reflex.

And yet at other times the harshness dissipates into a strangely elusive euphemism. "As you know, this is a not entirely benign procedure," some doctor will say, and that will be understood to imply agony, risk of complications, and maybe even a significant mortality rate.

The more extreme forms aside, one most important function of medical jargon is to help doctors maintain some distance from their patients. By reformulating a patient's pain and problems into a language that the patient doesn't even speak, I suppose we are in some sense taking those pains and problems under our jurisdiction and also reducing their emotional impact. This linguistic separation between doctors and patients allows conversations to go on at the bedside that are unintelligible to the patient. "Naturally, we're worried about adeno-CA," the intern can say to the medical student, and lung cancer need never be mentioned.

I learned a new language this past summer. At times it thrills me to hear myself using it. It enables me to understand my colleagues, to communicate effectively in the hospital. Yet I am uncomfortably aware that I will never again notice the peculiarities and even atrocities of medical language as keenly as I did this summer. There may be specific expressions I manage to avoid, but even as I remark them, promising myself I will never use them, I find that this language is becoming my professional speech. It no longer sounds strange in my ears—or coming from my mouth. And I am afraid that as with any new language, to use it properly you must absorb not only the vocabulary but also the structure, the logic, the attitudes. At first you may notice these new and alien assumptions every time you put together a sentence, but with time and increased fluency you stop being aware of them at all. And as you lose that awareness, for better or for worse, you move closer and closer to being a doctor instead of just talking like one. ▪

## Collaborative Activity 2.1

After reading "Learning the Language," work with classmates to describe the language doctors and nurses use to communicate. Why do doctors and nurses use the language that they do? What does the language they use tell us about the medical scene and the beliefs, assumptions, and objectives of the participants in that scene? In addition, what happens to Klass as she begins to learn the language? Why do you think this happens? Can members of your group relate to her experience? That is, have any of you had occasion to learn a new way of communicating, and if so, what kind of effect did that acquisition have on you? Be prepared to share your responses with the class.

## Writing Activity 2.3

Think of some group to which you belong: Perhaps a volunteer organization, an online discussion group, a fraternity or sorority, a club or team, or even a group of friends. What words do members of your group share that are not used the same way by other groups? Look at those words to see if you can discover reasons your group has chosen them. Do the reasons have something to do with the values, beliefs, and objectives of the group? What do the words mean to your group? Write a paragraph reporting your thoughts about the words and your group.

## THE SIGNIFICANCE OF SENTENCE STRUCTURES: PASSIVE VERSUS ACTIVE SENTENCES

Not only choices of words but also choices of sentence structures can reveal different points of view. In the same way that we can read the language of the medical and military scenes in order to learn something about the way people within them communicate and act, we can also read the language of the various academic scenes that we encounter in a college or university in order to communicate and act more effectively within them.

A great deal of writing in the sciences, for example, uses passive sentence constructions, such as "Twelve samples were studied," "The investigation was focused on the transmission of HIV," or "The ozone has traditionally been viewed as a protective layer." In each of these examples, the person or people performing the action—studying the samples, focusing the investigation, and viewing the ozone layer—are omitted so that the action seems to have occurred somehow on its own. The writer has constructed the sentence to eliminate reference to who is doing the action. You might recall English teachers who warned you against using the passive voice in your writing, preferring instead active sentences, such as "Professor Miller studied twelve samples" or "The team of scientists from MIT investigated the transmission of HIV." Participants in the humanities prefer the active voice because they believe **agency** (who is doing an action) is significant and because they focus on the human and the subjective. Their language reflects these values. In the sciences, however, different values and assumptions prevail.

In the sciences, the passive voice reinforces a scientific belief that the physical world exists objectively, independent of human intervention. A scientist traditionally assumes the role of someone who observes and records what happens, and the use of the passive voice reflects this process. Passive sentences suggest that actions occur mainly through their own accord, with the scientist simply *describing* them. Passive voice also allows the scientist to emphasize the physical world, the object of investigation, rather than the scientist, whose agency is less important. For the scientist who writes, "Five ounces of nitrate were added to a solution," it does not matter who actually added the nitrate; what matters is how the nitrate behaved after it was added to the solution. The passive voice not only linguistically reflects the objectivity that scientists desire; it also gives readers the impression that the action occurred on its own, free of human bias. This perspective is an important one for scientists to convey.

The difference between the active and the passive use of language enables us to recognize some of the differences between the scientific and the humanistic academic scenes. The active is not more effective or "better" than the passive; each just represents a different way of thinking, behaving, and communicating in different scenes. Similarly, "bed" is not better than "rack," and a medical student's vocabulary is not worse than a funeral director's. *As we learn to recognize the different uses of language in different scenes and situations, we can start to read the significance and meanings of those differences.* We come to realize that these different linguistic habits are not arbitrary or artificial; rather, they are adapted to and reflect their social scenes quite well. By learning to recognize and read the linguistic habits of each scene, we also learn how to position ourselves within it as social actors and as writers. In this way, the process of reading and the process of writing are dramatically connected.

## Writing Activity 2.4

Think of a scene in which you are currently participating and, using some of the observation strategies we described in Box 1.2 (pp. 44–45), observe the language used within that scene. For example, note the language used during a course you are currently taking; spend an hour in your workplace (when you are not working) and record the language you hear your fellow workers use; print copies of all the exchanges on your class electronic discussion list for a day; or observe the language used at a meeting of volunteers for a nonprofit agency for which you volunteer.

1. Record not just the specialist vocabulary of the participants but also how they use more ordinary words.
2. See what patterns you can recognize in the language you have recorded.
3. Speculate about what those patterns might mean, how they might reflect the values or goals or activities of the scene you observed.

Write for your teacher and classmates a one-page summary of your findings, including what scene you described, what language patterns you observed, and what their significance might be.

## Writing Activity 2.5

Study two Web sites from two different organizations. You might pick organizations having some common ground but different perspectives, like sites of a Republican and a Democratic organization, or sites of an animal breeding organization and an animal protection organization, or sites of a community college and an elite university. Look for different forms of language used on the two sites. Write a paragraph discussing how the different uses of language reveal the different perspectives of the two scenes.

## Collaborative Activity 2.2

You may already have begun to see the differing values and expectations among academic scenes. In small groups, trade textbooks that each of you brought in from a class in a different department, and compare these with this textbook. What different uses of language do you recognize in these two texts? Can you see more than just differences of technical or specialist vocabulary? List some examples of different language use, and speculate why these differences might exist.

# Reading Scenes and Situations through Genres

The language that people use reflects not only the scene but also the situation and genre within the scene. People adjust their language to the particular situation (involving certain participants, subjects, settings, and purposes) and the particular genre (the typical way of responding to the situation) in which they are participating. For example, scientists usually do not *speak* in passive voice no matter what situation they are in and what genre they are using. If they are instructing students how to perform an experiment, they will more likely use the imperative, saying "Pour the chemical into the beaker," not "The chemical was poured into the beaker." Passive constructions are prominent instead, as we've seen, in such genres as lab reports and research articles associated with a more reportive communication situation within the scientific scene. Similarly, medical students do not use the language Klass describes in all situations, but mainly when they are speaking with other medical personnel. And even Marines may shift from "rack" to "bed" when speaking to their families.

Once you learn to recognize how different situations and genres encourage different uses of language, you can use your understanding of these differences to make more effective writing choices within different situations and genres. In the remainder of this chapter, we will show you how to recognize and interpret features of genres; at the end of this chapter and then in the next one, we will show you how to turn that social understanding into making your own writing choices.

## GENRES AS SOCIAL SCRIPTS

As typical rhetorical ways of acting in different situations, genres function as social **scripts.** For instance, when you attend the first day of a typical college course, say this writing class, the first things you probably do are look around at the other students, check out the layout of the room, try to figure out what the teacher is like, and so on. In other words, you begin to read the scene in order to decide how best to act within it. But perhaps the best indication you will get about the nature of this scene is through the syllabus that the teacher distributes. As you know, the syllabus is a genre, one that teachers typically distribute on the first day of class. Beyond containing important information about the course goals, policies, and expectations, it helps *set the scene* of the course. By reading it carefully, you not only learn what you have to do in order to succeed in the course, when assignments are due, what the course policies are, and so on; you also learn something about how to behave in this scene; what kind of role your teacher will play and what kind of role she or he expects you to play; and what values, beliefs, and goals guide this course. The syllabus, in short, gives you early and important access to the "script" of the course. How well you read this script will impact how effectively you will act within the scene of the class and its various situations.

## Writing Activity 2.6

Select a course other than this one for which you have received a syllabus. Before looking back at the syllabus, describe the "personality" of that course—the nature of the course that is conveyed through the class structure, activities, assignments, teacher-student interactions, student-student interactions, etc. Now look at the syllabus for that course: Does the syllabus share any "personality traits" with the course? Could you tell from the syllabus what kind of course it is turning out to be? If so, find some features of the syllabus that reveal that personality. If not, find some features of the syllabus that suggest a different personality.

## Collaborative Activity 2.3

In a group of three or four other students, revise the syllabus for this writing course to create a "personality" quite different from the one the actual syllabus describes. Think about how different the role of students might be, what different kinds of information might be conveyed, how different the persona of the teacher might be. Your new syllabus should not change the requirements of the course, but it should significantly change the nature of its scene. Depending on what your teacher requests, write your new syllabus on an overhead transparency or your computer or post it to your class's Web site, and be prepared to explain to your classmates what aspects of the course's scene you changed by changing the syllabus script.

## READING THE PATIENT MEDICAL HISTORY FORM

For another example of how the language of genres reflects their situations, think about the scene of the doctor's office. Most of us can readily picture this scene, with its seating area, its coffee table piled with magazines, its reception desk, and its small examination rooms with health posters hanging on the walls. It is a familiar scene. What may be less familiar, however, is the role that genres play in scripting this scene.

The Patient Medical History Form (PMHF) is one such genre. You might recognize the form as the genre patients have to complete prior to meeting with the doctor on their initial visit to the doctor's office. The PMHF asks patients to provide critical information regarding their age, sex, weight, and height as well as their medical history, including prior and recurring physical conditions, past treatments, and, of course, a description of current physical symptoms. These questions are usually followed by a request for insurance information and then a consent-to-treat statement and a legal release statement that a patient signs. With these components, the PMHF is both a patient record and a legal document, helping the doctor treat the patient and at the same time protecting the doctor from potential lawsuits.

The PMHF does more than convey information from patient to doctor. In its content and visual design, it also tells us something about the scene that the patient is entering. Reading the genre, for instance, we notice that most if not all of its questions focus on a patient's physical symptoms. The genre is designed in such a way that there is very little space in which patients can describe their emotional state. The genre's focus on the physical reflects Western cultural views of medicine, which tend to separate the body and the mind. The medical assumption seems to be that doctors can isolate and then treat physical symptoms with little to no reference to the patient's state of mind and the effect that state of mind might have on these symptoms.

The attitude reflected in the language of this form resembles the description in Perri Klass's article earlier in this chapter of how doctors and nurses talk. As a genre, then, the PMHF reflects and preserves the habits of the medical community. It functions as one of the scripts by which the actors in this medical scene perform their roles and interact with one another. By completing the PMHF, an individual begins to assume the role of patient, one who has certain physical symptoms. And when the doctor meets the patient, the doctor will likely relate to the patient that way (it is not uncommon, for instance, for doctors and nurses to refer to patients by their physical symptoms, such as "I treated a knee injury today" or "the ear infection is in Room 3").

The Patient Medical History Form, thus, is one of the scripts that underwrites the scene of the doctor's office. Other genres within this scene (prescription notes, referral letters, patient files, letters to insurance companies, to name a few) set up other relations (between doctors and pharmacists,

## PATIENT HISTORY (Please Print)

THIS INFORMATION BECOMES PART OF YOUR CONFIDENTIAL MEDICAL RECORD

NAME _____ PRIOR PHYSICIAN _____
　　　　　　LAST　　　　　　　　　　FIRST　　　MIDDLE INITIAL

ADDRESS _____ TODAY'S DATE _____
　　　　　　　　　　　　　　CITY　　　　STATE　ZIP

TELEPHONE # (DAY)_____ (EVENING) _____ AGE _____ SEX  M  F

Chief Complaint and/or reason for visit _____

History of Present Illness - describe in detail _____

_____

_____

| Medical Conditions (Give names and dates) | Personal | Date | Family | Date | | Personal | Date | Family | Date |
|---|---|---|---|---|---|---|---|---|---|
| Hypertension | ❑ | ___ | ❑ | ___ | Anemia | ❑ | ___ | ❑ | ___ |
| Diabetes | ❑ | ___ | ❑ | ___ | Blood Disorders | ❑ | ___ | ❑ | ___ |
| Lung Disease | ❑ | ___ | ❑ | ___ | Obesity | ❑ | ___ | ❑ | ___ |
| Heart Disease | ❑ | ___ | ❑ | ___ | Ulcers | ❑ | ___ | ❑ | ___ |
| Cancer | ❑ | ___ | ❑ | ___ | Intestinal Disorders | ❑ | ___ | ❑ | ___ |
| Stroke | ❑ | ___ | ❑ | ___ | Jaundice | ❑ | ___ | ❑ | ___ |
| Chest Pain | ❑ | ___ | ❑ | ___ | Infertility | ❑ | ___ | ❑ | ___ |
| Abdominal Pain | ❑ | ___ | ❑ | ___ | Ear/Nose/Throat | ❑ | ___ | ❑ | ___ |
| Arthritis | ❑ | ___ | ❑ | ___ | High Cholesterol | ❑ | ___ | ❑ | ___ |
| Back Pain | ❑ | ___ | ❑ | ___ | Kidney Disease | ❑ | ___ | ❑ | ___ |
| Osteoporosis | ❑ | ___ | ❑ | ___ | Bladder Infections | ❑ | ___ | ❑ | ___ |
| Mental Disorders | ❑ | ___ | ❑ | ___ | TB Skin Tests | ❑ | ___ | ❑ | ___ |
| Phlebitis | ❑ | ___ | ❑ | ___ | Sleep Problems | ❑ | ___ | ❑ | ___ |
| Migraine | ❑ | ___ | ❑ | ___ | Alcoholism | ❑ | ___ | ❑ | ___ |
| Alcohol/Drug Abuse | ❑ | ___ | ❑ | ___ | Hepatitis C | ❑ | ___ | ❑ | ___ |
| Tobacco Abuse | ❑ | ___ | ❑ | ___ | Hepatitis B | ❑ | ___ | ❑ | ___ |
| Hereditary Disorders | ❑ | ___ | ❑ | ___ | Hepatitis Non A, Non B | ❑ | ___ | ❑ | ___ |
| Thyroid Disease | ❑ | ___ | ❑ | ___ | | | | | |

Surgical Procedures (Give names and dates) _____

Blood Transfusions (Give dates) _____

Hospitalizations (Give dates) _____

Injuries/Trauma (Give type and dates) _____

Allergies _____

### Immunization History
Influenza yearly  ❑ Y  ❑ N　　Pneumonia ❑ Y  ❑ N　　Tetanus  ❑ Y  ❑ N　　Hepatitis  ❑ Y  ❑ N

### Social History
Marital Status _____ Occupation _____

Education _____ Housing/source of drinking water _____

Status of immediate and extended family _____ Number living in the household _____

| | | | |
|---|---|---|---|
| Coffee/Tea intake? | ❑ Y | ❑ N | Amount? _____ |
| Difficulty sleeping? | ❑ Y | ❑ N | |
| Wear seatbelts? | ❑ Y | ❑ N | |
| Do you have a Living Will? | ❑ Y | ❑ N | |
| Do you have a Durable Power? | ❑ Y | ❑ N | |

**Social History (continued)**

| | | | | | |
|---|---|---|---|---|---|
| Cigarette use? | ❑Y | ❑N | Amount?_____ | Number of years?_____ |
| Pipe? Cigars? Chew? | ❑Y | ❑N | Amount?_____ | Number of years?_____ |
| If you smoke, do you want to stop? | ❑Y | ❑N | | |
| Alcohol use? | ❑Y | ❑N | Amount?_____ | Number of years?_____ |

I.V. drug or intranasal cocaine use, even if only once, at present or in the past? ❑Y ❑N
Have tattoos or extensive body piercing? ❑Y ❑N
Multiple sex partners (now or in the past?) ❑Y ❑N

Have you ever:
Had blood transfusions or any blood products? .......................... ❑Y ❑N
Been rejected for trying to donate blood? ................................ ❑Y ❑N
Been told that your liver function tests were elevated? ................... ❑Y ❑N
Been stuck with a needle or had an exposure to blood?.................. ❑Y ❑N
Had any sexually transmitted diseases (i.e. syphilis, chlamydia, gonorrhea)? ... ❑Y ❑N
Do you use condoms? ................................................. ❑Y ❑N

**Family History**

| | AGE IF LIVING | AGE AT DEATH | PRESENT CONDITION/CAUSE OF DEATH |
|---|---|---|---|
| Father | | | |
| Mother | | | |
| Children | | | |

**DRUGS FREQUENTLY OR PRESENTLY USED** (CHECK ALL THAT APPLY)

| | | | |
|---|---|---|---|
| ❑ Aspirin | ❑ Decongestants | ❑ Hormones | ❑ Diet Pills |
| ❑ Vitamins/Minerals/Herbals | ❑ Antibiotics | ❑ Diabetics | ❑ Antidepressants |
| Over the Counter Meds | ❑ Laxatives | ❑ Insulin | ❑ Sedatives |
| ❑ Water Pill | ❑ Antacids | ❑ Birth Control Pills | ❑ Sleeping Pills |
| ❑ Blood Pressure | ❑ Antihistamines | ❑ Heart | ❑ Cortisone |
| ❑ Asthma | ❑ Thyroid | ❑ Nitroglycerin | ❑ Anti-Inflammatory Pills |

Other _____

**Symptom and System Review**

| | | | |
|---|---|---|---|
| ❑ Headache | ❑ Shortness of Breath | ❑ Hemorrhoids | ❑ Muscle Cramps |
| ❑ Dizziness | ❑ Coughed up Blood | ❑ Abnormal EKG | ❑ Varicose Veins |
| ❑ Fainting | ❑ Night Sweats | ❑ Abnormal X-ray | ❑ Phlebitis |
| ❑ Seizures | ❑ Cough | ❑ High Blood Sugar | ❑ Goiter |
| ❑ Numbness | ❑ Wheezing/Asthma | ❑ Low Blood Sugar | ❑ Hot Flashes |
| ❑ Nervous | ❑ Loss of Appetite | ❑ Skin Rashes | ❑ Fluid Retention |
| ❑ Irritable | ❑ Indigestion | ❑ Dry Skin | ❑ Tired |
| ❑ Depressed | ❑ Heartburn | ❑ Heart Murmur | ❑ Trouble Sleeping |
| ❑ Ear Trouble | ❑ Nervous Stomach | ❑ Palpitations | ❑ Kidney Trouble |
| ❑ Sinus Trouble | ❑ Abdominal Pain | ❑ Irregular Heart Beat | ❑ Difficulty Urinating |
| ❑ Stuffy Nose | ❑ Diarrhea | ❑ Enlarged Heart | ❑ Urinary Burning |
| ❑ Nosebleeds | ❑ Constipation | ❑ Tire Easily | ❑ Frequent Urination |
| ❑ Vision Trouble | ❑ Change in Bowel Habits | ❑ Ankle Swelling | ❑ Middle of Night Urination |
| ❑ Nasal Allergies | ❑ Gall Bladder Trouble | ❑ Back Pain | |
| ❑ Hoarseness of Voice | ❑ Swallowing Trouble | ❑ Neck Pain | MEN - ❑ Impotence |
| ❑ Swallowing Trouble | ❑ Yellow Jaundice | ❑ Arm Pain | MEN - ❑ Loss of Libido |
| ❑ Sore Throat | ❑ Vomiting of Blood | ❑ Bursitis | WOMEN - ❑ Loss of Libido |
| ❑ Chest Pain/Pressure | ❑ Passing Blood by Rectum | ❑ Arthritis | WOMEN - ❑ PMS |

**Activity Level**
❑ Sedentary life with little exercise ❑ Mild exercise with job, house, or recreation (i.e. climb stairs)
❑ Occasional vigorous activity with work or recreation ❑ Regular vigorous exercise program or heavy manual work

---

**FOR WOMEN ONLY**

| | | | |
|---|---|---|---|
| Date last menstruated_____ | Any menstrual problems? | ❑Y | ❑N |
| Period every _____ days | Heavy periods | ❑Y | ❑N |
| Number of pregnancies_____ | Infrequent periods | ❑Y | ❑N |
| Number of miscarriages_____ | Irregular periods | ❑Y | ❑N |
| Birth control method_____ | Painful periods | ❑Y | ❑N |
| Date of last pap smear_____ | | | |

Check if you have had: ❑ D&C ❑ Toxemia ❑ Hysterectomy ❑ Ovarian Failure
❑ Difficulty with pregnancy ❑ with labor ❑ with delivery

doctors and other doctors, etc.), other actions, and other social roles. Together, the genres provide a kind of rhetorical map that we can read in order to chart how people behave and communicate within this scene.

## Collaborative Activity 2.4

Working with classmates, examine the visual elements of the sample PMHF we have included. Pay attention to the design of the document: The use of borders, boxes, headings and subheadings, font shape and size, color, etc. What else do these elements tell us about this genre and the scene in which it is used? In what ways do the visual elements support the claim we have been making about the PMHF?

## FROM READING TO ANALYZING GENRES

What we just did in reading the Patient Medical History Form to determine what it can tell us about how people behave and communicate in the doctor's office is called **genre analysis**. Genre analysis involves the close and critical reading of people's patterns of communication in different situations within scenes. As a process, it involves collecting samples of a genre, identifying patterns within it (recognizing, for example, that PMHFs focus almost exclusively on physical symptoms), and then drawing conclusions about what these patterns reveal about the situation or scene in which it is used. *By doing this kind of genre analysis, you will gain access to the patterns of communication that will enable you to write more effectively within different situations and scenes.*

Genre analysis involves close reading and some observation by

1. Collecting samples of a genre

2. Finding out where, when, by whom, why, and how the genre is used

3. Identifying rhetorical and linguistic patterns in the genre

4. Determining what these patterns tell us about the people who use it and the scene in which it is used

You might want to review our discussion of observing scenes in Chapter 1, especially Box 1.2 (pp. 44–45).

In order to demonstrate how genre analysis works, we will now move from our relatively informal reading of the PMHF genre to the formal process of analyzing the genre of the business complaint letter. After you practice analyzing genres yourself, we will show you how you can use your analysis of genre to make your own writing choices.

# A Sample Genre Analysis of the Complaint Letter

We have chosen the complaint letter as a model for our genre analysis in part because it is a genre you might have some experience with, and because it is short enough that we can include several samples (pp. 67–69). As noted above, the first step in doing genre analysis involves collecting samples of the genre. There are several ways to collect samples. You can ask participants in a scene you have been observing for copies of the genre they have been using. If the genre is a more public one, as in the case of greeting cards, classified ads, menus, Web sites, wedding announcements, etc., you can readily find samples of the genre. You can also collect samples from books about the genre. For the analysis that follows, we collected complaint letters from several business-writing textbooks that included examples of the genre.

The second step is to start collecting information about the genre's situation and scene. Before you look at the samples we have included, consider what you already know about the complaint letter as a genre:

- Who uses the genre?
- What is it about?
- Where is the genre used?
- When is it used?
- Why is it used?

There are several ways in which you can answer these questions before doing the deeper analysis of the genre samples. One way is to draw on what you already know about the genre. Another way is to observe the scene and situation in which the genre is used (see Box 1.2, pp. 44–45). The observation could include interviewing users of the genre, watching people use the genre, and observing what the genre does. In the case of the complaint letter, we know that, unlike a syllabus, a lab report, or a patient medical history form, the complaint letter is not solely used in just one concrete scene (a classroom, a lab, or a doctor's office, for instance). Individuals may write complaint letters from home, or an employee in a company's purchasing department may write a letter of complaint from the office. However, the general scene of this genre involves a group of participants (consumers) who have the shared objective of seeking restitution for a defective product or inadequate service.

Once we have identified the scene, we can consider the elements of situation (setting, subject, participants, purposes) that prompt and define complaint letters. Drawing on prior knowledge, we know that complaint letters are letters written in any setting, mailed or e-mailed, about some sort of problem that has arisen, be it a billing error, poor or inadequate service, a defective or falsely advertised product, and so on. We also know that a complaint letter is often written by someone who has been either directly affected by the problem or represents an organization that has been affected by the problem in some way. In turn, readers of complaint letters are ideally people who are in a position to address the problem, ranging from the owner of a small company to the consumer affairs department of a large organization. Finally, we know that the purposes of the complaint letter are to bring the problem to the attention of the person or organization responsible for it, to convince them that the complaint is justified, and to request some sort of fair settlement or correction, which, if settlement is reached, often arrives in the form of a related genre called the adjustment letter. Gathering information about use of a genre (in this case complaint letters), either through your prior knowledge, interview, or observation, is the second step, after collecting samples, in performing a genre analysis.

The third and fourth steps in genre analysis are a little more challenging. They involve identifying a genre's linguistic and rhetorical patterns and determining what these patterns reveal about the people who use it, including their behaviors and activities, and the situation and scene in which it is used. You are probably already familiar with most of these patterns from past English courses in which you practiced doing textual criticism and analysis of works of literature.

To begin identifying the rhetorical and linguistic patterns of a genre, we need to read it closely, looking for any recurrent features that all samples of the genre share. In identifying recurrent features, it is best to move from the general to the specific:

- Identify content
- Identify the appeals to the audience
- Identify the structure used
- Identify the format used
- Identify choice of sentence style and words

We begin by looking at the **content**, at the information that is typically included and excluded in the samples.

Then we look at the types of **rhetorical appeals** that are used. Rhetorical appeals are ways of trying to persuade an audience, the names of which—logos, pathos, and ethos—are based in the classical study of rhetoric in ancient Greece. *Logos* is appealing to an audience's rational mind, to the persuasiveness of logical and reasoned arguments and evidence. *Pathos* is appealing to an audience's emotions, persuading readers by making them feel the writer's position, whether through sympathy, compassion, anger, or any other emotion. *Ethos* is appealing to an audience's belief in the personal qualities of the writer, persuading the readers that the writer should be believed or agreed with on this subject. For example, writers may try to convince readers they are credible because of their expertise, sympathetic because of their experiences, or believable because they are in positions of power.

After the largest elements of content and rhetorical appeals, we look at the largest **structural patterns** (What are the various parts? How are they organized? In what order do they appear?) and then **format** (the layout of the sample texts, their appearance, length, etc.). Then we focus on the more specific linguistic features, on the **syntax** or sentence structure and the **diction** or word choices. Syntactic choices include sentence length and complexity and other patterns in sentence style, such as using the passive or active verbs, as we discussed earlier. We also look at the kinds of words that are used within the samples: What kinds of words are used to convey the subject matter? Are they mainly words used by specialists (jargon) or slang? What do the words connote? Recall our earlier discussion of the difference between the connotations of the words *bed* and *rack*. How would you describe the writer's voice (the personality or presence of the writer that is conveyed through the words)? *Everything from the content to the structure to the word choices within a genre makes up its rhetorical patterns.* With this brief overview in mind, we will now walk you through the process of identifying rhetorical and linguistic patterns typically found in complaint letters. As you read the samples on pages 67–69, see what rhetorical patterns you can identify.

## IDENTIFYING CONTENT

Beginning with content, we see that each complaint letter describes a specific complaint, something that went wrong or did not work as promised. The letters also include detailed information about the products or services that are the cause of the complaint, often listing invoice numbers, purchase dates, model numbers, etc. And each letter makes some request of the reader: Asking for a new product, a repair of the old product, or compensation to the writer for the bad service or product.

## Sample Complaint Letter 1

Rudi's Country Store
R.D. 1
Ft. Mark, PA 15540
August 22, 19

Mr. Franklin Morrison
American Paint Company
537 Schoolyard Road
Messina, PA 15540

Dear Mr. Morrison:

I am writing to you because I have been unable to reach you by phone, even after leaving messages on your machine. Your painting crew just finished painting my store and I am not entirely satisfied with the job or the bill.

Your workers tended to arrive late, about 9:30 a.m., and leave early, about 3:30 p.m. Once they missed a whole afternoon because, according to the foreman, they had another job to do. As a result, they were on site for four days instead of the estimated three.

The crew's behavior on the job was also unnecessarily disruptive. They worked with no shirts on and yelled to each other. My store stays open until 10:00 at night, and I would have appreciated it if they had cleared away their empty paint cans and other paraphernalia from around the front and sides of the store after work every day, but instead they left each afternoon without cleaning up.

I also seem to have been billed for a can of paint that the workers overturned, staining the parking lot. I fixed the stain, but I would like my bill adjusted accordingly. I hope you will pass these complaints on to your foreman. Because you are a successful company, I am sure that these practices are not normal. Your bid was low, and the paint job looks good. I look forward to doing business with you again, if you can assure me that the problems I mentioned will not arise.

Respectfully,

---

## Sample Complaint Letter 2

1390 Southwest Twentieth Street
Davie, FL 33326
22 September 2000

The Doubleday Store
Customer Service Department
501 Franklin Avenue
Garden City, NJ 07769

Re: Account #96-299-38934

Gentlemen:

Please review my account for a credit. On 12 July 2000 I received the Pierre Cardin canvas luggage set from your company which I ordered on 15 June 2000. When I received the luggage from your company, it was on a trial basis for 60 days. After examining the luggage, I determined that it was not substantial enough for my needs, and I returned the entire set on 12 August 2000.

The charge of $279.95 has continued to be shown on my last two monthly statements. I wrote a note on the statement each time indicating the date and return of luggage and sent the statement back to your company. Copies of these notes are attached to this letter. To date, I have not received an adjusted statement.

Would you please credit my account for $279.95 and send me an adjusted statement?

I will appreciate your prompt attention to this matter.

Very truly yours,

Ruth Burrows

---

## Sample Complaint Letter 3

**ROBBINS CONSTRUCTION, INC.**
**255 Robbins Place    Centerville, MO 65101    (417) 555-1850**

August 19, 19XX

Mr. David Larsen
Larsen Supply Company
311 Elmerine Avenue
Anderson, MO 63501

Dear Mr. Larsen:

As steady customers of yours for over 15 years, we came to you first when we needed a quiet pile driver for a job near a residential area. On your recommendation, we bought your Vista 500 Quiet Driver, at $14,900. We have since found, much to our embarrassment, that it is not substantially quieter than a regular pile driver.

We received the contract to do the bridge repair here in Centerville after promising to keep the noise to under 90 db during the day. The Vista 500 (see enclosed copy of bill of sale for particulars) is rated at 85 db, maximum. We began our work and, although one of our workers said the driver didn't seem sufficiently quiet to him, assured the people living near the job site that we were well within the agreed sound limit. One of them, an acoustical engineer, marched out the next day and demonstrated that we were putting out 104 db. Obviously, something is wrong with the pile driver.

I think you will agree that we have a problem. We were able to secure other equipment, at considerable inconvenience, to finish the job on schedule. When I telephoned your company that humiliating day, however, a Mr. Meredith informed me that I should have done an acoustical reading on the driver before I accepted delivery.

I would like you to send out a technician—as soon as possible—either to repair the driver so that it performs according to specifications or to take it back for a full refund.

Yours truly,

Jack Robbins, President

## IDENTIFYING RHETORICAL APPEALS

Second, we look for the kinds of rhetorical appeals the writers use. The writers of these complaint letters use a variety of rhetorical appeals to register their complaints in a forceful yet restrained and reasonable manner. They use *logos*, approaching the subject logically and treating the reader as a rational person who will surely see the problem and try to correct it. The writers offer facts and details about the situation and evidence of the problem to appeal to the reader's logical mind and to demonstrate that the writers are also rational and credible individuals. In order to create a credible and sympathetic *ethos*, or image of the writer, the letter writers portray themselves as reasonable people, who did what they should have done and yet encountered difficulty. Although the complaint letters rarely show anger (which might harm their sympathy or credibility), they do indicate how troubling or inconvenient the problem was, what pain and suffering was caused, appealing to *pathos* or to the reader's emotions for sympathy. In order to create sympathy between reader and writer, complaint letters often end on a note of optimism, suggesting that the writer believes the reader will respond conscientiously ("I will appreciate your prompt attention to this matter"). These complaint letters use logos, pathos, and ethos to try to persuade the reader to do what the writer is requesting.

## IDENTIFYING STRUCTURE

After describing what we can of the content and rhetorical appeals of the genre, we turn to describing the structure of the complaint letter—its parts and their order. We notice first that, for the most part, writers begin the genre by identifying themselves as customers of the company or organization being addressed. The first part of the complaint letter also sometimes includes the specific product or service that has caused the complaint, which the company or organization will need in order to issue repairs or refunds. The second part of the complaint letter provides a specific description of the nature of the problem. Included here is a description of what happened, especially what went wrong. This section does more than just describe, however; it also tries to convince the reader that the product is defective or the service is inadequate by giving detailed examples, primarily through personal testimony but sometimes supported by more objective data. The final part of these complaint letters usually proposes or requests some kind of action, solution, or adjustment in relation to the problem. Some conclude with a curt request; others conclude with a more courteous optimism, signaling the writer's hope that the reader will respond fairly and promptly.

## Identifying Format

In terms of format, layout, and appearance, these complaint letters generally follow standard business letter format, with a heading that includes the writer's address or letterhead as well as the date, an inside address with the name and address of the recipient, a salutation ("Dear Ms. Webber"), the body, the closing ("Sincerely" or "Respectfully"), and the signature. Although they are not represented among our samples, we have seen complaint letters that have been handwritten as well as typed, but even handwritten letters tend to follow the standard business letter format.

## Identifying Sentences, Words, and Tone

On the sentence and diction levels, we notice that complaint letters tend to be slightly formal and often direct. The writers of these letters use mostly active sentence constructions, such as "I ordered," "We have used your product for years," "Your workers arrived late," and "I think you will agree we have a problem." Writers of the complaint letters periodically use sentences that begin with introductory phrases, such as "As steady customers of yours for over 15 years, we came to you first . . . ," "On July 9, I ordered . . . ," and "Because you are a successful company, I am sure that . . ." These introductory phrases provide background to the claim that is about to be made in the sentence. As such, they serve as a way to create a narrative, a sort of cause-and-effect relationship that leads up to the point the writer is making. At the same time, they also help justify the credibility of both the writer and the complaint.

Because the complaint letter refers back to an event that already occurred, writers mostly use the past tense when describing the nature of the problem. In the final paragraph, however, when the writer shifts from a description of the problem to a request for settlement, the tense shifts as well, signaling future or conditional action often with the use of the auxiliary verb *would*. Overall, the sentences in these complaint letters tend to be slightly long and embedded, using a variety of transitions such as coordinating conjunctions (*and, but*), subordinating conjunctions (*because, after, though*), and interrupting phrases (phrases that add information or explanation such as "we were able to secure other equipment, *at considerable inconvenience,* to finish the job on schedule"). Such embedding creates a **narrative effect,** helping the writer describe a chain of interconnected events and their effects. Indeed, it seems that one of the rhetorical functions of the interrupting phrases in particular is to allow the writer to insert his or her feelings of annoyance into the description without drawing explicit attention to the annoyance.

A calm and rational tone, even when the writer may be annoyed, is perhaps the most typical feature of complaint letters, and it is evident at both the word and sentence levels. While moments of anger do appear, they are usually embedded within the larger description of the problem, as we saw in the embedding of "at considerable inconvenience." Even though first and second person pronouns (*I/we* and *you*) are primarily used—reflecting the relationship between writer and reader—the writers of these complaint letters temper this directness by depersonalizing the *you*. Rather than pinning the blame directly on the reader personally, writers instead often identify the reader as a representative of the company or organization or even the product that is to blame, hence we see phrases such as "because you are a successful company," "your Vista 500 Quiet Driver," "your painting crew," "your Newark, New Jersey parts warehouse," etc. Other examples of restraint and calmness include the selection of more formal words such as *informed* instead of *told*, *telephoned* instead of *called*, *arise* instead of *come up*, *paraphernalia* instead of *stuff*, *indicating* instead of *saying*, and so on.

## INTERPRETING GENERIC PATTERNS IN THE COMPLAINT LETTER

Now that we have described rhetorical patterns in the complaint letters, genre analysis turns to the *significance or meaning of those patterns:*

> What do these rhetorical patterns tell us about the genre of the complaint letter and the situation and scene in which it is used?
>
> What can we learn about the actions being performed through the genre by observing its language patterns?

These questions mark the final step in performing a genre analysis.

There are, of course, many ways we can answer these questions and many conclusions we can make and support. One argument we can make—our **thesis**, if you will—is that the genre of the complaint letter tries to create a situation that depersonalizes the relationship between the writer and the reader. In a relatively uncomfortable situation of complaint, the complaint letter genre enables the writer to complain without it "being personal." The writers present themselves not as the managers and company presidents that some of them are but as "customers." We see this especially at the beginning of the complaint letter, where the writer assumes the role of customer: "On July 9, I ordered nine TV tuner assembly units," "Your painting crew just finished painting my store," or "As steady customers of yours for over 15 years, we came to you. . . ." In this role of customer, the writer then presents his or her complaint in fairly *objective terms*. That is, he or she mainly describes how the service was inadequate or the product was defective rather than how he or she felt about the service or product. By couching any personal resentment or anger in a less emotional, relatively objective description of what happened to him or her as a "customer," the writer achieves credibility in the complaint letter. Likewise, the reader is also depersonalized. Rather than being addressed as personally responsible for the problem, the reader is addressed as the company or organization. This way, the reader is less likely to become defensive.

In mainstream U.S. culture, there are various "scenes" in which we can communicate our complaints. Some of them include genres with more emotional expression than others—for example, when a baseball player complains to an umpire about being called out. People in other cultures may treat complaints differently, and the genres that respond to their problems will reveal different attitudes and relationships, through different rhetorical patterns. When we write a complaint letter that reflects the habits and patterns that we have just analyzed, we probably are not even aware that the scene of writing is being shaped in a way that maintains a delicate and distancing relationship between the writer (customer) and the reader (company or organization). How we write about the problem and the sort of demands we make are all partly shaped by the genre we are using.

# Sample Genre Analysis

So that you can see an example of genre analysis, we include below an analysis written by a student, Nicole Rebernik, who here compares menus from two Italian restaurants to show how differences in their linguisitic and rhetorical patterns reveal differences in their customers. As you read this sample, note how the author discovers things about the genre by doing an analysis of the genre's patterns.

Note also how the author presents this interpretation in the form of some kind of argument about what the genre tells us. Such claims that focus a paper are called in academic writing a thesis or controlling idea.

The **controlling idea** is the main thing a writer wants to say, the point of the paper, the primary claim the writer wants to convey. The controlling idea controls the paper, working within a particular genre to help the writer determine what content is relevant and needed and how that content should be organized. The nature of the controlling idea varies in different genres, of course. As we will see in more detail in Part II, on academic genres, different kinds of ideas are important in different genres. In

genre analyses, the controlling idea makes a **claim** or interpretive statement about the significance of the genre patterns. For example, the student who analyzed the PMHF (p. 60) claimed that the genre emphasizes
physical symptoms to the exclusion of the whole patient. If we were to
write a genre analysis paper based on our analysis of the complaint letter,
we might construct a controlling idea that complaint letters depersonalize
the complaint situation, making it easier for people in U.S. society to register complaints. Genre analyses result in claims about the genre, situation,
or scene that become controlling ideas when written up in academic
papers.

As you read Nicole's analysis, pay attention to how she *supports her claim
with evidence* from the menus. Think also about any additional claims you
could make based on her analysis.

---

Rebernik 1

The Genre of Restaurant Menus: A Comparative Analysis

Nicole Rebernik

College students have many options throughout the
city when it comes to Italian dining. One popular spot near
campus is BelaRoma Pizza and Pasta, which caters to a college crowd and advertises on its menu the restaurant's goal
of "Satisfying Your Cravings." Located further from the campus strip is another Italian restaurant, Sicily's, that caters
more to the larger community and offers a more formal dining experience. On its menu, you will find a different advertisement: "Silver Platter Award Winner for Best Italian Food."
The differences in the implications of these quotations taken
from the menu covers show the differences in the communities these restaurants are trying to create and the customers
they are seeking to serve. BelaRoma's main purpose is to
serve takeout and delivery food to on-the-go students, while
Sicily's restaurant serves a sit-down clientele. Though Sicily's
Italian Restaurant and BelaRoma Deli are both restaurants

Rebernik 2

that offer Italian style dining, as demonstrated by their menus, the fact that they represent different communities is evident in the layout, items, pricing, and language of their menus.

Sicily's and BelaRoma, while being very different types of restaurants, share some basic similarities in their menus, reflecting the shared goals of the restaurant business. Each of the menus clearly displays the restaurant's name in large letters, with a graphic underneath the title to catch the customer's attention and to make the restaurant memorable to the customers so that they will keep coming back. When the customers first open the menus, a variety of food options are revealed, conveniently following the order that they usually are consumed, with appetizers listed first, followed by main dishes and then desserts. Each variety of food is broken down under different headings, such as "Appetizers" or "Pasta," thus making the menu easier to read and helping to guide customers as they make their choices.

Upon further examination, each of the food items then becomes a subheading, such as "Veggie Pita" or "Spinach Lasagna," with a description of the item underneath it; this is done so that the customers know precisely what they are ordering. The descriptions usually include vivid details and adjectives that try to sell customers on a particular dish with descriptions such as, "The lasagna is cooked until crusty brown and bubbling hot." The menus also include graphics throughout to make them more pleasing for the customer to peruse. The graphics include pictures of certain delectable food items that persuade customers to order that item. Finally, under each of the food descriptions is the price that the restaurant charges for the item, which is included after the description to downplay the cost as compared to the

Rebernik 3

deliciousness of the entrée. The menus also include payment options that the customer may use.

All of these similarities reflect the purposes and audiences of the genre being utilized. Each menu is trying to
attract a certain customer base. The purpose of the restaurant menu is to make the food presentable in a way that customers will want to order the offered menu items. The menus
need to explain the food that they are serving so that the customer will have an understanding of what they are ordering
and what it costs. The audiences that the restaurants are trying to attract and their purposes are similar in the sense that
they want to attract people who want the convenience of
eating out instead of preparing food themselves. They also
want the service and good food that goes along with this. All
of these strategies are reasons for the similarities in the
menus of Sicily's and BelaRoma.

Although the similarities in the menus reflect the
broader goals of restaurants to attract, serve, and maintain
customers, the differences in the menus reflect different situations. For instance, differences in the layout and organization of each menu become obvious just by looking at the
cover of each of the menus. BelaRoma's inexpensively
printed, flyer-like menu is printed on bright yellow paper
to attract the customer's eye when placed with other
takeout menus and is meant to be picked up or attached to
takeout orders so that customers can keep the flyer. "Free
Express Delivery" is displayed in bold lettering along with
BelaRoma's phone and fax numbers, hours of operations,
payment options, and location all on the cover of the
menu--all of which fits with their emphasis on takeout
business. The restaurant needs to make it as easy as
possible for the prospective client to find its phone number
and location; otherwise they could easily move on to

Rebernik 4

another takeout menu that more readily provides this information.

Sicily's restaurant's menu, on the other hand, is slicker and printed on heavier, more expensive paper and is colored in a somber dark green and red coloring of Italy, giving the feeling of a more formal eating environment. Sicily's does allow takeout ordering, but does not state this anywhere on their menu, which is meant only for in-restaurant use. The payment options, phone number, hours of operation, and location are all listed on the back cover of the menu in contrast with BelaRoma having all this on the front cover, demonstrating their different purposes. While BelaRoma has coupons for menu items such as pizza on the back of its menu, Sicily's lists the numerous awards it has received such as the Metro Weekly Award for "Best Italian Food" and "Most Romantic Restaurant." These differences in the cover layouts of the two menus reflect the differences between the communities in which Sicily's and BelaRoma participate. BelaRoma provides delivery services and takeout foods for a mostly campus clientele. The Sicily's menu reflects that they are looking for a more sophisticated clientele and not one that is looking for a fast takeout solution. Sicily's primary business comes from sit-down dining, and that is reflected in the more artistic and elaborate looking menu. Sicily's lists its awards on the back cover to give eating at the restaurant an aura of prestige and attract diners that are looking for quality food.

The menu items themselves are an accurate depiction of the differences between the two restaurants. Sicily's concentrates mainly on gourmet Italian food while BelaRoma offers Italian-type foods and also a wide variety of American fare. This is demonstrated by the statement on the front cover of BelaRoma's menu, "The diversity of our menu

Rebernik 5

enables us to cater to a wide range of tastes and cravings."
There is everything from Alfredo Pasta to a Mushroom
Swiss Burger on the BelaRoma menu. Sicily's offers a wine
list and champagne, while BelaRoma offers Coca-Cola
products. The differences between the items Sicily's and
BelaRoma carry reflect the different communities they are
trying to create. BelaRoma is trying to market a variety of
foods so that it can please almost everyone in a large group
of people, such as a large group of college students. Sicily's
has narrowed the group towards whom it is marketing its
items to a smaller demographic group that only wants
higher-quality foods.

The price differential between Sicily's restaurant's menu
and BelaRoma restaurant's menu further reflects the different
aims and audiences of the menus. The most expensive item
on BelaRoma's menu is $15.00 for a large pizza that will
feed a few people on average--perfect for college students
who don't have a lot of money--while Sicily's most expensive
item is an entrée entitled Filet Chianti at the cost of $19.99
and is meant to feed one person, a bit more out of the college student's range. A traditional Italian entrée of Lasagna
at BelaRoma costs $5.99 while at Sicily's restaurant it costs
the customer $9.99. The more expensive foods that are
served at Sicily's restaurant, along with the atmosphere and
service, justify the differences in prices. Sicily's offers more
select Italian foods than BelaRoma. The quality of ingredients
that go into making the dishes are part of the higher pricing
as is the preparation and artistry involved. BelaRoma is
focused on college students who would be more interested
in the types of food that they serve--pizza, quick pasta
dishes--and therefore need to price their items so that
the average college student would be able to afford
them.

Rebernik 6

The language on the menus fit the different price ranges and different clienteles of each restaurant. The use of elevated language in the Sicily's menu reflects the higher prices of its items and the more formal dining experience they provide. There are entrées on the menu at Sicily's such as "Zuppa del Giornio" and "Chicken Saltimboca." Most of the items on BelaRoma's menu consist of more familiar names like "Spaghetti" and "Reuben." This reflects the difference in types of food and claims to authenticity or ability to specialize in Italian food that each establishment offers as well as the different customers they are trying to attract. Sicily's restaurant is looking for more serious diners who would be interested in trying a menu item named "Linguine Pescatore" while BelaRoma is trying to attract customers-- most likely college students--who want to be able to order a "Bacon Swiss Burger" or "Cheese Sticks," in addition to Italian fare. The language of the menus, like the prices, lends a particular atmosphere to the foods offered by each restaurant.

The differences in the menus of BelaRoma Pizza and Pasta and Sicily's Italian Restaurant reflect the fact that these eateries belong to different communities of eating establishments. Each is using its menu to try to attract and appeal to a specific clientele: Sicily's is trying to attract a smaller group of people who are more selective and who only want Italian food while BelaRoma is trying to appeal to their diverse clientele of mostly college students with many different eating habits and tastes. While they share the similar goal of trying to get people to eat at their establishments and order their food, their strategies in menu layout, pricing, language, and menu items reflect differences in target customers.

## Collaborative Activity 2.5

Drawing on the sample menus reproduced here and your reading of the sample student paper, discuss with your classmates how you might extend the analysis. Note the visual elements of the menus and point out additional features of format as well as content, language, and structure that aren't mentioned in the sample paper. What other examples can be used to support the writer's claims? Next, compare and contrast the ways in which the two menus appeal to ethos, logos, and pathos. Then discuss with your group what other conclusions you might draw about the significance of the menus. What might your analysis of these menus (along with Rebernik's) lead you to conclude about the image of college students that the owners of BelaRoma appear to have, for example? Or what might you conclude about the larger scenes of these two restaurants?

## Collaborative Activity 2.6

Bring to class a copy of a sample menu (many of which can be found online) from the community in which your college/university is located and share the menus in your small group. Notice the visual elements of the menus as well as the other kinds of elements—content, structure, format, sentences, words. How do the menus reflect similar or different purposes and define similar or different roles for the restaurant and the customer? Based on the similarities and differences you found, what conclusions might you draw about menus as a genre? For example, what might you conclude about the role that menus play in setting the tone of a situation? Or in establishing behavior in a scene? Finally, based on your analysis of various menus, what might you conclude about the larger scene of restaurants in your college community?

# Practicing Genre Analysis

Having studied how genre analysis works and seen it in action in a couple of samples, you now have the opportunity to practice doing genre analysis yourself, using the guidelines for analyzing genre summarized in Box 2.1 on pages 93 and 94. The three activities that follow will guide you, individually and in groups, through the steps involved in analyzing genre. Then, in Writing Activity 2.8, you will have a chance to carry out a genre analysis on a genre of your own choosing, possibly one which you will then write about in Writing Project 2.1.

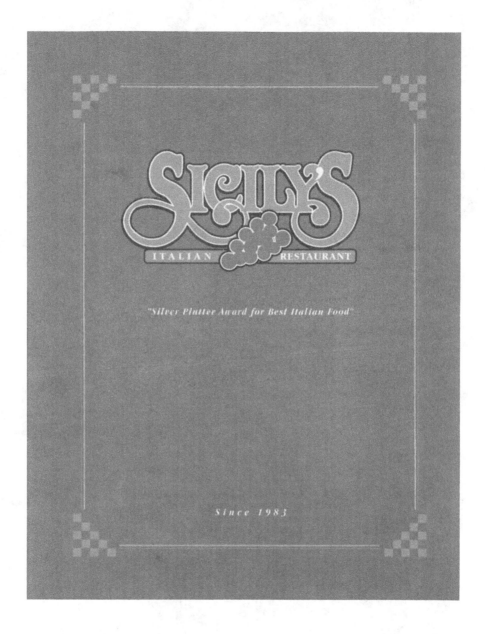

*"Silver Platter Award for Best Italian Food"*

## SOUPS

*Zuppa del Giornio* - Soup of the day, a fresh daily choice . . . . . . . . . . . . . . . . . . . . . . . . . . . . . . . . . . . . . . . .3.25
*Minestrone* - Hearty broth with fresh vegetables . . . . . . . . . . . . . . . . . . . . . . . . . . . . . . . . . . . . . . . . . . . . . . .3.75
*Seafood Soup* - Hearty broth with mixed seafood . . . . . . . . . . . . . . . . . . . . . . . . . . . . . . . . . . . . . . . . . . . .5.25

## APPETIZERS AND SALADS

*Bruschetta* - Toasted bread topped with diced tomatoes, garlic & fresh herbs . . . . . . . . . . . . . . . . . . . .3.59
*Roasted Garlic* - Garlic roasted in olive oil and served with toasted bruschetta . . . . . . . . . . . . . . . . . . .6.79
*Baked Clams* - Clams stuffed with homemade stuffing and herbs . . . . . . . . . . . . . . . . . . . . . . . . . . . . .7.59
*Stuffed Mushrooms* - Fresh mushrooms stuffed with bacon, cheese & onion . . . . . . . . . . . . . . . . . .7.59
*Fried Calamari* - Deep-fried calamari served with a spicy tomato sauce dip . . . . . . . . . . . . . . . . . . . .7.99
*Sicily's Salad* - Fresh romaine with shrimp & tomatoes in oil vinaigrette . . . . . . . . . . . . . . . . . . . . . .6.59
*Caesar Salad* - Romaine lettuce, bacon, cheese, croutons in chef's special blend . . . . . . . . . . . . . . .4.79
*Tomato Salad* - Fresh tomatoes with onions dressed in oil & vinegar . . . . . . . . . . . . . . . . . . . . . . . . .5.29

## PASTA

*Fettucine Alfredo* - Fettucine in a rich cream and parmesan sauce . . . . . . . . . . . . . . . . . . . . . . . . . . . .12.59
*Rotini alla Maria* - Pasta tossed with fresh broccoli and chicken in white wine garlic sauce . . . . . . . .10.59
*Gnocchi* - Homemade potato dumpling in a rich, creamy basil cream sauce . . . . . . . . . . . . . . . . . . .10.59
*Linguine Pescatore* - Pasta mixed with seafood and a "spicy" tomato or olive oil white wine sauce . . . .12.59
*Tortellini alla Pesto* - Tortellini tossed in an olive oil and pesto sauce . . . . . . . . . . . . . . . . . . . . . . . .9.79
*Lasagna* - Old country recipe, cooked until crusty brown and bubbling hot . . . . . . . . . . . . . . . . . . . .9.99
*Spinach Lasagna* - Filled with spinach and 3 cheeses, cooked until crusty brown and bubbling hot . . . . .9.79

## ENTRÉES

**Veal Parmigiana** - Veal cutlet topped with ham, cheese & tomato sauce ........................15.59

**Chicken Parmigiana** - Tender breast of chicken topped with tomato sauce and melted mozzerella .....14.99

**Chicken Rustico** - Pan-fried chicken in a "mouth-watering" rosemary, mushroom cream sauce ......14.99

**Chicken Saltimboca** - sauteed with Marsala wine, prosciutto ham, mozzarella, atop spinach ........12.99

**Veal Marsala** - Pan-fried veal sauteed with Marsala wine & mushrooms in a cream sauce ...........16.79

*\* All of the above entries are served with pasta \**

# HOUSE FAVORITES & SPECIALTIES

**Risotto Seafood** - Italian rice sauteed in white wine garlic & herbs mixed with fresh seafood .........13.99

**Spaghetti alla Sicily's** - Pasta tossed with sun-dried tomatoes, olive oil, garlic & cheese ...........11.59

**Filet Chianti** - 10 oz. cooked to perfection with wine sauce, served with rice and salad ...........19.99

**Pasta Primavera** - Linguine with vegetables and fresh tomatoes sauteed in a white wine garlic sauce ...16.99

**Ravioli alla Bolognese** - Fresh pasta filled with veal in homemade tomato meat sauce .............11.29

# DESSERTS

**Tartufi** - frozen Italian chocolate mousse ..................................................4.59

**Cannoli alla Sicily** - pastry shell filled with ricotta, cream cheese and chocolate chips ..............4.99

**Spumoni** - Italian chocolate, cherry, and pistachio ice cream, served with a cookie .................3.99

**Torta di Formaggio - Cheesecakes:**

   *Light Chocolate Cheesecake* - topped with peanuts and chocolate ...........................4.99

   *American Style Cheesecake* - topped with spiced apples and caramel sauce ....................4.99

   *Peanut Butter Pie* - layered with Reese's chocolate peanut butter and chocolate chips .............4.59

**Tiramisu** - lady fingers soaked in coffee and liqueur, layered with marscapone cheese ..............4.59

*Select a "dolce delizioso" from our delectable daily dessert specials*

*Ask your server about our extensive wine list*

**METRO WEEKLY AWARDS FOR**
*"Best Italian Food" and "Most Romantic Restaurant"*

**LOCATED ON "THE STRIP"**
4523 Volunteer Drive
Knoxville, TN 37932
Phone: 693-1716

**HOURS:**
*Monday-Thursday, 4-10 p.m.*
*Friday-Sunday, 1-midnight*

*Parties of six or more add 18% gratuity.*
*We accept VISA, Mastercard, American Express and Discover*

## Satisfying Your Cravings

We at BelaRoma are committed to the preparation of, presentation, and consistency of our products, and to the finest service possible. The diversity of our menu enables us to cater to a wide range of tastes and cravings. We are always open to any suggestions that could help us better serve you. And we always expedite your order with fast, free delivery.

## Free Express Delivery
# 522-1234
Or fax your order to 522-5221

### OPEN
Sunday–Thursday  11a.m.–2a.m.
Friday–Saturday  11a.m.–4a.m.

### CATERING
*Box Lunches • Coffees • Parties • Meetings • Groups*

### PAYMENT OPTIONS
Cash • Check • Visa • Master Card

We will be glad to accept your local check with proper I.D. and two phone numbers. There is a fifty cent (.50) charge for each check or credit card transaction. There is also a $20.00 returned check charge—no exceptions.

**715 17TH STREET, KNOXVILLE, TN 37916**
Cumberland Avenue at 17th Street (In the lower level beneath Threds)

## SPECIALTY SANDWICHES

**PHILLY STEAK & CHEESE**
Three-flavored sirloin steak, grilled with bell peppers & onions, topped with provolone cheese, and served in a french roll with a side of lettuce and tomato. ............... **$5.49**

**GYRO (HERO)**
Thin slices of beef and lamb, lettuce, tomatoes and onions, served in a warm gyro loaf with garlic cucumber sauce. ............... **$3.95**

**STEAK IN A SACK**
Grilled sirloin steak with onions, seasoned to perfection, and served with A-1 sauce, lettuce and tomato on the side. ............... **$5.49**

**VEGGIE PITA**
A variety of garden fresh vegetables. Lettuce, tomatoes, onions, spinach, bell peppers, cucumbers, black olives and carrots, served in a pita bread with balsamic oil and vinegar. **V** ............... **$3.50**

**FAJITAS (STEAK OR CHICKEN)**
Your choice of steak or chicken grilled with bell peppers, onions, herbs and spices, topped with spicy cheese and stuffed in a pita bread. Served with a side of lettuce, tomato, sour cream and guacamole. ............... **$4.99**

**CHICKEN SALAD**
Made from scratch, topped with provolone cheese, and served on a croissant with a side of tomatoes and sprouts. ............... **$5.49**

**HEALTHY CLUB**
Sliced ham, turkey, bacon, swiss and american cheeses piled high with lettuce and tomato on whole wheat slices. With mayo and mustard on the side. ............... **$4.95**

**THE ITALIAN SUB**
Ham, salami, pepperoni, swiss and provolone cheeses, all stuffed in a french roll and topped with lettuce, tomatoes, onions, herbs and spices. ............... **$4.50**

**MEATBALL SANDWICH**
Italian meatballs stuffed in a sub roll with marinara sauce and melted cheese. ...... **$5.49**

**REUBEN**
Lean corned beef, sauerkraut, swiss cheese and dressing served on a pumpernickel bread with a pickle on the side. ............... **$4.49**

**LITE TURKEY**
Served hot or cold. Gourmet turkey breast on a french roll with lettuce, tomato, mayo and mustard on the side. ............... **$3.99**
Add cheese ............... **$.50**

**ROAST BEEF (HOT OR COLD)**
Roast beef slices in a french roll with lettuce, tomato and onions on the side. ............... **$3.95**
Add cheese ............... **$.50**

**HAM & CHEESE**
Served hot or cold. Lean ham with your choice of american, swiss, or provolone cheese served in a french roll with sides of lettuce, tomato, onions, mustard and mayo. ............... **$4.49**

## SALADS

**ROMA SALAD**
A bed of mixed greens with tomatoes, cucumbers and carrots topped with croutons and served with garlic bread sticks. **V** .. **$3.50**

**LA PETTITE SALAD**
A smaller version of the Roma salad for the smaller appetite. **V** ............... **$1.75**

**CHEF SALAD**
Ham, turkey, bacon, mozzarella and cheddar cheeses on a bed of mixed greens with tomatoes, cucumbers and carrots. ...... **$6.99**

**CAESAR SALAD**
Romaine lettuce and croutons with Caesar dressing. **V** ............... **$3.50**

**GRILLED CHICKEN SALAD**
Grilled chicken breast strips seasoned lightly a top our Roma salad. ............... **$5.99**

**FRIED CHICKEN SALAD**
Lightedly breaded chicken breast filets deep fried then chopped a top our Roma Salad. ...... **$5.99**

**CHICKEN CAESAR SALAD**
Grilled chicken breast strips atop our Caesar salad garnished with tomatoes, olives, and mild krino peppers. ............... **$5.99**

**GREEK SALAD**
Mixed greens with feta cheese, black olives, krino peppers, red onions, tomatoes and anchovies with balsamic oil and vinegar. **V** ............... **$5.99**

**HUMMUS**
Garlic and chick pea dip served with olives, peppers and pita bread. **V** ............... **$3.95**

*Dressings*
*Lite Ranch, Honey Mustard, Lite Italian,*
*Bleu Cheese, Caesar, Thousand Island,*
*Balsamic Vinegar and Oil, and*
*Cholesterol and FAT FREE Honey French*

**V** = Vegetarian    **LF** = Low Fat

## BELA ROMA PIZZA

*Your Choice—Deep Dish or Regular Crust*

| LOW FAT CHEESE | Medium - 12" | DEEP DISH PIZZA |
|---|---|---|
| Available Upon Request | Large - 15" | For Large, Add $1.50 |
| | | For Medium, Add $1.00 |

### SIGNATURE GOURMET PIZZAS

**SEAFOOD PIZZA**

Shrimp and crabmeat in a light creamy white sauce with a secret seasoning and topped with parmesan, jack and mozzarella cheeses.

Large .................................. $12.99
Medium ................................. $9.49

**BBQ CHICKEN PIZZA**

Grilled bbq chicken breast with onions, jack and gouda cheeses and bbq sauce.

Large .................................. $12.99
Medium ................................. $9.49

**VEGETABLE PIZZA**

Broccoli, Zucchini squash, onions, mushrooms, artichokes and mozzarella and jack cheeses. **V**

Large .................................. $10.99
Medium ................................. $7.99

**JAMAICAN PEPPERED BEEF PIZZA**

Lean ground beef, onions, spices, mozzarella and hot pepper cheeses.

Large .................................. $10.99
Medium ................................. $7.99

**ROMA DELUXE CHEESE PIZZA**

In a white sauce with hot peppered cheese, mozzarella, provolone and jack cheese. **V**

Large .................................. $9.99
Medium ................................. $7.99

**VENUS PIZZA**

Vine ripened tomatoes, fresh basil, garlic and oregano with mozzarella cheese. **V/LF**

Large .................................. $9.99
Medium ................................. $6.99

**HOT CHICKEN PIZZA**

Select chicken breast marinated in a blend of spicy herbs topped with green onions, spinach, carrots and mozzarella and peppered cheeses.

Large .................................. $11.99
Medium ................................. $8.99

**FETA SPINACH PIZZA**

Spinach, feta cheese, mozzarella cheese, sundried tomatoes, onions and spices. **V**

Large .................................. $11.95
Medium ................................. $8.95

**GARDEN PESTO PIZZA**

Broccoli, carrots, mushrooms, tomatoes, basil pesto, parmesan and mozzarella cheeses. **V**

Large .................................. $11.00
Medium ................................. $9.00

**MEATBALL PIE**

Sliced Italian meatballs with mozzarella cheese.

Large .................................. $9.95
Medium ................................. $7.99

**ROMA DELUXE PIZZA**

Your choice of any 8 toppings

| | Medium | Large |
|---|---|---|
| Regular | $9.50 | $13.00 |
| Gourmet | $12.00 | $15.00 |
| 1/2 & 1/2 | $10.75 | $14.50 |

**SPINACH ARTICHOKE PIZZA**

Spinach and artichoke in a light, creamy white sauce, topped with provolone and mozzarella. **V**

Large .................................. $11.99
Medium ................................. $8.99

### CREATE YOUR OWN PIZZA

| | Cheese Pizza | Regular Items | Gourmet Items |
|---|---|---|---|
| Medium | $5.99 | $.75 | $1.00 |
| Large | $7.99 | $1.00 | $1.50 |

### BELAROMA'S POOR MAN'S PIZZA

When you have scraped up all your change and you only have a couple of bucks, don't worry. Just come on down to BelaRoma's and we'll feed you. Get a medium pizza with one regular topping for just **$3.99**. You can't take it with you, and we won't deliver it. But you're more than welcome to eat it here.

### TOPPINGS

| *Regular Items* | *Gourmet Items* |
|---|---|
| Cheese • Mushrooms • Bell pepper | Artichokes • Pesto • Genoa salami |
| Tomatoes • Black olives • Jalapenos • Bacon | Smoked gouda • Canadian bacon |
| Beef • Ham • Pepperoni • Onions • Anchovies | Sun dried tomatoes • Pineapple • Broccoli |
| Green olives • Italian sausage | Feta cheese • Fresh spinach • Shrimp |
| Banana peppers | |

## CALZONES

**MEAT CALZONE**
Ham, pepperoni, bell peppers and onions
with ricotta and mozarella cheeses. Marinara
sauce served on the side. . . . . . . . . . . .$5.95

**VEGGIEZONE**
Spinach, mushrooms, tomatoes, artichokes
and onions with ricotta and mozzarella
cheeses. Marinara sauce served on
the side. **V** . . . . . . . . . . . . . . . . . . . . .$5.95

**CHICKEN PARMESAN CALZONE**
Tender fried chicken, garlic, herbs &
spices with fresh parmesan and mozzarella
cheeses. . . . . . . . . . . . . . . . . . . . . . . .$6.50

**MEATBALL CALZONE**
Meatball slices with special spices served
with ricotta and mozzarella cheeses. . . .$5.95

**CHEESE CALZONE**
Mozzarella and ricotta cheeses with marinara
sauce. . . . . . . . . . . . . . . . . . . . . . . . . .$4.00

## PASTA

**SPAGHETTI**
Thin Spaghetti with our own marinara sauce
and parmesan cheese served with garlic
bread. . . . . . . . . . . . . . . . . . . . . . . .$4.79
With chicken or meatballs . . . . . . . . . . . . .$5.99

**LASAGNA**
Traditional old world style lasagna with
marinara and parmesan cheese. Served with
garlic bread
Meat . . . . . . . . . . . . . . . . . . . . . . . . . .$5.99

**FIVE CHEESE LASAGNA**
Our five cheese lasagna is low in fat only 6
grams per serving. Served with hot garlic
bread. . . . . . . . . . . . . . . . . . . . . . . . .$5.99

**RAVIOLI**
Tender stuffed pasta covered with marinara
sauce and served with hot garlic bread.
Meat or Cheese **V** . . . . . . . . . . . . . . . .$5.99

**ALFREDO**
A mixed blend of spinach and egg fettucini
made from scratch with fresh sweet basil,
oregano, swiss cheese and herbs and spices
in a creamy alfredo sauce. Served with
garlic bread sticks. . . . . . . . . . . . . . . .$4.95

**SEAFOOD ALFREDO**
Shrimp and crab meat in a creamy alfredo
sauce made from scratch with fresh sweet
basil, oregano, swiss cheese and herbs
and spices. Served with garlic bread
sticks. . . . . . . . . . . . . . . . . . . . . . . . . .$6.49

**CHICKEN ALFREDO**
Grilled chicken breast strips in our creamy
alfredo sauce. Served with garlic bread
sticks. . . . . . . . . . . . . . . . . . . . . . . . . .$6.49

**PRIMAVERA**
Zucchini squash, broccoli, carrots,
mushrooms, peppers and onions in our
creamy alfredo sauce. Served with garlic
bread sticks. **V/LF** . . . . . . . . . . . . . . . .$5.95

## BURGERS

**THE BELAROMA BURGER**
100% lean ground beef cooked to perfection
with all the trimmings. Served with lettuce,
tomato,onion, mustard, ketchup and mayo all
on the side. . . . . . . . . . . . . . . . . . . . .$2.49

**MUSHROOM SWISS BURGER**
The BelaRoma Burger with mushrooms
and swiss cheese, served with all the
trimmings. . . . . . . . . . . . . . . . . . . . . .$3.49
Add bacon . . . . . . . . . . . . . . . . . . . . . .$.50

**BACON SWISS BURGER**
The BelaRoma Burger with bacon and swiss
cheese, served with all the trimmings. .$3.49
Add mushrooms . . . . . . . . . . . . . . . . . . .$.50

**GARDEN BURGER**
The original GardenBurger made with whole
grains, nuts and mushrooms. Served with
lettuce, onion, tomato and pickle with our
chutney-yogurt sauce on the side. **V** . .$4.95

**WESTERN BURGER**
The BelaRoma Burger with southwestern
flair. Served with chili, onions and cheddar
cheese. All the trimmings come on
the side. . . . . . . . . . . . . . . . . . . . . . .$4.95

## APPETIZERS & SIDES

**LOADED POTATO SKINS**
Crispy potato skins loaded with cheddar and mozzarella cheeses, bacon and topped with chives served with sour cream on the side. ........................$4.99

**FRENCH FRIES**
Skin on fries seasoned with our own special spices. **V**.....................$1.50

**LOADED FRIES**
Our fries topped with bacon and chives and served with sour cream and melted cheese on the side. ........................$3.00

**CHEESE FRIES**
Our seasoned fries served covered in melted cheese. **V**.....................$2.00

**BEER BATTERED MUSHROOMS**
Deep fried battered mushrooms served with honey mustard sauce. **V** .............$2.75

**BEER BATTERED ONION RINGS**
You gotta try these! **V** ..............$3.25

**ARMADILLO EGGS**
Not really, they're just jalapeno peppers stuffed with cream cheese or cheddar cheese, then battered and deep fried. Served with honey mustard. **V** .......$3.99

**BAKED POTATO**
Baked Idaho Potato $1.49.**V**
Get it loaded $2.49.

**BUFFALO WINGS**
BelaRoma's nearly famous buffalo wings served with celery, hot or mild sauce, and your choice of bleu cheese, ranch, or honey mustard sauce.
10 for ..............................$3.99
20 for ..............................$7.49

**NACHOS & CHEESE**
Nacho chips served with cheese and sour cream. **V** .....................$2.99

**CHEESE BREAD STICKS**
Garlic bread sticks topped with lots of mixed cheeses. Seved with a side of marinara sauce. **V** ........................$3.99

**BREAD STICKS**
Garlic bread sticks served with marinara sauce. **V** ...................$1.99

**CHEESE STICKS**
Mozzerella cheese sticks served with marinara sauce. **V** .................$3.75

**CHIPS**
By the bag. Choose from a variety of flavors. **V**......................$.99 each

**CHILI OR VEGETARIAN CHILI**
Hearty homemade chili with ground beef, beans, olive oil, herbs and spices. Vegetarian chili is meatless, but with cracked wheat. Each bowl is served with cheese, onions and crackers. **V** .....................$2.95

## FRESH CHICKEN SANDWICHES

**MESQUITE CHICKEN SANDWICH**
A plump chicken breast grilled to perfection then served with lettuce, tomato and mayo on the side. ........................$4.99

**CAJUN CHICKEN SANDWICH**
A plump chicken breast grilled to perfection with rich cajun spices then served with lettuce, tomato and red onion.........$4.99

**BBQ CHICKEN SANDWICH**
A plump chicken breast grilled to perfection with bbq sauce then served with lettuce, tomato and red onion. ................$4.99

**CHICKEN QUESEDILLAS**
Chicken strips grilled with peppers, onions and mushrooms then served with lettuce, tomato and sour cream in a flour tortilla. ...........................$5.99

**CHICKEN TENDERS BASKET**
Chicken tenders fried golden brown and served with our seasoned fries. Served with honey mustard sauce on the side. .....$5.99

**CHICKEN TENDER SANDWICH**
Chicken breast filets lightly breaded then deep fried golden brown. Topped with hot pepper cheese and all the trimimngs on the side.............................$4.99

**BUFFALO TENDER SANDWICH**
Chicken breast filets light breaded then deep friend golden brown, dipped in our special wing sauce. Topped with hot pepper cheese and served with ranch or blue cheese dressing. ........................$5.49

## BEVERAGES

Coke . . . . . . . . . . . . . . . . . . . . . . . . . . . . . . . $.95
Diet Coke . . . . . . . . . . . . . . . . . . . . . . . . . $.95
Mellow Yellow . . . . . . . . . . . . . . . . . . . . . $.95
Dr Pepper . . . . . . . . . . . . . . . . . . . . . . . . . $.95
Iced Tea . . . . . . . . . . . . . . . . . . . . . . . . . . . $.95
Water or ice cup . . . . . . . . . . . . . . . . . . . $.25
Mountain Valley water, 1 litre . . . . . . . . . $1.29
2-litre Coke . . . . . . . . . . . . . . . . . . . . . . . $1.99
Fresh lemonade . . . . . . . . . . . . . . . . . . . . $.95

*Beer*
(No Beer Delivery)

|  | EACH | BUCKET(6) |
|---|---|---|
| Rolling Rock | $2.00 | $8.75 |
| Budweiser | $2.00 | $8.75 |
| Bud Light | $2.00 | $8.75 |
| Miller Lite | $2.00 | $8.75 |
| Michelob Light | $2.00 | $8.75 |
| Heineken | $2.50 | $11.25 |
| Samuel Adams | $2.50 | $11.25 |

## DESSERTS

Chocolate Suicide Cake . . . . . . . . . . . . . . $3.50
Apple pie . . . . . . . . . . . . . . . . . . . . . . . . . $2.00
French silk pie . . . . . . . . . . . . . . . . . . . . . $2.25
Vanilla ice cream . . . . . . . . . . . . . . . . . . . $1.35
Gourmet cookies . . . . . $.50 ea. . . . $5.50 dz.
(chocolate chip, white chocolate
macadamia nut)

Brownie supreme with lots of ice cream
and fudge . . . . . . . . . . . . . . . . . . . . . . . . . $3.50
Carrot cake . . . . . . . . . . . . . . . . . . . . . . . . $2.25
Cheese cake . . . . . . . . . . . . . . . . . . . . . . . $2.25
Brownies . . . . . . . . . . . . . . . . . . . . . . . $1.35 ea.

*Toppings*

*Strawberry, Chocolate* . . . . . . . . . . . . . . . . *$.50*
*Hot Fudge* . . . . . . . . . . . . . . . . . . . . . . . . . *$.60*

## DRUG STORE

**Bayer Aspirin** 24 tablets
**Nuprin** 24 tablets
**Tylenol** 24 tablets
**Rolaids** 12 tablets
**Alka Seltzer** 12 tablet box
**Alka Seltzer Plus** 12-tablet box
**Robitussin DM** 4 oz. bottle
**Gillette Razors** 3 pk.
**Band-Aids** 10, 3/4" strips
**No-Doz** 16 tablets
**Crest Toothpaste** 2.7 oz.
**Tampons** regular, box of 8
**Children's Bayer** 36 tablets
**Midol** max. strength, 8 tablets
**Goody's Powders** 6 pieces
**Pepto Bismol** 4 oz. bottle
**Toilet Tissue** 1 roll

**Nyquil** 6 oz. bottle
**Playing Cards** Aviator
**Shaving Cream** 11 oz. can
**Visine** regular, 1/2 oz.
**Deodorant** Sure, 1.7 oz.
**Tooth Brush** Oral-B
**Condoms** lubricated, 3 pk.
**Knoxville News Sentinel** daily or Sunday

*Tobacco Products*

Marlboro . . . . . . . . . . . . . . . . . . . . . . . .Mkt Price
Marlboro Mediums . . . . . . . . . . . . . . . .Mkt Price
Marlboro Lights . . . . . . . . . . . . . . . . . .Mkt Price
Camel, Camel Lights . . . . . . . . . . . . . .Mkt Price
Disposable lighters . . . . . . . . . . . . . . . . .$1.99
Cigarette papers . . . . . . . . . . . . . . . . . . .$2.49
Cigarette tobacco, pouch . . . . . . . . . . . .$2.99

### FREE EXPRESS DELIVERY

Yes, we do deliver, and we will be happy to bring you any of the non-food items that we carry in
our drug store. However, without a food order, a $10 minimum order is required for delivery.

ITS THE LAW: You MUST be 21 to purchase alcohol products! You MUST be 18 to purchase tobacco products!

## Collaborative Activity 2.7

This next set of three activities is your opportunity to work with classmates to conduct a genre analysis of a genre of your own choosing. First, collect and review samples of the genre. Then list everything your group can think of that you might know about the scene in which this genre is used—where it is used and the beliefs, values, assumptions, and objectives of the people who use it. (For guidelines about how to study and describe a scene, refer back to Box 1.2, pp. 44–45.) Then list everything your group knows about the situation of the genre, using the questions on situation in Box 2.1, Step 2. What do you know about the setting, subject, participants, and purposes of the genre?

## Writing Activity 2.7

For this next step, work individually before sharing your results with your group so that you learn how many patterns in the genre you can in fact see on your own. Reread samples of the genre, looking for patterns in the genre's features. For this activity, work your way methodically through the list of features in Box 2.1 Step 3, from content through diction. List any patterns you see in these samples. Be prepared to share your results with others in your group.

## Collaborative Activity 2.8

Share your list of genre patterns with the group, adding to your list the patterns others saw that you did not. After compiling a group list, your final task is to analyze what the patterns you noticed might tell you about the situation and scene in which the genre is used. Again for this activity, your group should work methodically, writing down answers for each of the questions we suggest for analysis in Box 2.1, Step 4: From what the participants have to know through what attitude is implied. Remember, you are working to discover what might be significant about these patterns, what they might reveal to you about what the genre, situation, and scene is about and what people within it are trying to do. There is not only one good answer to these questions. Different analysts will discover different things, so explore all the different interpretations your group members suggest. Be prepared to share your discoveries with your teacher and other groups.

## Writing Activity 2.8

Choose a genre that you would like to know something about, perhaps one that is related to your academic major or your future profession or one you encounter in your job, in volunteer work, or in other parts of your life outside of school. Then perform a genre analysis on it, following the guidelines and questions in the preceding activities and Box 2.1 (pp. 93–94). In the past, our students have chosen such genres as the lab report, the resumé, the psychology research paper, the graduate school writing sample, the sweepstakes letter, the wedding invitation, the personal ad, the petition, and the school yearbook. In fact, this chapter's analysis of the Patient Medical History Form is based on the analysis work of one of our students who was preparing to be a doctor. If you want to analyze a professional genre but are uncertain about what genres are used in your academic major or future profession, we encourage you to ask a professor or a graduate teaching assistant, an upper-division student in the major, or a professional in that field.

Whatever genre you choose, make sure to keep track of your findings—either in your class journal or notebook. You might need to refer to these notes later, when you translate your analysis into writing for Writing Project 2.1. For now, though, concentrate on trying to learn as much as you can about your genre. When your research is complete, be prepared to report and discuss your findings with your teacher and classmates.

---

When you learn to perform a genre analysis, you are not just learning how to read a piece of writing. You are also learning how to read people's activities and behaviors within a scene. By doing the kind of genre analysis you practiced in the preceding activities, you are, in a way, uncovering the script of a scene; you are using the language of a scene to examine how people interact, think, and communicate within it. You are, in short, reading a scene through its patterns of writing.

# Turning Reading into Writing

Now that you have practiced doing genre analysis, how can you use what you know about genre to make more effective writing choices? Identifying a genre's patterns and analyzing what they mean does not give writers a ready-made syllabus or complaint letter. Just as readers bring their own knowledge and beliefs to their reading and can choose to resist the roles defined for them by genres, writers also do more than just copy these patterns. Unlike a script for a play, where actors have all their lines written and need to choose only how to perform those lines, a genre's pattern or "script" does not tell us, as writers, exactly what actions to take, what roles to perform, or what sentences and words to use. What it does give us is a *general* sense of the scene and situation and some general rhetorical patterns, and we can use this knowledge of the scene and people's rhetorical behaviors within it to make more effective and informed writing choices.

## Box 2.1    *Guidelines for Analyzing Genres*

### 1. Collect Samples of the Genre

If you are studying a genre that is fairly public, such as wedding announcements, you can look at samples from various newspapers. You can also locate samples of a genre in textbooks and manuals about the genre, as we did with the complaint letters. If you are studying a less public genre, such as the Patient Medical History Form, you might have to visit several doctors' offices to collect samples. If you are unsure where to find samples, use our strategies for observing scenes in Chapter 1 (p. 25) to ask a user of that genre for assistance. Try to gather samples from more than one place (for example, wedding announcements from different newspapers or medical history forms from different doctors' offices) so that you get a more accurate picture of the complexity of the genre. The more samples of the genre you collect, the more easily you will be able to notice patterns within the genre.

### 2. Identify the Scene and Describe the Situation in Which the Genre Is Used

Following the guidelines in Box 1.2, Step 1 (p. 40), try to identify the larger scene in which the genre is used. Seek answers to questions about the genre's situation. Consider:

- **Setting:** Where does the genre appear? How and when is it transmitted and used? With what other genres does this genre interact?
- **Subject:** What topics, issues, ideas, questions, etc. does the genre address? When people use this genre, what is it that they are interacting about?
- **Participants:** Who uses the genre?
  *Writers:* Who writes the texts in this genre? Are multiple writers possible? What roles do they perform? What characteristics must writers of this genre possess? Under what circumstances do writers write the genre (e.g., in teams, on a computer, in a rush)?
  *Readers:* Who reads the texts in this genre? Is there more than one type of reader for this genre? What roles do they perform? What characteristics must readers of this genre possess? Under what circumstances do readers read the genre (e.g., at their leisure, on the run, in waiting rooms)?
- **Purposes:** Why do writers write this genre and why do readers read it? What purposes does the genre fulfill for the people who use it?

*(continued on next page)*

### 3. Identify and Describe Patterns in the Genre's Features

What recurrent features do the samples share? For example:

- What **content** is typically included? What excluded? How is the content treated? What sorts of examples are used? What counts as evidence (personal testimony, facts, etc.)?
- What **rhetorical appeals** are used? What appeals to logos, pathos, and ethos appear?
- How are texts in the genres **structured**? What are their parts, and how are they organized?
- In what **format** are texts of this genre presented? What layout or appearance is common? How long is a typical text in this genre?
- What types of **sentences** do texts in the genre typically use? How long are they? Are they simple or complex, passive or active? Are the sentences varied? Do they share a certain style?
- What **diction** (types of words) is most common? Is a type of jargon used? Is slang used? How would you describe the writer's voice?

### 4. Analyze What These Patterns Reveal about the Situation and Scene

What do these rhetorical patterns reveal about the genre, its situation, and the scene in which it is used? Why are these patterns significant? What can you learn about the actions being performed through the genre by observing its language patterns? What arguments can you make about these patterns? As you consider these questions, focus on the following:

- What do participants have to know or believe to understand or appreciate the genre?
- Who is invited into the genre, and who is excluded?
- What roles for writers and readers does it encourage or discourage?
- What values, beliefs, goals, and assumptions are revealed through the genre's patterns?
- How is the subject of the genre treated? What content is considered most important? What content (topics or details) is ignored?
- What actions does the genre help make possible? What actions does the genre make difficult?
- What attitude toward readers is implied in the genre? What attitude toward the world is implied in it?

Rather than staring at a blank page or screen and guessing about how to begin writing or what to write about, you can turn to your knowledge of genres. Writing becomes choosing, not guessing. By analyzing any given genre, for example, you can make choices regarding major rhetorical elements:

### Your purpose as writer

Knowing what genres are available in a given scene and how and why they are used will help you decide which one can best accomplish your purpose in writing. On the other hand, if you are *assigned* a genre to write and are not sure about your purpose for writing it, studying the genre can show you the purposes other writers have pursued with that genre. In either case, purpose and genre are interrelated: Your purpose for writing affects your choice of genre and your choice of genre affects your purpose.

### Your role as a writer

Your role as a writer has to do with the kind of persona you choose to present in order to be persuasive as a speaker or writer. For example, should you be aggressive, soft-spoken, excited, subdued, or confident? The persona you choose will have a great deal to do with how effectively you write within a specific scene, as we saw in the example of the complaint letter. The patterns of behavior and communication within a genre will help you choose the role within that scene that will be the most appropriate in fulfilling your purpose.

### Your readers

Certain genres are geared toward certain readers (the syllabus is geared toward students, the resumé toward an employer). By analyzing the genre, you learn something about your readers even though they may not be physically present. What do readers *expect* from the genre? For instance, do they expect to be treated with respect? Do they expect you to assume authority? Do they expect to laugh or cry or both? Do they expect you to be detailed, technical, and complicated, or do they expect simple and direct communication? Knowing something about your readers as revealed through the genre will help you "see" your audience, much like we began to "see" the audience during our analysis of the complaint letter. Such knowledge will help you decide what genre most suits your purpose.

### Your subject matter

Any given subject can be treated in different ways depending on the genre used. A writer who analyzes the genres first is in a better position to decide which genre to write and then how to treat the subject matter. Using your knowledge of these genres, contemplate your subject matter: How should you introduce it? Should you treat it objectively or personally? Do you need to explain it in detail or is such explanation unnecessary? Should you present it logically or emotionally or sarcastically, etc.? Do you need to provide examples? Should you be descriptive, argumentative, or both? Should you present both sides of the subject? Do you need to quote experts on the subject or can you depend on your own authority? And so on. Knowledge of the genre will help you make some of these decisions about what and how to write.

### *Your format and organization*

On a very obvious level, knowledge of a genre's patterns will help you decide how to format your writing. A resumé, for example, is formatted differently from a complaint letter. Knowing this, you begin to conceptualize the appearance of your text so that what may have begun as a blank page or screen suddenly has a shape. You can decide if you should present your content in the form of tables and charts, graphics, lists, prose, or poetry. The structural features of a genre will help you decide not only how to format the physical appearance of your writing; they will also help you decide how to present and organize your ideas. For example, by learning the patterns of a genre, you can decide what to mention first, second, third, and so on. You can learn whether the main ideas are stated at the beginning or at the end, whether to move from generalities to particularities or from particularities to generalities. You can also decide what kinds of transitions, if any, to use between different sections of the text. In short, not only will your genre knowledge help you approach your subject matter, but it will also help you present your subject matter in certain ways.

### *Your sentences and word choices*

Having read samples of your genre should have given you a sense of the typical style used in that situation, a feel for what texts in that genre sound like. You can imitate that style, trying to make your text sound like the ones you studied. As you revise your draft and take a more explicit and conscious approach, knowing something about the genre's sentence and diction patterns will help you decide, for instance, whether to use active or passive sentences. It will also help you decide how long your sentences should be and what kind of complexity and variation is expected. In the resumé, for example, sentences often begin with a verb rather than a subject and need to be consistent ("Managed the sales department," "Served as liaison between employer and employees"). In other genres, of course, different sentence styles are preferred. The same applies to word choices. In scientific research articles, for example, the people being studied are often referred to as "subjects" while the pronoun "you" appears frequently in business letters. By looking at the patterns in word choice within a genre, you will be able to make more effective decisions about what words to use and why.

What we have just presented is meant only as a set of guidelines for using your knowledge of a genre to make more effective writing choices within that genre. There is no exact formula. The more you practice genre analysis, the more skillful you will become at reading genre scenes and situations. The better you are able to read and understand the patterns of a genre, the better you will become at knowing what purpose these patterns serve and how to make use of them in your writing.

## Writing Activity 2.9

Review the genre you analyzed collaboratively in the last sets of activities or the genre of your choice in Writing Activity 2.8 (p. 91), including the samples you collected, your notes, and your conclusions. Based on your analysis, describe what a writer needs to understand about the scene and situation in order to write that genre. Use our suggested guidelines in Box 2.1 (pp. 93–94) and be as specific as you can. As a writer of this genre, what choices would you make regarding your role as writer, your readers, your subject matter, your format and structure, and your sentences and word choices? Record your responses and be prepared to share them with your teacher and classmates. Think of this activity as an exercise in prewriting, planning, and invention.

## Writing Projects

### Writing Project 2.1

To demonstrate to your teacher and classmates your understanding of genre analysis and to share your perspective on a particular genre, write your own genre analysis paper, either of the genre which you studied in Collaborative Activities 2.7 and 2.8 (p. 91) or of the genre you chose to study in Writing Activity 2.8 (p. 91). Much of this chapter has been teaching you how to perform a genre analysis. Now you have a chance to write a paper based on that analysis (we recommend you review the sample genre analysis paper and our discussion of it in this chapter). For this assignment, write a paper (4 to 5 pages) for your instructor and classmates that makes a claim about what the genre you have chosen tells us about the people who use it and the scene in which it is used. Be sure that your paper makes a claim and has a controlling idea about what you think the genre reveals about some aspect of the situation or scene: How people behave, their goals and beliefs, or the actions they perform. (You might wish to review the description of controlling idea and how the sample genre analysis paper used its controlling idea, pp. 73–74.) Your controlling idea will also need to be supported by specific examples and explanations taken from your analysis of the genre.

## Writing Project 2.2

Write a complaint letter of your own. First, select a subject (an actual problem you have had with a product or service). Then decide on an audience (someone who can address your problem, perhaps researching the name of the head of Customer Service for a specific company or the boss of someone whose service was inadequate—checking a company's Web site is a good starting place for researching such information). Drawing on the analysis of the complaint letter and the samples in this chapter, write your own complaint letter. Finally, write a cover memo (a brief, straightforward description) addressed to your teacher that explains what choices you had to make about such things as your letter's content, appeals, structure, format, sentences, and words and how your choices reflected your particular situation and scene.

## Writing Project 2.3

As we mentioned earlier in the chapter, there are various ways to register complaints, the genre of the business complaint letter being one of them. Imagine a situation in which you wanted to register a complaint within the scene of your college or university, say about the availability of parking on campus or the cost of tuition or the lack of funding for student activities, etc. First identify an actual complaint and then decide to whom and where to address the complaint. Then choose a genre that would best accomplish your purpose for your situation and compose that genre. When you are finished, submit the genre along with a cover memo to your teacher explaining why you chose the genre you did and how it is an effective response given the scene and your purpose, audience, and subject.

Taken from *Having Your Say: Reading and Writing Public Arguments*
by Davida H. Charney and Christine M. Neuwirth with David S. Kaufer
and Cheryl Geisler

# CHAPTER 3

# Mapping a Conversation

In this chapter, you will develop an understanding of the public debate about your issue, find a focal point for your own interests, and identify controversial points about the problem or potential solutions. Points of controversy are chances for you to contribute your own arguments. The exploratory strategy presented here involves synthesizing the positions of a variety of authors, a task in which you will characterize their views fairly and draw plausible inferences about how they might respond to challenges or questions.

Synthesis differs from analysis. Analyzing means taking apart the elements of an argument in order to look at its overall structure and find its strengths and weaknesses. You practiced analysis while working with the chapters in Part I; you may also have written an argument analysis using the strategies. In contrast, synthesizing means creating something new by looking at a group of separate items and connecting them into a coherent pattern or map.

## Relating Your Position to Others'

If you think of a public debate as an expedition of individuals and groups, then synthesizing would be like taking a bird's eye view of the entire scene. Imagine that you are sitting on a hillside watching a crowd of people in a forest below searching for the way out. From the distance of your perspective, you can see where everyone is even though they may not be able to see each other. You can tell which searchers are closest together and which are furthest apart, which are headed in the same direction and which are covering old ground, who has wandered off and who is sitting waiting to be rescued. You can even pick out a promising spot that everyone has overlooked so far and identify who is "getting warmer."

You may never have considered the relationships among authors this way. Faced with a complicated array of positions on a controversial issue, you might be tempted simply to divide authors into groups, good guys against bad guys, or extremists against moderates. You might avoid authors whose views seem strange or ignore those points in an author's argument that would disrupt your neat picture. Public policy is not that simple. People who are opponents on one issue may be allies on another. Allies frequently disagree among themselves about what to do first and how to proceed.

In order to have your say taken seriously, you must understand how your position relates to those of many others involved in the issue. Only then will you seem informed and credible enough to deserve attention. Only then can you figure out which points your readers will find controversial, the ones that need the most development and support. Only then can you invent ways to make opponents more receptive to your ideas.

## Synthesis Defined

A synthesis is a form of argument, not a collection of dry information. Synthesizing an issue requires you to be imaginative, to think beyond the positions you have already taken on an issue. Even though you will write from a distanced perspective rather than arguing your own view from the ground, any map that you draw of an issue will be your description, made from where you are sitting, not some kind of cosmic photograph that accurately depicts every detail. No matter what your perspective is, you have reached it through a lifetime of experiences and lessons that were not shared by everyone else. From your viewpoint, you might not be able to see everyone; you might misinterpret where a group is headed; you may not know how things look from the ground. By synthesizing, you will focus on details you overlooked and seek explanations for points that seemed misguided or irrelevant.

Even though it will differ from how everyone else sees the debate, your synthesis can have value for yourself and for others. It will help you develop and articulate your position by highlighting the specific points on which you must decide whether you agree or disagree. A fully developed synthesis of an issue can also help everyone involved see more of the big picture; they may be convinced to accept your view and take your recommendations more seriously. Strategies for writing a full-length synthesis paper are presented.

Writing a synthesis is also an important step if you plan to intervene directly in the debate by persuading the stakeholders to adopt your approach to the problem or the solution. The stakeholders will have already heard many arguments. To write convincingly you have to avoid rehashing positions that have already been rejected and address the disputes that are hot right now.

You are ready to try the strategies in this chapter if you have already used one or more of the strategies. You should have explored your own experiences and beliefs concerning the issue, searched a variety of sources to find out more about the issue, and searched out published arguments about the issue from a variety of authors and stakeholders.

Synthesizing requires that you develop a good understanding of each author's argument. Before you begin, you should read the texts carefully, following the strategies for segmenting an author's entire paper into spans (Issue, Problem, Solution), segmenting each span into stases (Existence, Definition, Value, Cause, Action), and each stasis into a series of points with claims and supporting appeals (Ethos, Pathos, Logos). You should then map out the main points of the authors' lines of argument. Following these strategies, you should end up with a rough sketch for each article like the ones provided for Castleman and Chivers.

## Selecting a Relevant Set of Authors

The first step is to select authors to include in your synthesis. This chapter illustrates a synthesis of the six readings printed on each topic in this book.

You are likely to have a larger set of articles to choose from, including articles that you or your class have chosen. Ideally, the authors you choose will represent a wide range of positions, but almost any set of argumentative articles within your topic area will do. Select 6 to 8 articles using these strategies:

- Start with as many "on-topic" authors as you can find who directly address the specific issue that concerns you, articles from people they cite, and articles in which they are cited.
- Include additional articles that address any general points raised by the on-topic authors, such as prevention, human rights, or the role of the media.
- If you have not yet selected eight authors, choose from the remaining articles the ones with which you most strongly agree or disagree.

Do not hesitate to choose authors whose positions seem unrelated. Surprisingly enough, you can develop important new insights by synthesizing authors who are not explicitly addressing the same problem.

Next, compare the articles looking for points that most of the authors address. The most thorough way to find points of comparison would be to list out every point in every article and then draw connections, but this process is too burden-some. A better approach is to focus your attention on the points that matter most to you. The next sections offer strategies for using graphics to sketch out different connections and review them at a glance.

## What Are Synthesis Trees?

A synthesis tree is a branching diagram that illustrates groupings of authors. Each main branch represents a point on which a set of authors agrees. A group of allied authors all appear under the same main branch. Opposing groups are represented with their own main branches.

As a branch extends, it divides into smaller and smaller branches representing subgroups within a set of allies. The subgroups keep dividing until each author is represented on his or her own twig. Each branch separates authors who agree the most from those with other positions.

The synthesis trees discussed throughout this chapter are shown in Figures 3.1A–3.1F.

### Alternative Synthesis Trees

*Environment*

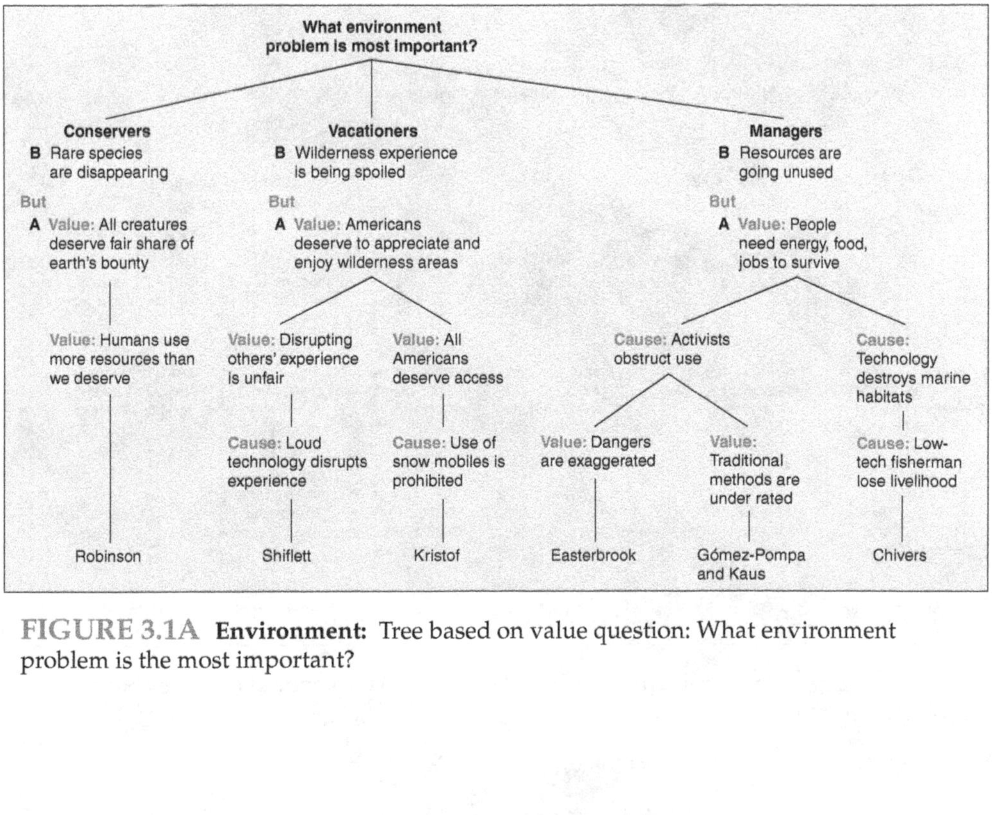

**FIGURE 3.1A  Environment:** Tree based on value question: What environment problem is the most important?

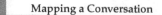

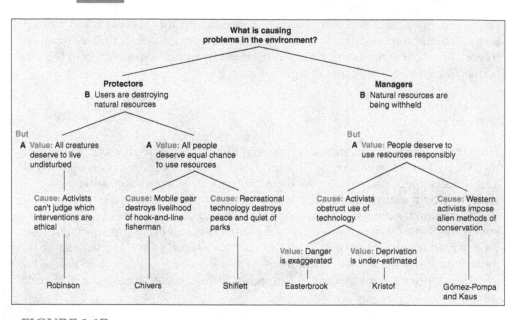

FIGURE 3.1B  **Environment:**  Tree based on cause question: What is causing problems in the environment?

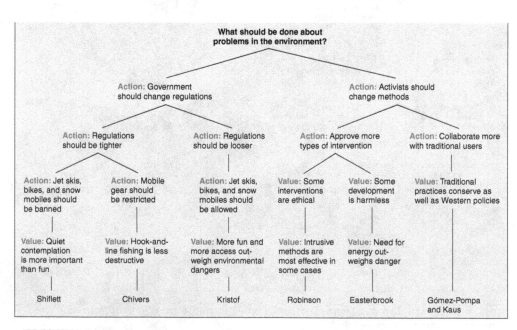

FIGURE 3.1C  **Environment:**  Tree based on action: What should be done about problems in the environment?

*Crime*

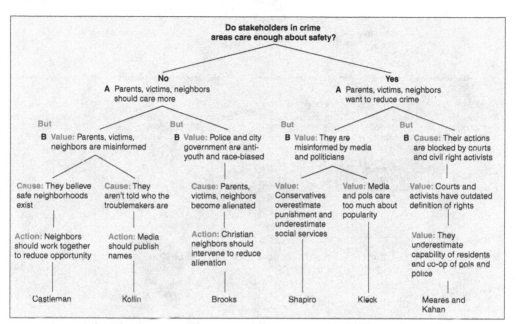

FIGURE 3.1D **Crime:** Tree based on value question: Do stakeholders in high crime areas care enough about safety?

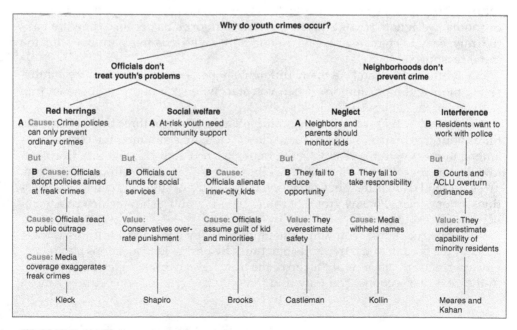

FIGURE 3.1E **Crime:** Tree based on cause question: Why do youth crimes occur?

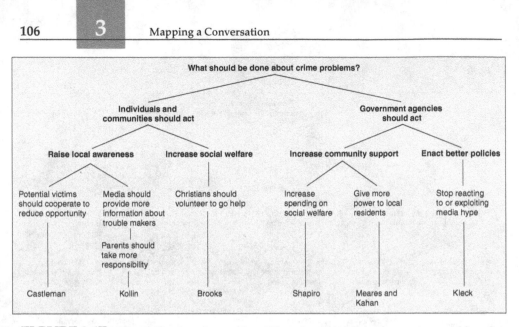

FIGURE 3.1F  **Crime:**  Tree based on action: What should be done about crime problems?

A synthesis sketch looks like an inverted tree. Sketches like these are used by designers to summarize a lot of information in a small space. A similar type of sketch is the floorplan of a dreamhouse. Floorplans record different ways for dividing up the space available, for creating and connecting different types of rooms. Designers try out many alternative floorplans because they are easy to draw, easy to change, and easy to compare. Synthesis trees are used for the same reasons.

A synthesis tree can take many different shapes, especially as you try synthesizing more and more authors. When you start with six authors, you can end up with any of the shapes shown in Figure 3.2.

The most useful synthesis trees branch off at least two or three times. The more times your tree branches off, the more closely you are examining the connections among authors within a group. Of the trees sketched above, Tree a is far too shallow; it shows a collection of six authors lined up with no connections spelled out. Trees b, c, and d are better; they show separate groups of allies with no further relations among them. For any group of three, Trees e, f, and g show which two members are closest together.

To construct a tree, you will sometimes work by comparing authors to each other at the bottom of the tree and sometimes by posing key questions about general approaches to an issue at the top of the tree. These two strategies are explained in the next two sections. You may find that you prefer to use one strategy most.

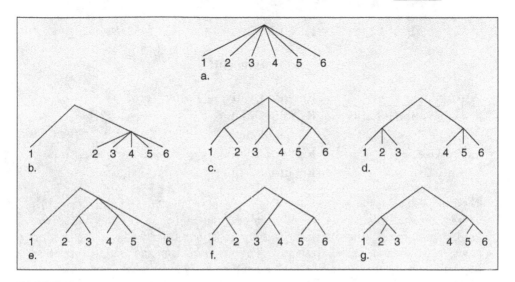

FIGURE 3.2   Possible shapes of a tree with six authors.

However, the best way to use them is by working back and forth between the top and bottom levels. Whatever strategies you use, you must be careful to treat all authors fairly.

# Identifying Common Approaches

The easiest way to begin a synthesis is to select two or three articles that seem to be closely related and compare them. After you sketch out the common points and differences of a few authors, you will find it easier to consider additional articles and decide how they relate to the sketch.

## Grouping Authors

The first step is create some preliminary groupings of your authors. Try out a few sample groupings by asking yourself any of these questions: Which author or authors are your allies and which your opponents? Which authors agree with each other the most? Which authors address the most similar issues? Each question will lead you to create different clusters. Usually it will be easy to assign two or three authors to a cluster. Some authors will not fit easily anywhere; don't force them into a group. Some sample clusters are shown in "Preliminary Clusters of Authors."

## PRELIMINARY CLUSTERS OF AUTHORS

### *Environment*

| | |
|---|---|
| **Animals** | Robinson, Chivers, Easterbrook |
| **U.S. National Parks** | Kristof, Shiflett |
| **Crops** | Gómez-Pompa |
| **Pro-Use** | Kristof, Easterbrook, Gómez-Pompa and Kaus |
| **Anti-Use** | Robinson, Shiflett |

These alternative clusterings lead in different directions. The Pro- and Anti-Use groups address the same basic issue, use of resources, but from opposite sides. Within the Pro-Use group, the authors are all critical of restrictions called for by environmental activists. On the other hand, the Anti-Use authors Robinson and Shiflett agree that human activities can be harmful. This branching is likely to reveal differences among the allies on each side over which restrictions should be changed.

The clusterings around Animals, Parks, and Global Use topics do not build on basic agreements. Robinson and Easterbrook are not natural allies; Robinson is an environmental activist while Easterbrook criticizes "enviros." Shiflett and Kristof are direct opponents on using vehicles in park. None of these authors comment directly on the overall importance of the problems they address. This clustering, however, may still produce insights that lead to a valuable synthesis.

### *Crime*

| | |
|---|---|
| **Media** | Kollin, Kleck, Shapiro |
| **Civil Liberty** | Brooks, Meares and Kahan, Castleman |
| **Individualists** | Castleman, Kollin |
| **Governmentalists** | Kleck, Meares and Kahan, Shapiro |

These alternative clusterings lead in different directions. The Individualist and Governmentalist clusters address the same basic issue, responsibility for preventing crime, from opposite sides. The Individualists, Castleman and Kollin, agree that citizens should take action to prevent crime. On the other hand, the three Governmentalists believe that it is up to legislators to adopt better laws. This branching is likely to reveal differences among the allies on each side over which restrictions should be changed.

The remaining two clusters, Media and Civil Liberty, do not unite authors with basic agreements. While Brooks and Meares and Kahan focus on civil rights, they are not natural allies; Brooks is against curfews and gang laws while Meares and Kahan favor them. The authors in the Media cluster also disagree; Kollin favors more media coverage while Kleck and Shapiro consider media attention harmful. This clustering, however, may still produce insights that lead to a valuable synthesis.

No two authors will ever make exactly the same claims. But if the authors you have chosen are allies, then there are many points on which they would probably agree. They may share the same goals and disagree only on priorities and methods.

## Branching Out Groups and Subgroups

The branches in a tree signal disagreement over a claim. The group on one side agrees with the claim and the other group disagrees with it. Your branchings should represent the most central or important points on which your authors disagree. To branch out your tree, you will work creatively to compare authors and to articulate claims.

Of all your authors, ask yourself which two are in closest agreement. Write out some important claims on which this pair of authors agrees. Then consider the other authors one by one. An author who also agrees with these claims fits into a group with that pair; an author who disagrees does not. Considering the outsiders, create a group of authors who would agree to an opposing claim. As you continue, look at any grouping of three or more authors; try to generate claims to which two would agree and the third would not.

Using the strategies for inventing and naming groups, write a descriptive term at each point where the tree branches.

Deciding which authors belong closer together along the entire tree is not easy. It takes persistence and creativity. However, that effort provides the key benefit of exploring with a synthesis. Expect the original groupings to change as you discover better or more important relationships.

"Reasoning about an Author's Assignment" illustrates different decisions on where to assign an author.

### REASONING ABOUT AN AUTHOR'S ASSIGNMENT

#### Environment

In the clusters in "Preliminary Synthesis Trees," Chivers has not been assigned to either the pro- or anti-use clusters. He is close to the pro-users because he is allied with fishermen's organizations, but in wanting to preserve habitat and keep out destructive technologies, he is close to the anti-users. To be fair to Chivers, both aspects must be reflected in the synthesis.

Figure 3.1 shows two ways to assign Chivers. In Tree A, Chivers is grouped with the Managers because he is not for banning fishing or even banning mobile gear, just restricting where mobile gear is allowed. He is separated from the other Managers because he approves of environmental activism. In Tree B, Chivers is grouped with the Protectors who want to slow or eliminate the destruction of natural resources. Within this grouping, he is paired with Shiflett; both consider human use of the environment appropriate, within limits.

## Crime

In the clusters in "Preliminary Synthesis Trees," Brooks has not been assigned to either the Individualist or Governmentalist clusters. He is close to the Individualists because he is writing to churchgoers to urge them to volunteer to help kids; however, in opposing the passage of new curfew and gang ordinances, he is close to the Governmentalists. To be fair to Brooks, both aspects must be reflected in the synthesis.

Figure 3.1 shows two ways to assign Brooks. In Tree D, he is grouped with those who consider civil liberties to be important. Within this grouping, however, he is on his own in arguing that civil liberties violations increase crime. In Tree F, Brooks is grouped with the Individualists because he calls for personal intervention, not changes in the laws. Within the Individualists, he is on his own because he urges individuals (Christians) from outside the neighborhood to take action.

As you create groupings, you are likely to notice many points where authors in different groups share common ground. Keep track of these claims. Common ground is often the starting point for an author's proposal of a new way to see the problem or discover solutions.

## Drawing Fair Inferences

A crucial skill involved in synthesizing is drawing inferences about positions that your authors might take or assumptions that they might have made. Inferencing is necessary because the authors in your set are unlikely to address each other's points directly, unless you have chosen articles on a very narrow issue. To find points of agreement and disagreement, then, you have to infer an author's position. As you do so, an author comes to represent one case out of a category of very close allies who take the same approach.

For your synthesis to be of use in solving real-world problems, you must act as fairly as you can toward all the authors. If you mischaracterize an author, you open yourself to charges of demagoguery, the willingness to use any means, including inaccurate and inflammatory claims, to win public support. Demagogues are good at stirring up allies and repelling opponents. However, their inaccurate descriptions of the problem lead to faulty solutions that fail to address its underlying causes.

The basic strategies needed for fair representations are the same as those introduced for disagreeing with an opponent: identify the authors, summarize their positions in a way they would agree is fair, make concessions, and state rebuttals. In a synthesis, your inferences describe the possible rebuttals that your authors would make to each other's arguments. Be prepared to support the plausibility of your inferences with evidence from the authors' own words.

"Representing Authors Fairly" provides examples of fair and unfair inferences drawn from the synthesis trees presented in this chapter.

## REPRESENTING AUTHORS FAIRLY

### Environment

In Figure 3.1A, Shiflett and Kristof are grouped together as agreeing on the importance of the wilderness experience.

#### Unfair Inference

Shiflett and Kristof think their own enjoyment as vacationers is more important than protecting endangered species. This makes them similar to the Managers who want resources extracted, no matter what the harm would be caused to the environment.

#### Fairer Inference

Shiflett and Kristof focus on the place of tourists in National Parks. They agree that a vacationer's enjoyment of the wilderness is important, even though they differ on what activities should be allowed. Neither of them says how they feel about the dangers to animal or plant life. However, because they both love being in nature, they probably disagree with the Conservers about the urgency of the dangers.

### Crime

In Figure 3.1C, Kleck is usually allied with Shapiro in criticizing current government approaches to crime.

#### Unfair Inference

Even though terrorists worldwide are usually turning out to be students, Kleck opposes the regulations that give federal investigators secret access to the library records, bookstore purchases, health records, and electronic communication of U.S. college students. He thinks the 9/11 bombing was a "freakish event," not an everyday, common occurrence; therefore, it is an inappropriate model for preventing terrorism. He would insist that universities be allowed to keep student records confidential.

### Fairer Inference

Kleck would probably agree that government action is needed for detecting potential terrorists in U.S. colleges. Nowadays, the most common perpetrators of terrorism worldwide are students; therefore, students deserve extra attention. But Kleck would probably oppose the regulations that give federal investigators secret access to the library records, bookstore purchases, health records, and electronic communication of U.S. college students. He would consider the 9/11 bombings to be a "freakish event" and an inappropriate model for preventing terrorism. He would support the colleges that want to keep student records confidential.

## Asking Argument-Based Questions

Another way to develop a synthesis tree is to treat each branching point as a question that authors must address in a public policy argument.

Policy arguments often have three main sections, an issue span, a problem span, and a solution span. Each span is developed with points about existence, definition, value, cause, and action claims. These points are the author's responses to questions such as these:

**Issue span**

| | |
|---|---|
| Existence | Has something happened? What is the current situation? Are there cases of a problem? |
| Value | Why is the issue worth attention? So what? Why should we care? |
| Action | What do we need to know about it? What new angle or approach do we need to take? |

**Problem span**

| | |
|---|---|
| Existence | Is there a problem? |
| Definition | What kind of event is it? Have cases of the problem been misclassified? |
| Cause | What causes it? How did it get this way? |
| Value | How serious is it? |
| Action | Should we try to solve it? |

**Solution span**

| | |
|---|---|
| **Existence** | Are any solutions possible? Have any solutions been tried or proposed already? |
| **Definition** | What kinds of solutions are they? |
| **Cause** | Will the solutions make the problem go away? Will they at least make the problem less frequent or less serious? |
| **Value** | What are the advantages and disadvantages of each solution? Which solution will cost the least and produce the most benefits? |
| **Action** | Who should act on the solution and how? |

Just as the points in a policy argument represent the views of one author on these questions, a synthesis tree captures the responses of groups of authors. The groups represent different approaches to a major question about the problem or the solution. The authors in each group share the same basic outlook on a major question but differ on specific points.

Focusing on these questions will help you decide on the most important ways in which authors disagree.

## Problem Trees and Solution Trees

A synthesis tree can contain points about both the problem and solution or it can focus on just one of these spans.

- **Environment.** Trees A and B in Figure 3.1 focus on the problem span: "What is environment problem is most important?" and "What is causing problems in the environment?" A synthesis tree can also focus on the solution span, like the tree entitled "What should be done about problems in the environment?" in Figure 3.1.

- **Crime.** Trees D and E in Figure 3.1 focus on the problem span, "Do stakeholders in crime areas care enough about safety?" and "Why do youth crimes occur?" A synthesis can also focus on the solution span, like the tree entitled "What should be done about crime problems?" in Figure 3.1F.

Your choice of a focus depends on the authors you are working with, the type of paper you are planning to write, and the aspects of the issue that interest you the most.

## Trees Based on Stases

The question that starts off a tree will itself represent a claim at one of the five stases: existence, definition, value, cause, or action. The claims at the major branches will also be at one of the stases.

As you can see in Figure 3.1, stasis labels can be attached to the question at the very top of the tree. The questions "What is the most important problem?" and "Do people care enough?" ask about values. The questions "What is causing the problems?" or "Why do problems occur?" ask about agents, factors, and changes. As you trace through the positions within a group, you will see that allies will often disagree on questions of value, cause, and action.

As you work on describing a disagreement between authors, it is helpful to ask:

Do they agree that there is a problem?

Do they count the same cases as problematic?

Do they have different priorities?

Do they appeal to different ethical principles?

Do they blame different factors?

Do they disagree on the effects of a change?

Do they recommend different actions?

Write down an inference describing how each author would answer these questions.

## Testing the Tree

Before finalizing your tree, it is important to test it to see whether you have characterized the authors' positions accurately and fairly, whether the tree captures different ways that groups would treat a problem case, and whether the tree is balanced and coherent.

### Role-Playing

In creating a synthesis tree, it is often helpful to imagine that the authors are all in a room talking. "Role-playing" presents part of a conversation among students who were asked to take on the role of an author, to ask questions that he or she would ask other authors and to answer their questions.

---

### ROLE-PLAYING

#### *Environment*

**John Robinson**        What are our rights and obligations when having a wilderness experience? I think our obligation is to protect wildlife by any means possible.

| | |
|---|---|
| **Dave Shiflett** | We all have the right to enjoy the peace and serenity of nature. We are all also therefore obliged to respect the peace and serenity of others. |
| **C. J. Chivers** | I would recommend enjoying the wilderness and doing whatever you please as long as you do not destroy the wilderness permanently. |
| **Nicholas Kristof** | Robinson, by "any means possible," do you mean reducing our opportunity to enjoy the wilderness? Do you mean banning all transport? |
| **Robinson** | Kristof, if you mean limiting access, yes, if that is what it takes to protect a rare animal's habitat. Snowmobiles and mountain bikes allow access to otherwise unattainable areas where animals find sanctuary and scare them off into perhaps less beneficial areas. |
| **Shiflett** | Absolutely. We need to keep motorized vehicles out of our wilderness areas. |
| **Gregg Easterbrook** | Robinson, aren't you exaggerating the danger from these vehicles? Most animals would be fine after moving their habitats and other ones would come in to fill up in the gaps. |
| **Robinson** | It depends on which animals we are talking about. Individual animals that are not rare should still be available to the public even if they are harmed. Access to animals keeps people interested in their plight and willing to help preserve them. |

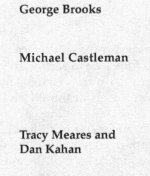

## Crime

| | |
|---|---|
| **George Brooks** | Castleman, I think we disagree in our assumptions about youth. Do you think we should treat every young person with suspicion? |
| **Michael Castleman** | Brooks, I do not think every young person should be regarded as a potential criminal or lawbreaker. I think you should take people as you meet and know them personally, just lock your doors at night. |
| **Tracy Meares and Dan Kahan** | Castleman, do you agree with us that people who live in high-crime areas need to cooperate more with the police? |
| **Castleman** | Yes. |
| **Bruce Shapiro** | I think the police do a lot to help crime in my neighborhood but not high-crime areas. What about |

| | |
|---|---|
| | placing the police in "hot spots" or specific areas where crime seems more prevalent? |
| Meares and Kahan | We think the *entire* American public should show some support for the enforcement of laws. This country is only as good as we [the public] allow it to be. We have no starting place without the ideas, support, and respect of the people. |
| Brooks | It is hard for someone to do that when your only interaction with the police is when they show up to take away your mother, brother, uncle, or best friend. |
| Castleman | Neighbors in any area can help change kids' lives; reducing opportunity in the first place reduces alienation and they won't commit the crimes. |
| Joe Kollin | I agree. Neighbors need to know which kids are the troublemakers. |

Role-playing conversations can help you discover points on which your authors agree or disagree, as long as the inferences underlying an author's response are fair.

When using these insights in your writing, be careful to signal clearly that these are hypothetical responses. Some useful phrases include "might argue," "might respond," and "would probably say."

## Testing with Problem Cases

A good way to test your tree is to select a problem case and infer how each group would treat it. For each group, try to answer these questions: Is this case relevant to their position? Would it be seen as an ideal case or a problem case?

## Looking for Coherence and Balance

Once you have finished a sketch of a complete tree, test it for coherence. Read through the sequence of claims leading from the top of the tree to each individual author's position. The sequence should make sense for each author. General points should precede specific points. An author's position on one claim should lead naturally to the claims following it.

To check the tree for balance, read across the branches at each level. The claims at a single level should all make sense as alternative answers to the same question. The branches should come in a sensible sequence so that the authors who agree the most are closest together and the ones who disagree the most are farthest apart.

# EXERCISES

## Backtalk: What Do You Say?

Come to class prepared to pretend to role-play one of the authors your class has been discussing. Reread the author's article carefully. Prepare a list of one or two questions your author would ask the other authors. Write a list of questions that you anticipate an author might ask you.

## Recognize/Evaluate

### A. Environment

Consider each statement in the following role-playing conversations. Which statements are fair to the authors who are speaking and which are unfair? Support your answers by referring to passages in the authors' articles.

1. **Kristof:** OK, Shiflett, I agree with you that the wilderness can be a serene place where silence is golden. But how are we to enjoy these places if we can't get to them? There are thousands of miles of trails in other parts of the country. Would it be okay if the transportation users stayed in areas designated for them?

2. **Shiflett:** If you can enjoy it without ruining it for anyone else, more power to you. But if technology disrupts other people's enjoyment, then the person using that technology is in the wrong. You have to be concerned with other people's wilderness experiences, not just your own. It's impossible to keep loud mountain bikes from ruining trails for hikers.

3. **Easterbrook:** Since when are mountain bikes loud? The wilderness can rebuild itself, so what about having trails in a kind of rotation system where every year a different bunch of trails is opened while some remain closed?

4. **Robinson:** Does one person's enjoyment cancel out the other's ruined experience? A resounding NO. Snowmobilers and mountain bikers can enjoy nature just as well from the ground without causing harm. Why not just take the simple route and say no to snowmobiles?

5. **Kristof:** Because they are fun. We all want to have fun in the wilderness, right? What about the people who do not want to rough it or who are disabled or out of shape? Don't they have the right to enjoy the wilderness?

6. **Shiflett:** The mountain bike itself isn't loud. The person enjoying his ride with his buddies is loud. So get rid of the people and leave the bikes, as long as I don't trip over them and ruin my experience or something.

7. **Chivers:** How can the wilderness unpave a paved road? Even with bikes, it would take more than a few years to erase the marks on the trails. Simply switching trails every few years would not leave nature enough time to properly heal herself.

8. **Easterbrook:** Agreed! Humans have to go in and restore trails. There is nothing wrong with filling in ruts with rocks and topsoil. It does not harm a thing. After a couple of years it will be back to the way it was before it was torn up by human contact.

## B. Crime

Students in this role-playing exercise were asked to respond to a case as they inferred their author would. Consider each statement in detail. Which statements are fair to the authors who are speaking and which are unfair? Support your answers by referring to passages in the authors' articles.

*How do you respond to this problem case: A seventh-grader brought a can of beer to school and gave it to a classmate. The classmate was caught drinking from the beer and expelled from school, due to a zero-tolerance policy for drugs and alcohol.*

1. **Kleck:** Harsh zero-tolerance policies are another misguided attempt provoked by media coverage and resulting public pressure due to the Columbine tragedy. Administrators and the public waste time overreacting instead of looking at individual cases and specifics. By overreacting to the situation (just one sip of alcohol, and by accident), the system drives kids to an all or nothing mentality on alcohol.

2. **Brooks:** This case shows a clear example of bias against a completely undeserving, innocent young woman. Her civil rights were obviously violated. If a boy had done the same, the punishment wouldn't have been nearly as severe. Zero-tolerance policies are like curfew laws in that they do nothing to curb crime while hurting young people. Instead we should put mentoring programs in place to prevent the problem of underage drinking altogether.

3. **Meares and Kahan:** Certainly the punishment was unfair in this particular case, but perhaps in agreeing to go to public school students must give up some rights. Appropriate suspensions and even zero-tolerance policies may be necessary to keep schools safe.

4. **Castleman:** The policy is foolish in the first place and likely won't prevent kids from drinking because it's often an impulse decision. Parents should instead team up to watch their children's behavior and stop drinking. The severity of this punishment smacks of the conservative let's-put-all-our-eggs-in-one-basket approach to sentencing.

5. **Shapiro:** This exemplifies why harsher regulations won't work. We need to work within the school systems to make sure kids don't fall through the cracks and start new antidrinking and violence programs in schools.

## Detect

### A. Environment

1. Edward Abbey, an environmental activist, wrote an article entitled, "The Damnation of a Canyon." Fit Abbey into one of the trees in Figure 3.1. To complete this exercise, you will probably have change the branchings and relabel them.

2. Read the following description of a problematic case concerning a rare species of seal in Alaska:

   Marine biologists in Alaska noticed a sharp drop in the population of Steller seals. Greenpeace and other environmentalist groups argued that fishing in the seals' habitat was a plausible cause. Fishermen argued that they weren't catching the kinds of fish that these seals eat. The federal judge in charge barred fishing temporarily to test whether fishing was the cause.

   Choose one of the trees in Figure 3.1. For each group, write a brief description of what the authors would probably say about this case.

### B. Crime

1. Nicolas Kristof, a pundit for the *New York Times*, wrote an article entitled, "Lock and Load," proposing a different approach to gun control. Fit Kristof into one of the trees in Figure 3.1. To complete this exercise, you will probably have to change the branchings and relabel them.

2. Read the following description of a problematic case concerning racial profiling:

   A group of teenagers playing a pick-up game of basketball got into a shoving match. A police officer driving by stopped the fight. He searched the trucks of the two Hispanic players, found a weapon, and arrested Roberto for possession of a firearm in public. Roberto, a high school senior and member of the basketball team, had never been in trouble before. He was kicked off the team and eventually expelled from school.

Choose one of the trees in Figure 3.1. For each group, write a brief description of what the authors would probably say about this case.

## Produce

Draw a synthesis tree for a group of six authors. At least three of the authors should be different from the ones discussed in this book.

# CHAPTER 4

# Critical Reading Process

Many students read texts looking for valuable nuggets of information to remember for an exam or to use in a writing assignment. To argue on an issue, however, you need to read actively and critically, with multiple goals in mind:

- To formulate a position of your own, not simply to find information.
- To find allies and opponents to respond to, instead of looking for quotes to fill out your paper.
- To find important points of dispute, instead of points the experts all agree on.

To understand a complex argument thoroughly, you will have to read it more than once. You might end up reading parts of it five or six times, looking at different aspects each time. This chapter will give you ideas for what to do while preparing to read, reading a text for the first time, reading to deepen your understanding, reading to map out the argument, and following through after reading. These strategies focus on different goals; the best ones to follow depend on how difficult you find the article and what you want to do with it.

These strategies are used every day by professionals, academics, and successful students. Using them does not guarantee that you will develop perfect understanding of the text; because texts allow for more than one reasonable interpretation, you can't check an answer key to see if your interpretation is right. But these strategies will help you build a thorough and coherent interpretation. Along the way, you may consider and reject several shaky ones.

## Preparing to Read

The best way to learn something new is to connect it to something you already know, something that you already have in mind. When you are first starting to read a new article, you may not have anything in mind that relates to it at all. You may be thinking about dinner or about an assignment in another class. So some good strategies before you read are to start thinking about the article in advance and to build up some expectations about it. The strategies in this section will help you focus on the topic, notice aspects of the text, and decide how much effort you will need to invest. Two of the best ways to prepare are to preview the text and to check out the author and the forum.

## Previewing

Previewing the text is a quick and easy strategy. It begins with glancing through the text, looking for clues about what conversation the author is joining and what the author wants to say. Read the title carefully. Look at the authors' names. Look at the title of the journal and the date when the article was published. Look for headings and read them carefully. Look for a list of references or works cited and see what kinds of articles or books are included. Look at any pictures or diagrams. Read an abstract if it is available.

Then, form some hypotheses about the author, the kind of article this is, its probable audience, and its topic. Scan your memory to think of things you already know or feel about this topic or about people like the author and probable readers. Recalling what you know activates the most relevant areas of your mental knowledge base and makes the new information in the article easier to understand and remember.

Finally, set some expectations. What do you think the author will say about the issue? The problem? The solution? Will this be an easy read? An interesting one? Are you likely to agree with this author? Setting expectations helps you notice both the strengths and weaknesses of the argument as you read.

## Checking

To understand the author's point of view, you need answers to these questions: Who is the author (name, job, stake in the issue, age, etc.)? What inspired him or her to enter the conversation at this particular time? How does the author's background relate to his or her position on the issue? Who are the author's allies and opponents? Who are the intended readers of this article?

To find information about the author, look for biographical information in a note at the beginning or end of the article, or on a separate "Contributors" page in a book or journal. Or search for the author's name on the Internet. "Check Out the Author" illustrates the types of biographical information to look for.

---

### CHECK OUT THE AUTHOR

#### Environment: Easterbrook's Background

Gregg Easterbrook has been a contributing editor at *Newsweek* and *U.S. News & World Report*. A senior editor of *The New Republic* and a contributing editor for *Atlantic Monthly* and *Washington Monthly*, Easterbrook is a two-time winner of the Investigative Reporters and Editors Award and a distinguished fellow of the

Fulbright Foundation. He is the author of several critically acclaimed books, including *Beside Still Waters: Searching for Meaning in an Age of Doubt*. This information was found at the Website "Gregg Easterbrook: Beliefnet Columnist," www.beliefnet.com/author/author_78.html.

### Crime: Kleck's Background

Gary Kleck is a Professor in the School of Criminology and Criminal Justice at Florida State University. His research centers on violence and crime control with special focus on gun control and crime deterrence. Dr. Kleck is the author of *Point Blank: Guns and Violence in America* (Aldine de Gruyter, 1991), which won the Michael J. Hindelang Award of the American Society of Criminology, for the book which made "the most outstanding contribution to criminology" in the preceding three years. This information was found at the Website "Who is Gary Kleck?" www.guncite.com/gcwhoGK.html.

To check out the forum where the article appeared, use the strategies. Find out as much information as you can about the aims and goals of the periodical or Web site and evaluate its trustworthiness. Remember that a forum can be trustworthy and useful even if it takes a strong stance on one side of an issue.

With all these recollections and ideas in mind, you will find the article easier to understand. The topics and approach won't all seem new and unexpected. You will also find it easier to respond to the author and to assess the strength of her arguments. The strategies described here work best in advance of reading, but you can also use them at other times. For example, you will use these strategies to find and choose additional sources.

## Reading a Text for the First Time

The first time you read an article, don't try to work out every detail. Plan to give yourself more opportunities to keep refining your understanding of the argument. Follow these strategies:

- **Focus on the big picture.** Read to get the main ideas of the argument. Check the expectations you set before reading. While some of your expectations were probably right, others may have been off-target. Adjust your expectations. Don't worry if the argument doesn't all make sense right away. Stop and reread as needed to follow the main ideas.

- **Note questions.** If you are having trouble understanding some passages, write questions (or even just a question mark) in a nearby margin. Similarly, mark any passage or section that seems pointless or irrelevant. Then you can come back to these sections later to see if they make more sense after you have additional information provided further on in the article.

- **Note surprises, frustrations, and unmet expectations.** It is important to note these experiences early, while they are fresh in your mind. Perhaps you are picking up on a point that the author should have included or on a tone that turns you (and other readers) off.

Trust your reactions to the text. All readers, even experts, invest effort figuring out the meaning of confusing passages. Any passage can be confusing because any piece of writing allows multiple interpretations, because authors don't always explain themselves clearly, and because readers differ in what they know and why they are reading. What is clear to one reader can confuse another.

Later on, if you are writing an analysis of the argument or a response to the author, these points may give you important clues to weaknesses in the article.

## Reading to Deepen Your Understanding

An initial reading is enough to give you a good picture of the author's entire argument. However, to analyze the argument, you need a deeper understanding of how the argument is put together.

Begin by reading the article again more slowly. Slowing down gives you more time to think about what you are reading. Think about how the current point fits in with the ones that came before. Think about how the points relate to your own knowledge of the topic.

Then return to any passage you had marked as confusing. Try summarizing or restating it in your own words. Here is how one reader used this strategy to figure out a confusing technical passage about a car recall. Below is the original passage. The second paragraph is a transcript of the reader saying out loud everything he was reading and thinking. The words that he is reading from the text are printed in plain typeface and his comments and paraphrases are in italics:

**Original passage:**
This plate (front suspension pivot bar support plate) connects a portion of the front suspension to the vehicle frame, and its failure could affect vehicle directional control, particularly during heavy brake application.

**Example of a person reading and thinking aloud:**
This plate (front suspension pivot bar support plate) *I guess that's another way of saying what this plate is*—connects a portion of the front suspension to the vehicle frame, *OK the plate connects the suspension to the vehicle frame*—and its failure could affect vehicle directional control, *so if this plate messes up, you lose the ability to steer I suppose*—directional control *I guess means steering*—particularly during heavy brake application . . . *so when you apply the brakes you could lose control of the car if you have a problem with this plate hmm*—

This reader restates the difficult phrases as a story about a real person experiencing the problem. His paraphrase is actually much clearer than the original and would be a good basis for a revision of the passage.

Depending on the article, you may have to read it several times in its entirety to understand the main points of the argument. While you do not need to understand every word or idea, you should see a purpose to every section. Going on to map the argument will also help you understand it.

## Reading to Map Out the Argument

Mapping out the line of argument means identifying a sequence of sections and claims that the author has laid out to steer the reader towards her destination. No matter where an article is published, authors face pressures to be as concise as possible, so you can assume that the author has a reason for including every passage. A good approach is to treat the article as a puzzle. Your job is to figure out how each section of the text contributes to the author's overall purpose. Two useful techniques for mapping the argument are annotating the text and creating a sketch.

### Annotating the Text

Annotating is the familiar process of writing in the margins, circling or underling text, or using a highlighter. For this process to be effective, be selective in what you mark.

- Highlight references to authors, experts, witnesses, and groups. These references will help you identify the author's allies and opponents.

- Highlight descriptions or references to real-world cases in which a problem has occurred, including place names, dates, and names of officials and agencies. These references will help you later on as you explore the problem and invent possible solutions.

- Write a brief phrase in the margin that sums up the main topic of a paragraph or group of paragraphs.

### Creating a Sketch

Your goal is to create a sketch that divides the text into the major sections of a public policy argument, the spans (issue, problem, and solution) and the stases (existence, definition, value, cause, and action). Your sketch can look like the ones provided for Castleman and Chivers. To create such a sketch, follow these steps:

1. Number the paragraphs in the text.

2. Write a list of the numbers on a separate piece of paper.

3. Draw a line between the paragraph numbers to represent the breaks between the issue and problem spans and another for the break between the problem and solution spans.

4. Look at consecutive paragraphs within a span to see if they are about the same topic or point. Paragraphs on a topic repeat important phrases. Draw a bracket around these paragraph numbers on your list and label it with a descriptive word or phrase.

5. Join up consecutive groupings if they all belong to the same stasis. For example, in the Castleman article, a large causal argument runs from par. 17–29, made up of subgroupings for liberal and conservative causes (such as the family or punishment) and for Castleman's causes, impulse, alienation, and opportunity.

Remember that a grouping may be very short or very long. Authors pick and choose among the possible stasis points, spending more time on some than others. An author spends most time on the points he or she thinks are most important and most controversial at the moment.

By the end of this process, every paragraph should belong to a topical grouping under a stasis, the set of stases should extend across an entire span, and the spans should extend across the entire article.

With so much flexibility in the framework, mapping out the line of argument is a real challenge. It is not a matter of clear-cut right or wrong answers; instead it takes reasoned interpretation about what makes sense.

## Identifying Spans and Passages within Spans

Figuring out the size and shape of a passage takes informed judgment. The important clues to the purpose of a passage are those that you can point to by underlining words or phrases. Review the "Words to Watch For" and keep those pages handy as you read.

The appeals that support a claim can themselves be claims. For this reason, the process of identifying passages becomes frustrating if you try to classify units of text that are too small, such as individual sentences. Here are several strategies for looking for spans and passages:

*Supersize It*

- Don't try to classify each sentence; you will lose sight of the big picture. Start by looking for spans and then for stases within a span.

- For spans, look at big units of text, as short as a paragraph and as long as several pages.

- Assume for the time being that the issue span starts with the first paragraph of the article. Find the halfway point in the article. Look near or before it for the start of the problem span. Look near or after it for the start of the solution span.

- Assume for the time being that a span is a sequence of passages developing each stasis: existence, definition, value, cause, and action. Consider whether a passage is developing an idea related to a stasis. For example, definition claims develop ideas about cases and categories, value claims compare cases within a category to each other or to a standard, and cause claims involve items that change over time due to factors.

- Look at the neighboring paragraphs to see if they are about the same stasis. Group together the biggest possible number of connected sentences or paragraphs on one stasis before assuming that you have entered a passage on a different stasis.

## Find the Edges

- Read headings and subheadings to see if they signal the beginning of a span or a stasis.

- Look for the solution span first; it is often the easiest to find.

- Find a clear case of a span or stasis; then work forward and backward to find where it starts or end.

- Within the spans, work back and forth to find text segments at the stases. Once you spot keywords for a stasis in one paragraph, see if the surrounding paragraphs are about the same topic and belong in the same segment. Then look for a new segment before or after that one. The stasis segments should cover all the paragraphs within the span.

- Mark where segments begin and end by drawing lines or writing a label in the margin. Draw these in pencil so you can change your mind.

## Allow for Absences and Extras

- Be sure that your proposed spans cover the entire article. Be sure that every segment within a span relates to a stasis or purpose.

- Don't assume that you will find all three spans. Some issues don't need much introduction. At times, analyzing a problem is more useful than trying to solve it.

- Don't assume that you will find every kind of stasis. Not all stases are used equally often. An issue span may simply be one big existence claim. Definition arguments are relatively rare.

- Spans and stases can be used more than once. You might find a sequence of alternative series of solutions, each with its own existence-cause-value claims, before one is recommended.

# Tying It All Together

Once you have identified passages and labeled them at least tentatively, you can begin working out the puzzle of how every passage contributes to the author's overall conclusion.

- Assume that the line of argument has to make sense—that it all fits together. Look for a consistent theme or position that connects all the segments. Figure out what happens to topics raised at the beginning. If the argument starts with a problem case, figure out how the solution would affect it.

- Look for connections at the level of stases (existence, definition, value, cause, action) to get to the guts of the argument. Some articles seem easy and clear at the top level of spans; the stases are where the real action is.

- Sometimes, a passage that seems irrelevant to you may be aimed at a specific audience. Look again at the information you found out about the journal or Web site. Why would the author think that this audience would need to read this passage?

- Summarize the argument in your own words to test the coherence of your interpretation. Be sure to use span and stasis keywords. Consider whether the author would agree that your summary or interpretation is fair. Do you exaggerate any of the author's claims? Adjust your summary to make it sound fair.

# Following Through After Reading

Critical reading doesn't end when you put down an author's article. Even after you stop looking at it, you should continue thinking about it from time to time. Tell a friend or relative about an interesting point. Keep an eye out for related information on the news, in conversation, or in other class discussions. Jot down any new ideas or new sources of related information. These follow-up strategies are valuable, no matter whether your goal is to remember the article for an exam, to learn background information on an issue, or to write your own argument on the issue.

When you read about a controversial issue, you may feel as if you are in a room with a lot of people arguing, talking quickly, getting off track, answering some questions and not others. To figure out how to jump in, you need a way to keep the authors and their positions straight by actively creating a mental reminder for each author.

Find a memory hook for each article. Come up with a catch phrase that sums up the topic of the article and the author's position. Concentrate on associating the phrase with the author's name. The goal is to remember the main line of the argument whenever you hear or think of the author's name.

- **Environment.** Chivers: dredging the ocean floor; Shiflett: jet skis and dirt bikes; Gómez-Pompa and Kaus: Western and non-Western conservation.

- **Crime.** Castleman: street crime and opportunity; Shapiro: being stabbed on TV; Meares and Kahan: civil rights, curfews, Chicago.

Try to remember a case that the author cares a lot about. Try to remember what he or she talks most about. If you have more than one article from the same author, come up with another catch phrase and another case to set it apart.

When you read an article from a different author, take time to compare the two authors. Try to remember an earlier author by recalling your catch phrase. Then think about where these authors would agree/disagree.

# 5

# Writing an Argument

When your instructor gives you a writing assignment, look closely at what you are asked to do. Assignments typically contain a great deal of information, and you have to sort that information. First, circle all the instructions about the length, the due date, the format, the grading criteria, and anything else about the production and conventions of the assignment. This information is important to you, but it doesn't tell you what the paper is supposed to be about.

Often your assignment will contain key words such as *analyze, define, evaluate,* or *propose* that will assist you in determining what direction to take. *Analyze* can mean several things. Your instructor might want you to analyze a piece of writing or the causes of something (see pages 176–188). *Define* usually means writing a **definition argument**, in which you argue for a definition based on the criteria you set out (see pages 161–176). *Evaluate* indicates an **evaluation argument**, in which you argue that something is good, bad, the best, or the worst in its class according to the criteria that you set out (see pages 188–194). An assignment that contains the instructions *Take a position in regard to a reading* might lead you to write a **rebuttal argument** (see pages 194–202). *Propose* means that you should identify a particular problem and explain why your solution is the best one (see pages 202–214).

If you remain unclear about the purpose of the assignment after reading it carefully, talk with your instructor.

## FIND A TOPIC THAT INTERESTS YOU

If your assignment does not provide a specific topic but instead gives you a wide range of options and you don't know what to write about, look first at the materials for your course: the readings, your lecture notes, and discussion boards. Think about what subjects came up in class discussion.

## WHAT IS NOT ARGUABLE

- **Statements of fact.** Most facts can be verified by doing research. But even simple facts can sometimes be argued. For example, Mount Everest is usually acknowledged to be the highest mountain in the world at 29,028 feet above sea level. But if the total height of a mountain from base to summit is the measure, then the volcano Mauna Loa in Hawaii is the highest mountain in the world. Although the top of Mauna Loa is 13,667 feet above sea level, the summit is 31,784 above the ocean floor. Thus the "fact" that Mount Everest is the highest mountain on the earth depends on a definition of *highest*. You could argue for this definition—assuming you can find someone who cares.

- **Claims of personal taste.** Your favorite food and your favorite color are examples of personal taste. If you hate fresh tomatoes, no one can convince you that you actually like them. But many claims of personal taste turn out to be value judgments using arguable criteria. For example, if you think that *Alien* is the best science-fiction movie ever made, you can argue that claim using evaluative criteria that other people can consider as good reasons. Indeed, you might not even like science fiction and still argue that *Alien* is the best science-fiction movie ever.

- **Statements of belief or faith.** If someone accepts a claim as a matter of religious belief, then for that person, the claim is true and cannot be refuted. Of course, people still make arguments about the existence of God and which religion reflects the will of God. Whenever an audience will not consider an idea, it's possible but very difficult to construct an argument. Many people claim to have evidence that UFOs exist, but most people refuse to acknowledge that evidence as even being possibly factual.

If you need to look outside class for a topic, think about what interests you. Subjects we argue about often find us. There are enough of them in daily life. We're late for work or class because the traffic is heavy or the bus doesn't run on time. We can't find a place to park when we get to school or work. We have to negotiate through various bureaucracies for almost anything we do—making an appointment to see a doctor, getting a course added or dropped, or correcting a mistake on a bill. Most of the time we grumble and let it go at that. But sometimes we stick with a subject and come up with a solution. Neighborhood groups in cities and towns have been especially effective in getting something done by writing about it—for example, stopping a new road from being built, getting better police and fire protection, and getting a vacant lot turned into a park.

If you are still stuck for an idea, consider writing about the issues that are engaging others in your community. Is there an issue on campus that people are riled up about? Is your local city council or school board debating a topic that is engaging the community? Are two of your friends always at odds on certain issues? Then you might want to enter into those debates yourself. Even if those issues aren't especially compelling to you individually, you will find yourself learning plenty in the course of entering the conversation.

## List and Analyze Issues

A good way to get started is to list possible issues to write about. Make a list of questions that can be answered "YES, because..." or "NO, because...." (Check the following lists for some suggestions to get you started.) Think about issues that affect your campus, your community, the nation, and the world. Which issues interest you? About which issues could you make a contribution to the larger discussion?

**Campus**
- ✔ Should smoking be banned on campus?
- ✔ Should varsity athletes get paid for playing sports that bring in revenue?
- ✔ Should admissions decisions be based exclusively on academic achievement?

✔ Should knowledge of a foreign language be required for all degree plans?

✔ Is there any way to curb the dangerous drinking habits of many students on your campus?

**Community**

✔ Should people who ride bicycles and motorcycles be required to wear helmets?

✔ Should high schools be allowed to search students for drugs at any time?

✔ Should bilingual education programs be eliminated?

✔ Should bike lanes be built throughout your community to encourage more people to ride bicycles?

✔ Should more tax dollars be shifted from building highways to funding public transportation?

**Nation/World**

✔ Should driving while talking on a cell phone be banned?

✔ Should capital punishment be abolished?

✔ Should the Internet be censored?

✔ Should beef and poultry be free of growth hormones?

✔ Should people who are terminally ill be allowed to end their lives?

*Narrowing a list*

1. Put a check beside the issues that look most interesting to write about or the ones that mean the most to you.

2. Put a question mark beside the issues that you don't know very much about. If you choose one of these issues, you will probably have to do in-depth research—by talking to people, by using the Internet, or by going to the library.

3. Select the two or three issues that look most promising. For each issue, make another list:

   • Who is most interested in this issue?

   • Whom or what does this issue affect?

- What are the pros and cons of this issue? Make two columns. At the top of the left one, write "YES, because." At the top of the right one, write "NO, because."

- What has been written about this issue? How can you find out what has been written?

## Find a Topic on the Web

Online subject directories can help you identify the subtopics of a large, general topic. Try the subject index of your library's online catalog. You'll likely find subtopics listed under large topics. Also, your library's Web site may have a link to the *Opposing Viewpoints* database.

One of the best Web subject directories for finding arguments is Yahoo's Issues and Causes directory (dir.yahoo.com/Society_and_ Culture/Issues_and_Causes/). This directory provides subtopics for major issues and provides links to the Web sites of organizations interested in particular issues.

## EXPLORE YOUR TOPIC

When you identify a potential topic, make a quick exploration of that topic, much as you would walk through a house or an apartment you are thinking about renting for a quick look. One way of exploring is to visualize the topic by making a map.

If you live in a state on the coast that has a high potential for wind energy, you might argue that your state should provide financial incentives for generating more electricity from the wind. Perhaps it seems like a no-brainer to you because wind power consumes no fuel and causes no air pollution. The only energy required is for the manufacture and transportation of the wind turbines and transmission lines. But your state and other coastal states may not have exploited potential wind energy for three reasons:

1. **Aesthetics.** Some people think wind turbines are ugly, akin to power lines.
2. **Hazard to wildlife.** A few poorly located wind turbines have killed birds and bats.

3. **Cost.** Wind power costs differ, but wind energy is generally more expensive than electricity produced by burning coal.

To convince other people that your proposal is a good one, you will have to answer these objections.

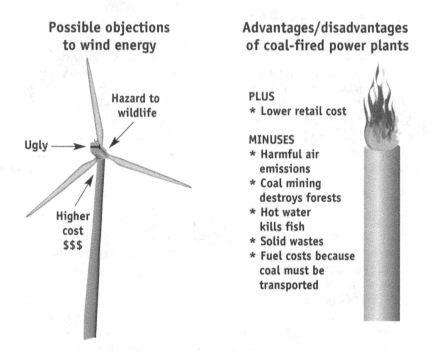

### Possible objections to wind energy

Hazard to wildlife

Ugly

Higher cost $$$

### Advantages/disadvantages of coal-fired power plants

PLUS
* Lower retail cost

MINUSES
* Harmful air emissions
* Coal mining destroys forests
* Hot water kills fish
* Solid wastes
* Fuel costs because coal must be transported

The first two objections are relatively easy to address. Locating wind farms ten kilometers offshore keeps them out of sight and away from most migrating birds and all bats. The third objection, higher cost, is more difficult. One strategy is to argue that the overall costs of wind energy and energy produced by burning coal are comparable if environmental costs are included. You can analyze the advantages and disadvantages of each by drawing maps.

These maps can help you organize an argument for providing financial incentives for wind energy.

## Advantages/disadvantages of wind energy

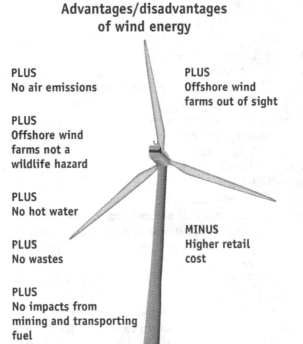

**PLUS**
No air emissions

**PLUS**
Offshore wind
farms not a
wildlife hazard

**PLUS**
No hot water

**PLUS**
No wastes

**PLUS**
No impacts from
mining and transporting
fuel

**PLUS**
Offshore wind
farms out of sight

**MINUS**
Higher retail
cost

## READ ABOUT YOUR TOPIC

Much college writing draws on and responds to sources—books, articles, reports, and other material written by other people. Every significant issue discussed in today's world has an extensive history of discussion involving many people and various points of view. Before you formulate a claim about a significant issue, you need to become familiar with the conversation that's in progress by reading about it.

One of the most controversial and talked-about subjects in recent years is the outsourcing of white-collar and manufacturing jobs to low-wage nations. Since 2000 an estimated 400,000 to 500,000 American jobs each year have gone to cheap overseas labor markets. The Internet has made this migration of jobs possible, allowing companies to outsource not only low-skilled jobs but also highly skilled jobs in fields such as software development, data storage, and even examining X-rays and MRI scans.

You may have read about this or another complex and controversial topic in one of your courses. Just as in a conversation with several people who hold different views, you may agree with some people, disagree with some, and with others agree with some of their ideas up to a point but then disagree.

CNN commentator Lou Dobbs has been sharply critical of outsourcing. In *Exporting America: Why Corporate Greed Is Shipping American Jobs Overseas* (2006), Dobbs blames large corporations for putting profits ahead of the good of the nation. He accuses both Republicans and Democrats of ignoring the effects of a massive trade deficit and the largest national debt in American history, which Dobbs claims will eventually destroy the American way of life.

Thomas Friedman, columnist for *The New York Times*, takes a different viewpoint on outsourcing in *The World Is Flat: A Brief History of the Twenty-first Century* (2006). By *flat*, Friedman means that the nations of the world are connected like never before through the Internet and the lowering of trade barriers, putting every nation in direct competition with all the others. Friedman believes that outsourcing is not only unstoppable but also desirable. He argues that Americans need to adapt to the new reality and rethink our system of education, or else we will be left hopelessly uncompetitive.

If you decide to write an argument about the issue of outsourcing, you might use either Dobbs's or Friedman's book as your starting point in making a claim. You could begin by using either book to disagree, to agree, or to agree up to a point and then disagree.

## *No:* Disagreeing with a Source

It's easy to disagree by simply saying an idea is dumb, but readers expect you to be persuasive about why you disagree and to offer reasons to support your views.

> **X claims that _____, but this view is mistaken because _____.**

### Example claim: Arguing against outsourcing resulting from free-trade policies
Thomas Friedman claims that the world is "flat," giving a sense of a level-playing field for all, but it is absurd to think that the millions of starving children in the world have opportunities similar to those in affluent countries who pay $100 for basketball shoes made by the starving children.

### Example claim: Arguing in favor of outsourcing resulting from free-trade policies
Lou Dobbs is a patriotic American who recognizes the suffering of manufacturing workers in industries like steel and automobiles, but he neglects to realize that the major cause of the loss of manufacturing jobs in the United States and China alike is increased productivity—the 40 hours of labor necessary to produce a car just a few years ago has now been reduced to 15.

## *Yes:* Agreeing with a Source with an Additional Point
Sources should not make your argument for you. With sources that support your position, indicate exactly how they fit into your argument with an additional point.

> **I agree with _____ and will make the additional point that _____.**

### Example claim: Arguing against outsourcing resulting from free-trade policies
Lou Dobbs's outcry against the outsourcing of American jobs also has a related argument: We are dependent not only on foreign oil but also foreign clothing, foreign electronics, foreign tools, foreign toys, and foreign cars and trucks—indeed, just about everything—which is quickly eroding the world leadership of the United States.

**Example claim: Arguing in favor of outsourcing resulting from free-trade policies**
Thomas Friedman's claim that the Internet enables everyone to become an entrepreneur is demonstrated by thousands of Americans, including my aunt, who could retire early because she developed an income stream by buying jeans and children's clothes at garage sales and selling them to people around the world on eBay.

## *Yes,* But: Agreeing and Disagreeing Simultaneously with a Source

Incorporating sources is not a matter of simply agreeing or disagreeing with them. Often you will agree with a source up to a point, but you will come to a different conclusion. Or you may agree with the conclusions, but not agree with the reasons put forth.

> I agree with _____ up to a point, but I disagree with the conclusion _____ because _____.

**Example claim: Qualifying the argument against outsourcing resulting from free-trade policies**
Lou Dobbs accurately blames our government for giving multinational corporations tax breaks for exporting jobs rather than regulating the loss of millions of jobs, but the real problem lies in the enormous appetite of Americans for inexpensive consumer products like HD televisions, an appetite that is supported by borrowing money from overseas to the point that our dollar has plummeted in value.

**Example claim: Qualifying the argument in favor of outsourcing resulting from free-trade policies**
Thomas Friedman's central claim that the world is being "flattened" by globalization and there is not much we can do to stop it is essentially correct, but he neglects the social costs of globalization around the world, where the banner of free trade has been the justification for devastating the environment, destroying workers' rights and the rights of indigenous peoples, and even undermining the laws passed by representative governments.

## RECOGNIZE FALLACIES

Recognizing where arguments go off track is one of the most important aspects of critical reading. What passes as political discourse is often filled with claims that lack evidence or substitute emotions for evidence. Such faulty reasoning often contains one or more **logical fallacies.** For example, politicians know that the public is outraged when the price of gasoline goes up, and they try to score political points by accusing oil companies of price gouging. It sounds good to angry voters—and it may well be true—but unless the politician defines what *price gouging* means and provides evidence that oil companies are guilty, the argument has no more validity than children calling each other bad names on the playground.

### *Fallacies of logic*

- **Begging the question** *Politicians are inherently dishonest because no honest person would run for public office.* The fallacy of begging the question occurs when the claim is restated and passed off as evidence.

- **Either-or** *Either we eliminate the regulation of businesses or else profits will suffer.* The either-or fallacy suggests that there are only two choices in a complex situation. Rarely, if ever, is this the case.

- **False analogies** *Japan quit fighting in 1945 when we dropped nuclear bombs on them. We should use nuclear weapons against other countries.* Analogies always depend on the degree of resemblance of one situation to another. In this case, the analogy fails to recognize that circumstances today are very different from those in 1945. Many countries now possess nuclear weapons, and we know their use could harm the entire world.

- **Hasty generalization** *We have been in a drought for three years; that's a sure sign of climate change.* A hasty generalization is a broad claim made on the basis of a few occurrences. Climate cycles occur regularly over spans of a few years. Climate trends, however, must be observed over centuries.

(Continued on next page)

- **Non sequitur** *A university that can raise a billion dollars from alumni should not have to raise tuition.* A non sequitur (a Latin term meaning "it does not follow") ties together two unrelated ideas. In this case, the argument fails to recognize that the money for capital campaigns is often donated for special purposes such as athletic facilities or scholarships and is not part of a university's general revenue.

- **Oversimplification** *No one would run stop signs if we had a mandatory death penalty for doing it.* This claim may be true, but the argument would be unacceptable to most citizens. More complex, if less definitive, solutions are called for.

- **Post hoc fallacy** *The stock market goes down when the AFC wins the Super Bowl in even years.* The *post hoc* fallacy (from the Latin *post hoc ergo propter hoc,* which means "after this, therefore because of this") assumes that events that follow in time have a causal relationship.

- **Rationalization** *I could have finished my paper on time if my printer had been working.* People frequently come up with excuses and weak explanations for their own and others' behavior. These excuses often avoid actual causes.

- **Slippery slope** *We shouldn't grant citizenship to illegal immigrants now living in the United States because then no one will want to obey our laws.* The slippery slope fallacy maintains that one thing inevitably will cause something else to happen.

### Fallacies of emotion and language

- **Bandwagon appeals** *It doesn't matter if I copy a paper off the Web because everyone else does.* This argument suggests that everyone is doing it, so why shouldn't you? But on close examination, it may be that everyone really isn't doing it—and in any case, it may not be the right thing to do.

- **Name-calling** Name-calling is frequent in politics and among competing groups. People level accusations using names such as *radical,* *tax-and-spend liberal, racist, fascist, right-wing ideologue.* Unless these terms are carefully defined, they are meaningless.

- **Polarization** *Feminists are all man haters.* Like name-calling, polarization exaggerates positions and groups by representing them as extreme and divisive.

- **Straw man** *Environmentalists won't be satisfied until not a single human being is allowed to enter a national park.* A straw man argument is a diversionary tactic that sets up another's position in a way that can be easily rejected. In fact, only a small percentage of environmentalists would make an argument even close to this one.

## FIND GOOD REASONS

Get in the habit of asking the following questions every time you are asked to write an argument.

### Can You Argue by Definition?

Probably the most powerful kind of good reason is an **argument from definition**. You can think of a definition as a simple statement: _____ *is a* _____. You use these statements all the time. When you need a course to fulfill your social-science requirement, you look at the list of courses that are defined as social-science courses. You find out that the anthropology class you want to take is one of them. It's just as important when _____ *is not a* _____. Suppose you are taking College Algebra, which is a math course taught by the math department, yet it doesn't count for the math requirement. The reason it doesn't count is because College Algebra is not defined as a college-level math class. So you have to enroll next semester in Calculus I.

Many definitions are not nearly as clear-cut as the math requirement. If you want to argue that cheerleaders are athletes, you will need to define what an athlete is. You start thinking. An athlete competes in an activity, but that definition alone is too broad, since many competitions do not require physical activity. Thus, an athlete must participate in a competitive physical activity and must train for it. But that definition is still not quite narrow enough, since soldiers train for competitive physical activity. You decide to add that the activity must be a sport and that it must require special competence and precision: *Cheerleaders are athletes because true athletes train for and compete in physical sporting events that require special competence and precision.*

If you can get your audience to accept your definitions, you've gone a long way toward convincing them of the validity of your claim. That is why the most controversial issues in our culture— affirmative action, gay rights, pornography, women's rights, privacy rights, gun control, the death penalty—are argued from definition. Is pornography protected by the First Amendment, or is it a violation of women's rights? Is the death penalty just or cruel and inhumane? You can see from these examples that definitions often rely on deeply held beliefs.

Because people have strong beliefs about controversial issues, they often don't care about the practical consequences. Arguing that it is much cheaper to execute prisoners who have been convicted of first-degree murder than to keep them in prison for life does not convince those who believe that it is morally wrong to kill. (See pages 161–176.)

## Can You Argue from Value?

A special kind of argument from definition, one that often implies consequences, is the **argument from value**. You can support your claim with a "because" clause (or several of them) that includes a sense of evaluation. Arguments from value follow from claims like _____ *is a good* _____, or _____ *is not a good* _____.

Evaluation arguments usually proceed from the presentation of certain criteria. These criteria come from the definitions of good and bad, of poor and not so poor, that prevail in a given case. A great burger fulfills certain criteria; so does an outstanding movie, an excellent class, or the best laptop in your price range. Sometimes the criteria are straightforward, as in the burger example. A great burger has to have tasty meat—tender and without gristle, fresh, never frozen—a fresh bun that is the right size, and your favorite condiments. But if you are buying a laptop computer and want to play the latest games along with your school tasks, you need to do some homework. For realistic graphics the best laptop will have a fast processor, a long-lasting battery, connectivity to your wireless accessories, and sturdy construction. The keys for evaluation arguments are finding the appropriate criteria and convincing your readers that those criteria are the right criteria (see pages 188–194).

## Can You Argue from Consequence?

Another powerful source of good reasons comes from considering the possible consequences of your position: Can you sketch out the good things that will follow from your position? Can you establish that certain bad things will be avoided if your position is adopted? If so, you will have other good reasons to use.

**Causal arguments** take the basic form of _____ *causes* _____ (or _____ *does not cause* _____). Very often, causal arguments are more complicated, taking the form _____ *causes* _____ *which, in turn, causes* _____ and so on. The pesticide DDT was banned in the United States as the result of an effective causal argument set out in Rachel Carson's *Silent Spring*, which makes powerful arguments from consequence. The key to Carson's argument is the causal chain that explains how animals and people are poisoned. Carson describes how nothing exists alone in nature. When a potato field is sprayed with DDT, some of that poison is absorbed by the skin of the potatoes and some washes into the groundwater, where it contaminates drinking water. Other poisonous residue is absorbed into streams, where it is ingested by insect larvae, which in turn are eaten by fish. Fish are eaten by other fish, which are then eaten by waterfowl and people. At each stage, the poisons become more concentrated. (See pages 176–188.)

**Proposal arguments** are future-oriented arguments from consequence. In a proposal argument, you cannot stop with naming good reasons; you also have to show that these consequences would follow from the idea or course of action that you are arguing. For example, if you are proposing designated lanes for bicycles on the streets of your city, you must argue that they will encourage more people to ride bicycles to work and school, reducing air pollution and traffic congestion for everyone. (See pages 202–214.)

## Can You Counter Objections to Your Position?

Another good way to find convincing good reasons is to think about possible objections to your position. If you can imagine how your audience might counter or respond to your argument, you will probably include in your argument precisely the points that will address your readers' particular needs and objections. If you are successful, your readers will be convinced that you are right. You've no doubt had the experience of mentally saying to a writer in the course of your reading, "Yeah, but what about this other idea?"—only to have the writer address precisely this objection.

You can impress your readers if you've thought about why anyone would oppose your position and exactly how that opposition would be expressed. If you are writing a proposal argument for a computer literacy requirement for all high school graduates, you might think about why anyone would object, since computers are becoming increasingly important to our jobs and lives. What will the practical objections be? What about philosophical ones? Why hasn't such a requirement been put in place already? By asking such questions in your own arguments, you are likely to develop convincing reasons.

Sometimes, writers pose rhetorical questions such as, "You might say, 'But won't paying for computers for all students make my taxes go up?'" Stating objections explicitly can be effective if you make the objections as those of a reasonable person with an alternative point of view. But if the objections you state are ridiculous or contrived, then you risk being accused of setting up a **straw man**—that is, making the position opposing your own so simplistic that no one would likely identify with it. (See pages 194–202.)

## FIND EVIDENCE TO SUPPORT GOOD REASONS

Good reasons are essential ingredients of good arguments, but they don't do the job alone. You must support or verify good reasons with evidence. **Evidence** consists of hard data, examples, personal experiences, episodes, or tabulations of episodes (known as **statistics**) that are seen as relevant to the good reasons you are putting forward. Thus, a writer of arguments puts forward not only claims and good reasons but also evidence that those good reasons are true.

How much supporting evidence should you supply? How much evidence is enough? As is usual in the case of rhetoric, the best answer is, "It depends." If a reader is likely to find one of your good reasons hard to believe, then you should be aggressive in offering support. You should present detailed evidence in a patient and painstaking way. As one presenting an argument, you have a responsibility not just to *state* a case but to *make* a case with evidence. Arguments that are unsuccessful tend to fail not because of a shortage of good reasons; more often, they fail because the reader doesn't agree that there is enough evidence to support the good reason that is being presented.

When a writer doesn't provide satisfactory evidence to support a reason, readers might feel that there has been a failure in the reasoning process. In fact, earlier in this chapter you learned about various **fallacies** associated with faulty arguments (see pages 143–145). But strictly speaking, there is nothing false about these so-called logical fallacies. The fallacies most often refer to failures in providing evidence; when you don't provide enough good evidence to convince your audience, you might be accused of committing a fallacy in reasoning. You will usually avoid such accusations if the evidence that you cite is both *relevant* and *sufficient*.

**Relevance** refers to the appropriateness of the evidence to the case at hand. Some kinds of evidence are seen as more relevant than others for particular audiences. On the one hand, in science and industry, personal testimony is seen as having limited relevance, while experimental procedures and controlled observations have far more credibility. Compare someone who defends the use of a particular piece of computer software because "it worked for me" with someone who defends it because "according to a journal article published last month, 84 percent of the users of the software were satisfied or very satisfied with it." On the other hand, in writing to the general public on controversial issues such as gun control, personal experience is often considered more relevant than other kinds of data.

**Sufficiency** refers to the amount of evidence cited. Sometimes a single piece of evidence or a single instance will carry the day if it is especially compelling in some way—if it represents the situation well or makes a point that isn't particularly controversial. More often, people expect more than one piece of evidence if they are to be convinced of something. Convincing readers that they should approve a state-wide computer literacy requirement for all high school graduates will require much more evidence than the story of a single graduate who succeeded with her computer skills. You will likely need statistical evidence for such a broad proposal.

If you anticipate that your audience might not accept your evidence, face the situation squarely. First, think carefully about the argument you are presenting. If you cannot cite adequate evidence for your assertions, perhaps those assertions must be modified or qualified in some way. If you remain convinced of your assertions, then think about doing more research to come up with additional evidence.

## STATE AND EVALUATE YOUR THESIS

Once you have identified a topic and have a good sense of how to develop it, the next critical step is to write a **working thesis**. Your **thesis** states your main claim. Much writing that you will do in college and later in your career will require an explicit thesis, usually placed near the beginning.

### Focus Your Thesis

The thesis can make or break your paper. If the thesis is too broad, you cannot do justice to the argument. Who wouldn't wish for fewer traffic accidents, better medical care, more effective schools, or a cleaner environment? Simple solutions for these complex problems are unlikely.

Stating something that is obvious to everyone isn't an arguable thesis. Don't settle for easy answers. When a topic is too broad, a predictable thesis often results. Narrow your focus and concentrate on the areas where you have the most questions. Those are likely the areas where your readers will have the most questions too.

The opposite problem is less common: a thesis that is too narrow. If your thesis simply states a commonly known fact, then it is too narrow. For example, the growth rate of the population in the United States has doubled since 1970 because of increased immigration. The U.S. Census Bureau provides reasonably accurate statistical information, so this claim is not arguable. But the policies that allow increased immigration and the effects of a larger population—more crowding and higher costs of health care, education, and transportation—are arguable.

> **Not arguable:** The population of the United States grew faster in the 1990s than in any previous decade because Congress increased the rate of legal immigration and the government stopped enforcing most laws against illegal immigration in the interior of the country.
>
> **Arguable:** Allowing a high rate of immigration helps the United States deal with the problems of an increasingly aging society and helps provide funding for millions of Social Security recipients.
>
> **Arguable:** The increase in the number of visas to foreign workers in technology industries is a major cause of unemployment for U. S. citizens in those industries.

## Evaluate Your Thesis

Once you have a working thesis, ask these questions:

- Is it arguable?
- Is it specific?
- Is it manageable given your length and time requirements?
- Is it interesting to your intended readers?

*Example 1*

> **Sample thesis.** We should take action to resolve the serious traffic problem in our city.

> **Is it arguable?** The thesis is arguable, but it lacks a focus.
>
> **Is it specific?** The thesis is too broad.
>
> **Is it manageable?** Transportation is a complex issue. New highways and rail systems are expensive and take many years to build. Furthermore, citizens don't want new roads running through their neighborhoods.
>
> **Is it interesting?** The topic has the potential to be interesting if the writer can propose a specific solution to a problem that everyone in the city recognizes.

When a thesis is too broad, it needs to be revised to address a specific aspect of an issue. Make the big topic smaller.

**Revised thesis.** The existing freight railway that runs through the center of the city should be converted to a passenger railway because this is the cheapest and quickest way to decrease traffic congestion downtown.

*Example 2*
**Sample thesis.** Over 60 percent of Americans play computer games on a regular basis.

**Is it arguable?** The thesis states a commonly acknowledged fact. It is not arguable.

**Is it specific?** The thesis is too narrow.

**Is it manageable?** A known fact is stated in the thesis, so there is little to research. Several surveys report this finding.

**Is it interesting?** The popularity of computer games is well established. Nearly everyone is aware of the trend.

There's nothing original or interesting about stating that Americans love computer games. Think about what is controversial. One debatable topic is how computer games affect children.

**Revised thesis.** Computer games are valuable because they improve children's visual attention skills, literacy skills, and computer literacy skills.

## THINK ABOUT YOUR READERS

Thinking about your readers doesn't mean telling them what they might want to hear. Instead, imagine yourself in a dialogue with your readers. What questions will they likely have? How might you address any potential objections?

## Think About What Your Readers Know—and Do Not Know

Your readers' knowledge of your subject is critical to the success of your argument. If they are not familiar with the background information, they probably won't understand your argument fully. If you know that your readers will be unfamiliar with your subject, you have to supply background information before attempting to convince them of your position. A good tactic is to tie your new information to what your readers already know. Comparisons and analogies can be very helpful in linking old and new information.

## Think About Your Readers' Attitudes Toward You

Readers trust writers who know what they are talking about and take a balanced view. Readers respect writers who have done their homework and represent opposing viewpoints fairly. Readers also respect writers who write well. Nothing undermines your credibility faster than numerous errors and sloppy sentences.

## Think About Your Readers' Attitudes Toward Your Subject

People have prior attitudes about controversial issues. You must take these attitudes into consideration as you write or speak. Imagine, for instance, that you are preparing an argument for a guest editorial in your college newspaper. You are advocating that your state government should provide parents with choices between public and private schools. You plan to argue that the tax dollars that now automatically go to public schools should go to private schools if parents so choose. You have evidence that the sophomore-to-senior dropout rate in private schools is less than half the rate in public schools. Furthermore, students from private schools attend college at nearly twice the rate of public-school graduates. You intend to argue that one of the reasons private schools are more successful is that they spend more money on instruction and less on administration. And you believe that school choice speaks to the American desire for personal freedom.

Not everyone on your campus will agree with your position. How might the faculty at your college or university feel about this issue? How about the administrators, the staff, other students, and interested community members who read the student newspaper? What are their attitudes toward public funding of private schools? How are you going to deal with the objection that many students in private schools do better in school because they come from more affluent families? And what will the faculty think about you? Will they think you have enough expertise to sound off reliably on the topic? How will you have to buttress your credibility?

Even when you write about a much less controversial subject, you must think carefully about your audience's attitudes toward what you have to say or to write. Sometimes your audience may share your attitudes; other times, your audience may be neutral. At still other times, your audience will have attitudes that differ sharply from your own. Anticipate these various attitudes and act accordingly. If these attitudes are different from yours, you will have to work hard to counter them without insulting your audience.

## ORGANIZE YOUR ARGUMENT

Asking a series of questions can generate a list of good reasons, but even if you have plenty, you still have to decide which ones to use and in what order to present them. Thinking about your readers' knowledge, attitudes, and values will help you to decide which reasons to present to your audience.

Writing plans often take the form of outlines, either formal outlines or working outlines. A **formal outline** typically begins with the thesis statement, which anchors the entire outline.

MANAGING THE RISKS OF NANOTECHNOLOGY
WHILE REAPING THE REWARDS

THESIS: The revolutionary potential of nanotechnology has arrived in an explosion of consumer products, yet our federal government has yet to recognize the potential risks or to fund research to reduce those risks.

   I.  Nanotechnology now is in many consumer products.
      A. The promise of nanotechnology to revolutionize medicine, energy production, and communication is years in the future, but consumer products are here now.
      B. Nanotechnology is now in clothing, food, sports equipment, medicines, electronics, and cars.
      C. Experts predict that 15 percent of manufactured products worldwide will contain nanotechnology in 2014.
      D. The question that hasn't been asked: Is nanotechnology safe?

  II.  Americans have little awareness of nanotechnology.
      A. Companies have stopped mentioning and advertising nanotechnology.
      B. Companies and the insurance industry paid $250 billion in asbestos claims in the United States alone.
      C. Companies fear exposure to lawsuits if nanotechnology is found to be toxic.

A **working outline** is a sketch of how you will arrange the major sections.

MANAGING THE RISKS OF NANOTECHNOLOGY
WHILE REAPING THE REWARDS

SECTION 1: Begin by defining nanotechnology—manipulating particles between 1 and 100 nanometers (nanometer is a billionth of a meter). Describe the rapid spread of nanotechnology in consumer products including clothing, food, sports equipment, medicines, electronics, and cars. State projection of 15 percent of global manufactured goods containing nanotechnology in 2014.

SECTION 2: Most Americans know nothing about nanotechnology. Companies have stopped advertising that their products contain nanotechnology because of fear of potential lawsuits. Asbestos, once thought safe, now is known to be toxic and has cost companies $250 billion in lawsuits in the United States alone.

SECTION 3: Almost no research has been done on the safety of nanotechnology, only $11 million in federal research. No testing is required for new products because the materials are common, but materials behave differently at nano-scale (e.g., aluminum is normally inert but combustible at nano-scale).

SECTION 4: Nanoparticles are highly mobile and can cross the blood-brain barrier and through the placenta. They are toxic in brains of fish and may collect in lungs.

SECTION 5: Urge that the federal government develop a master plan for identifying and reducing potential risks of nanotechnology and provide sufficient funding to carry out the plan.

## WRITE AN ENGAGING TITLE AND INTRODUCTION

Many writers don't think much about titles, but they are very important. A good title makes the reader want to see what you have to say. Be specific as you can in your title, and if possible, suggest your stance.

Get off to a fast start in your introduction. Convince your reader to keep reading. Cut to the chase. Think about how you can get your readers interested. Consider using one of the following.

- a concisely stated thesis
- a hard-hitting fact
- a question
- a vivid description of a problem
- a contradiction or paradox
- a scenario

---

### MANAGING THE RISKS OF NANOTECHNOLOGY WHILE REAPING THE REWARDS

The revolutionary potential of nanotechnology for medicine, energy production, and communication is now at the research and development stage, but the future has arrived in consumer products. Nanotechnology has given us products we hardly could have imagined just a few years ago: socks that never stink; pants that repel water yet keep you cool; eyeglasses that won't scratch; "smart" foods that add nutrition and reduce cholesterol; DVDs that are incredibly lifelike; bandages that speed healing; tennis balls that last longer; golf balls that fly straighter; pharmaceuticals that selectively deliver drugs; various digital devices like iPads, digital cameras, and smart phones that have longer battery lives and more vivid displays; and cars that are lighter, stronger, and more fuel efficient. These miracle products are now possible because scientists have learned how to manipulate nano-scale particles of 1–100 nanometers (a nanometer is a billionth of a meter; a human hair is about 100,000 nanometers in width). Experts estimate that 15 percent of all consumer products will contain nanotechnology by 2014. In the rush to create new consumer products, however, one question has not been asked: Is nanotechnology safe for those who use the products and the workers who are exposed to nanoparticles daily?

## WRITE A STRONG CONCLUSION

Restating your thesis usually isn't the best way to finish a paper. Conclusions that offer only a summary bore readers. The worst endings say something like "in my paper I've said this." Effective conclusions are interesting and provocative, leaving readers with something to think about. Give your readers something to take away besides a straight summary; if you must offer a summary, at least offer it in a new and memorable way. Instead of summarizing, try one of these approaches.

- Issue a call to action.
- Discuss the implications.
- Make recommendations.
- Project into the future.
- Tell an anecdote that illustrates a key point.

---

The potential risks of nanotechnology are reasonably well known. Among the more obvious research questions are the following:

- How hazardous are nanoparticles for workers who have daily exposure?
- What happens to nanoparticles when they are poured down the drain and eventually enter streams, lakes, and oceans?
- How readily do nanoparticles penetrate the skin?
- What happens when nanoparticles enter the brain?
- What effect do airborne nanoparticles have on the lungs?

Nanotechnology promises untold benefits beyond consumer goods in the fields of medicine, energy production, and communication, but these benefits can be realized only if nanotechnology is safe. In January 2012, the National Research Council reported that little progress has been made in understanding the health effects of nanotechnology and little research has been done on new nanotechnology products coming on the market. The federal government needs to create a master plan for risk research and to increase spending at least tenfold to ensure sufficient funding to carry out the plan.

When you finish your conclusion, read your introduction again. The main claim in your conclusion should be clearly related to the main subject, question, or claim in your introduction. If they do not match, revise your introduction so that it prepares your readers for where you will end. Your thinking evolves and develops as you write; thus often you need to adjust your introduction if you wrote it first.

# 6

# Constructing an Argument

Imagine that you bought a new car in June and you are taking some of your friends to your favorite lake over the Fourth of July weekend. You have a great time until, as you are heading home, a drunk driver—a repeat offender—swerves into your lane and totals your new car. You and your friends are lucky not to be hurt, but you're outraged because you believe that repeat offenders should be prevented from driving, even if that means putting them in jail. You also remember going to another state that had sobriety checkpoints on holiday weekends. If such a checkpoint had been at the lake, you might still be driving your new car. You live in a town that encourages citizens to contribute to the local newspaper, and you think you could get a guest editorial published. The question is, how do you want to write the editorial?

- You could tell your story about how a repeat drunk driver endangered the lives of you and your friends.
- You could define driving while intoxicated (DWI) as a more legally culpable crime.
- You could compare the treatment of drunk drivers in your state with the treatment of drunk drivers in another state.
- You could cite statistics that alcohol-related accidents killed nearly 11,000 people in the United States in 2009.
- You could evaluate the present drunk-driving laws as insufficiently just or less than totally successful.
- You could propose taking vehicles away from repeat drunk drivers and forcing them to serve mandatory sentences.
- You could argue that your community should have sobriety checkpoints at times when drunk drivers are likely to be on the road.
- You could do several of the given points.

You're not going to have much space in the newspaper, so you decide to argue for sobriety checkpoints. You know that they are controversial. One of your friends who was in the car with you said that the checkpoints are unconstitutional because they involve search without probable cause. However, after doing some research to find out whether checkpoints are defined as legal or illegal, you learn that on June 14, 1990, the U.S. Supreme Court upheld the constitutionality of using checkpoints as a deterrent and enforcement tool against drunk drivers.

But you still want to know whether most people would agree with your friend that sobriety checkpoints are an invasion of privacy. You find opinion polls and surveys going back to the 1980s that show that 70 to 80 percent of those polled support sobriety checkpoints. You also realize that you can argue by analogy that security checkpoints for alcohol are similar in many ways to airport security checkpoints that protect passengers. You decide you will finish by making an argument from consequence. If people who go to the lake with plans to drink know in advance that there will be checkpoints, they will find a designated driver or some other means of safe transportation, and everyone else will also be safer.

The point of this example is that people very rarely set out to define something in an argument for the sake of definition, to compare for the sake of comparison, or to adopt any of the other ways of structuring an argument. Instead, they have a purpose in mind, and they use the kinds of arguments that are discussed in this chapter—most often in combination—as means to an end. Most arguments use multiple approaches and multiple sources of good reasons. Proposal arguments in particular often analyze a present situation with definition, causal, and evaluative arguments before advancing a course of future action to address that situation. The advantage of thinking explicitly about the structure of arguments is that you often find other ways to argue. Sometimes you just need a way to get started writing about complex issues.

## DEFINITION ARGUMENTS

The continuing controversies about what should be defined as art, free speech, pornography, and hate crimes (to name just a few) illustrate why definitions often matter more than we might think. People argue about definitions because of the consequences of something being defined in a certain way. The controversies about certain subjects also illustrate three important principles that operate when definitions are used in arguments.

First, people make definitions that benefit their interests. Early in life you learned the importance of defining actions as "accidents." Windows can be broken through carelessness, especially when you are tossing a ball against the side of the house, but if it's an "accident," well, accidents just happen (and don't require punishment).

Second, most of the time when you are arguing about a definition, your audience will either have a different definition in mind or be unsure of the definition. Your mother or father probably didn't think breaking the window was an accident but rather was carelessness, so you had to convince Mom or Dad that you were really being careful, and the ball just slipped out of your hand. It's your job to get them to accept your definition.

Third, if you can get your audience to accept your definition, then usually you succeed. For this reason, definition arguments as a rule are the most powerful arguments.

## Understand How Definition Arguments Work

Definition arguments set out criteria and then argue that whatever is being defined meets or does not meet those criteria.

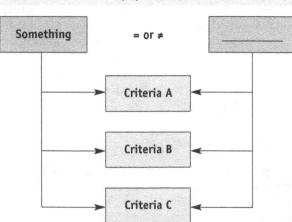

*Example*

**Graffiti is art** because *it is a means of self expression, it shows an understanding of design principles*, and *it stimulates both the senses and the mind.*

## Recognize Kinds of Definitions

Rarely do you get far into an argument without having to define something. Imagine that you are writing an argument about the decades-old and largely ineffective "war on drugs" in the United States. We all know that the war on drugs is being waged against drugs that are illegal, like cocaine and marijuana, and not against the legal drugs produced by the multibillion-dollar drug industry. Our society classifies drugs into two categories: "good" drugs, which are legal (though often controlled), and "bad" drugs, which are illegal.

How exactly does our society arrive at these definitions? Drugs would be relatively easy to define as good or bad if the difference could be defined at the molecular level. Bad drugs would contain certain molecules that define them as bad. The history of drug use in the United States, however, tells us that it is not so simple. In the twentieth century, alcohol was on the list of illegal drugs for over a decade, while opium was considered a good drug and was distributed in many patent medicines by pharmaceutical companies. Similarly, LSD (lysergic acid diethylamide) and MDMA (methylenedioxymethamphetamine, known better by its street name *ecstasy*) were developed by the pharmaceutical industry but later made illegal. In a few states, marijuana is now legal for medicinal use.

If drugs cannot be classified as good or bad by their molecular structure, then perhaps society classifies them by their effects. It might be reasonable to assume that addictive drugs are illegal, but that's not the case. Nicotine is highly addictive and is a legal drug, as are many prescription medicines. Drugs taken for the purpose of pleasure are not necessarily illegal (think of alcohol and Viagra), nor are drugs that alter consciousness or change personality (such as Prozac).

Whether a drug is defined as legal or illegal apparently is determined by example. The nationwide effort to stop Americans from drinking alcohol during the first decades of the twentieth century led to the passage of the Eighteenth Amendment and the ban on sales of alcohol from 1920 to 1933, known as Prohibition. Those who argued for Prohibition used examples of drunkenness, especially among the poor, to show how alcohol broke up families and left mothers and children penniless in the street. Those who opposed Prohibition initially pointed to the consumption of beer and wine in many cultural traditions. Later they raised examples of the bad effects of Prohibition—the rise of organized crime, the increase in alcohol abuse, and the general disregard for laws.

When you make a definition argument, it's important to think about what kind of definition you will use.

- **Formal definitions** typically categorize an item into the next-higher classification and provide criteria that distinguish the item from other items within that classification. Most dictionary definitions are formal definitions. For example, fish are cold-blooded aquatic vertebrates that have jaws, fins, and scales and are distinguished from other cold-blooded aquatic vertebrates (such as sea snakes) by the presence of gills. If you can construct a formal definition with specific criteria that your audience will accept, then you will likely have a strong argument. The key is to get your audience to agree to your criteria.

- **Operational definitions** are often used when a concept cannot be easily defined by formal definitions. For example, researchers who study binge drinking among college students define a binge as five or more drinks in one sitting for a man, and four or more drinks for a woman. Some people think this standard is too low and should be raised to six to eight drinks to distinguish true problem drinkers from the general college population. No matter what the number, researchers must argue that the particular definition is one that suits the concept.

- **Definitions from example** are used for many human qualities such as honesty, courage, creativity, deceit, and love. Few would not call the firefighters who entered the World Trade Center on September 11, 2001, courageous. Most people would describe someone with a diagnosis of terminal cancer who refuses to feel self-pity as courageous. But what about a student who declines to go to a concert with her friends so she can study for an exam? Her behavior might be admirable, but most people would hesitate to call it courageous. The key to arguing a definition from example is that the examples must strike the audience as typical of the concept, even if the situation is unusual.

## Build a Definition Argument

Because definition arguments are so powerful, they are found at the center of some of the most important debates in American history. Definition arguments were at the heart of the abolition of slavery, for example, and many of the major arguments of the civil rights movement were based on definitions. Martin Luther King Jr.'s "Letter from Birmingham Jail" is one eloquent example.

King was jailed in April 1963 for leading a series of peaceful protests in Birmingham, Alabama. While he was being held in solitary confinement, Rev. King wrote a letter to eight white Birmingham clergymen. These religious leaders had issued a statement urging an end to the protests in their city. King argued that it was necessary to act now rather than wait for change. His purpose in writing the argument was to win acceptance for the protests and protestors and to make his audience see that the anti-segregationists were not agitators and rabble-rousers, but citizens acting responsibly to correct a grave injustice. A critical part of King's argument is his definition of "just" and "unjust" laws.

Supporters of segregation in Birmingham had obtained a court order forbidding further protests, and the eight white clergymen urged King and his supporters to obey the courts. Our society generally assumes that laws, and the courts that enforce them, should be obeyed. King, however, argues that there are two categories of laws and that citizens must treat one category differently from the other. Morally just laws, King argues, should be obeyed, but unjust ones should not. But how are just laws to be distinguished from unjust ones? By distinguishing two different kinds of laws, King creates a rationale for obeying some laws and disobeying others.

His argument rests on the clear moral and legal criteria he uses to define just and unjust laws. Without these criteria, people could simply disobey any law they chose, which is what King's detractors accused him of advocating. King had to show that he was in fact acting on principle, and that he and his supporters wanted to establish justice, not cause chaos. First, King states that a "just law is a man-made code that squares with the moral law of God" and "an unjust law is a code that is out of harmony with the moral law." Second, King notes that "any law that degrades human personality is unjust." Finally, King states that just laws are ones that hold for everyone because they were arrived at through democratic processes, while unjust laws are those that are inflicted on a minority that, because they were not permitted to vote, had no participation in approving them.

The definitions that King offers promote his goals. He maintains in his famous "Letter" that people have a moral responsibility to obey just laws, and, by the same logic, "a moral responsibility to disobey unjust laws." He then completes his definitional argument by show-ing how segregation laws fit the definition of "unjust" that he has laid out. Once his audience accepts his placement of segregation laws in the "unjust" category, they must also accept that King and his fellow protestors were right to break those laws. He answers to his critics effectively through a powerful definition argument.

Note how King's three definitions all fit the structure described at the beginning of this chapter:

> **Something is (or is not) a _____ because it has (does not have)**
> **features A,B, and C.**

Building an extended definition argument like King's is a two-step process. First, you have to establish the criteria for the categories you wish to define. In King's letter, consistency with moral law and uplifting of the human spirit are set forth as criteria for a just law. King provides arguments from St. Thomas Aquinas, a religious authority likely to carry significant weight with Birmingham clergymen and others who will read the letter.

Second, you must convince your audience that the particular case in question meets or doesn't meet the criteria. King cannot simply state that segregation laws are unjust; he must provide evidence showing how they fail to meet the criteria for a just law. Specifically, he notes the segregation "gives the segregator a false sense of superiority and the segregated a false sense of inferiority." These false senses of self are a distortion or degradation of the human personality.

Sometimes definition arguments have to argue for the relevance and suitability of the criteria. King, in fact, spent a great deal of his letter laying out and defending his criteria for just and unjust laws. While he addressed his letter to clergymen, he knew that it would find a wider audience. Therefore, he did not rely solely on criteria linked to moral law, or to Thomas Aquinas, or the "law of God." People who were not especially religious might not be convinced by those parts of his argument. So, King presents two additional criteria for just laws that he knows will appeal to those who value the democratic process.

When you build a definition argument, often you must put much effort into identifying and explaining your criteria. You must convince your readers that your criteria are the best ones for what you are defining and that they apply to the case you are arguing.

---

### KING'S EXTENDED DEFINITION ARGUMENT

After establishing criteria for two kinds of laws, *just* and *unjust*, King argues that citizens must respond differently to laws that are unjust, by disobeying them. He then shows how the special case of *segregation laws* meets the criteria for unjust laws. If readers accept his argument, they will agree that segregation laws belong in the category of unjust laws, and therefore must be disobeyed.

| Criteria for Just Laws | Criteria for Unjust Laws | Segregation Laws |
|---|---|---|
| Consistent with moral law | Not consistent with moral law | ✓ |
| Uplift human personality | Damage human personality | ✓ |
| Must be obeyed by all people | Must be obeyed by some people, but not others | ✓ |
| Made by democratically elected representatives | Not made by democratically elected representatives | ✓ |
| Appropriate response to just laws: All citizens should obey them. | Appropriate response to unjust laws: All citizens should disobey them. | |

## SAMPLE STUDENT DEFINITION ARGUMENT

Conley 1

Patrice Conley

Professor Douglas

English 101

28 April 2012

Flagrant Foul: The NCAA's Definition of Student
Athletes as Amateurs

Every year, thousands of student athletes across
America sign the National Collegiate Athletic Association's
Form 08-3a, the "Student-Athlete" form, waiving their
right to receive payment for the use of their name and
image (McCann). The form defines student athletes as
amateurs, who cannot receive payment for playing their
sports. While their schools and coaches may make millions
of dollars in salaries and endorsement deals and are the
highest-paid public employees in many states, student
athletes can never earn a single penny from their college
athletic careers. Former Nike executive Sonny Vacarro
sums it up: "Everybody has a right except for the player.
The player has no rights" ("Money").

Make no mistake: college athletics are big business.
The most visible college sports—big-time men's football
and basketball—generate staggering sums of money.
For example, the twelve universities in the Southeastern
Conference receive $205 million each year from CBS
and ESPN for the right to broadcast its football games
(Smith and Ourand). Even more money comes in from
video games, clothing, and similar licenses. In 2010, the
*New York Times* reported, "the NCAA's licensing deals
are estimated at more than $4 billion" per year (Thamel).

Conley 2

While the staggering executive pay at big corporations has brought public outrage, coaches' salaries are even more outlandish. Kentucky basketball coach, John Calipari, is paid over $4 million a year for a basketball program that makes about $35-40 million a year, more than 10% of the entire revenue. Tom Van Riper observes that no corporate CEO commands this large a share of the profits. He observes that if Steve Ballmer, the CEO at Microsoft, had Calipari's deal, Ballmer would make over $6 billion a year.

How can colleges allow advertisers, arena operators, concession owners, athletic gear manufacturers, retailers, game companies, and media moguls, along with coaches and university officials, to make millions and pay the stars of the show nothing? The answer is that colleges define athletes as amateurs. Not only are student athletes not paid for playing their sport, they cannot receive gifts and are not allowed to endorse products, which may be a violation of their right to free speech. The NCAA, an organization of colleges and schools, forces student athletes to sign away their rights because, it says, it is protecting the students. If student athletes could accept money from anyone, the NCAA argues, they might be exploited, cheated, or even bribed. Taking money out of the equation is supposed to let students focus on academics and preserve the amateur status of college sports.

The definition of amateur arose in the nineteenth century in Britain, when team sports became popular. Middle-class and upper-class students in college had ample time to play their sports while working-class athletes had only a half-day off (no sports were played on Sundays in

Conley 3

that era). Teams began to pay top working-class sportsmen for the time they had to take off from work. Middle-class and upper-class sportsmen didn't want to play against the working-class teams, so they made the distinction between amateurs and professionals. The definition of amateur crossed the Atlantic to the United States, where college sports became popular in the 1880s. But it was not long until the hypocrisy of amateurism undermined the ideal. Top football programs like Yale had slush funds to pay athletes, and others used ringers—players who weren't students—and even players from other schools (Zimbalist 7).

The Olympic Games maintained the amateur-professional distinction until 1988, but it was long evident that Communist bloc nations were paying athletes to train full-time and Western nations were paying athletes through endorsement contracts. The only Olympic sport that now requires amateur status is boxing. The college sports empire in the United States run by the NCAA is the last bastion of amateurism for sports that draw audiences large enough to be televised.

Colleges might be able to defend the policy of amateurism if they extended this definition to all students. A fair policy is one that treats all students the same. A fair policy doesn't result in some students getting paid for professional work, while other students do not. Consider the students in the Butler School of Music at the University of Texas at Austin, for example. Many student musicians perform at the professional level. Does the school prevent them from earning money for their musical performances? No. In fact, the school runs a referral service that connects its students with people and businesses who want to hire

Conley 4

professional musicians. The university even advises its students on how to negotiate a contract and get paid for their performance ("Welcome").

Likewise, why are student actors and actresses allowed to earn money from their work and images, while student athletes are not? Think about actress Emma Watson, who enrolled at Brown University in Rhode Island. Can you imagine the university officials at Brown telling Watson that she would have to make the next two Harry Potter films for free, instead of for the $5 million she has been offered? Can you imagine Brown University telling Watson that all the revenue from Harry Potter merchandise bearing her likeness would have to be paid directly to the university, for the rest of her life? They would if Watson were an athlete instead of an actress.

In fact, compared to musicians and actors, student athletes have an even greater need to earn money while they are still in college. Athletes' professional careers are likely to be much shorter than musicians' or actors'. College may be the only time some athletes have the opportunity to capitalize on their success. (Indeed, rather than focusing student athletes on their academic careers, the NCAA policy sometimes forces students to leave college early, so they can earn a living before their peak playing years are over.) Student athletes often leave school with permanent injuries and no medical insurance or job prospects, whereas student musicians and actors rarely suffer career-ending injuries on the job.

Student athletes are prevented from profiting from their name and image. The NCAA says this rule preserves their standing as amateurs and protects them from the

Conley 5

celebrity and media frenzy surrounding professional sports stars. Search for a "Tim Tebow Jersey" online, and you can buy officially branded Florida Gators shirts, ranging in price from $34.99 to $349.99 (autographed by Tebow). The NCAA, the University of Florida, Nike, and the other parties involved in the production and sale of these products get around the problem of using an amateur's name by using his team number instead. Tebow's name doesn't appear anywhere on the jerseys—just his number, fifteen. Yet all these jerseys are identified as "Official Tim Tebow Gators merchandise," and they are certainly bought by fans of Tebow rather than people who just happen to like the number fifteen. Nobody is saying how much money these jerseys have made for Nike, or for the University of Florida. What we do know for sure is the amount Tim Tebow has made off the jerseys: nothing.

Defenders of the current system argue that student athletes on scholarships are paid with free tuition, free room and board, free books, and tutoring help. The total package can be the equivalent of $120,000 over four years. For those student athletes who are motivated to take advantage of the opportunity, the lifetime benefits can be enormous. Unfortunately, too few student athletes do take advantage of the opportunity. Seldom does a major college football and men's basketball program have a graduation rate at or close to the overall student body. A study by the University of North Carolina's College Sports Research Institute released in 2010 accuses the NCAA of playing fast and loose with graduation rates by counting part-time students in statistics for the general student body, which makes graduation rates for athletes look better in a

Conley 6

comparison. Student athletes must be full-time students; thus they should be compared to other full-time students. The North Carolina Institute reports that 54.8% of major college (Football Bowl Subdivision) football players at 117 schools graduated within six years, compared to 73.7% of other full-time students. The gap between basketball players was even greater, with 44.6% of athletes graduating compared to 75.7% of the general student body (Zaiger). For the handful of talented athletes who can play in the National Football League or the National Basketball Association, college sports provide training for their future lucrative, although short-lived, profession. But as the NCAA itself points out in its ads, the great majority of student athletes "go pro in something other than sports." For the 55% of college basketball players who fail to graduate, the supposed $120,000 package is an air ball.

    The NCAA would be wise to return to the older definition of amateur, which comes from Latin through old French, meaning "lover of." It doesn't necessarily have to have anything to do with money. Whether it's a jazz performer or dancer or an athlete, an amateur ought to be considered someone in love with an activity—someone who cares deeply about the activity, studies the activity in depth, and practices in order to be highly proficient. NBA players, Olympians, college athletes, high school players, and even bird watchers, star gazers, and open-source programmers: they're all amateurs. If they are lucky enough to be paid, so be it.

Conley 7

Works Cited

McCann, Michael. "NCAA Faces Unspecified Damages, Changes in Latest Anti-Trust Case." *SI.com.* Time, Inc., 21 July 2009. Web. 6 Apr. 2012.

"Money and March Madness." *Frontline.* PBS, 29 Mar. 2011. Web. 3 Apr. 2012.

National Collegiate Athletic Association. Advertisement. *NCAA.org.* NCAA, 13 Mar. 2007. Web. 3 Apr. 2012.

Smith, Michael, and John Ourand. "ESPN Pays $2.25B for SEC Rights." *SportsBusiness Journal.* Smith and Street, 25 Aug. 2008. Web. 1 Apr. 2012.

Thamel, Pete. "N.C.A.A. Fails to Stop Licensing Lawsuit." *New York Times.* New York Times, 8 Feb. 2010. Web. 1 Apr. 2012.

Van Riper, Thomas. "The Highest-Paid College Basketball Coaches." *Forbes.com.* Forbes, 8 Mar. 2010. Web. 6 Apr. 2012.

"Welcome to the Music Referral Service." *Butler School of Music.* Univ. of Texas at Austin, n.d. Web. 5 Apr. 2012.

Zaiger, Alan Scher. "Study: NCAA Graduation Rate Comparisons Flawed." *ABC News.* ABC News, 20 Apr. 2010. Web. 1 Apr. 2012.

Zimbalist, Andrew. *Unpaid Professionals: Commercialism and Conflict in Big-Time College Sports.* Princeton UP, 2001. Print.

## WRITE A DEFINITION ARGUMENT

### Step 1 Make a claim
Make a definitional claim on a controversial issue that focuses on a key term.

***Template***
> _____ is (or is not) a _____ because it has (or does not have) features A, B, and C (or more).

***Examples***
- Hate speech (or pornography, literature, films, and so on) is (or is not) free speech protected by the First Amendment because it has (or does not have) these features.
- Hunting (or using animals for cosmetics testing, keeping animals in zoos, wearing furs, and so on) is (or is not) cruelty to animals because it has (or does not have) these features.

### Step 2 Think about what's at stake
- Does nearly everyone agree with you? If so, then your claim probably isn't interesting or important. If you can think of people who disagree, then something is at stake.
- Who argues the opposite of your claim?
- Why or how do they benefit from a different definition?

### Step 3 List the criteria
- Which criteria are necessary for _____ to be a _____?
- Which are not necessary?
- Which are the most important?
- Does your case in point meet all the criteria?

### Step 4 Analyze your potential readers
- Who are your readers?
- How does the definitional claim you are making affect them?
- How familiar are they with the issue, concept, or controversy that you're writing about?

- What are they likely to know and not know?
- Which criteria are they most likely to accept with little explanation, and which will they disagree with?

## Step 5 Write a draft

### Introduction
- Set out the issue, concept, or controversy.
- Give the background that your intended readers need.

### Body
- Set out your criteria and argue for the appropriateness of the criteria.
- Determine whether the criteria apply to the case in point.
- Anticipate where readers might question either your criteria or how they apply to your subject.
- Address opposing viewpoints by acknowledging how their definitions differ and by showing why your definition is better.

### Conclusion
- Do more than simply summarize. You can, for example, go into more detail about what is at stake or the implications of your definition.

## Step 6 Revise, edit, proofread
- For detailed instructions.
- For a checklist to use to evaluate your draft

---

## CAUSAL ARGUMENTS

Why did the driver who passed you on a blind curve risk his life to get one car ahead at the next traffic light? Why is it hard to recognize people you know when you run into them unexpectedly in an unfamiliar setting? Why does your mother or father spend an extra hour, plus the extra gas, driving to a supermarket across town just to save a few pennies on one or two items on sale? Why do some of your friends keep going to horror films when they can hardly sit through them and have nightmares afterward?

Life is full of big and little mysteries, and people spend a lot of time speculating about the causes. Most of the time, however, they don't take the time to analyze in depth what causes a controversial trend, event, or phenomenon. But in college and in the workplace, you likely will have to write causal arguments that require in-depth analysis. In a professional career you will have to make many detailed causal analyses: Why did a retail business fail when it seemed to have an ideal location? What causes cost overruns in the development of a new product? What causes people in some circumstances to prefer public transportation over driving?

## Understand How Causal Arguments Work

Causal arguments take three basic forms.

*1. One cause leads to one or more effects.*

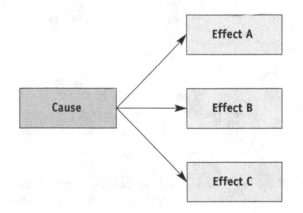

*Example*

The **invention of the telegraph** led to the *commodities market, the establishment of standard time zones,* and *news reporting as we know it today.*

*2. One effect has several causes.*

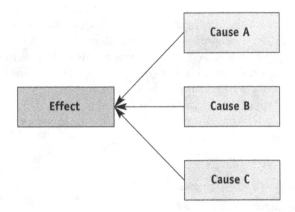

*Example*

**Hurricanes are becoming more financially destructive** to the United States because of *the greater intensity of recent storms, an increase in the commercial and residential development of coastal areas,* and *a reluctance to enforce certain construction standards in coastal residential areas.*

*3. Something causes something else to happen, which in turn causes something else to happen.*

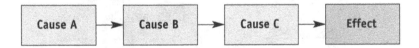

*Example*

*Making the HPV vaccination mandatory for adolescent girls* will make *unprotected sex seem safer, leading to greater promiscuity,* and **resulting in more teenage pregnancies.**

## Find Causes

The causal claim is at the center of a causal argument. Therefore, to get started on a causal argument, you need to propose one or more causes. The big problem with causal arguments is that any topic worth writing about is likely to be complex, making identifying causes difficult. The philosopher John Stuart Mill recognized this problem long ago and devised four methods for finding causes:

- **The Common Factor Method.** Sometimes causes can be identified because two or more similar events share a common factor. The common factor may be the cause. For example, if two people in two different states both develop a rare disease, and both of them recently traveled to Madagascar, they were probably exposed to the illness while there.

- **The Single Difference Method.** Causes can often be identified when two situations or events have different outcomes. If there is a single difference in the two scenarios, that difference may be the cause. At the 1998 Winter Olympics in Nagano, Japan, the speed skating team from the Netherlands introduced a technological innovation to the sport—clap skates, which improve skaters' performance by keeping the skate blade in contact with the ice longer. Racing against the best skaters in the world, the Dutch on their clap skates won eleven of thirty medals, five of which were gold. By the 2002 Winter Olympics, all speed skaters had switched over to the new skates, and the medal count was much more evenly distributed. That year the United States, the Netherlands, and Germany each won three gold medals, and a total of eight medals apiece. Clap skates were the most likely cause of the Netherlands' dominance four years earlier.

- **Concomitant Variation.** Some causes are discovered by observing a shared pattern of variation in a possible cause and possible effect. For example, scientists noticed that peaks in the eleven-year sunspot cycle have predictable effects on high-frequency radio transmission on the earth.

- **Process of Elimination.** Many possible causes can be proposed for most trends and events. If you are a careful investigator, you have to consider all causes that you can think of and eliminate the ones that cannot be causes.

To understand how these methods might work for you, consider this example. Suppose you want to research the causes of the increase in legalized lotteries in the United States. You might discover that lotteries go back to colonial times. Lotteries were common before and after the American Revolution, but they eventually ran into trouble because they were run by private companies that failed to pay the winners. After 1840, laws against lotteries were passed, but they came back in the South after the Civil War. The defeated states of the Confederacy needed money to rebuild the bridges, buildings, and schools that were destroyed in the Civil War, and they turned to selling lottery tickets throughout the nation (ironically, the tickets were very popular in the North). Once again, the lotteries were run by private companies, and scandals eventually led to their being banned.

In 1964, the voters in New Hampshire approved a lottery as a means of funding education—in preference to an income tax or a sales tax. Soon other northeastern states followed this lead and established lotteries with the reasoning that if people were going to gamble, the money should remain at home. During the 1980s, other states approved not only lotteries but also other forms of state-run gambling such as keno and video poker. By 1993, only Hawaii and Utah had no legalized gambling of any kind.

If you are analyzing the causes of the spread of legalized gambling, you might use the **common factor method** to investigate what current lotteries have in common with earlier lotteries. That factor is easy to identify: it's economic. The early colonies and later the states have turned to lotteries again and again as a way of raising money that avoids unpopular tax increases. But why have lotteries spread so quickly and seemingly become so permanent since 1964, when before that, they were used only sporadically and were banned eventually? The **single difference method** points us to the major difference between the lotteries of today and those of previous eras: Lotteries in the past were run by private companies, and inevitably someone took off with the money instead of paying it out. Today's lotteries are owned and operated by state agencies or contracted under state control, and while they are not immune to scandals, they are much more closely monitored than lotteries were in the past.

Many effects don't have causes as obvious as the spread of legalized gambling. The **process of elimination method** can be a useful tool when several possible causes are involved. Perhaps you have had the experience of your television not turning on. To identify the problem, if you checked first to see if it was plugged in, then plugged it into another socket to make sure the socket was on, and then checked the surge suppressor to see if it worked, you used a process of elimination to diagnose the cause of the problem. Major advances in science and medicine have resulted from the process of elimination. For centuries, soldiers on long campaigns and sailors on long sea voyages suffered horrible deaths from scurvy until 1747, when James Lind demonstrated that scurvy could be treated and prevented with a diet that includes lemons and limes. Nevertheless, people proposed various causes for scurvy including poor hygiene, lack of exercise, and tainted canned food. Finally, in 1932, the cause of scurvy was proven to be a vitamin C deficiency.

## Build a Causal Argument

A pitfall common in causal arguments using statistics is mistaking correlation for causation. For example, the FBI reported that in 1995 criminal victimization rates in the United States dropped 13 percent for personal crimes and 12.4 percent for property crimes—the largest decreases ever. During that same year, the nation's prison and jail populations reached a record high of 1,085,000 and 507,000 inmates, respectively. The easy inference is that putting more people behind bars lowers the crime rate, but there are plenty of examples to the contrary. The drop in crime rates in the 1990s remains quite difficult to explain.

Others have argued that the decline in SAT verbal scores during the late 1960s and 1970s reflected a decline in literacy skills caused by an increase in television viewing. But the fact that the number of people who took the SAT during the 1970s greatly increased suggests that the major cause was a great expansion in the population who wanted to go to college.

## SAMPLE STUDENT CAUSAL ARGUMENT

Tansal 1

Armadi Tansal
Professor Stewart
English 115
28 October 2011

Modern Warfare: Video Games' Link to<br>Real-World Violence

"John" is a nineteen-year-old college student who gets decent grades. He comes from a typical upper-middle-class family and plans to get his MBA after he graduates. John is also my friend, which is why I'm not using his real name.

John has been playing moderately violent video games since he was nine years old. I started playing video and console games around that age too, and I played a lot in junior high, but John plays more than anyone I know. John says that over the past year he has played video games at least four hours every day, and "sometimes all day and night on the weekends." I have personally witnessed John play *Call of Duty: Modern Warfare 2* for six hours straight, with breaks only to use the bathroom or eat something.

I've never seen John act violently, and he's never been in trouble with the law. But new research on violent video games suggests that John's gaming habit puts him at risk for violent or aggressive behavior. Dr. Craig Anderson, a psychologist at the University of Iowa, says "the active role required by video games...may make violent video games even more hazardous than violent television or cinema" (Anderson). When people like John play these games, they get used to being rewarded for violent behavior. For example, in the multiplayer version of *Modern Warfare 2,* if

Tansal 2

the player gets a five-kill streak, he can call in a Predator missile strike. If you kill twenty-five people in a row, you can call in a tactical nuclear strike. Missile strikes help you advance toward the mission goals more quickly, so the more people you kill, the faster you'll win.

Along with *Modern Warfare 2,* John plays games like *Left 4 Dead, Halo,* and *Grand Theft Auto.* All these games are rated M for Mature, which according to the Entertainment Software Rating Board means they "may contain intense violence, blood and gore, sexual content and/ or strong language." Some M-rated games, like *Grand Theft Auto,* feature random violence, where players can run amok in a city, beat up and kill people, and smash stuff for no reason. In others, like *Modern Warfare 2,* the violence takes place in the context of military action. To do well in all of these games, you have to commit acts of violence. But does acting violently in games make you more violent in real life?

Anderson says studies show that "violent video games are significantly associated with: increased aggressive behavior, thoughts, and affect [feelings]; increased physio-logical arousal; and decreased prosocial (helping) behavior" (Anderson). He also claims that "high levels of violent video game exposure have been linked to delinquency, fighting at school and during free play periods, and violent criminal behavior (e.g., self-reported assault, robbery)."

Being "associated with" and "linked to" violent behavior doesn't necessarily mean video games cause such behavior. Many people have argued that the links Anderson sees are coincidental, or that any effects video games might have on behavior are so slight that we shouldn't worry about them. Christopher Ferguson and John Kilburn, professors of criminal justice at Texas A&M International University, feel that the existing research does not support Anderson's claims. In a report published in the *Journal of Pediatrics,* they point out that in past studies, "the closer aggression measures got to actual violent behavior, the weaker the effects seen."

From what I can tell, John doesn't have any more violent thoughts and feelings than most men his age. When I asked him if he thought the games had made him more violent or aggressive in real life, he said, "I'm actually less violent now. When we were kids we used to play 'war' with fake guns and sticks, chasing each other around the neighborhood and fighting commando-style. We didn't really fight but sometimes kids got banged up. No one ever gets hurt playing a video game."

Anderson admits that "a healthy, normal, nonviolent child or adolescent who has no other risk factors for high aggression or violence is not going to become a school shooter simply because they play five hours or 10 hours a week of these violent video games" (qtd. in St. George). But just because violent video games don't turn all players into mass murderers, that doesn't mean they have no effect on a player's behavior and personality. For example, my friend John doesn't get into fights or rob people, but he doesn't display a lot of prosocial "helping" behaviors either. He spends most of his free time gaming, so he doesn't get out of his apartment much. Also, the friends he does have mostly play video games with him.

Even though the games restrict his interactions with other humans and condition him to behave violently

Tansal 4

onscreen, John is probably not at high risk of becoming
violent in real life. But according to researchers, this low
risk of becoming violent is because none of the dozens
of other risk factors associated with violent behavior are
present in his life (Anderson et al. 160). If John were a high
school dropout, came from a broken home, or abused alcohol and other drugs, his game playing might be more likely
to contribute to violent behavior.

Anderson contends that violent video games are a
"causal risk factor" for violence and aggression—not that
they alone cause violent aggression. In other words, the
games are a small piece of a much larger problem. People
like my friend John are not likely to become violent because of the video games they play. But Anderson's research indicates that some people do. Although there is no
simple way to tell who those people are, we should include
video games as a possible risk factor when we think about
who is likely to become violent.

Even if the risk contributed by violent video games
is slight for each individual, the total impact of the games
on violence in society could be huge. *Call of Duty: Modern
Warfare 2* is the third-best-selling video game in the United
States (Orry). Its creator, Activision Blizzard, had $1.3 billion
in sales in the just first three months of 2010 (Pham). Millions
of people play this game and games like it, and they aren't all
as well-adjusted as John. If video games contribute to violent
tendencies in only a small fraction of players, they could still
have a terrible impact.

Tansal 5

Works Cited

Anderson, Craig. "Violent Video Games: Myths, Facts,
    and Unanswered Questions." *Psychological Science
    Agenda* 16.5 (2003): n. pag. Web. 6 Oct. 2011.

Anderson, Craig, et al. "Violent Video Game Effects
    on Aggression, Empathy, and Prosocial Behavior
    in Eastern and Western Countries." *Psychological
    Bulletin* 136.2 (2010): 151–73. Print.

Entertainment Software Rating Board. *Game Ratings
    and Descriptor Guide.* Entertainment Software
    Association, n.d. Web. 7 Oct. 2011.

Ferguson, Christopher J., and John Kilburn. "The Public
    Health Risks of Media Violence: A Meta-Analytic
    Review." *Journal of Pediatrics* 154.5 (2009): 759–63.
    Print.

John (pseudonym). Personal interview. 4 Oct. 2011.

Orry, James. "Modern Warfare 2 the 3rd Best-Selling
    Game in the US." *Videogamer.com.* Pro-G Media
    Ltd., 12 Mar. 2010. Web. 6 Oct. 2011.

Pham, Alex. "Call of Duty: Modern Warfare 2 Propels
    Revenue, Profit for Activision Blizzard." *Los Angeles
    Times.* Los Angeles Times, 6 May 2010. Web. 7 Oct.
    2011.

St. George, Donna. "Study Links Violent Video Games,
    Hostility." *Washington Post.* Washington Post, 3 Nov.
    2008. Web. 5 Oct. 2011.

## WRITE A CAUSAL ARGUMENT

### Step 1 Make a claim

Make a causal claim on a controversial trend, event, or phenomenon.

***Template***

SOMETHING does (or does not) cause SOMETHING ELSE.
-or-
SOMETHING causes SOMETHING ELSE, which, in turn, causes SOMETHING ELSE.

***Examples***

- One-parent families (or television violence, bad diet, and so on) are (or are not) the cause of emotional and behavioral problems in children.

- Firearms control laws (or right-to-carry-handgun laws) reduce (or increase) violent crimes.

- Putting grade school children into competitive sports teaches them how to succeed in later life (or puts undue emphasis on winning and teaches many who are slower to mature to have a negative self-image).

### Step 2 What's at stake in your claim

- If the cause is obvious to everyone, then it probably isn't worth writing about.

### Step 3 Think of possible causes

- Which are the immediate causes?
- Which are the background causes?
- Which are the hidden causes?

### Step 4 Analyze your potential readers

- Who are your readers?
- How familiar are they with the trend, event, or phenomenon that you're writing about?
- What are they likely to know and not know?
- How likely are they to accept your causal explanation?
- What alternative explanation might they argue for?

### Step 5 Write a draft

*Introduction*
- Describe the controversial trend, event, or phenomenon.
- Give the background that your intended readers need.

*Body*
- Explain the circumstances of a trend, event, or phenomenon that are unfamiliar to your readers. Remember that providing facts is not the same thing as establishing causes, although facts can help to support your causal analysis.
- Set out the causes that have been offered and reject them one by one. Then you can present the cause that you think is most important.
- Treat a series of causes one by one, analyzing the importance of each.

*Conclusion*
- Do more than simply summarize. Consider describing additional effects beyond those that have been noted previously.

### Step 6 Revise, edit, proofread
- For detailed instructions.
- For a checklist to use to evaluate your draft.

## EVALUATION ARGUMENTS

People make evaluations all the time. Newspapers and magazines have picked up on this love of evaluation by running "best of" polls. They ask their readers to vote on the best Chinese restaurant, the best pizza, the best local band, the best coffeehouse, the best dance club, the best neighborhood park, the best swimming hole, the best bike ride (scenic or challenging), the best volleyball court, the best place to get married, and so on. If you ask one of your friends who voted in a "best" poll why she picked a particular restaurant as the best of its kind, she might respond by saying simply, "I like it." But if you ask her why she likes it, she might start offering good reasons such as these: the food is good, the service prompt, the prices fair, and the atmosphere comfortable. It's really not a mystery why these polls are often quite predictable or why the same restaurants tend to win year after year. Many people think that evaluations are matters of personal taste, but when we begin probing the reasons, we often discover that different people use similar criteria to make evaluations.

The key to convincing other people that your judgment is sound is establishing the criteria you will use to make your evaluation. Sometimes it will be necessary to argue for the validity of the criteria that you think your readers should consider. If your readers accept your criteria, it's likely they will agree with your conclusions.

## Understand How Evaluation Arguments Work

Evaluation arguments set out criteria and then judge something to be good or bad or best or worst according to those criteria.

Something is a good (bad, the best, the worst) _____ if measured by certain criteria (practicality, aesthetics, ethics).

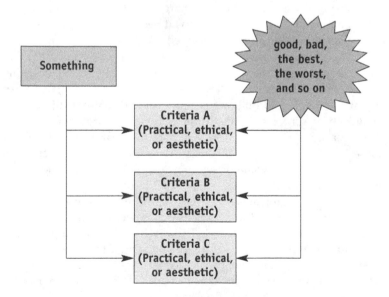

*Example*

**Google Maps is the best mapping program** because *it is easy to use, it is accurate*, and *it provides entertaining and educational features such as Google Earth.*

## Recognize Kinds of Evaluations

Arguments of evaluation are structured much like arguments of definition. Recall that the criteria in arguments of definition are set out in *because* clauses: SOMETHING is a _____ because it has these criteria. The key move in writing most evaluative arguments is first deciding what kind of criteria to use.

Imagine that the oldest commercial building in your city is about to be torn down. Your goal is to get the old store converted to a museum by making a proposal argument. First you will need to make an evaluative argument that will form the basis of your proposal. You might argue that a downtown museum would be much better than more office space because it would draw more visitors. You might argue that the stonework in the building is of excellent quality and deserves preservation. Or you might argue that it is only fair that the oldest commercial building be preserved because the oldest house and other historic buildings have been saved.

Each of these arguments uses different criteria. An argument that a museum is better than an office building because it would bring more visitors to the downtown area is based on **practical criteria**. An argument that the old building is beautiful and that beautiful things should be preserved uses **aesthetic criteria**. An argument that the oldest commercial building deserves the same treatment as the oldest house is based on fairness, a concept that relies on **ethical criteria**. The debate over the value of sending people versus sending robots into space employs all these criteria but with different emphases. Both those who favor and those who oppose human space travel make practical arguments that much scientific knowledge and many other benefits result from space travel. Those who favor sending humans use aesthetic arguments: space travel is essential to the way we understand ourselves as humans and Americans. Those who oppose sending humans question the ethics of spending so much money for manned space vehicles when there are pressing needs at home, and they point out that robots can be used for a fraction of the cost.

## Build an Evaluation Argument

Most people have a lot of practice making consumer evaluations, and when they have enough time to do their homework, they usually make an informed decision. Sometimes, criteria for evaluations are not so obvious, however, and evaluations are much more difficult to make. Sometimes one set of criteria favors one choice, while another set of criteria favors another. You might have encountered this problem when you chose a college. If you were able to leave home to go to school, you had a potential choice of over 1600 accredited colleges and universities. Until thirty years ago, there wasn't much information about choosing a college other than what colleges said about themselves. You could find out the price of tuition and what courses were offered, but it was hard to compare one college with another.

In 1983, the magazine *U.S. News & World Report* began ranking U.S. colleges and universities from a consumer's perspective. These rankings have remained highly controversial ever since. Many college officials have attacked the criteria that *U.S. News* uses to make its evaluations, calling for a national boycott of the *U.S. News* rankings (without much success). *U.S. News* replies in its defense that colleges and universities themselves do a lot of ranking. Schools rank students for admissions, using SAT or ACT scores, high school GPA, high school class rank, quality of high school, and other factors, and then grade the students and rank them against each other when they are enrolled in college. Furthermore, schools also evaluate faculty members and take great interest in the national ranking of their departments. They care very much about where they stand in relation to each other. Why, then, *U.S. News* argues, shouldn't people be able to evaluate colleges and universities, since colleges and universities are so much in the business of evaluating people?

Arguing for the right to evaluate colleges and universities is one thing; actually doing comprehensive and reliable evaluations is quite another. *U.S. News* uses a formula in which about 25 percent of a school's ranking is based on a survey of reputation in which the president, provost, and dean of admissions at each college rate the quality of schools in the same category, and the remaining 75 percent is based on statistical criteria of quality. These statistical criteria fall into six major categories: retention of students, faculty resources, student selectivity, financial resources, alumni giving, and graduation rate performance—the difference between the number of students who are expected to graduate and the number that actually do. These major categories are made up of factors that are weighted according to their importance. For example, the faculty resources category is determined by the size of classes (the proportion of classes with fewer than twenty students to classes with fifty or more students), the average faculty pay weighted by the cost of living in different regions of the country, the percentage of professors with the highest degree in their field, the overall student-faculty ratio, and the percentage of faculty who are full-time.

Those who have challenged the *U.S. News* rankings argue that the magazine should use different criteria or weight the criteria differently. *U.S. News* explains its ranking system on its Web site (colleges. usnews.rankingsandreviews.com/best-colleges). If you are curious about where your school ranks, take a look.

## WRITE AN EVALUATION ARGUMENT

### Step 1 Make a claim
Make an evaluative claim based on specific criteria.

#### Template
SOMETHING is good (bad, the best, the worst) if measured by certain criteria (practicality, aesthetics, ethics).

#### Examples
- A book or movie review.
- A defense of a particular kind of music or art.
- An evaluation of a controversial aspect of sports (e.g., the current system of determining who is champion in Division I college football by a system of bowls and polls) or a sports event (e.g., this year's WNBA playoffs) or a team.

- An evaluation of the effectiveness of an educational program (such as your high school honors program or your college's core curriculum requirement) or some other aspect of your campus.
- An evaluation of the effectiveness of a social policy or law such as legislating 21 as the legal drinking age, current gun control laws, or environmental regulation.

## Step 2 Think about what's at stake

- Does nearly everyone agree with you? If so, then your claim probably isn't interesting or important. If you can think of people who disagree, then something is at stake.
- Who argues the opposite of your claim?
- Why do they make a different evaluation?

## Step 3 List the criteria

- Which criteria make something either good or bad?
- Which are the most important?
- Which criteria are fairly obvious, and which will you have to argue for?

## Step 4 Analyze your potential readers

- Who are your readers?
- How familiar are they with what you are evaluating?
- What are they likely to know and not know?
- Which criteria are they most likely to accept with little explanation, and which will they disagree with?

## Step 5 Write a draft

### *Introduction*
- Introduce the person, group, institution, event, or object that you are going to evaluate. You might want to announce your stance at this point or wait until the concluding section.
- Give the background that your intended readers need.

### *Body*
- Describe each criterion and then analyze how well what you are evaluating meets that criterion.
- If you are making an evaluation according to the effects someone or something produces, describe each effect in detail.

- Anticipate where readers might question either your criteria or how they apply to your subject.
- Address opposing viewpoints by acknowledging how their evaluations might differ and by showing why your evaluation is better.

### Conclusion
- If you have not yet announced your stance, conclude that, on the basis of the criteria you set out or the effects you have analyzed, something is good (bad, the best, the worst).
- If you have made your stance clear from the beginning, end with a compelling example or analogy.

### Step 6 Revise, edit, proofread
- For detailed instructions.
- For a checklist to use to evaluate your draft.

---

## REBUTTAL ARGUMENTS

When you hear the word *rebuttal*, you might think of a debate team or the part of a trial when the attorney for the defense answers the plaintiff's accusations. Although rebuttal has those definitions, a rebuttal argument can be thought of in much larger terms. Indeed, much of what people know about the world today is the result of centuries of arguments of rebuttal.

### Understand How Rebuttal Arguments Work

When you rebut the argument of someone else, you can do one of two things. You can refute the argument, or you can counterargue. In the first case, **refutation**, you emphasize the shortcomings of the argument that you wish to undermine without really making a positive case of your own. In the second case, **counterargument**, you emphasize not the shortcomings of the argument that you are rebutting but the strengths of the position you wish to support. Often there is considerable overlap between refutation and counterargument, and often both are present in a rebuttal.

**Refutation: The opposing argument has serious shortcomings that undermine the claim.**

*Example*

*The great white shark gained a reputation as a "man eater"* from the 1975 movie *Jaws*, but in fact **attacks on humans are rare** and **most bites have been "test bites,"** which is a common shark behavior with unfamiliar objects.

**Counterarguments: The opposing argument has some merit, but my argument is superior.**

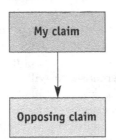

*Example*

*Those who argue for tariffs on goods from China claim that tariffs will protect American manufacturing jobs,* but **tariffs would increase prices on clothing, furniture, toys, and other consumer goods for everyone and would cause the loss of retailing jobs.**

## Recognize Kinds of Rebuttal Arguments

*Refutation*

There are two primary strategies for refutation arguments. First, you can challenge the assumptions on which a claim is based. Until about five hundred years ago, people believed that the sky, and everything in it, moved, while the Earth remained still. In the early sixteenth century, the Polish astronomer Nicolaus Copernicus challenged this assumption and argued that the Earth and other planets circle around the Sun.

Second, you can question the evidence supporting the claim. Sometimes the evidence presented is simply wrong. Sometimes the evidence is incomplete or unrepresentative, and sometimes counterevidence can be found. Often when you refute an argument, you make the case that your opponent has been guilty of one or more fallacies of arguments (see pages 143–145). A lively debate has developed in recent years over the impacts of *Web 2.0*, a term that has come to stand for a Web-based social phenomenon characterized by open communication and a decentralization of authority. Various new genres and social media are associated with Web 2.0, including wikis, blogs, YouTube, Facebook, eBay, craigslist, Twitter—anything that encourages participation and can exist only on the Internet.

From the beginning the Internet inspired grand visions of a better society through access to information and instant communication. The initial enthusiasm declined after the Web turned into a giant home-shopping network and the potential for dialogue among different groups was lost in the proliferation of political and advocacy sites. But Web 2.0 rekindled that enthusiasm with the potential of connecting billions of human minds. Wikipedia is held up as a glorious example of the age of participation because it allows us to pool the collective wisdom of all our brains. Amateurism is celebrated. Anyone can publish writing, videos, songs, photographs, and other art for everyone else connected to the Internet to see and hear, and millions of people are doing just that.

Not surprisingly, the hype over Web 2.0 has drawn critics. In June 2007, Andrew Keen published *The Cult of the Amateur: How Today's*

*Internet Is Killing Our Culture*, which upholds the authority of the expert against the thousands of amateurs who contribute to YouTube and Wikipedia. He challenges the assumptions of those who inflate the promise of Web 2.0:

> The Web 2.0 revolution has peddled the promise of bringing more truth to more people—more depth of information, more global perspective, more unbiased opinion from dispassionate observers. But this is all a smokescreen. What the Web 2.0 revolution is really delivering is superficial observations of the world around us rather than deep analysis, shrill opinion rather than considered judgment. The information business is being transformed by the Internet into the sheer noise of a hundred million bloggers all simultaneously talking about themselves. (16)

Keen repeats several of the frequent charges against the Internet: identity theft is made easy, pornographers and gamblers thrive, personal data is vulnerable, and political and corporate interests spread propaganda. What bothers him the most, however, is how all the "free information" will eventually destroy traditional media—magazines, newspapers, recording studios, and book publishers—with their resources of writers, editors, journalists, musicians, and reporters. Amateurs, according to Keen, do not have the resources to produce in-depth reporting or great music or great books, and even if they did, how could anyone find it? The sheer number of amateurs publishing on the Web makes it next to impossible to sort the good from the bad.

Keen begins by recalling the hypothetical example that if an infinite number of monkeys were given typewriters to pound, eventually one of them will type out a masterpiece. He writes, "today's amateur monkeys can use their networked computers to publish everything from uninformed political commentary, to unseemly home videos, to embarrassingly amateurish music, to unreadable poems, reviews, essays and novels" (3).

Keen's comparison of bloggers to millions of monkeys with typewriters drew the ire of bloggers even before the book appeared. Lawrence Lessig wrote in his blog (www.lessig.org/blog/) in May 2007 that Keen's book is no more reliable than the typical blog. Lessig goes after Keen's evidence:

> [W]hat is puzzling about this book is that it purports to be a book attacking the sloppiness, error and ignorance of the Internet, yet it itself is shot through with sloppiness, error and ignorance. It tells us that without institutions, and standards, to signal what we can trust (like the institution, Doubleday, that decided to print his book), we won't know what's true and what's false. But the book itself is riddled with falsity—from simple errors of fact, to gross misreadings of arguments, to the most basic errors of economics.

If an edited book from a major publisher contains errors and misreadings, Lessig contends, it undermines Keen's claim that experts save us from these inaccuracies.

The Web 2.0 debate is a series of rebuttal arguments in which the debaters attempt to knock the evidence out from under the competing claims.

## Counterargument

Another way to rebut is to counterargue. In a counterargument, you do not really show the shortcomings of your opponent's point of view; you may not refer to the details of the other argument at all. Rather, you offer an argument of another point of view in the hope that it will outweigh the argument that is being rebutted. A counterarguer, in effect, says, "I hear your argument. But there is more to it than that. Now listen while I explain why another position is stronger."

The counterarguer depends on the wisdom of her or his audience members to hear all sides of an issue and to make up their minds about the merits of the case. In the following short poem, Wilfred Owen, a veteran of the horrors of World War I trench warfare, offers a counterargument to those who argue that war is noble, to those who believe along with the poet Horace that "dulce et decorum est pro patria mori"— that it is sweet and fitting to die for one's country. The vast amount of destruction and enormous loss of lives that occurred during the "war to end all wars" led people to question the belief that it is always noble to die for one's country.

### Dulce Et Decorum Est

Bent double, like old beggars under sacks,
Knock-kneed, coughing like hags, we cursed through sludge,
Till on the haunting flares we turned our backs
And towards our distant rest began to trudge.
Men marched asleep. Many had lost their boots
But limped on, blood-shod. All went lame; all blind;
Drunk with fatigue; deaf even to the hoots
Of disappointed shells that dropped behind.

Gas! Gas! Quick, boys!—An ecstasy of fumbling,
Fitting the clumsy helmets just in time;
But someone still was yelling out and stumbling
And floundering like a man in fire or lime.—
Dim, through the misty panes and thick green light
As under a green sea, I saw him drowning.
In all my dreams, before my helpless sight,
He plunges at me, guttering, choking, drowning.

If in some smothering dreams you too could pace
Behind the wagon that we flung him in,
And watch the white eyes writhing in his face,
His hanging face, like a devil's sick of sin;
If you could hear, at every jolt, the blood
Come gargling from the froth-corrupted lungs,
Obscene as cancer, bitter as the cud
Of vile, incurable sores on innocent tongues,—
My friend, you would not tell with such high zest
To children ardent for some desperate glory,
The old Lie: Dulce et decorum est
Pro patria mori.

Owen does not summarize the argument in favor of being willing
to die for one's country and then refute that argument premise by
premise. Rather, his poem presents an opposing argument, supported
by a narrative of the speaker's experience in a poison-gas attack, that he
hopes will more than counterbalance what he calls "the old lie." Owen

simply ignores the good reasons that people give for being willing to die for one's country and argues instead that there are also good reasons not to do so. And he hopes that the evidence that he summons for his countering position will outweigh for his audience ("My friend") the evidence in support of the other side.

Rebuttal arguments frequently offer both refutation and counterargument. In short, people who write rebuttals work like attorneys do in a trial: they make their own cases with good reasons and hard evidence, but they also do what they can to undermine their opponent's argument. In the end the jury, the audience, decides.

## Build a Rebuttal Argument

Rebuttal arguments begin with critical interrogations of the evidence underlying claims. In the era of the Internet, many writers use what turns up on the first page of a Google search. Google reports the most popular sites, however, not the most accurate ones. Mistakes and outright falsehoods are repeated because many writers on the Internet do not check their facts.

Look up a writer's sources to judge the quality of the evidence. Also, check if the writer is reporting sources accurately. Do your own fact checking. Having access to your library's databases gives you a great advantage because database sources are usually more reliable than the information you can find on the Internet.

Treat facts like a detective would. Sometimes there are alternative explanations. For example, arguments that schools are getting worse and students are getting dumber often use standardized test scores as evidence. On close inspection, however, you will find that writers often use these test scores selectively, quoting some scores and ignoring others that don't support their arguments. Furthermore, writers who quote test scores rarely take into account the population of test takers, which seldom remains constant from year to year.

When you write a counterargument with the goal of convincing readers that you have the stronger argument, your readers will appreciate your being fair about other arguments. Remember that you don't have to demolish the other person's argument, just establish that yours is better. Often you can be convincing by showing that you have thought about an issue in more depth and have taken into account more of its complexity.

## WRITE A REBUTTAL ARGUMENT

### Step 1 Identify an argument to argue against, as well as the argument's main claim(s)

- What exactly are you arguing against?
- Are there secondary claims attached to the main claim?
- Include a fair summary of your opponent's position in your finished rebuttal.

#### *Examples*

- Arguing against raising taxes for the purpose of building a new sports stadium (examine how proponents claim that a new sports facility will benefit the local economy).
- Arguing for raising the minimum wage (examine how opponents claim that a higher minimum wage isn't necessary and negatively affects small-business owners).

### Step 2 Examine the facts on which the claim is based

- Are the facts accurate and current?
- Is there another body of facts that you can present as counterevidence?
- If the author uses statistics, can the statistics be interpreted differently?
- If the author quotes from sources, how reliable are those sources?
- Are the sources treated fairly, or are quotations taken out of context?

### Step 3 Examine the assumptions on which the claim is based

- What are the primary and secondary assumptions of the claim you are rejecting?
- How are those assumptions flawed?
- Does the author resort to name-calling, use faulty reasoning, or ignore key facts?

### Step 4 Analyze your potential readers

- To what extent do your potential readers support the claim that you are rejecting?
- If they strongly support that claim, how might you appeal to them to change their minds?
- What common assumptions and beliefs do you share with them?

## Step 5 Write a draft

### *Introduction*
- Provide background if the issue is unfamiliar to most of your readers.
- Give a quick summary of the competing positions even if the issue is familiar to your readers.
- Make your aim clear in your thesis statement.

### *Body*
- Challenge the facts in the argument you are rejecting.
- Question how statistical evidence is presented and interpreted.
- Challenge the credibility of sources and authorities cited.
- Present counterevidence and countertestimony.

### *Conclusion*
- Conclude on a firm note by underscoring your objections.
- Consider ending with a counterproposal.

## Step 6 Revise, edit, proofread
- For detailed instructions.
- For a checklist to use to evaluate your draft.

---

# PROPOSAL ARGUMENTS

Proposal arguments make the case that someone should do something: "The federal government should raise grazing fees on public lands." "The student union should renovate the old swimming pool in Butler Gymnasium." "All parents should secure their children in booster seats when driving, even for short distances." Proposals can also argue that something should *not* be done, or that people should stop doing something: "The plan to extend Highway 45 is a waste of tax dollars and citizens should not vote for it." "Don't drink and drive."

The challenge for writers of proposal arguments is to convince readers to take action. It's easy for readers to agree that something should be done, as long as they don't have to do it. It's much harder to get readers involved with the situation or convince them to spend their time or money trying to carry out the proposal. A successful proposal argument conveys a sense of urgency to motivate readers and describes definite actions they should take.

## Understand How Proposal Arguments Work

Proposal arguments call for some action to be taken (or not to be taken). If readers are convinced that the proposal serves their interests, they will take action. Proposal arguments take this form:

**SOMEONE should (or should not) do SOMETHING because \_\_\_\_.**

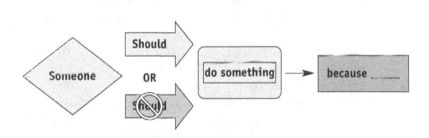

*Example*

We should convert existing train tracks in the downtown area to a light-rail system and build a new freight track around the city *because we need to relieve traffic and parking congestion downtown.*

## Recognize Components of Proposal Arguments

Proposal arguments are often complex and involve the kinds of arguments that are discussed earlier in this chapter. Successful proposals have four major components:

- **Identifying the problem.** Sometimes, problems are evident to your intended readers. If your city is constantly tearing up the streets and then leaving them for months without doing anything to repair them, then you shouldn't have to spend much time convincing the citizens of your city that streets should be repaired more quickly. But if you raise a problem that will be unfamiliar to most of your readers, first you will have to argue that the problem exists. You also will have to define the scope of the problem. Some of the bad roads in your city might be the responsibility of the state, not the city, government.

- **Stating a proposed solution.** A strong proposal offers a clear, definite statement of exactly what you are proposing. Vague statements that "Something must be done!" may get readers stirred up about the issue, but are unlikely to lead to constructive action. A detailed proposal also adds credibility to your argument, showing that you are concerned enough to think through the nuts and bolts of the changes to be made. You can state your proposed solution near the beginning of your argument, or introduce it later—for example, after you have considered and rejected other possible solutions.

- **Convincing readers that the proposed solution is fair and will work.** Once your readers agree that a problem exists and a solution should be found, you have to convince them that your solution is the best one. Perhaps you want your city to fire the planning committee members who are responsible for street repair. You will need to show that those officials are indeed responsible for the delays, and that, once they are fired, the city will be able to quickly hire new, more effective planners.

- **Demonstrating that the solution is feasible.** Your solution not only has to work; it must be feasible, or practical, to implement. You might be able to raise money for street repairs by billing property owners for repairs to the streets in front of their houses, but opposition to such a proposal would be fierce. Most Americans will object to making individuals responsible for road repair costs when roads are used by all drivers.

You may also have to show how your proposal is better than other possible actions that could be taken. Perhaps others believe your city should hire private contractors to repair the streets more quickly, or reward work crews who finish quickly with extra pay or days off. If there are multiple proposed solutions, all perceived as equally good, then there is no clear course of action for your audience to work for. Very often, that means nothing will happen.

# BUILD A PROPOSAL ARGUMENT

At this moment, you might not think that you feel strongly enough about anything to write a proposal argument. But if you write a list of things that make you mad or at least a little annoyed, then you have a start toward writing a proposal argument. Some things on your list are not going to produce proposal arguments that many people would want to read. If your roommate is a slob, you might be able to write a proposal for that person to start cleaning up more, but who else would be interested? Similarly, it might be annoying to you that where you live is too far from the ocean, but it is hard to imagine making a serious proposal to move your city closer to the coast. Short of those extremes, however, are many things that might make you think, "Why hasn't someone done something about this?" If you believe that others have something to gain if a problem is solved, or at least that the situation can be made a little better, then you might be able to develop a good proposal argument.

For instance, suppose you are living off campus, and you buy a student parking sticker when you register for courses so that you can park in the student lot. However, you quickly find out that there are too many cars and trucks for the number of available spaces, and unless you get to campus by 8:00 a.m., you aren't going to find a place to park in your assigned lot. The situation makes you angry because you believe that if you pay for a sticker, you should have a reasonable chance of finding a place to park. You see that there are unfilled lots reserved for faculty and staff next to the student parking lot, and you wonder why more spaces aren't allotted to students. You decide to write to the president of your college. You want her to direct parking and traffic services to give more spaces to students or else to build a parking garage that will accommodate more vehicles.

When you start talking to other students on campus, however, you begin to realize that the problem may be more complex than your first view of it. Your college has taken the position that if fewer students drive to campus, there will be less traffic on and around your campus. The administration wants more students to ride shuttle buses, to form car pools, or to bicycle to campus instead of driving alone. You also find out that faculty and staff members pay ten times as much as students for their parking permits, so they pay a very high premium for a guaranteed space—much too high for most students. If the president of your college is your primary audience, you first have to argue that a problem really exists. You have to convince the president that many students have no choice but to drive if they are to attend classes. You, for example, are willing to ride the shuttle buses, but they don't run often enough for you to make your classes, get back to your car that you left at home, and then drive to your job.

Next, you have to argue that your solution will solve the problem. An eightstory parking garage might be adequate to park all the cars of students who want to drive, but parking garages are very expensive to build. Even if a parking garage is the best solution, the question remains: who is going to pay for it? Many problems in life could be solved if you had access to unlimited resources, but very few people— or organizations—have such resources at their command. It's not enough to propose a solution that can resolve the problem. You have to be able to argue for the feasibility of your solution. If you want to argue that a parking garage is the solution to the parking problem on your campus, then you must also propose how to finance the garage.

## SAMPLE STUDENT PROPOSAL ARGUMENT

Kim Lee
Professor Patel
RHE 306
10 May 2012

Let's Make It a Real Melting Pot with Presidential
Hopes for All

The image the United States likes to advertise is a
country that embraces diversity and creates a land of equal
opportunity for all. As the Statue of Liberty cries out,
"give me your tired, your poor, your huddled masses yearn-
ing to breathe free," American politicians gleefully evoke
such images to frame the United States as a bastion for all
things good, fair, and equal. As a proud American, however, I must nonetheless highlight one of the cracks in this
façade of equality. Imagine that a couple decides to adopt
an orphaned child from China. They follow all of the legal
processes deemed necessary by both countries. They fly
abroad and bring home their (once parentless) six-month-
old baby boy. They raise and nurture him, and while teaching him to embrace his ethnicity, they also teach him to
love Cap'n Crunch, baseball, and *Sesame Street*. He grows
and eventually attends an ethnically diverse American
public school. One day his fifth-grade teacher tells the class
that anyone can grow up to be president. To clarify her
point, she turns to the boy, knowing his background, and
states, "No, you could not be president, Stu, but you could
still be a senator. That's something to aspire to!" How do
Stu's parents explain this rule to this American-raised child?
This scenario will become increasingly common, yet as the

Lee 2

Constitution currently reads, only "natural-born" citizens may run for the offices of president and vice president. Neither these children nor the thousands of hardworking Americans who chose to make America their official homeland may aspire to the highest political position in the land. While the huddled masses may enter, it appears they must retain a second-class citizen ranking.

The issue arose most recently when bloggers, media personalities, and some elected officials alleged that Barack Obama was born in Kenya, not Hawaii, and that his birth certificate is a forgery. The release of a certified copy of Obama's Certificate of Live Birth (the "long form") and other evidence including birth announcements in two Hawaii newspapers in August 1961 answered Donald Trump and other prominent "birthers" (Shear). Lost in the controversy was the question: Should it matter where Obama or any other candidate was born? In a land where everyone but American Indians are immigrants or descendants of immigrants, why should being born in the United States be considered an essential qualification for election as President?

The provision arose from very different circumstances than those of today. The "natural-born" stipulation regarding the presidency stems from the self-same meeting of minds that brought the American people the Electoral College. During the Constitutional Convention of 1787, the Congress formulated the regulatory measures associated with the office of the president. A letter sent from John Jay to George Washington during this period reads as follows:

"Permit me to hint," Jay wrote, "whether it would not be wise and seasonable to provide a strong check to the admission of foreigners into the administration

Lee 3

of our national government; and to declare expressly
that the Commander in Chief of the American
army shall not be given to, nor devolve on, any but
a natural-born citizen." (Mathews A1)

Shortly thereafter, Article II, Section I, Clause V, of the
Constitution declared that "No Person except a natural born
Citizen, or a Citizen of the United States at the time of the
Adoption of this Constitution, shall be eligible to the Office
of President." Jill A. Pryor states in the *Yale Law Journal*
that "some writers have suggested that Jay was responding
to rumors that foreign princes might be asked to assume the
presidency" (881). Many cite disastrous examples of foreign
rule in the eighteenth century as the impetus for the "natural-
born" clause. For example, in 1772—only 15 years prior to
the adoption of the statute—Poland had been divided up by
Prussia, Russia, and Austria (Kasindorf). Perhaps an element of self-preservation and not ethnocentrism led to the
questionable stipulation. Nonetheless, in the twenty-first
century this clause reeks of xenophobia.

The Fourteenth Amendment clarified the difference
between "naturalborn" and "native-born" citizens by spelling out the citizenship status of children born to American
parents outside of the United States (Ginsberg 929). This
clause qualifies individuals such as Senator John McCain—
born in Panama—for presidency. This change, however,
is not adequate. I propose that the United States abolish
the natural-born clause and replace it with a stipulation
that allows naturalized citizens to run for president. This
amendment would state that a candidate must have been
naturalized and must have lived in residence in the United
States for a period of at least twenty-five years. The present

Lee 4

time is ideal for this change. This amendment could simultaneously honor the spirit of the Constitution, protect and ensure the interests of the United States, promote an international image of inclusiveness, and grant heretofore-withheld rights to thousands of legal and loyal United States citizens.

In our push for change, we must make clear the importance of this amendment. It would not provide special rights for would-be terrorists. To the contrary, it would fulfill the longtime promises of the nation. Naturalized citizens have been contributing to the United States for centuries. Many nameless Mexican, Irish, and Asian Americans sweated and toiled to build the American railroads. The public has welcomed naturalized Americans such as Bob Hope, Albert Pujols, and Peter Jennings into their hearts and living rooms. Individuals such as German-born Henry Kissinger and Czechoslovakian-born Madeleine Albright have held high posts in the American government and have served as respected aides to its presidents. The amendment must make clear that it is not about one man's celebrity. Approximately seven hundred foreign-born Americans have won the Medal of Honor, and over sixty thousand proudly serve in the United States military today (Siskind 5). The "natural-born" clause must be removed to provide each of these people—over half a million naturalized in 2003 alone—with equal footing to those who were born into citizenship rather than working for it (United States).

Since the passing of the Bill of Rights, only 17 amendments have been ratified. This process takes time and overwhelming congressional and statewide support. To alter the Constitution, a proposed amendment must pass

Lee 5

with a two-thirds "supermajority" in both the House of
Representatives and the Senate. In addition, the proposal
must find favor in two-thirds of the 50 state legislatures. In
short, this task will not be easy. In order for this change to
occur, a grassroots campaign must work to dispel misin-
formation regarding naturalized citizens and to force the
hands of senators and representatives wishing to retain their
congressional seats. We must take this proposal to ethnicity-
specific political groups from both sides of the aisle, business organizations, and community activist groups. We
must convince representatives that this issue matters. Only
through raising voices and casting votes can the people
enact change. Only then can every American child see the
possibility for limitless achievement and equality. Only then
can everyone find the same sense of pride in the possibility
for true American diversity in the highest office in the land.

Lee 6

Works Cited

Epstein, Edward. "Doubt about a Foreign-Born
President." *San Francisco Chronicle* 6 Oct. 2004: A5.
*LexisNexis Academic.* Web. 16 Apr. 2012.

Ginsberg, Gordon. "Citizenship: Expatriation: Distinction
between Naturalized and Natural Born Citizens."
*Michigan Law Review* 50 (1952): 926–29. *JSTOR.*
Web. 16 Apr. 2012.

Lee 7

Kasindorf, Martin. "Should the Constitution Be Amended for Arnold?" *USA Today* 2 Dec. 2004. *LexisNexis Academic*. Web. 18 Apr. 2012.

Mathews, Joe. "Maybe Anyone Can Be President." *Los Angeles Times* 2 Feb. 2005: A1. *LexisNexis Academic*. Web. 16 Apr. 2012.

Pryor, Jill A. "The Natural Born Citizen Clause and Presidential Eligibility: An Approach for Resolving Two Hundred Years of Uncertainty." *Yale Law Journal* 97.5 (1988): 881–99. Print.

Shear, Michael D. "With Document, Obama Seeks to End 'Birther' Issue." *New York Times*. New York Times, 27 Apr. 2011. Web. 28 Apr. 2012.

Siskind, Lawrence J. "Why Shouldn't Arnold Run?" *Recorder* 10 Dec. 2004: 5. *LexisNexis Academic*. Web. 10 Apr. 2012.

United States. Dept. of Commerce. Census Bureau. "The Fourth of July 2005." *Facts for Features*. U.S. Dept. of Commerce, 27 June 2005. Web. 17 Apr. 2012.

## WRITE A PROPOSAL ARGUMENT

### Step 1 Make a claim

Make a proposal claim advocating a specific change or course of action.

***Template***

• We should (or should not) do SOMETHING.

### *Examples*

In an essay of five or fewer pages, it's difficult to propose solutions to big problems such as persistent poverty. Proposals that address local problems are more manageable, and sometimes they get actual results.

- Redesigning the process of registering for courses, applying for financial aid, or making appointments to be more efficient.
- Creating bicycle lanes to make cycling safer and to reduce traffic.
- Streamlining the rules for recycling newspapers, bottles, and cans to encourage increased participation.

## Step 2 Identify the problem

- What exactly is the problem?
- Who is most affected by the problem?
- Has anyone tried to do anything about it? If so, why haven't they succeeded?
- What is likely to happen in the future if the problem isn't solved?

## Step 3 Propose your solution

- State your solution as specifically as you can.
- What exactly do you want to achieve?
- How exactly will your solution work?
- Can it be accomplished quickly, or will it have to be phased in over a few years?
- Has anything like it been tried elsewhere? If so, what happened?

## Step 4 Consider other solutions

- What other solutions have been or might be proposed for this problem, including doing nothing?
- Why is your solution better?

## Step 5 Examine the feasibility of your solution

- How easy is your solution to implement?
- Will the people most affected by your solution be willing to go along with it? (For example, lots of things can be accomplished if enough people volunteer, but groups often have difficulty getting enough volunteers to work without pay.)
- If your solution costs money, how do you propose to pay for it?
- Who is most likely to reject your proposal because it is not practical enough?
- How can you convince your readers that your proposal can be achieved?

## Step 6 Analyze your potential readers

- Whom are you writing for?
- How interested will your readers be in this problem?
- How much does this problem affect them?
- How would your solution benefit them directly and indirectly?

## Step 7 Write a draft

### *Introduction*
- Set out the issue or problem, perhaps by telling about your experience or the experience of someone you know.
- Argue for the seriousness of the problem.
- Give some background about the problem if necessary.

### *Body*
- Present your solution. Consider setting out your solution first, explaining how it will work, discussing other possible solutions, and arguing that yours is better. Or consider discussing other possible solutions first, arguing that they don't solve the problem or are not feasible, and then presenting your solution.
- Make clear the goals of your solution. Many solutions cannot solve problems completely. If you are proposing a solution for juvenile crime in your neighborhood, for example, you cannot expect to eliminate all juvenile crime.
- Describe in detail the steps in implementing your solution and how they will solve the problem you have identified. You can impress your readers with the care with which you have thought through this problem.
- Explain the positive consequences that will follow from your proposal. What good things will happen, and what bad things will be avoided, if your advice is taken?
- Argue that your proposal is feasible and can be put into practice.

### *Conclusion*
- Issue a call to action—if your readers agree with you, they will want to take action.
- Restate and emphasize exactly what readers need to do to solve the problem.

## Step 8 Revise, edit, proofread
- For detailed instructions.
- For a checklist to use to evaluate your draft.

Taken from *Scenes of Writing: Strategies for Composing with Genres*
by Amy Devitt, Mary Jo Reiff, and Anis Bawarshi

# 7 Critiquing and Changing Genres

We have asked you to analyze genres for what they can tell you about the communication and behavior of participants within scenes of writing, and we have encouraged you to apply your genre knowledge in order to make more informed and effective choices as you begin to participate as writers within these scenes. In short, we have described strategies for using genre to make sense of and function effectively within various scenes of writing. In this chapter, we will take up the question of how genres can also be used to critique and change not only how participants communicate but also how they behave within some of the scenes making up our lives.

Because genres carry with them particular strategies for writing, you might assume that, as writers, you have little say in creating new genres or changing scenes of writing. However, since we are always making choices as we write within a genre, we are, in a sense, always being creative. An appropriate analogy would be actors on a stage. Even though they are given a script from which to perform, different actors will necessarily perform the same script differently. The constraints of the script would be the same, but different actors will make different choices about how to present the personality of their character, how to interact with others on the stage, even how to read their lines. Although a dramatic script is much more limiting than a genre script, the kind of creative control that exists for actors is available to writers. Different writers will make different writing choices within the same genre. The degree of variation depends on the genre, of course. There is more room for choice in the free-verse poem, for example, than there is in the sonnet, more room for individual creativity in an e-mail message to a friend than in a message to a newsgroup or discussion list. Nevertheless, within the patterns of each genre, writers always have to make choices, and *all* of these choices are creative.

How do writers make creative choices within genres? Writers' creativity depends in large part on their knowledge of the existing conventions. This assertion may sound like a contradiction, especially since we tend to think of creativity as being the opposite of conventionality. But in a very important sense, *writers cannot resist or modify conventions unless they know what these conventions are and what they do.* We can recognize an innovative mystery only if we know the conventions of a traditional mystery. We recognize that a Web site is especially well designed only if we can see how well it works compared to others we have visited. In this way, the constraints that already exist within the patterns of a genre and which limit the writing choices we can make are also what enable writers to be creative.

Writers are not creative by accident, nor do they make creative writing choices simply for the heck of it. Very often, their choices are informed and purposeful. They have a reason for making the choices that they do, and, what is more, they know which patterns within the genre they can modify and which ones they had better not. This knowledge is important since, if writers modify too many essential elements of the genre at once, the audience will no longer be able to recognize the genre at all, defeating the purpose. That strategy might also backfire since users of the genre would likely reject such a wholesale revision of their habits of communication and behavior. Consider, for example, the French artist Marcel Duchamp, who in the early twentieth century submitted a porcelain urinal for an art exhibition, titling it *Fountain*. While this innovative act challenged the conventional understanding of what constitutes art—resisting the traditional presentation of genres and the conventions of "good taste" and aesthetic beauty in art— it also stirred a great deal of controversy and led to the rejection of his "art" in the exhibit and his ensuing resignation from the Society of Independent Artists. This example illustrates the need to examine the patterns of a genre and the scene itself in order to gauge how far you can expand your choices without losing your credibility. But the example also demonstrates how resisting the expectations of a genre can lead to genre change. While not everyone begins with the credibility of a Marcel Duchamp—who, despite the controversy (or perhaps because of it), has become associated with the transformation of art in the twentieth century—his example nevertheless illustrates how you can use the conventions of a genre and your variations from those conventions to make a statement about and to critique existing conventions.

We have shown you how learning to read a genre is an important first step in gaining the experience to write it effectively and creatively, this chapter will explore further how the genres we read and write might fail to serve the goals of a situation and, consequently, might need to be revised. You will have an opportunity to revisit and critique some of the genres we have examined, including such genres as the Patient Medical History

Form, the complaint letter, the syllabus, or any of the other genres you have explored so far. We will examine several approaches to genre critique:

- What a critique of genre might look like
- How some genres may not work equally well for everyone within certain scenes
- How genres change as the needs of their users and their scenes change
- What happens to scenes of writing when we change the genres that exist and are used within them

# From Thinking Critically to Critiquing Genres

Because genres can give us access to how people act and interact within scenes of writing, they serve not only as sites for **thinking critically** about these scenes, but also as sites for **critiquing** them. Although the words *critically* and *critiquing* are related, each represents a different level of engagement.

The strategy for performing genre analysis (see Box 2.1, pp. 93–94) that we have described and practiced so far in this book asks you to read genres critically. *Critically* in this case means looking below the surface to identify the patterns of various genres and then to use these patterns to gain insight into the scenes in which they are used—using these patterns, in other words, to uncover what they can tell us about some of a scene's assumptions, values, beliefs, and goals. *Critiquing*, however, asks you to do something more. It asks you to *question and evaluate* assumptions. To critique means to engage in **judgment,** to examine and then determine the strengths and shortcomings of certain genres. As such, critiquing genres enables you to examine not just how genres function within their scenes, but also how they might support and/or fail to serve the needs of their users within these scenes. This is the kind of critique that we will now examine in more detail.

As an example of the difference between critically reading and critiquing a genre, let us return to a genre we examined in Chapter 2: the Patient Medical History Form (PMHF). (See pages 61–62.) The PMHF is a commonly used genre in the scene of the doctor's office, a genre that you yourself have probably filled out on your initial visit to a doctor's office. As you might recall from our earlier discussion, the PMHF asks patients to describe their physical characteristics such as age, sex, weight, height, etc.; their medical history, highlighting prior and/or recurring physical conditions; and, most importantly, their current physical symptoms. In performing our critical reading of the PMHF, we noted that a prominent characteristic of the genre is that it focuses mainly on a patient's physical symptoms, while soliciting very little, if any, information about the patient's emotional state. Based on this critical reading, we concluded that the PMHF as a genre reflects Western views of medicine, views that tend to separate the mind from the body in treating illness. The use of the PMHF, then, reveals something about how doctors treat patients by focusing mainly on their physical symptoms, the assumption being that doctors can isolate and then treat physical symptoms with little to no reference to the patient's state of mind. This critical reading of the PMHF helps us describe how the PMHF as a genre reflects the ways doctors and patients communicate. Through our critical reading, we come to see how the PMHF acts as a kind of social script for how patients and doctors typically act and communicate within the scene of the doctor's office.

Critiquing a genre takes the above critical reading of the PMHF one step further. It also allows us to *question the practices* that the genre reflects and enables. For example, a **genre critique** might draw attention to the fact that the PMHF actually reduces patients to physical objects in a way that limits the extent to which they can be treated. In other words, by discouraging patients from describing their emotional states and how these emotional states might be connected to their physical symptoms, the PMHF could very well encourage doctors to ignore the full extent of a patient's physical symptoms. In this case, the critique of the PMHF becomes a part of *a larger critique of the medical community* and its typical assumptions, beliefs, and practices. Such a critique involves pointing out the PMHF's shortcomings, especially the ways in which it fails to represent the patient fully and, therefore, fails to serve more completely the needs of the patient (as well as the doctor, perhaps).

On the other hand, a critique of the PMHF might also explore how in fact the PMHF does indeed work effectively in the scene of the doctor's office. You could argue, for example, that by separating the patient's physical symptoms from his or her emotional state, the PMHF actually enables doctors to treat patients more effectively. Reducing the patient to a physical object allows the doctor to keep an emotional distance from the patient, a distance that is necessary, some would argue, for the doctor to maintain objectivity. In this case, the critique reveals the PMHF's positive effects for the doctor.

Genre critique, thus, can take many forms. It can examine whose needs a genre serves or does not serve within a specific scene. It can also question the ways that a genre or genres might fail to serve the objectives and practices of a scene—how, that is, a genre or genres might limit what individuals can and cannot do within certain scenes. Whatever argument you might choose to make about the effects of a genre, keep in mind that a critique of a genre must be based on a critical reading of a genre; the two go hand in hand. As our above example of the PMHF indicates, you need to know how a genre works and what it reveals before you can examine its effects, including its strengths and weaknesses.

## WHY IT IS IMPORTANT TO CRITIQUE GENRES

Since genres reflect the typical strategies for communicating and behaving, we might be tempted to assume that this means genres reliably and equitably serve the needs of all their users. This in fact is not always the case. Some genres privilege the needs of some users over the needs of other users. In supporting some of the values, beliefs, and assumptions of members of a scene, genres may limit other possible values and beliefs. Sometimes, people misinterpret or misuse these generic strategies. Furthermore, not everyone within a scene of writing will always agree on these strategies, especially when such strategies may not serve their needs. As a result, genres do not always operate smoothly or effectively within their scenes of writing. They do not always communicate what we intend or expect them to, or we may not want to communicate what genres encourage us to.

Critiquing genres and the scenes in which they are used helps us detect any dissonance between a genre's purposes and the objectives and assumptions of the scene it functions within. For instance, a writer may choose an inappropriate genre for a given occasion, or in some cases someone might confuse one genre for another. Sweepstakes companies use such genre confusion to their advantage by sending sweepstakes letters that look temptingly like legal documents telling us that we have "won" 25 million dollars or a fancy car or a 10-day vacation. Banking on the fact that we will be fooled by the legal-sounding language, such companies try to convince us to take their offers seriously. So well can the sweepstakes promoter make the genre of the sweepstakes letter resemble a legal document that some recipients have responded as if they indeed have received notification of their winnings: Recipients have undergone hardship and expense to claim their prizes and, when the truth is discovered, have filed real lawsuits against the sweepstakes promoters. The strategy of this sweepstakes letter genre is based, in part, on its misuse of another genre and on the recipients' mis-recognition. A critique of genres can work to expose such misuse and misrecognition.

Critiquing genres can also help explain how and why some genres might fail to function effectively in a scene of writing. One of us, for example, has studied why jurors might have trouble following jury instructions given them by the judge. Among other things, she discovered that the language used in these instructions was written by and between lawyers and judges to specify legal details to achieve shared objectives of *their* professional legal scene. As a result, the jurors, who were not members of that professional scene, could not fully understand the legal nuances of terms such as *mitigating* or the responsibility implied in a use of passive voice. The genre of jury instructions in this case worked for lawyers and judges but failed to function effectively for those who relied on it most, the jurors. Genre critique can help explain why certain genres fail to produce their desired effects or achieve their writers' purposes.

## Writing Activity 7.1

Think about a time when a genre has either failed you or failed to function effectively in one of your scenes of writing. For example, you might have expected a genre to help you communicate something but then you found that it could not (such as the use of the five-paragraph essay in your college-level writing courses). Or perhaps your use of a genre did not produce the desired effect, or your or someone else's use of a genre created controversy within a scene of writing. As you reflect on this occasion, think about how the genre failed. Was it a failure of the genre to meet the needs of its scene and situation; or did you mistakenly choose an inappropriate genre for your situation? What do you think may have contributed to this failure?

## EXAMPLES OF CRITIQUING GENRES

Genres, then, can reveal how people communicate and behave within certain scenes, but they can also reveal the potential—and sometimes less obvious—tensions and limitations within certain scenes; such tensions and limitations can lead to misrecognition, miscommunication, and unequal practices. By becoming aware of and then examining these tensions and limitations as they are revealed through genres, you can begin to develop possible strategies for revising genres and changing the scenes in which they are used. Before we describe such strategies for revising genres and changing their scenes, we will now provide some examples of genre critique: one from a student and one from a genre scholar. In both cases, the genre critique functions as a precursor for changing the genre and its scene.

What follows is an analysis paper, an academic paper that breaks something into its parts and examines how those parts relate. This paper was written by a student who identifies and examines tensions within the genre of the wedding invitation. In it, the student writer performs what we have been calling genre critique. The paper is by no means flawless, but it does serve as a helpful example of what a genre critique might look like written by a student who, perhaps like you, is attempting a genre critique for the first time. As you read it, notice how the writer employs a critical reading of the genre in order to critique the genre. That is, she first describes how the genre works and then evaluates its effects—both in terms of what the genre does and in terms of the effect it has on those who use it.

---

Devine 1

For the Bride or Groom?

Theresa Devine

Invitations are used for a variety of events such as a birthday, christening, anniversary celebration, party, and, in my case, a wedding. Each event brings with it a different kind of invitation with its own set of conventions. For each of these invitations a different genre exists, each being a written form of the American culture. Since an invitation is a written representation of the American culture, it can tell us about our culture. The genre I would like to discuss is the genre of the wedding invitation.

A major decision that a bride and groom face to initiate the first step toward their big event is choosing the wedding invitations. There are many issues a couple has to consider when deciding upon the perfect invitation. For example, what kind of pattern should they pick? What color should be used? What type of writing? And what should the invitation say? All

Devine 2

of these questions contribute to the genre of the wedding invitation. However, who does the genre of the invitation usually appeal to most? Are the invitations really appealing to both the bride and groom? Wedding invitations are looked at as an invitation that represents a joint union between two people. But when analyzed, wedding invitations seem to represent an unequal union. The invitations themselves are more appealing to the bride than the groom. And when the invitation arrives at a couple's house, who is more likely to look at it and view the invitation, the man or the woman? By examining such questions, I have come to the conclusion that the genre of wedding invitations is gender biased through the colors, patterns, writing, and dialogue displayed in it.

To begin supporting this claim I would like to examine the colors of wedding invitations. By looking at invitations in the catalogs "Wedding Treasures," "Now and Then," and "Rexcraft," the predominant colors appear to be soft feminine pastels like: pink, green, and blue. Other colors displayed in the catalogs are vibrant, bright, and shiny, for example hot pink, silver, teal, and red. It is hard to find invitations that could appeal to a man using masculine associated colors like: navy blue, forest green, and maroon. The colors used are colors that are directed to the eyes of most women. The colors are soft and bright, not bold and dark. The softness of the invitations is made to appeal to women and not to many men. The colors used on the majority of the invitations and displayed in these catalogs supports the claim that the genre of wedding invitations is gender biased.

Next, I would like to draw attention to the patterns or drawings used on wedding invitations. Drawings that predominantly appear on the invitations are flowers, bows, roses, small children, a fairy tale castle, a dancing man and

Devine 3

woman, and hearts. Almost all of the invitations that I viewed contained at least one of these drawings or symbols. As a woman, I've been taught to find these symbols cute, pretty, and feminine. What symbol here could possibly be considered appealing to a man? How often in our culture do men recognize the beauty of flowers, or ask for them as a gift? Who always dreams about the fairy tale castle? There is not much to be found as masculine in the form of a wedding invitation. The simplest, and I would consider most appealing invitation to a man, is found only five times throughout the wedding catalogs. The detail on the invitation is just a silver outline around the invitation, with no patterns or pastel colors. This invitation is in the middle of most of the catalogs. This invitation will be easily missed and overlooked among the flowers, colors, and bows, once again reinforcing the gender bias within the genre of wedding invitations.

The lettering and the content of the invitations also support their gender bias. Cultural views of women generally perceive them as writing a soft flowing bubbled yet clear print. The writing on each and every invitation used in the wedding catalog is very similar to most writing styles of women. In fact, out of twenty and some odd types of writing styles to choose from in the different catalogs, only four of them are in a traditional print that could be considered as unisex writing. Likewise, looking over the dialogue used in invitations, again it can be seen that wedding invitations are gender biased. I have gone through the different catalogs and found that the majority of the invitations use fairly similar dialogue. Within three catalogs averaging fifty-eight pages and displaying approximately four types of invitations a page, only seven in each book were worded differently than the following:

Devine 4

Mr. And Mrs. Benjamin Sharpe
request the honor of your presence
at the marriage of **their daughter**
Michelle Louise
to
Mr. Christopher R. Botham
on Sunday the fifth of October
nineteen hundred and ninety-seven
at twelve noon
St. Etc . . .

Just by looking at the above example it can be seen that this invitation clearly represents the bride. Look at the bolded letters **their daughter**. What about the other parents' son? The groom is briefly mentioned with no long introduction like the bride and right after his name is the date, time, and place. So I ask, who is the invitation really appealing to and who does it represent? I clearly see the answer to be the BRIDE.

What does this say about our culture, values, and the way that we view this announcement? As a culture we see this event as a moment where the bride, or "their daughter" is giving up a part of her identity. "Their daughter" is giving up a name that has represented her over the past eighteen years or more. The value of that name and change of names is extremely important to the bride and her parents. The bride mentioned on the invitation will always be "their daughter." However, the bride's name is most likely changing and she will no longer be recognized as "their daughter" just by looking at her name. More information needs to be known about this woman in order to find out who her parents are. A wedding invitation allows parents to formally recognize their daughter through this type of dialogue before she then gives up her name.

Devine 5

Also, the dialog often represents who is contributing a lot of time and effort in this event. Recognizing the parents of the bride and their daughter first reflects that they have built on the initiation of this event (the engagement) and see this as the moment in which they give away their most precious gift of all, their daughter. As such, the invitation remains gender biased.

Our culture seems to view this event as a feminine and traditional celebration. The genre of the invitations represents the femininity of the occasion. I am not saying that the groom is not important and not involved in this process of choosing an invitation. However, I am saying that the female usually does play more of a role in this process. When asking five future spouses, "Who generally initiates the planning and decision making in the wedding, you or your fiancé, the answer is a unanimous me (the bride) or me and my mom (the other woman).

I recognize that there are other styles of writing on invitations and not all women like the flowers, bows, and heart patterned invitations; and in some situations the groom plays an equal role in deciding on wedding invitations. However, I am making the claim that the majority of wedding invitations are gender biased and are more appealing to the female eye. Invitations display this feminine bias using the types of colors, patterns, style of writing, and dialogue displayed on them. As a result of my analysis of wedding invitations, my fiancé and I have chosen to use the single male-appealing invitation using a feminine style of writing-- just so that we can balance the gender inequality a little.

## Writing Activity 7.2

In "For the Bride or Groom?" distinguish between the parts that perform a critical reading of the genre and the parts that perform a critique of the genre. Give examples of each and explain how they differ.

Because genres, as Theresa Devine observes above, are indeed reflections of our culture, they can be critiqued in order to expose some of the entrenched cultural assumptions and practices they reflect. In the case of wedding invitations, in addition to making the assumption that weddings are for the bride and her parents, we notice a cultural irony at work, an irony the student critique points out but does not fully address. The irony goes something like this: The wedding invitations are meant mainly to appeal to the bride, yet it is ultimately the bride's self-interests that are least served by these invitations since these invitations reduce the bride to a piece of property that is being transferred from parents to husband. In this case, the student critique suggests that the genre of wedding invitations not only reflects but reinforces gender inequalities. *Genre critique can help reveal shortcomings in the ways we communicate and act in our various scenes. Such critique can also potentially lead to changing the genre to make it more equitable.*

## Collaborative Activity 7.1

Working with classmates, think about how the wedding invitation could be changed to address the critique that "For the Bride or Groom?" raises. What would it take to correct the inequality between bride and groom? Write a wedding invitation that reflects this equality.

Genre scholar Randall Popken has performed a similar critique of another popular genre, one: the resumé. In his scholarly article "The Pedagogical Dissemination of a Genre: The Resumé in American Business Discourse Textbooks, 1914–1939," Popken traces the evolution of the resumé from its beginnings to the present. In its current state, he argues, the resumé works to erase the presence of the individual who writes it. By downplaying the voice and persona of resumé writers, the resumé depersonalizes job seekers, portraying them as commodities that can be sold. To prove his claim, Popken turns to the genre itself and its rhetorical patterns. The following patterns, he argues, all help erase the presence of the resumé writer, thus limiting his or her ability to present a personality:

- The use of subjectless sentences to describe a person's work history, sentences such as: "managed a large budget" instead of "I managed a large budget," etc.
- The physical constraints of the resumé, which is usually limited in length from one to two pages.

- The overall structure of the resumé and its prescribed categories such as "career objective," "work experience," "education," etc.
- The kind of "acceptable topics" the resumé writer can include, which tends to be limited to his or her previous positions, educational accomplishments, and career success, while excluding topics such as the writer's home life, nonwork interests, or philosophy of life.
(Popken 92–93)

The above characteristics all contribute to the exclusion of personality in the resumé. This exclusion reveals a possible shortcoming in the way that individuals communicate and interact within business scenes of writing, reinforcing an artificial and potentially detrimental split between the personal and the professional. Such a split also contributes to the reduction of individuals to the sum of the work they do, a reduction that in some cases helps turn employees into commodities that can be bought and sold.


## PERFORMING YOUR OWN GENRE CRITIQUE

To perform a genre critique like the ones we describe above, first follow the guidelines for conducting genre analyses we outlined in Box 2.1, pp. 93–94. These guidelines will help you identify the scene or scenes in which the genre is used, the key patterns within the genre itself, and what these patterns tell us about the scene or scenes. After you have completed the above analysis, you are ready to determine what you see as the effects of the genre, including its strengths and weaknesses. Keep the questions in Box 7.1 in mind as you consider the effects of the genre.

Box 7.1 offers just a sampling of the possible questions you could ask to help you gauge a genre's effects. Notice how the questions invite you to engage the genre not so much on its own terms (by describing its features and explaining how and why they function within a scene of writing) but rather on *your* own terms. That is, the questions lead you to look beyond how and why the genre works so that you can assess how well it works based on standards you hold. For instance, someone else might agree with Popken that the resumé indeed does depersonalize its writer, but that same person might not agree that such depersonalization is necessarily a limitation of the genre. When you are critiquing a genre, then, you need to be sure to make compelling **arguments**—specific claims, supported by reasons and evidence—about how and why the genre does in fact fail or succeed in some way.

## Box 7.1   *Questions for Critiquing Genres*

- What does the genre allow its users to do and what does it not allow them to do?
- Whose needs are most served by the genre? Whose needs are least served?
- In what ways does the genre succeed the most? In what ways does it fail?
- Does the genre enable its users to represent themselves fully?
- Does the genre effectively accomplish what its users intend it to do?
- Does the genre limit the way in which its users can do their work?
- Does the genre create inequalities among its users that lead to imbalances of power?
- Do the assumptions that the genre reflects privilege certain ways of doing things?
- Do those privileged ways of doing things run counter to the supposed objectives of those who use it and the scene in which it is used?
- Does the genre allow its users to do certain things at the expense of others? And if so, at what cost?

### Writing Activity 7.3

Choose a new genre or look back on a genre that either you or we have analyzed in an earlier chapter. For example, this can be the genre you analyzed in Chapter 2 (Writing Activity 2.8, p. 91, and Writing Project 2.1, p. 97) or any of the genres we have analyzed throughout the book so far, such as the syllabus or the complaint letter. Your teacher might assign one of these genres. Whatever genre you choose or are assigned, carefully examine its features and, using some of the questions we listed in Box 7.1, work to develop a critique of the genre. In the process of developing your critique, identify those features of the genre that support your critique, much like Popken identified those features of the resumé that limit the expressions of the writer's personality. Keep careful notes of your findings as you might need to use them to develop your argument.

Having described what we mean by a genre critique and having invited you to practice doing such a critique, we will now further address what is gained by doing such a critique. Critique even for the sake of critique can be enlightening since it exposes some of the entrenched and sometimes hidden limitations within a genre and its scene of writing. Indeed, as the above examples of the PMHF, the wedding invitations, and the resumé demonstrate, genre critique can reveal how genres do not always function smoothly or effectively for all their users—how, in fact, genres can be sites of controversy as much as sites of communication. *If you understand a genre's limitations when you write it, you might be able to resist its embedded assumptions.* In addition to exposing some of the limitations and complexities of genres, however, a genre critique can also serve as the starting point for changing already existing genres and developing new genres. The next section will describe how genre critique can lead to such potential genre transformation.

## Changing Genres

Genres are not static entities. At times, they may appear to be unchanging, especially when they become entrenched in how and why people act and interact within certain scenes. But the reality is that genres do change as the people who use them and the scenes in which they are used change. *As attitudes, ways of knowing, and goals change, people revise already existing genres and sometimes develop new ones that more effectively reflect these new attitudes, ways of knowing, and goals.* Likewise, as the technologies for communication change, new genres emerge to accommodate them (for example, personal computer technology has enabled writers to incorporate more design and images into their writing, leading to such genres as Web pages). In this way, genres *evolve* over time, so that, by tracing the evolution of a genre within a certain scene, scholars can actually trace the evolution of people's assumptions within that scene.

For instance, one such genre scholar, Charles Bazerman, has traced the historical evolution of the genre of the experimental report in the first English scientific journal, the *Philosophic Transactions of the Royal Society of London*. In his book *Shaping Written Knowledge: The Genre and Activity of the Experimental Article in Science,* his research shows how the experimental report genre, which began as an informative letter exchanged among scientists, developed and changed between the years 1665 and 1800 as a result of changes in assumptions regarding what nature is and how it can be studied. For example, Bazerman observed that the genre developed over the period of those years, from being a way of simply describing an unusual phenomenon (for example, how mercury expands when heated) and, in some cases, showing readers how to re-create the phenomenon; to being a more conscious investigation of phenomena that involves some manipulation of the phenomena (for example, testing how mercury reacts under different conditions); to being more driven by a specific goal, such as the testing of a hypothesis or the resolving of a debate. The changes in the genre during these early years, Bazerman explains, reflect changing attitudes about nature, from a view of nature as a "given" to a view of nature as a subject of contention. In other words, in the earliest stages of the experimental report, "nature was portrayed as speaking for itself" and so the report was simply a way of describing nature and telling readers what happened (Bazerman 77). Later, as assumptions about nature changed, so too did the way scientists report their experiments. As Bazerman explains,

> experiments stop being a clear window to a self-revealing nature, but become a way of tying down uncertain claims about an opaque and uncertain nature. The meaning of an experiment is no longer the simple observation of what happens. An experiment is to be understood only in terms of the ideas that motivate it, for nature is no longer considered to be so easy to find. (67-8)

So what we recognize today as an experimental report with its testing and proof and description of methods and results is a reflection of our current attitudes about what nature is and how it can be studied. Each genre contains ways of thinking that have evolved over its history.

## FROM CRITIQUE TO CHANGE

Genres are always changing as the assumptions and needs of their users change. Genres do not change magically on their own; *people* change genres, usually slowly and imperceptibly, as they begin to recognize the ways in which genres no longer fully serve their needs. The genre of the experimental report, for instance, did not evolve overnight into the genre we recognize today. It took nearly 150 years to do so, and it in fact still continues to evolve with the influence of new scientific technologies and greater knowledge about nature. In each stage of the experimental report's development, some scientist or group of scientists would likely have encountered and identified a limitation caused by existing genre conventions and attempted to revise the genre. While they may not consciously have performed a genre analysis and decided on a needed change, their actions in writing the genre differently created changes so that the genre would accommodate their new perspective. In this way, genre critique and genre change work hand in hand.

We can observe how genre critique might lead to genre change if we look once again at the genre of the Patient Medical History Form (PMHF). We discussed one possible critique of the PMHF earlier in this chapter. If enough patients and doctors begin to complain about the PMHF's limitations, then it is quite possible that the American Medical Association will recommend revising the genre so that it solicits more information about a patient's emotions, especially in terms of how the patient's emotional state might affect his or her physical symptoms. Such changes might occur slowly at first, with a few doctors adding questions that ask patients to describe their state of mind. Eventually, these changes, especially if they are sanctioned by the AMA, could become new conventions.

The following student's researched position paper, an academic argument based on the writer's research, provides a real-world example of how a new genre evolves from an already existing genre to meet new conditions and needs. The student, an education major, chose to examine how the report card as a genre has changed over the years as assumptions about how students learn have changed. In particular, she explores how a new genre of student assessment, the grade continuum, is emerging to reflect these new assumptions. As you read her researched position paper, think about what it teaches us about how and why genres change and what such generic change means for the people and scenes that use them. How, for example, do changes in the genre reflect changes in education philosophies? What reasons does the writer give for supporting these changes?

Weishaar 1

Changing Forms

Amy J. Weishaar

What is the purpose of attending school? One might answer that the ultimate goal of education is to promote the intellectual, social, physical, and even spiritual growth of an individual to achieve at least a minimum set of criteria in order to maximize the individual's personal quality of life and contribution to society. Assuming that this type of response is accurate, how does the education community formally communicate, to the individual as well as to society, an evaluation of the individual's progress and achievements? In America since the late 1800s, the answer has been the almighty grade card. The grade card, also referred to as a progress report, is a genre, the "typified response" of the education community to the "recurring rhetorical situation" of reporting a student's progress in education. Currently the traditional grade card evaluation practice is undergoing revision throughout the United States. In particular, Quail Run Elementary School in Lawrence, KS, is leading the reform of this genre in the Lawrence Public Schools. What do the changes being made to this genre tell the public about the education community? This reform reflects the education community's commitment to continually revise and implement educational strategies in order to maximize the quality and effectiveness of student instruction.

In each decade it seems that the government and educators come up with a new emphasis for education. For example, in the late 1950s and 1960s the educational push in America was to emphasize mathematics and science in order to compete in the booming field of technology such as space exploration. Then came the segregation of students with like abilities or disabilities (i.e., learning disabled, behavior disorders, educable mentally handicapped, gifted/talented/creative) in order to give individualized, specialized attention to each child. What led to changes such as these? The answer is assessment of students. Assessment influences and often changes instruction. Assessments such as state-required proficiency tests, "multiple choice" in design, as well as the individualized grade card show that students are not measuring up to the set standards of the state, the schools, or the teachers. Test scores measuring American students' intellectual development are constantly being compared to that of Japanese children. The results rarely seem promising. Observations such as these lead educators to wonder: Are we evaluating students fairly? Are our assessments constructed

Weishaar 3

to give a fair analysis of students' performances? Do our current forms of evaluation influence teachers' means and emphases of instruction so that student work and progress can easily be converted to a weighted measure required by the grade card genre? The grade card, due to its physical and textual form, presents those reviewing a child's progress with a concise list of the skills which the child should acquire in each particular grade level. This genre reflects the assessments of the educational community, pre-constructed ideas which are considered most important in a child's education. The feedback that students and parents receive about the student's performance is contained within the grade card genre, and unless a parent-teacher conference is held, the grade card is solely responsible for reporting the child's educational progress. Thus, the grade card genre is a powerful instrument. What exactly does it tell the reader?

Currently the standardized report card for elementary schools utilizes the seventy-nine-year-old A, B, C, D, and F grading scale in conjunction with symbols (i.e., +, –) and/or other terms such as satisfactory and unsatisfactory to report student achievement. These forms subdivide the curriculum by subject, and assign a letter grade or symbol to each subject. The graded subjects include math, language arts, reading, writing, social studies, science, music, art, physical education, and behavioral attributes. Subdivisions for each of the categories include more specific statements about the curriculum of the subject (i.e., "The student knows addition facts through 100"). Blanks next to the more specific statements are checked with a "+," indicating that the child has mastered the skill, or a "–" indicating that the child needs to improve or has failed to learn that knowledge. Students are then placed into categorical grades such as A--outstanding effort, B--above average, C--average, D--below average, and

Weishaar 4

F--failed; other categories might include a less-harsh wording system such as satisfactory or unsatisfactory. What meaning do these terms actually hold? Is the student's performance average when compared to that of her peers, or is the student failing to meet the state and school criteria of achievement for that grade? Does "average" achievement for one teacher translate to "above average" achievement for another teacher in terms of expectations? Does the student's grade reflect the information that he/she has actually learned, or is the grade a type of punishment, a reflection of a lack of responsibility on the student's part to turn in assignments? With the current type of report card assessment, educators, parents, and students cannot be sure.

Assessment, especially the genre which presents the assessment, influences and often changes instruction. The standard type of report card fails to explain exactly what is expected of the students and what the degrees (i.e., +, −, average, etc.) of a child's performance actually mean. Assessment is being altered so that it is reflective of the curriculum which is to be taught. The genre is being altered to communicate a more thorough evaluation of a child's development, accomplishments, and goals. Thus, the means of instruction are changing to complement the new evaluation. The products and specific skills which teachers require students to master are geared toward meeting the requirements of the new genre of evaluation.

This is not to say that because student performance is not skyrocketing the charts of our current forms of assessment, that educators are changing the way they assess in order to make our students appear more intelligent. Instead, educators are asking, "Do our forms of assessment (genres) accurately measure the knowledge that our students have mastered?" For example, does a multiple-choice test

Weishaar 5

necessarily reflect a child's ability to write a well-developed paragraph, or even ask a child if he or she can explain how he or she interprets a concept? If the answer is no, then a grade drawn from a multiple choice assessment is equally lacking in accurately reflecting a child's knowledge. Furthermore, assessment should not just be a measure of what the student can memorize for a test and then forget ten minutes later. Instruction today is valued as it applies to the student's application of knowledge, skills, and understanding in important, real-world contexts.

One of the newest forms of assessment, called Performance Based Education, measures what really counts-- it measures how students apply their knowledge, skills, and understanding to real-world contexts. What is assessed should be what is important to learn. Principal Harold London of Ridgewood High School, Norridge, Ill., in an article in the NASSP Bulletin of May 1996, writes that: "Our purpose for grades is to communicate progress to students and parents. If we want to communicate accurately, we need to expand the choices available for teachers to use [for giving assessments, the genre used] so the purpose can be realized. If we have high expectations for our students, we need to establish the expectations early and demand that students meet the expectations" (119).

Because education is turning toward Outcomes Based/Performance Based Education (P.B.E.), the methods of assessment, and therefore the genre of reporting these assessments, must be reformed. Why? One of the greatest flaws of assessments such as the standardized report card is that these types of assessments often provide an evaluation of a student's achievements without any documentation of the achievements. P.B.E. calls for educators to define content standards and learner outcomes and then to make these con-

Weishaar 6

tent standards and learner outcomes available to the public. Along with this documentation of what students will be expected to learn, a criteria and high standards must be established to measure the student's performance because the student's achievement will be assessed on his or her performance. This type of assessment also demands that schools develop a curriculum and instruction to fit the content standards.

Obviously, the current standardized grade card cannot accurately reflect or give a documentation, an ongoing flow chart, of the student's achievements. Therefore, schools like Quail Run Elementary are reforming the traditional grade card, the genre of student assessment. Currently Quail Run teachers are perfecting a new type of "grade card," specific to general subjects (for now writing and reading), called continuums. A continuum is unlike a traditional grade card in design, content, and even in its range of function.

The continuums are divided by general subjects such as writing and reading which overlap many content areas. With the new push for measuring a student's application of his or her knowledge to real-world situations, many subject/content areas overlap. For example, writing ability might be measured in a social studies unit which might also include scientific investigation and mathematical problem solving. Standard grade cards do not facilitate the combining of subject areas because a grade must be given for each area. Continuums are designed in levels of development; each level of development has content standards and objectives which a student must demonstrate a command of before moving to the next development category. In the writing continuum, for example, the categories include: (For Primary students) Pre-Emerging Writer, Emerging Writer, Developing Writer, Expanding Writer, and Accomplishing Writer; (For

Weishaar 7

Intermediate students) Expanding Writer, Accomplishing Writer, Maturing Writer, and Distinguishing Writer. These categories are laid out horizontally across an 8" × 14" page. Under each development category are the criteria for assessment.

With this change in assessment, new criteria and scoring tools have been developed which allow teachers to evaluate a student's performance based on his/her application of his/her knowledge, The new scoring tools reflect the real-world idea that there is not necessarily one correct answer (a concept which was not enforced in the standard grade card genre). Grading rubrics, rating scales, and performance lists are scoring tools composed of the criteria which list the qualities educators consider to be most significant in student work. In the Quail Run writing continuum, the criteria are based on the Six Trait Writing model. This model measures the quality of a student's work by looking for six writing traits: Idea, Organization, Voice, Word Choice, Sentence Fluency, and Conventions. The new continuum also explains this model of evaluation on the backside of the continuum. Also, teachers are required to keep a portfolio of each student's work. As projects, papers, etc. are completed, the student along with the teacher selects pieces to be placed in the portfolio. Through these writing pieces, the teacher documents examples of a child's ability or difficulty with meeting a listed criteria. The portfolios, although not attached to the continuums, are used in direct conjunction with the continuums. They are the documentation of the student's progress. The continuum genre demands that instruction be geared towards the standards of the continuum and that examples of the students' applications/demonstrations of these specific skills be documented. Portfolios, because of the function of the genre, are now a necessity in evaluation. They back up

Weishaar 8
everything that the new genre, the continuum, reports. In
fact, this reformed genre does not limit what we ask or learn
about a student to the simple question and measurement
standard of "what grade did I get?" The continuums,
instead, call upon other sources, such as the portfolio, to
prove the report.

The continuums hold teachers accountable for giving
accurate, detailed evaluations because they must keep an up-
to-date portfolio of each child's work. Parents and students
are exposed to a clearly defined curriculum early on, and
because the development levels are laid out, they are aware
of not only what the student has already accomplished but
also where the student is heading. The continuums have a
"time line" of sorts running horizontally across the top of the
development categories. At each marking period, after determining the category of development that the child falls under
as demonstrated by his or her performance recorded by the
portfolios, the teacher will mark an approximate place of current development status. This mark, if found to remain in the
same area over several grading periods, will indicate to the
teacher that this student could need specialized attention in a
specific area.

With the movement towards the inclusion of all learning abilities within one classroom, the continuum in this way
fills the need for individualized attention or a way to check on
student progress. The development categories of the continuum, along with the rubrics used as scoring tools, provide a
flexibility within this genre that allows teachers to give a per-
sonalized critique of individual students in what could pose to
be a class with extremely diverse learning abilities. This flexibility was not found in the old genre of report cards with a
rigid five-category letter grade approach. The continuums do
not end with a development level anything less than the

Weishaar 9

abilities of an adult writer. Thus, students and parents are asked together to write goals for improvement at each marking period, and because of the "continuous" format they always have an idea of what goals are appropriate to aim towards.

Furthermore, the continuums generate flexibility among schools to accommodate new students. In this highly mobile world, students often transfer schools throughout districts and across the country. The continuum not only is designed to travel with the student from year to year, but in the case of a transfer, the new school and teacher will be able to see how the student has progressed, the curriculum he/she studied (from portfolios), and will immediately be able to tell the student's current learning state.

Educators, in their commitment to maximize the quality of student instruction, are developing a tool for evaluation, a genre which sets clear educational standards and requires that students demonstrate that they have met these standards. The revision of the standard, limiting grade card genre has evolved into a flexible form of communication which enhances student performance and does not just measure it.

Weishaar 10

Works Cited

Goodrich, Heidi. "Understanding Rubrics." Educational Leadership (Dec. 1996/ Jan. 1997): 14-17.

Guskey, Thomas R. "Making the Grade: What Benefits
    Students?" Educational Leadership (Oct. 1994): 14-19.
Hartenbach, David, and Joan Ott, and Sue Clark.
    "Performance-Based Education in Aurora."
    Educational Leadership (Dec. 1996/ Jan. 1997): 51-55.
Kirby-Linton, Kate, and Nancy Lyle, and Susan White.
    "When Parents and Teachers Create Writing
    Standards." Educational Leadership (Dec. 1996/ Jan.
    1997): 30-32.
Claffidge, Pamela Brown, and Elizabeth M. Whitaker.
    "Implementing a New Elementary Progress Report."
    Educational Leadership (Oct. 1994): 7-13.
London, Harold. "Do Our Grading Systems Contribute to
    Dumbing Down?" NASSP Bulletin (May 1996):117-
    121.
McTighe, Jay. "What Happens Between Assessments?"
    Educational Leadership (Dec. 1996/ Jan. 1997): 6-12
Meisels, Samuel J. "Using Work Sampling in Authentic
    Assessments." Educational Leadership (Dec. 1996/Jan.
    1997): 60-65.
Wiggins, Grant. "Practicing What We Preach in Designing
    Authentic Assessments." Educational Leadership (Dec.
    1996/ Jan. 1997): 18-25.

## Collaborative Activity 7.2

Think about what the above researched position paper—as well as our earlier discussions of the PMHF and the experimental report—teach us about how and why genres evolve or new genres emerge. What factors seem to encourage genres to change? How does that change come about? As a group, generate a list of your findings. Be prepared to share and discuss your findings with your classmates.

As we observe in the examples of the experimental report, the PMHF, and the report card, the new genres that develop out of new conditions and/or needs are most often revisions and refinements of already existing genres. This is the case even with genres that seem to be completely "new" such as the various kinds of e-mail that have emerged as a result of Internet technologies. Although the medium for communicating in e-mail might be new, the genres of e-mail that are developing—such as messages to friends, shared jokes, office communications, and spam or unsolicited e-mail advertisements—are themselves revisions of more traditional, already existing genres. Language scholars are beginning to study the characteristics of e-mail writing, and, in the future, we might be able to characterize its genres more fully.

Even now, however, we know that some e-mail messages combine characteristics of speaking and writing, giving them somewhat of a conversational quality. Messages in an e-mail thread are often responses, sometimes with the previous message included in the response, making such messages resemble conventional turn-taking conversations. However, unlike face-to-face conversations, the technological medium of e-mail—quicker than sending a letter to someone but slower than a face-to-face conversation—results in some written genres that use abbreviated language and shorthand (such as "BTW" for "By the way" or "IMHO" for "In my humble opinion") or symbols known as "emoticons" such as smiles :), frowns :(, or winks ;) that convey missing visual cues, tone, and body language. At the same time, e-mail genres draw on a variety of already existing written genres, such as memoranda, business letters, personal letters, reports, and so on. As such, we notice how some e-mail messages begin and end with greetings and salutations much as traditional letters do, while others use the subject line and memo headings as reports do.

## Writing Activity 7.4

Think about the ways that you write e-mail messages. What genres do you find yourself drawing on, even unconsciously, as you compose your messages? How would you characterize your e-mail writing style, and how does this differ as you write in different e-mail genres? How many different kinds of e-mail genres do you think you write? What characteristics distinguish those different e-mail genres? In what ways do you find yourself writing differently when you write in e-mail genres (such as a note to a friend) as opposed to when you write more traditional genres (such as snail-mail letters to friends)?

## REVISING OLD GENRES TO DEVELOP NEW ONES

There are reasons that new genres usually develop as revisions of previous ones. Genres reflect habitual ways of communicating and behaving in various scenes, and habits, as we all know, are difficult to break, especially when we rely on them to function in various scenes. If a completely unprecedented genre were to emerge, people would simply not know how to engage with it. And, even if people *were* able to make sense of a completely new genre, the question remains, can someone actually create a completely new genre without borrowing from other genres? Scholars who study the development of genres claim that it is unlikely. In fact, even genres that appear to be radically different from those that preceded them often result from combining already existing genres with a new scene or medium, just as we saw in the case of e-mail genres.

The genre of the resumé provides a case in point for how genres change. Earlier, we discussed how Randall Popken has argued that the resumé depersonalizes its writers, turning them into commodities that can be sold. As Popken explains, this was not always the case. Originally, job seekers relied solely on letters of application, which allowed them to write in full prose paragraphs about themselves and their qualifications. When the earliest versions of the resumé began to appear between 1914 and 1924, they were embedded in these letters of application. Popken refers to them as "resumé-in-letter." Here is an example of one such "resumé-in-letter." As you read it, notice how the "resumé-in-letter" is different from and similar to today's resumés.

---

X462 Tribune,
   Chicago.

Dear Sir:
   This is in answer to your advertisement for a stenographer:
   My education experience and qualifications, briefly, are: I am a graduate of the shorthand department of Brown's Business College, Peoria, and also of the Peoria High School, a school that is on the accredited list of the State University. I can take dictation rapidly and transcribe it quickly and accurately—spelling correctly, and placing the punctuation and capitals properly.
   I know how—
   To arrange a letter tastefully on the letterhead.
   To file a letter properly—or to find one that has been filed.
   To use the mimeograph and other duplicating devices.

To fold a letter.

To make out a bill correctly.

To meet callers.

To keep the affairs of the office to myself.

To attend to the mailing so that the right enclosures will go with the right letters.

I fully understand the uses of common business papers, such as drafts, checks, receipts, invoices, statements, etc.

I am twenty years old and live at home.

I have no experience, but my course of training has been thorough and has duplicated as closely as possible actual business conditions.

May I not have an opportunity to demonstrate my ability? The salary question we can safely leave open until you have had a chance to see what I can do.

Very truly yours,

From Randall Popken, "The Pedagogical Dissemination of a Genre: The Resumé in American Business Discourse Textbooks, 1914–1939" *JAC: A Journal of Composition Theory* 19.1 (1999): 91–116.

---

Notice how in the above example, the list of facts about the applicant is embedded within the sentence framework of the letter, thereby giving the applicant an opportunity to at least present himself or herself as more than just a list of facts. Popken notes that by 1924, the resumé begins to appear as a separate genre, one not embedded within an application letter. This separation reduced the self that could be presented more fully in the letter mainly to a set of facts that are depicted in the resumé. Here is a version of an early freestanding resumé from 1924. Notice how the genre has changed from the earlier version of the resumé-in-letter:

---

## Qualifications of Mr. Samuel Crompton

*Personal:*

Age, 25; unmarried; height, 5ft. 7in.; weight, 156 lbs.

Habits: good; does not drink; smokes moderately; likes outdoor sports.

Associations: member of St. John's Episcopal Church; active in the Elks and Odd Fellows, and a member of the Arts Association.

Health: very good, rarely sick.

Personality: see photograph attached.

*Education:*
Textile Arts School, graduated, 1917.
Temple College, attended night sessions, winters, 1913, 14, 16, 18.
Massachusetts Institute of Technology, finished night course in design, 1915.
Home Study Course, Correspondence Institute, pursued courses in carpet designing, show card writing, textile weaves and design, 1912-16.

*Experience:*

| | | | |
|---|---|---|---|
| General Design work, | The Textile Mills, | 1917-23 | $2500 |
| Asst. Carpet Designer, | Frankford Mills, | 1915-17 | 1800 |
| Ornamental Designer, | Clay Pottery Works, | 1914-15 | 1500 |
| Architectural Drafting, | Christopher Wren Co., | 1912-14 | 1400 |
| Teaching and Drafting, | Christopher Wren Co., | 1910-12 | 1000 |

*References:*
Mr. Theodore Lee, General Manager, Textile Mills, Philadelphia
Mr. John Mercer, Ass. Supt., Frankford Mills, Philadelphia
Mr. Joseph Aspdin, Pres. Clay Pottery Works, Philadelphia
Mr. Richard Artwright, Instructor, Drexel Institute, Philadelphia
Rev. Samuel Benedict, Philadelphia
Address: 19752 Gloucester Avenue, Philadelphia; Telephone, 469J, Germantown

From Randall Popken, "The Pedagogical Dissemination of a Genre: The Resumé in American Business Discourse Textbooks, 1914–1939" *JAC: A Journal of Composition Theory* 19.1 (1999): 91–116.

---

In this early precursor of the modern resumé, we notice features that we recognize in today's resumé, including the subjectless sentences and the categories of education, experiences, and references. We also recognize the list of facts and dates, arranged in an outline format. Today's resumé, however, generally allows even less personal information. It is not common for applicants to disclose their health, personality, height, weight, or even personal hobbies. Yet in the evolution of the genre from a letter, to a resumé-in-letter, to a free-standing resumé that allows some personal information, to the present-day resumé that allows less personal information, we can see a chain of interconnections that link each new genre to a prior one. And, even today, the genre of the resumé is undergoing more changes as new technologies allow more creative use of design and visuals and Internet technologies allow applicants to create online resumés with links to other sites, such as their professional portfolios.

**Collaborative Activity 7.3**

Working with a group of classmates, find a sample contemporary resumé, either one of your own or one from someone you know, or find one on the Internet), and compare its features to that of the early resumés we described above. What strikes you as being similar and different? What might account for these differences?

**Collaborative Activity 7.4**

This activity invites you to change an already existing genre. In your group, and while working with the same contemporary resumé that you examined in the previous activity, try to revise the resumé in ways that make it more reflective of its writer's personality as you imagine it. What changes would you make? What would you add and/or delete? How creative can you be without risking the effectiveness of the resumé in helping its writer get the desired job? After making your revisions, reflect on them. What strategies did you use? What risks did you take and what risks did you avoid? Why? What do you think will be the effects of your revisions?

# Using the Power of Genre for Change

As we have demonstrated with our ongoing example of the PMHF, genre critique can lead to genre change. But this is not all genre critique can do. Genre change can, in turn, lead to changes in the ways that people communicate and interact. For example, the new questions added to the PMHF, which ask patients to describe their mental state in relation to their physical symptoms, would change the genre; they might also change the ways doctors treat patients and what patients feel comfortable discussing with their doctors. Changing the genre *reflects* but can also *affect* changes in assumptions and practices. This is what we mean when we say that genres have power. Genres are not just sites for communicating and acting within scenes of writing; they are also potentially sites for changing the scenes themselves.

The emergence of Web sites and other hypertext genres in the last couple of decades shows how the power of genre can affect how people communicate and interact. James Sosnoski has studied these effects, focusing in particular on how genres written in hypertext, such as Web sites, are changing the way people read and interact with texts. He describes eight characteristics that define what he calls "hyper-reading." They are:

1. Filtering: a higher degree of selectivity in reading

2. Skimming: less text actually read

3. Pecking: a less linear sequencing of passages read

4. Imposing: less contextualization derived from the text and more from readerly intention

5. Filming: the ". . . but I saw the film" response which implies that significant meaning is derived from graphical elements as from verbal elements of the text

6. Trespassing: loosening of textual boundaries

7. De-authorizing: lessening sense of authorship and authorly intention

8. Fragmenting: breaking texts into notes rather than regarding them as essay, articles, or books

   From James Sosnoski, "Hyper-readers and their Reading Engines." *Passions, Pedagogies, and 21st Century Technologies*. Eds. Gail E. Hawisher and Cynthia L. Self. (Logan, UT: Utah State UP, 1999, 161–77.)

Sosnoski argues that these new characteristics of reading and interacting with texts mark a departure from more traditional ways of reading in that they shift authority from the writer to the reader. As a result, reading a Web site becomes a more constructive act than, say, reading a magazine article: Readers pick and choose different portions of text, and they "create" the texts as they select and navigate through various links. The reading of and interaction with texts becomes less linear and more three-dimensional, so that the dividing line between image and text as well as between reading and writing begins to blur. Eventually, Sosnoski argues, these hyper-reading characteristics will not be limited to hypertext genres. As children grow up internalizing these ways of reading, they will transfer them to the reading of other, nonelectronic genres, thereby changing the ways we use and interact with a great many genres.

   The power of genre to enact change, however, does not have to be as dramatic as what Sosnoski describes. We see people using the power of genre to effect change without having to depend on major developments in technology. For example, people use genres like petitions to gain support for new policies and write letters to the editor to try to change public opinion.

People can also add genres where they didn't exist before to effect change. For example, a teacher who is having difficulty getting the parents of her students involved in their education might decide to create a newsletter that the students help to write and that parents can then read in order to stay connected to their children's learning. The presence of this new genre, the classroom newsletter, might facilitate better interaction between parents, students, and teacher.

In a similar gesture, two students in one of our advanced writing courses decided to use the power of genre to create a more balanced relationship between the needs of learning-disabled students and their parents, and the needs of the teacher and the school. To create such a balance, the two students modified an existing genre called the Individual Education Plan (IEP). Signed into law in 1975, the IEP requires that learning-disabled students who are mainstreamed into traditional classrooms must have an individual education plan drawn up for them that is appropriate for their learning abilities and needs. At the start of each school year, the classroom teacher, special education teacher, parents, school principal, and other specialists meet to develop the student's individual education plan. As a result of their critique of the IEP, the two students in our class concluded that these IEP sessions were mainly one-sided, with parents playing a small role in developing the IEP and the students themselves (who have the most to gain and lose) playing no role at all. To address this lack of participation, our two students created an extra dimension to the IEP, a friendly-looking form (unlike the very institutional-looking IEP) with the heading: "This Year I Would Like To:" followed by enough space for the learning-disabled student to list five personal goals. As stated in their rationale for this addition, our two students hoped that such an inclusion might allow the student's voice and goals to play a part in the IEP.

### Writing Activity 7.5

Think about a time when either you or someone you know used the power of genre to make a difference, great or small. If you cannot draw from an immediate experience, then think about a time in history when a genre was used to make a difference. How was the genre used? What difference did it make? Why?

### Writing Activity 7.6

Think about how the genres that you use might be changed to suit you better. Consider genres you use at work, in school, in your public life, or in your private life. Select one that you would most like to see change and briefly describe how the genre works currently, the specific changes that might make the genre work better for you, and what these changes could achieve.

We end this chapter by describing an incident in which the power of genre actually did make a difference in the world—and in the process ignited a large controversy around the power of genre.

In 1983, Rigoberta Menchú, with the assistance of anthropologist Elizabeth Burgos-Debra, published her memoir called *I, Rigoberta Menchú*. A "memoir," as the name suggests, is a genre based in "memory"—a recollection of past lived experiences that hold some significance for the present. In her memoir, Menchú recounts her struggle as a Mayan peasant growing up in war-torn Guatemala, including her father's battles with oppressive landlords, the murder of members of her family, and the peasants' courageous attempts at resistance. The power of Menchú's memoir drew the world's attention to the suffering of Guatemalan peasants and won her critical acclaim as a human rights advocate. The memoir itself became an international best-seller and, in 1992, won the Nobel Prize. More significantly, by bringing attention to the suffering of poor Guatemalans, Menchú's memoir did something even more powerful: It helped force the Guatemalan government to sign an agreement to stop violating human rights.

The story does not end here, however. In 1999, David Stoll, an anthropologist, published a book called *Rigoberta Menchú and the Story of All Poor Guatemalans*. In the book, Stoll proves that many of the incidents Menchú recounts either did not actually happen to her or have been exaggerated for effect. The human rights violations that Menchú describes did occur, but not always in the versions she tells them and not always to her or her family. As you can imagine, Stoll's book ignited a controversy, with some people calling for a ban of Menchú's memoir from college reading lists and others hailing her work for its literary strength and ability to create change in the world. This controversy will not likely be resolved anytime soon, but what we do know is that Menchú's memoir *did* make a difference in the world. It helped bring attention to a people's suffering in a way that other attempts had not been able to accomplish, and it ultimately helped to curb the Guatemalan government's human rights violations. And it could be argued that it made the difference it did in part because it *was* presented as a memoir and yet did not remain true to all the expectations of a memoir.

This argument, however, raises the question of what it means to change genre conventions. Because they touch us on a personal level, memoirs can have a great effect on us, much like Menchú's did. At the same time, we expect that memoirs should depict events truthfully, and, when we find that they do not, we feel cheated, as many readers of Menchú's memoir did. Some could argue, though, that Menchú used the genre of the memoir because she knew it would make a powerful impact, but that she stretched its boundaries because she had to tell a powerful story, one more powerful even than her own story. In this, we could see Menchú using the power of genre (a genre that already has certain power in our culture) by adapting it to fit better her purpose and ultimately change her scene: to change the horrible conditions in which poor Guatemalans live.

We leave it up to you to decide where you stand in relation to this controversy. But most of all we hope that you find evidence in this controversy of the power of genre. Indeed, as we argue throughout this book, genre can give us access to the world in which we live and the various scenes of writing we participate in and negotiate. At the same time, genre can also enable us to critique the world in which we live while holding out the possibility that, through such critique, we can change the ways people communicate, interact, and live in the world. As you study the situations and genres of other scenes, keep in mind the power of genre not only to limit what you can communicate but also to critique those limitations. As you perform your critical reading of various genres in your life, take the time also to perform a critique of those genres, to reflect on their power over you and how you can use their power.

## Writing Projects

### Writing Project 7.1

Write a critique of the genre you have begun to examine, with your classmates and instructor as your audience. Make sure to state and then develop a **claim** that evaluates some aspect of the genre's effects. Then support your claim with **evidence** taken from the genre, evidence that you have already identified. In the process of developing your claim, keep in mind that you will need not only to describe the effects a genre has, but also to evaluate the strengths and/or limitations of these effects. To help you get started, read again the sample student paper, "For the Bride or Groom?", which performs a similar critique to the one we are asking you to perform.

### Writing Project 7.2

Using the list of findings about generic change that you developed as your guide, trace the development of some genre for your teacher and classmates. You can investigate a genre you have already analyzed in earlier activities and assignments or a genre you have not examined yet but which you would like to learn more about. Try, if possible, to determine how the genre came into existence, and then explore how and why it has evolved over the years. In order to research your chosen genre, you might gather samples of the genre used in different periods of time, interview long-time users of the genre, or find books/articles written about the genre and its development and use. When your research is complete, choose what you consider the most effective way to present it (given your subject matter, purpose, and audience). Various genres lend themselves to such a presentation of research, including a poster board, a Power-Point presentation, a Web site, or a researched position paper. The genre you use to present your research will affect how you organize and describe your research; it will also affect how your audience relates to the research; take some time to consider which genre to use.

## Writing Assignment 7.3

Find a genre that you are familiar with and that usually is no longer than one page. Various forms fit this specification, but so do everyday genres like bills, obituaries, party invitations, and flyers. After analyzing how this genre operates, write your own version of the genre so that you change its conventions (as the students rewrote the IEP or the teachers rewrote the grade report). Write a cover letter to your teacher explaining what conventions you changed and how you think those changes have altered the genre's situation (subject, participants, setting, purposes) and scene.

# Understanding Academic Scenes and Writing Courses

# 8

Among the recurring roles you have played in a variety of scenes as a writer are the multiple performances that have taken place within academic scenes and against the backdrop of the classroom setting. Some of you may even recall your debut performances as writers in this scene — forming your first letters and words or writing your first "story" in elementary school—and gradually moving to more challenging roles, like writing book reports in middle school and term papers or literary analyses in high school. All of your writing experiences over the course of your academic career, but particularly your more recent high school experiences, have served as rehearsals of sorts for the college or university scene.

Anytime you enter new scenes of writing, like the university and its various disciplines, you are likely to experience some uncertainty about how to communicate within them. You may feel a little like an outsider, out of place in an unfamiliar setting. The way people interact within these academic scenes, the choices they make when they speak and write, and their habits of mind may seem mysterious at first because you do not really know the reasons they are making the choices they are making. Academic writing does not need to be this mysterious, however. This chapter and the following one will help you become more familiar with academic scenes, the rhetorical interactions or situations within those scenes, and the academic genres that frame those scenes.

Chapters 1 and 2 of this book taught you to define and observe scenes of writing (Chapter 1) and to analyze the genres or patterns of communication within scenes in order to gain access to scenes of writing (Chapter 2). Next, we will draw on what you have learned in the previous chapters about communication within scenes and apply it specifically to reading and writing within academic scenes and academic genres, especially those that you will most likely encounter in your first-year writing course. This chapter will situate the particular scene of the college writing course within the broader academic scene of the college or university. We will explore the shared goals of the writing course (and how these goals reflect the larger shared goals of the college or university), the rhetorical interactions that make up the situations in this scene, and the genres used to interact within the situations of the writing class scene. In Chapters 8 and 9 you will be able to use your knowledge of academic scenes and genres to participate more effectively in your writing course and, building on that experience, to read and write your way through other scenes in the university or college more effectively and confidently.

## The Objectives of Colleges and Universities

In Chapter 1, *we defined scene as a place where communication happens among groups of people with some shared objectives.* The college or university is a scene that involves a place (a campus) in which communication happens among groups of people (students, faculty, staff, administrators) with some shared objectives (to facilitate the pursuit, production, and exchange of knowledge). While colleges and universities are diverse, with differing traditions and missions, they share essential overarching objectives. Colleges or universities generally encourage the pursuit of knowledge (its creation and application), critical inquiry and research, and openness to diverse experiences, worldviews, and values. Underlying the pursuit of knowledge is the shared idea that knowledge is not something that one can find simply by looking, and not something one can achieve alone. Rather, knowledge is something *constructed*, most often through a process of social interaction and collaborative inquiry.

The shared objectives of higher education thus go beyond career preparation or job training to include the teaching of habits and strategies for working with others to acquire, create, and apply knowledge. Many university mission statements, for example, contain language referring to "a lifetime of learning" or to making students "lifelong learners." Most higher education institutions see their mission as preparing students not for one career but for a multiplicity of potential careers as well as preparing them to play critical and thoughtful roles as citizens in a complex, changing society.

This vision of a "well-rounded" education that shapes a responsible, reflective citizenry dates back to classical Greek and Roman times and the earliest models of an educated society. In *The Republic*, the ancient Greek philosopher Plato argued that a good education combines intellectual development with spiritual, social, and artistic growth, laying the foundations for what we have come to know as a "liberal arts" education. While there are a number of liberal arts colleges that make this their sole mission, many universities try to integrate the breadth of the liberal arts with the depth of specialized training. These shared goals of professional training combined with the development of "lifelong learning" are even reflected in the organization of institutions of higher education, with their separation into Colleges of Arts and Sciences and Colleges of Law, Agriculture, Business, Engineering, etc. Even the physical layout of a university campus—often with separate buildings for different disciplines (such as the "Humanities Building") or separate floors/offices for individual departments (such as the English Department or the Psychology Department)—reveal this attempt to provide "coverage" of a wide array of disciplinary knowledge while also allowing concentration in a particular major.

Within this overarching scene of shared goals and systems of organization that carry out and reflect these goals, different colleges and universities, of course, form their own distinct scenes. Some colleges, for example, which began as teaching colleges, continue strongly to emphasize teacher training. Other regional schools may have programs tailored to meet the particular needs of citizens in that area—for example, strong agricultural programs in schools in solidly agricultural regions. Religious colleges or universities may highlight moral or religious values in their mission, while technical colleges may emphasize the development of technical skills over a "liberal arts" background. And although all universities and colleges share in the pursuit and production of knowledge, some may highlight the application of knowledge over its production, while others may highlight different aspects of knowledge and specialize in different kinds of knowledge making.

## Writing Activity 8.1

Check your university or college's Web site or catalogue for a statement of the mission and goals of your college or university. Based on the stated goals/objectives, how would you describe the scene of your institution? Which statements seem like goals that could be met by institutions anywhere, and which seem specific to the particular scene of your university/college?

# Multiple Scenes within Colleges and Universities

While a university or college is itself an overarching scene—a place where communication happens among groups of people with some shared objectives—it is also made up of multiple scenes that both share in the overarching objectives and have their own more particular objectives. The various administrative offices, the different schools, disciplines and departments, and the multiple curricular and extracurricular organizations and clubs are all *scenes,* because they each involve a place in which communication happens among groups of people with some shared objectives. For example, members of English departments are likely to pursue knowledge as it is produced and interpreted in texts, while members of sociology departments are likely to pursue knowledge as it takes place within social groups and cultures. Each department thus becomes a more particular scene within the larger academic scene.

Even within the more particular scenes of disciplines and departments, there are more specific scenes such as specializations, tracks, and courses. In the department of English, for instance, there may be specialized tracks and courses in literature, rhetoric-composition, technical writing, creative writing, or linguistics. As we mentioned in Chapter 1, each course you take is its own scene in that it, too, involves a place in which communication happens among groups of people with some shared objectives. In the department of English, each course, while sharing the objectives of the larger department, has its own more specific objectives, which are often outlined in the course syllabus.

As you make your way through the multiple scenes of your university or college, try to identify and define the particular scene you are in, but also remember that the scene is itself part of a larger scene which might very well be part of an even larger scene. The more you can situate the scene in which you are participating within the larger scenes that influence it, the more fully you will be able to understand and carry out its objectives.

## Writing Activity 8.2

Log on to the Internet, and visit the home page of your college or university. What do the features of the Web site indicate about the overarching scene of the college or university and the multiple scenes within it? How are different scenes indicated (through different kinds of links, for example, or other kinds of structures)? What are some of the various scenes that you can identify?

# Multiple Situations within Colleges and Universities

Each of the multiple social and academic scenes within a college or university has its own particular *situations,* defined in Chapter 1 as *the rhetorical interactions happening within a scene, involving participants, purposes, subjects, and settings.* Each course, in fact, is a scene made up of multiple situations, so that in any given course you will find students and teachers engaged in different types of interactions. Examples of these situations, as we described in Chapter 1, include class discussions, students working in peer groups, student and teacher engaged in one-on-one conferencing, students writing in-class papers, etc.

You have probably already encountered a variety of academic situations, where participants are discussing a variety of subjects and are using language to accomplish various purposes in various settings. While walking to class you have probably observed a variety of situations, from students gathered on the quad chatting about the band that is playing on Saturday night to students sitting in hallways reading the student newspaper or studying class notes. Or you might have passed classrooms where teachers are giving a class lecture as students furiously scribble notes or where students are gathered in a science laboratory taking notes on an experiment. Or maybe you have passed a professor's office and found him or her conferring with a student.

The multiple situations taking place within academic scenes are too numerous to mention here and may range from situations outside the classroom (students filling out financial aid forms or registering for classes, fans cheering at a basketball game, or students debating a proposal before the student government), to a multitude of academic situations that vary according to different disciplines and departments. Whether theater majors rehearsing on a stage in the university auditorium, computer science students working collaboratively to write new software in a computer lab, faculty and deans from the school of business gathered in a conference room to discuss new internship requirements, or students and faculty gathered in an auditorium to hear a poetry reading or political lecture, these rhetorical interactions accomplish some shared objectives and carry out the actions and activities of various university scenes.

## Writing Activity 8.3

Drawing on Box 1.2: Guidelines for Observing and Describing Scenes (pp. 44–45), choose a situation within an academic scene and write a one-page description of the situation. You might observe a situation in a class you are taking, such as a lecture, class discussion, group work assignment, or oral presentation. Or you might observe a group of students studying in the library, a meeting of a student group or organization, or a group of fans at a sporting event. In a paragraph or two, describe the participants in the situation, the setting of their interaction, the subject of their interaction, and their purposes for interacting and the type of language and tone used. What is the nature of their communication, and how is it shaped by the situation and scene?

# Academic Genres

In order to carry out their shared objectives within an academic scene or to accomplish a particular purpose within an academic situation, participants draw on genres. *Genres are the typical rhetorical ways of responding to a situation that repeatedly occurs within a scene.* Within academic scenes that share the overarching missions of cultivating learning and gauging the effectiveness of that learning, teaching situations and evaluation procedures tend to repeat themselves semester after semester, year after year, leading to typical responses. For instance, teachers—regardless of discipline—rely on certain typical rhetorical interactions to carry out their instructional goals, whether through the genres of assignments, lectures, class discussions, visual presentations (such as overheads), conferences with students, or even textbooks such as this one. In addition, to gauge whether they are effectively transferring this knowledge, teachers ask students to participate in proven patterns of action such as oral presentations, journals, quizzes, term papers, tests, and exams. Because educational institutions at all levels participate in a scene that increasingly values accountability, you, as student have no doubt become more than familiar with the many genres of testing, whether true/false, multiple choice, or essay exams. Analyzing the genres used in the college or university scene is one strategy for better understanding that scene and learning how to participate in it. Here, we will focus on two genres that are used across multiple academic scenes: the syllabus and the writing assignment.

## The Syllabus

As writers, we can begin to understand and communicate in different academic scenes of writing by identifying their central assumptions. Since assumptions are embedded in the genres people use within these academic scenes, we can use genres not only as scripts, but also as maps for gaining access to these academic scenes. The *syllabus* is one such map. One immediate way to begin navigating new academic landscapes is by carefully reading your different courses' syllabi, which help frame each course's scene of writing. Doing so will help you identify some of the assumptions that shape the values and goals of these courses, knowledge that will help you start making more informed choices as a writer when it is time for you to perform within these different scenes of writing. Following is a sample syllabus from an advanced writing course, which we will use to illustrate how this genre can help you uncover the assumptions and expectations of a course.

---

### English 355: Rhetoric and Writing

## COURSE GOALS

English 355 is an advanced writing course designed to develop your writing proficiency and to further refine your writing skills, with emphasis on development of ideas, analysis of style, and clarity of thought and expression. Through analysis of the rhetorical situations that motivate your writing and roles as writers, you will learn to adapt and adjust your messages to particular audiences, purposes, and contexts for writing. You will plan, draft, and revise papers that address a variety of situations within academic, professional, and public contexts. In addition, you will critically read and discuss both published texts and the writing of your peers and will learn to analyze and evaluate writing based on its appropriateness to the rhetorical situation (audience, purpose, persona) and to guide its revision.

## COURSE ORGANIZATION

Based on the principle that writers learn to write by writing, the class will be organized as a writing workshop, with a large portion of our class periods spent on in-class writing projects, discussion of works in progress and planning, drafting, and revision of written assignments. In addition, because writing is a dynamic social process and learning to interact with other writers is central to every writer's development, you will also collaborate in small-group workshops as well as participate in full-group workshops and discussions. As a writer, you are responsible for bringing copies of your paper for each member of your group on the class period scheduled. As a responder, you will be responsible for carefully and critically reading and commenting on your classmates' papers. All response sheets will be handed in with final drafts of papers.

## WRITTEN WORK

You will plan, draft, and revise four papers and will complete a final revision project, in addition to peer responses (both written and oral) and other informal in-class writings and style exercises. You will choose your own topic areas and will determine the genres that would be most appropriate (for example, a letter, proposal, report, editorial, article, newsletter, brochure, etc.). For each assignment, you will develop an analysis of the writing situation (both the social and the rhetorical situation) surrounding that piece of writing and will target a specific audience and forum for publication. That analysis will be submitted with each paper. At the end of the semester, you will revise some aspect of your rhetorical situation and will rewrite a fitting response for this new situation.

## COURSE POLICIES

Since English 355 will be conducted as a writing workshop, its success depends upon active and informed involvement and participation. You are expected to submit rough drafts for peer response on time. Written and oral responses to the writing of others are significant components of this course—activities for which you will receive credit. As a result, regular attendance is necessary in order to perform successfully in this course.

## GRADING

Paper 1—10%        Paper 3—20%        Revision Project—15%
Paper 2—15%        Paper 4—25%        Workshop Grade—15%

## ENGLISH 355: DAILY SYLLABUS

| | | |
|---|---|---|
| Wed. | 1/10 | Introduction to Course |
| Fri. | 1/12 | In-class Writing: Writing Background Analysis |
| Mon. | 1/15 | Martin Luther King Day: No Classes |
| Wed. | 1/17 | Ch. 1 "Writing in College" & Ch. 2 "What Is Good Writing?" |
| Fri. | 1/19 | Ch. 3 "What Happens When People Write?"; Assign Paper 1 |
| Mon. | 1/22 | Ch. 4 "What Is your Writing Situation?"; Rhetorical Situation; Appeals |
| Wed. | 1/24 | Ch. 5 "Drafting Your Paper"; Writing Situation Analysis Due |
| Fri. | 1/26 | Ch. 7 "Holding Your Reader"; Bring draft-in-progress |
| Mon. | 1/29 | **Draft Due: Paper 1**; Ch. 8 "Writing Clearly" |
| Wed. | 1/31 | Draft Workshop (Bring copies for small group); Ch. 6 "Revising" |
| Fri. | 2/2 | Style Workshop (Bring copies—small group); Ch. 9 "Crafting Paragraphs" |
| Mon. | 2/5 | **Final Due: Paper 1**; Prewriting for Paper 2: Exploratory Paper |
| Wed. | 2/7 | Planning/Drafting: Paper 2 |

| Fri. | 2/9 | Writing Situation Analysis: Analyzing the Rhetorical Situation/Social Community |
| Mon. | 2/12 | Group Troubleshooting Workshop: Paper 2; Voice: Ch 1–2 |
| Wed. | 2/14 | **Draft Due: Paper 2** (Bring copies for full-class workshop); Ch. 3 |
| Fri. | 2/16 | Draft Workshop: Full-Class Discussion |
| Mon. | 2/19 | Draft Workshop: Full-Class Discussion |
| Wed. | 2/21 | Draft Workshop: Full-Class Discussion |
| Fri. | 2/23 | Draft Workshop: Full-Class Discussion |
| Mon. | 2/26 | **Final Due: Paper 2**; Prewriting for Paper 3: Rhetorical Analysis |
| Wed. | 2/28 | Doing Nonlibrary Research |
| Fri. | 3/2 | Analyzing Communities/Rhetorical Actions |
| Mon. | 3/5 | "Learning the Language" (handout) |
| Wed. | 3/7 | Sample Analysis: Political Speech |
| Fri. | 3/9 | Planning/Drafting: Paper 3 |
| Mon. | 3/12 | Group Troubleshoot: Paper 3 (bring intro, tentative thesis, rough outline & questions) |
| Wed. | 3/14 | **Draft Due: Paper 3**; Draft Workshop (bring copies for small group) |
| Fri. | 3/16 | Conference on College Composition and Communication; Coherence: Ch. 6 |
| Mon. | 3/19– | Spring Break: No Classes |
| Fri. | 3/23 | |
| Mon. | 3/26 | Draft Due: Paper 3; Style Workshop; Structural Variety: Ch. 10 |
| Wed. | 3/28 | Editing Workshop; Ch. 10 |
| Fri. | 3/30 | **Final Due: Paper 3**; Prewriting for Paper 4: brochure/magazine article |
| Mon. | 4/2 | Planning/Drafting: Paper 4 |
| Wed. | 4/4 | Writing Situation Analysis |
| Fri. | 4/6 | Sample Genres |
| Mon. | 4/9 | Bring in draft in progress; Actors and Actions: Ch. 9 |
| Wed. | 4/11 | Bring in draft in progress: Word Choice: Ch. 4–5 |
| Fri. | 4/13 | Easter Break: No Classes |
| Mon. | 4/16 | **Draft Due: Paper 4** (bring copies for full-class workshop); Ch. 11 |
| Wed. | 4/18 | Draft Workshop: Full-Class Discussion |
| Fri. | 4/20 | Draft Workshop: Full-Class Discussion |

| Mon. | 4/23 | Draft Workshop: Full-Class Discussion |
| Wed. | 4/25 | Draft Workshop: Full-Class Discussion |
| Fri. | 4/27 | **Final Due: Paper 4**; Planning for Revision Project |
| Mon. | 4/30 | Workshop: Revision Project |
| Mon. | 5/7 | Final 8–10 a.m.—Turn in Revision Project |

The syllabus is a genre that not only contains helpful information about the course policies and schedule; it also contains important information about the course's underlying logic—information that frames the course's scene of writing. What, for instance, are the stated objectives of the syllabus? How does your instructor describe these objectives? You can usually find these statements at the beginning of the syllabus, where the instructor often includes a description of the course and its goals. The sample syllabus begins with a section called "Course Goals," which mentions specific objectives, such as development of writing proficiency and style, practice with writing processes, and awareness of rhetorical situations.

Next, you can examine the syllabus in order to identify how your instructor plans on accomplishing these objectives. You might look at the daily assignments and readings as well as any writing assignments or major projects for clues to this. Do the assignments and activities outlined in the syllabus build on one another? If so, how? If not, then how do they relate? What does your instructor expect you to practice and learn in each assignment and activity? In the syllabus, there are several clues to how the objectives will be carried out: assigned readings, papers, and class discussions that develop critical thinking skills; various workshop activities such as "planning/drafting" and "draft workshops" that emphasize writing processes; and oral responses, writing assignments, and collaborative activities that ask students to implement rhetorical strategies. The reference to revision projects under the heading "Written Work" as well as the many references to planning and drafting on the daily schedule emphasize the instructor's expectation that students will develop processes for writing and will spend a significant amount of time revising their work. In addition, the fact that each writing assignment is weighted more heavily than the one preceding it (see "Grading") indicates the increased complexity of assignments as well as the underlying belief that student writing will improve throughout the course.

As you continue to uncover the underlying assumptions and expectations of the course in your analysis of the syllabus, look for key words and phrases, words and phrases that might be underlined or repeated often. Think about what these words reveal about how the course will treat the subject of study. In the sample syllabus, there are repeated references to "process," "workshops," "peer response," "rhetorical situations," and to the stages of "planning," "drafting," and "revision." These terms reflect the course's focus on learning to write by writing (rather than by lecturing about writing) and the expectation that students will actively participate in the learning process through their participation in the writing process activities and collaborative activities of peer review.

Learning to analyze your syllabus in this way is a first step in becoming an active academic participant rather than a passive receiver of information, and it is a first step in beginning to make more effective learning choices in the academic scene. Of course, the syllabus alone does not contain all the answers, but as a genre that reflects and reveals the goals and objectives of a course, it does offer a map of the course scene that can help you begin navigating the class and locating yourself in this scene.

## Collaborative Activity 8.1

Bring in sample syllabi from courses that you are taking, and share these syllabi in small groups. Drawing on the Guidelines for Analyzing Genres in Box 2.1 (pp. 93–94), *identify* the rhetorical patterns of the syllabus genre (content, format, language, tone, organization). Then *analyze* what these patterns reveal about the academic scene and the roles of participants within this scene. What is expected of students in college courses, for example? How are they expected to behave, according to the syllabi's assumptions? What kinds of roles are teachers expected to take, as reflected in the syllabus genre? What kinds of things do the syllabi seem to stress, and what does that say about the expectations within the academic scene?

Next, drawing on the Questions for Critiquing Genre in Box 7.1 (p. 229), *critique* the genre of the syllabus. What does the genre enable its users (both teachers and students) to do, and what does it not allow them to do? Whose needs are most and least served by the genre? What limitations does the genre place on participation in the writing course scene and the larger academic scene? Be prepared to share your responses with the rest of the class.

## Collaborative Activity 8.2

In small groups, share the syllabi you collected for the previous activity, but this time analyze the differences among the different versions of the academic scene. Note not only the variation possible in the syllabus genre, since every genre allows variation, but attend also to how those differences may reflect disciplinary differences. Do the syllabi from the humanities (like English, history, philosophy) differ from those of the sciences or social sciences? How does the general academic scene vary in different disciplines?

---

**Box 8.1**    *Questions for Analyzing Writing Assignments*

1. *Setting:* What kind of course is this assignment for? Does this kind of course or this field have expectations I can anticipate? Is this one of a set of assignments? If so, how does this particular assignment fit in?
2. *Subject:* Does the assignment specify a subject? If so, what is it? If not, what subjects are most appropriate? Whatever subject I choose, how am I being asked to treat it? What does the assignment want me to do with the subject—describe it, analyze it, argue about it, research it? What should my goals be in addressing the subject?
3. *Writers:* What kind of role does the assignment ask me to play as a writer? What sort of stance should I take? (Should it be critical, questioning, accepting?) What kind of tone shall I present?
4. *Readers:* Who should I assume will be my readers? What kind of information does the assignment provide about the readers? What else do I need to know about the readers for me to address them effectively? What are my readers' expectations—of me and the subject matter?
8. *Purposes:* Other than to get a grade, why am I writing this assignment? What does the teacher want me to gain from this assignment? What do I want to gain?
6. *Genre Features:* Are there certain expectations about organization and format? If so, what are those? If not, then where can I go to find out? What about style? Does the assignment specify a certain style or am I permitted to choose a style? Given the role I will be taking on, my readers, and the subject matter, what style will be most appropriate?

---

## THE WRITING ASSIGNMENT

While the syllabus helps frame a course's general scene of writing by containing some of its basic objectives and assumptions, writing assignments are genres that specify some of the situations that will occur in the course's scene. Writing assignments help to frame the situation for writing by specifying, to some extent, the subject, setting, audience, and purpose for writing. So yet another way to access and participate effectively in academic scenes is by identifying the expectations regarding subject, setting, audience, and purpose for writing that are embedded in your assignment.

The first and most important step you can take as a writer is to position yourself within the assignment as a reader, to make sense of the writing assignment. "Reading" an assignment is just like reading other genres that we described in Chapter 2. Before you decide how to act in a situation, you need to read what the genre tells you about that situation. The more you can figure out what the underlying assumptions and expectations are, the more likely you will be able to make informed writing choices.

When you are given a writing assignment, try to identify its expectations and assumptions by asking yourself the questions in Box 8.1, which are based on our analysis of situations in Chapter 1.

By asking yourself such questions before you begin writing, you not only begin to understand your writing situation better, but you also begin to situate your writing choices more knowingly within it.

### Writing Activity 8.4

Take a writing assignment, either from your current writing course or from any other course, and analyze it using the questions in Box 8.1 as your guidelines. What do you learn about your writing situation as a result? What kinds of writing choices would be most appropriate for you to make as you begin to write?

## The Objectives of Writing Courses

Like many new college students, chances are you might have had some trepidation about writing in college, especially as you entered your first-year writing course, which is an unfamiliar scene. You might have heard horror stories about the required writing course (or courses): how it is a "weed-out" or "boot camp" course, how its teachers' standards are so much higher than those you encountered before in school, how it is a course you just have to get out of the way before you get to the "real" classes that have "real" subjects, and so on. College-level writing courses really do not deserve such stigmas. Indeed, by the time they are ready to graduate, an overwhelming number of surveyed students consistently single out their first-year writing courses as being among the most beneficial and rewarding of their college experience. These students cite the small class size, the opportunity to receive one-to-one instruction as well as to work collaboratively with peers, the close attention to their writing, and the transferable writing skills that they can use throughout their college careers and beyond as contributing to the positive experience. In fact, when they reflect back on their writing courses, most students realize what we hope to convince you of here: That writing courses like the one you are taking are in fact not "weed-out" but "weed-*in*" courses; they introduce you to and help you learn how to function more effectively as readers and writers within the scene of the university.

In many ways, college writing courses are transitional courses. They function in part as "ports of entry" into the ways of thinking and interacting that are common in the university, with its emphasis on critical analysis, inquiry, and research. You already possess—and have most likely practiced—some of the thinking and interacting skills that are valued in the university, and writing courses such as the one you are currently taking help you build on and refine these skills so that you can function more effectively as college writers. Thinking of writing courses metaphorically as "ports of entry" can be a helpful way of imagining how such courses let you develop the rhetorical skills that will enable you to move with more agility and awareness through the various scenes of writing that await you.

If writing courses are ports of entry, then language use and genre knowledge are kinds of passports for entering into and navigating these often unfamiliar landscapes of the college and university scene. In addition, the metaphor of passports—which entitle their bearers to participate in the scene they are entering as well as the scenes they leave behind—suggests that you enter the writing class with a knowledge of language and of genres already in place and don't just show up to your college writing course as blank slates.

Writing researcher and college professor Anne DiPardo, in her research study entitled *A Kind of Passport*, uses this passport metaphor to describe students' struggles with writing as they move from the scene of their home cultures into academic scenes, particularly the scene of the college writing classroom. In the reading that follows, DiPardo—drawing on some of the techniques for observing scenes that we discussed in Chapter 1—closely observes and interviews students as they adjust to the academic scene of "Dover Park University" (DPU). The following excerpt from DiPardo's study focuses on how one writer, "Sylvia," uses language to negotiate multiple situations and rhetorical interactions within this scene. As you read, consider the nature of the struggles that Sylvia faces as she attempts to adjust to the demands of college life, particularly her struggles with communicating within unfamiliar academic scenes.

▦ ▦ ▦

# Sylvia

Anne DiPardo

## Cultural and Linguistic Background

Sylvia's family immigrated from Mexico when she was eight months old, settling in a prosperous, traditionally Anglo farming community that was then in a process of demographic transformation. While Sylvia recalled that some of the local Anglos "began to hate the idea that Latinos might take over," the town gradually became a place where families from widely varied backgrounds peaceably coexisted. She seemed particularly eager to dispel any suspicion that it was an impoverished ghetto:

> The town where I live is an urban area, and it's middle class, upper-middle class. There is the lower class, but I mean, I don't see it, because I'm not around it all the time and stuff. It's not *that* bad. I grew up with, I don't know, a variety of people, you know, Mexicans, blacks, Asians, whatever.

Sylvia's parents had never become fully proficient in English, and Spanish remained the language of home: "they've picked up a little English here and there," she explained, "but like fluently, no." Although both held relatively low-paying jobs—her father working in the fields and her mother doing housecleaning and childcare—they had managed to purchase some lucrative farmland, send money home to relatives, and save for Sylvia's education.[1] Still, as Sylvia explained in an essay entitled "My Dream," she "felt sorry" for her parents, who "didn't have the opportunity to make choices" that she now possessed:

> When they were my age, times were hard for them and life was pretty much planned out for them . . . Well, in this day and age I have choices. I can go to college, or I could quit school altogether and work. It is my decision. I also have the choice of the field to go into. I could be an engineer, a teacher, or a mathematician. It is entirely up to me. The jobs are out there, I just have to choose which one I will pursue.

Elsewhere in the essay, Sylvia explained that while her own life was already rather different from her parents', she would always share their commitment to family: "my family would be the most important thing in my life," she wrote, "because they will always be there for me, and they will always stand beside me."

But already, Sylvia's dual commitment to family and worldly achievement was fraught with paradox. Even as her parents boasted of their daughter's presence at a four-year college, they worried that she was losing touch with her roots; and even as Sylvia was trying to recapture an earlier sense of ethnic identity, she longed to break away from the typecasting that had long plagued her, to be perceived "just like any other American." In one of her essays she described the "many barriers" that she had crossed, the "many negative messages" that she had overcome:

> . . . my family back in Mexico is proud that I am going to school, but some members put me down. They can not understand that I am doing something worthwhile with my life. They feel that I should do things the traditional way, which is to stay home until I get married. My family sees me as an independent woman that left home and will never get married.

Although Sylvia's parents had helped force her to take the first big step into the Anglo world—when they sent her, then a five-year-old girl who could speak only Spanish, to a local kindergarten—they had ample cause to regret her cultural and linguistic estrangement. The problem first became evident during Sylvia's second-grade year, when she made an abrupt and disruptive switch from a bilingual classroom to an English-immersion program. For a time, she was gripped with "the fear of speaking in either English or Spanish," and had trouble communicating at home and school alike:

> So by the time they said, "Well, here's English," I was like, "Whoa, wait a minute, slow down here!" It was just like a big switch, it was kind of hard for me. And ever since then I've had that [writer's] block kinda thing . . . I didn't even know the basics of my own language, you know, when they said, "Boo, here's English." You know. And the funny thing is, I *lost* my Spanish. I couldn't speak it no more. And you know, my parents, it was a really . . . *[exasperated sigh]* it was so tough to communicate.

"I lost it," she repeated softly, as if still amazed that such a thing could happen. "I could have lost it completely," she added, "and not even speak Spanish right now, and really be called 'coconut.'"[2]

Deeply concerned, Sylvia's parents arranged a month's stay in Mexico between her second- and third-grade years—this in the hopes that she might recover the ability to speak her native language, and might also realize the link it represented to her extended family. Sylvia found the experience disorienting and somewhat disturbing: even as she basked in the warmth of her relatives' hugs and eager chatter, she was literally speechless. At first, her brother was her translator and emissary—then, as Sylvia recalled, "reality hit. I said [to myself], 'You've gotta learn it.'" At first, she was halting and awkward, but by the end of that pivotal month she was once again comfortable speaking Spanish to relatives and Hispanic friends. Even as Sylvia approached young adulthood,

Spanish remained the language spoken at home, especially when one of her parents was present—"to show respect," as her father had always said.

Sylvia remained apprehensive, however, about her ability to communicate in Spanish with strangers: "My fear," she explained, "is that I cannot pronounce the words and they won't know what I'm talking about." While she felt somewhat uncertain about her English writing, she was even more insecure about composing in her native language: "I just can't write it properly," she maintained. Flicking aside playful criticism from non-Spanish-speaking friends, she had futilely scanned the schedule of classes for a course that would help her speak and read her native language with renewed confidence. Sylvia spoke longingly of her nine-year-old sister back home: "she can speak better Spanish than I can," she explained, "and that's because they speak it in the house all the time."

Sylvia felt fully competent in neither language—in both, she was keenly aware of her foreigner's accent and uneasy about her abilities as a writer. It would be inadequate to say that Sylvia had made an incomplete transition from Spanish to English, the reality being vastly more complex, more tangled with dilemma. As Sylvia described her sense of being caught between languages, she inevitably described her sense of being caught between cultures as well: "It's funny, because like when I go to Mexico, I don't feel I'm part of them. I don't feel any less, either. It's just like I have two different cultures in me, but I can't choose."

While she felt more at home in the States than in her native Mexico, Sylvia was as concerned about recovering a sense of her family's culture as she was about retaining her first language: "I don't know my culture that well, to tell you the truth. I know more American culture than I know about my own. But everyday I'm learning, you know, and I like it . . . my friend is always joking with me, saying, 'You're not a real Mexican.' I say, 'But a proud one, though.'"

Although Sylvia's path had been far from easy, she was pleased with her progress, and quick to point out that her experiences in two worlds had helped her toward a number of important realizations. She had begun to see her bilingualism as a resource, and was fast overcoming her habitual shyness about speaking Spanish in public: whenever she overheard someone struggling to assemble fragments of broken English, she explained, "I see myself when I was a kid," and she was stepping in to help wherever she could. She had also acquired a certain easygoing open-mindedness, an ability to consider diverse perspectives but ultimately chart her own course—this from growing up in a multiethnic, multilingual community, and from her struggle to come to terms with the assumptions and values of her extended family back in Mexico. Finally, her own experiences in school had convinced her of the value of bilingual education, a topic that she took up in her last essay of the semester:

> My opinion for bilingual education is that there should be programs funded by the government . . . How is a student going to be able to comprehend a second language, if the student has not had a strong foundation of his first language? By studying and understanding the basics such as grammar and structure, the student will be able to switch to another language.

Sylvia's argument was informed by knowledge of Cummins's (1979, 1981) "interdependence hypothesis," and by an abiding belief that she was living evidence of its truth. With her family's support, she had long struggled toward an "additive" bilingualism, toward a facility in two languages that would empower her in new ways without diminishing the importance of the old. Only as an insightful and ambitious young woman was she beginning to grasp the full complexity of that struggle, and to cast a discerning eye upon the lingering effects of what had happened to her—to her sense of linguistic competence, to her sense of identity—in second grade.

## Adjustment to DPU

When asked if she were happy at DPU, Sylvia was decidedly upbeat: "I'm *very* happy here," she assured me; "I'm glad that I came, and for many reasons." Her father, she explained, had always wanted her to learn to be independent, and the experience of being away gave her a newfound confidence in her ability to get along on her own. While she admitted to fleeting moments of homesickness, Sylvia also boasted of her 2.9 G.P.A. and her ambition to "really push," to become a "better person," to fill in deficiencies in her academic preparation and build from existing strengths. If her glowing score on an initial placement exam was any indication, some of her greatest strengths were in mathematics, which she was "looking into" as a possible major. "Ever since I was a kid," she explained, "mathematics came easy to me—I get a thrill doing math." She could see herself going on for graduate work in math or engineering and possibly teaching at the college level.

Sylvia often spoke of the need for equity students to "get out of their cliques," noting that her upbringing in a multiethnic community had provided the sorts of experiences that were allowing her to thrive at DPU. Of Sylvia's closest friends on campus, two were Mexican and two African-American: "We can joke about race and not get offended," she emphasized, noting that she had learned much from their many discussions "about who we are and where we come from." Although her membership in M.E.Ch.A. initially opened a number of important doors, she had recently distanced herself somewhat from the organization. She was, however, continuing to serve as a DPU recruiter under the auspices of M.E.Ch.A.—leading campus tours and talking to local high school students "about what it's like to be away from home, in college." Sylvia spoke of this community service with particular pride, reporting that these highly positive experiences were helping to banish her lifelong fear of public speaking.

On the one hand, Sylvia felt a strong need to spend time with other Hispanic students—to speak Spanish ("music to my ears," as she described one recent conversation), and to reflect together upon the rewards and challenges of life at DPU; on the other hand, she worried that campus Anglos might regard her close association with the Hispanic community as a sort of protective cocooning, a shield that she insisted she neither wanted nor needed. Having grown up among people of many backgrounds, she was untroubled to find herself the only non-Anglo student in many of her classes. In a beginning-of-term interview, Sylvia flicked aside the many complaints she heard from others: "Sometimes if they feel that they're a minority," she speculated, "they feel real low or, like, low self-esteem. Who knows, you know? I'm a minority, I don't have a problem."

By the end of the semester, however, Sylvia's perception of ethnic relations at DPU had shifted somewhat. In an initial interview, she had insisted that she saw no signs of prejudice on campus, emphasizing that she refused to "look for trouble"; in a final interview, however, she noted that one of the most important lessons she had learned during her first year at DPU concerned the reality of discrimination. When an article in the county newspaper included the accusation that DPU equity students were recruiting for inner-city street gangs, this young woman who liked to avoid "trouble" joined the protest march downtown. In the attitudes of security personnel and newspaper staff, Sylvia saw undeniable evidence of the same entrenched biases displayed in the article. This new awareness was, she admitted, initially shocking:

> I wasn't aware of what's out there when I was in high school. And then when I come here, it was a whole new world for me, you know, and I've never really been—well, I've been discriminated, but not to my face . . . and for me to actually see something like that, the first time it was really shocking to me. I thought, "damn," you know?

While Sylvia saw community attitudes as part and parcel of what she had observed on campus, she was especially disturbed to find DPU students—particularly students of color—discriminating against one another: "I thought we were all here to do something for ourselves," she mused, "not to put someone else down." Too many students, she observed, "see the outside first," missing the person within:

> I don't see the color. I mean, I can see the color, but I don't use it, like, "Oh, okay, she's white, she's this and this and this," or "She's black, she must be this and this and this," you know what I mean? I just look at them as the person.

Sylvia continued to regard racial prejudice as a hallmark of ignorance, of a failure to understand that human destinies are inextricably interwoven. Sobered by what she had observed during her year on campus, she was neither dejected nor sorry. While she had had to "cross many barriers," her ethnic identity was not associated in her mind with disempowerment or disadvantage. As far as she was concerned, her people were—like Sylvia the individual—up and coming:

> Like they say, "minorities." But I heard in the year 2000, that minorities are gonna be the majority, okay? Then why are we still being called "minorities"? Why can't we be called underrepresented"? I like that better, you know, than "minority." I am not no minority. I am not in one of those little groups—I'm *underrepresented.*

## Struggles with Writing

On the basis of her low score on an initial placement test, Sylvia had been assigned to a two-semester basic writing course. Impressed by her early work, course instructor Susan Williams gave Sylvia the option of moving into freshman composition after completing only the first semester—an offer Sylvia declined, electing to enroll in Williams's English 90 course. Although Williams saw Sylvia as the strongest writer in the second-semester class, she complained that Sylvia "doesn't go as much into depth as she needs to," and, lacking confidence in her writing ability, "sticks to real simple forms." Sylvia seemed well aware of these weaknesses, and spoke often of her desire to move beyond the five-paragraph essay, which she had first encountered in a writing workshop for Hispanic high school students; she also explained that while she had been influenced by her father's frequent reminders to "hurry up and get to the point," "writing teachers always want more detail."

When Williams asked for a written description of the "basic ingredients of an essay," Sylvia gamely recited the well-worn precepts she had heard again and again:

> The three basic ingredients of an essay are thesis, sufficient support for the thesis, and logical arrangement of that support. The thesis is the main point that the author wants to get across to the reader. Sometimes the thesis is mentioned, somewhere in the essay or the reader has to determine what it is from the reading. Sufficient support for the thesis is giving backup evidence to the thesis. The support could be factual or not. Logical arrangement is how the author wants to arrange his thoughts. The arrangement makes the paper flow.

But as the semester drew to a close, Sylvia was still somewhat unsure of how to offer "sufficient support" or to make her papers "flow." Here, for instance, is a paragraph from a five-paragraph essay on "stereotypes" that she turned in during the final weeks:

> Society has stereotyped Latina women through the use of the media in television shows and movies. Sometimes the media shows Latinas as hookers that the white men prefer because they think that the women can give the men "good sex". Young Latinas have also been portrayed as being pregnant with two kids. The young women are also shown as having an abusive husband that beats her for the smallest reason, like a spot of dirt on the wall. Latinas are rarely cast into the roles of college students or graduates. I am a Latina woman who is in a four-year college, making something of my life. I don't have an abusive husband or children, but I am still fighting these stereotypes.

As with most of Sylvia's work, Williams felt that while this piece was adequate, it seemed a bit lackluster, as if she had stopped short—short of the livelier way with words that seemed well within her grasp, and short of expressing the vital emotions that lay just beneath the surface.

When asked on a beginning-of-term questionnaire if she liked to write, Sylvia had replied, "Not much. When I feel like writing, I write about things that interest me." But even when writing about matters of profound personal concern, Sylvia tended to rush, hurrying through the gist of a story or argument rather than providing the sorts of detail that her writing teachers always seemed to want. This tendency was evident in an essay describing her mother's battle with cancer, which began with stage-setting realism, but soon sped through long and significant stretches of time:

> Seven years ago a major change came into my mother's life and swept the family with her. One day I arrived at home after dance practice. I walked in the house, it was pitch dark, there were no lights on. Usually the stove light is on, but not this day. As I walked into the house, I got a strange feeling in my body. My mother was in her bedroom asleep. When she woke up, she looked as if she had seen a ghost. She was yellow, and her eyes were blood shot from crying. She did not want to tell me what was wrong. Eventually, she told me she had cancer. My mother said she had to make a decision whether to get an operation or not. She decided to go through with the operation. After the operation, my mother had to go through chemotherapy. The first day after chemotherapy, she came home all drained out. She felt as if her spirit was sucked out by a vacuum cleaner. I felt as if I also had cancer because I was defenseless to help or stop her suffering.

In an interview, Sylvia traced her struggles with writing to her troubled linguistic background—to the fact that she had first learned to write in an atmosphere of linguistic conflict and confusion, and at a time when she was being prematurely immersed in an all-English classroom environment. Written words came forth more easily in English than in Spanish, but somehow her composing still felt hidebound and unnatural; somehow she had never come to visualize the reader over her shoulder, to see composing as an opportunity to express or convey meanings. "I was always ashamed of my writing," she recalled. "My writing experiences are not as vivid as it might be to other people," she wrote in an in-class paper. "Ever since a kid, I did not like to write much. I would only write papers because they were assign to me." Only once, when a high school teacher had carefully led her step-by-step through a term paper assignment, had she felt both engaged and accomplished: "for the first time in a long time, I had confidence," she recalled. An ambitious paper which involved drawing upon secondary sources to compare three American writers, the assignment was more rigorous than anything Sylvia had yet been asked to do in college.

Describing Sylvia as a "very, very bright young woman," Williams remained puzzled by her acceptable but undazzling performance as a writer, surmising that Sylvia had developed "a little bit of a negative attitude about writing"; since "everything else comes pretty easily to her," Williams speculated, perhaps Sylvia was "a little upset that the writing doesn't." While Williams believed Sylvia had problems with "second language input," she held that "it's more in her case just a kind of a lack of interest in writing," since "her language interference problems aren't that severe." "I'd love to see something she's written in Spanish," she added hopefully.

Meanwhile, Sylvia's description of her enduringly troubled relationship with both English and Spanish belied the assumption that her writing was plagued by a clear-cut case of first-language "interference." Although Sylvia believed that her struggle to bring forth words in written English was rooted in the trauma of her early schooling, she only dropped hints to that effect in the presence of her teacher or group leader. Her written words remained mere kernels, the germs of ideas that might be encouraged to grow in the warm light of conversation and engaged feedback, but Sylvia was not particularly eager to move in that direction. When asked if her writing had improved over the semester, she replied, "not what I was looking forward to, or hoping. But that's only because of myself, because I brought it upon myself."

## Group Leader's Response: Morgan

Morgan saw many similarities between herself and Sylvia—in their shared struggle against those who would accuse them of ethnic disloyalty, and in their propensity for stubborn resistance. While Sylvia's small-group attendance was about average for the class as a whole (she was present for twenty sessions and missed thirteen), Morgan considered her absenteeism excessive. Even when

Sylvia was present, Morgan was often frustrated at Sylvia's level of participation—at her frequent reluctance to share writing and, occasionally, to participate in group discussions. One morning, as Morgan struggled to generate a brainstorming session, she paused to meet Sylvia's gaze: "You're giving me a bored look," Morgan observed; "You've got an intimidating look—I thought I was the only one with that took." At the last session of the semester, Morgan was a bit more direct: after Sylvia declined to read aloud the essay that she had been scanning silently, Morgan observed, "You're so feisty sometimes, I just want to, like, grab you by that hair." Unperturbed, Sylvia explained that she had a lot on her mind. "I'm teasin' you," Morgan quickly explained, if somewhat unconvincingly.

On those rare occasions when Sylvia brought in rough drafts of her essays, Morgan was an engaged and inquisitive reader, playing back her understandings of the text and encouraging Sylvia to extend her ideas. Late in the term, for instance, Sylvia handed Morgan a rough draft of an essay about her mother and asked her to read it silently. Sensing Sylvia's dissatisfaction with the piece, Morgan asked Sylvia what she felt was wrong. When Sylvia replied that it "wasn't balanced," Morgan worked to describe what she saw as the essay's controlling theme, and then asked a series of questions to help Sylvia clarify her purpose. Having agreed that the piece would contrast the mother's and daughter's differing aesthetic sensibilities, Morgan and Sylvia brainstormed details that would help bring alive these differences. Although they sometimes seemed to be lapsing into informal banter, Morgan periodically brought their conversation back to a focus, reminding Sylvia that the instances she was bringing up needed to illustrate a larger point: "What's the significance of that?" she asked repeatedly.

More often, however, Sylvia brought in only preliminary ideas, and they lapsed into mutually supportive discussions about life, often with no direct reference to writing. As she began to brainstorm an essay about stereotyping, for instance, Sylvia observed that many of her Latino friends back home "kind of feel jealous," openly criticizing her decision to go to a predominantly white college; "I'm doing something for myself and they're putting me down," she asserted. This struck a responsive chord in Morgan, who went on to describe her own struggle to overcome the conception that she was somehow "not black enough." The discussion continued in a later group, when Sylvia described how relatives back in Mexico often assumed that she was leading an Anglicized existence of ease and wealth, and Morgan spoke at length of how estranged she would feel in the presence of African natives. Both displayed a sense of pride at the people they were becoming, at the paths they were pursuing, at their defiance of cultural conventions that both found rigidly prescriptive. One morning, when Sylvia was to speak to a group of Hispanic high school students, she noted that she "didn't care who was out there," that her goal was simply to communicate that she was happy to be pursuing an education. An appreciative Morgan literally cheered.

At other times, however, Morgan's strong identification with Sylvia interfered with her understanding of how their backgrounds diverged, and possibly impeded her efforts to help Sylvia formulate her own thoughts in writing. When Sylvia began brainstorming ideas for her essay about her mother's battle with cancer, for instance, Morgan mistakenly assumed that Sylvia's mother, like her own, had died of the disease: "My mom had cancer and died, too," she said, adding that when she tried to write about the experience for a timed essay exam, she had felt "too emotional" and found she "couldn't do it." "Oh, she didn't die!" Sylvia quickly explained, adding that while she might feel somewhat emotional about the subject, she was sure she could write about it. "Always be that critical writer," Morgan warned, "the objective writer . . . try to put yourself outside of the situation and look at it in terms of writing a story." In an interview, Sylvia explained that she found the cautionary note unnecessary; she, too, was a private person, she maintained, but before she could write on a subject, she had to feel personally connected to it.

In a final interview, Morgan observed that Sylvia seemed more receptive to her comments and a bit more open about bringing in her work. Still, Morgan shared Williams's feeling that although Sylvia had "complex ideas," she was readily frustrated by the effort it took to express them in writing:

> She tends to be a perfectionist. And so, when her writing isn't really, really good, uh, her writing is simple in a lot of ways, very simple. And it's, she doesn't like anybody to see it, you know, until it's really perfect. And then, I, I think that's her roadblock—she likes to do something, put it out and it's done, and it's nice and it's set out. And she looks nice all the time—her hair's always done nice, her makeup's always on, you know. And I think with her writing, she wants to do it once and here it is, it's nice and it's all done, and it's all wrapped up and it's tidy. It bothers her that, you know, she doesn't have it down the first time.

There's "something in her personality that comes out in her writing," Morgan observed—a tendency to "just present things," to forego "a deeper analysis." Morgan saw something of this same "black-and-white" approach in Sylvia's attitude toward the group:

> She doesn't worry about anybody else's trips, you know. We've had conversations before on tapes where she's like, oh, when we were talking one time about the students not showing up, she's like, "It doesn't bother me if they show up or not, I'm still gonna get ahead, I'm still gonna do my own thing," you know? So it's very clear: "These are my goals, these are what I'm doing, it doesn't bother

me if anybody else does or not." She doesn't feel a need to bring the whole group along—if she's getting along, then that's fine.

Operating under the assumption that Sylvia was a native speaker of English, Morgan's analysis did not include attention to how Sylvia's linguistic background might play into her present difficulties with writing. What Morgan and Williams suspected was probably true to a point: embarrassed that her writing was not stronger, Sylvia was reluctant to share her preliminary efforts, and admittedly spent inadequate time revising her essays. An understanding of the psychological and linguistic reasons behind this behavior might have helped Morgan provide more consistently engaging and appropriate help; but such insight proved elusive, as Sylvia remained in Morgan's mind an intellectually gifted young woman whose problems with writing could be ascribed to a perfectionistic slant of character and, perhaps, a touch of basic laziness.

## Perspective on the Adjunct Sessions

Sylvia began the semester with buoyant optimism, glad that Morgan was so much more personable than the critical, often-patronizing group leader that she had the previous semester. "I know I need help with my writing," Sylvia wrote in her journal after an early group session; "I feel this class is going to help because there is more of an individual help . . . the group leaders here are willing to help the students, if the students want help." The possibility that the adjunct sessions might foster peer response and discussion did not seem to occur to Sylvia, who described the small groups as a cost-effective but somewhat inefficient means of providing one-on-one assistance:

> I think one-on-one you get more out of it. Because you can spend an hour and go through a lot . . . and with a group, a small group, you could only get to two or three people, and the other two or three are left. And they need, they might need more help, or less help, or whatever.

When asked about the effectiveness of group sessions, Sylvia's answers always focused upon her perceptions of her relationship with Morgan. In the beginning, Sylvia explained that especially since Morgan did not assign grades, she seemed less threatening and therefore more approachable than Williams: "I see her as a friend, but with the skills of a teacher," she explained, "and I'm not afraid of asking her, 'Morgan, what do you think of this?'" While Sylvia believed that she would ultimately have to overcome her writer's block on her own, she thought that her group leader could help by "having patience" and by understanding the source of her seeming resistance. It is important, she emphasized, that both teachers and group leaders "don't give up on the students—'cause that's what I think a lot of teachers do, just give up on the student, and say, 'Well, they're not gonna do it, or they don't wanna do it.'"

In a final interview, Sylvia admitted that she had not attended the small groups as often as she had initially thought she would, explaining that she had gradually "lost interest." When I asked why, she began by assuming full responsibility ("I wasn't taking advantage of it, when I should have"), but she soon confessed her disappointment in Morgan's shifting attitude:

> I don't know, I mean, I guess because the leaders lost the interest—not to all of us, but kind of lost the interest in working with some of us. And so, I mean, we're not that blind, if we see, if I see that Morgan's not that interested that day, you know, we'll just talk about things, you know. And I guess that's what happened.

Morgan's enthusiasm was "really off and on," Sylvia observed, noting particularly Morgan's tendency to get frustrated when the group seemed unresponsive: "Sometimes she would come to the group all pumped up and ready to go, and we wouldn't be all pumped up with her, but that's how reality goes." Although Sylvia felt that she understood Morgan's reaction to the group, she was still troubled by it:

> I think she had high expectations of all of us in the beginning. But then when she got to know us, I guess through our writing and through our discussions, she, I don't think she had high expectations. I mean, I don't know—to me, when someone has high expectations and the person doesn't please them, or whatever, then the other person will be all, like, down and, like, "I didn't do my job right," or whatever.

Although Sylvia sometimes enjoyed the group's talks about issues and assigned readings, she generally preferred whole-class discussions, noting that they encompassed more perspectives. When it came time to share writing, however, Sylvia found even the small group a daunting audience:

> I'd rather have one person criticize me, and I know I can take that, than on a group basis. Because I remember in the beginning we would do, like, freewrites or whatever, and Morgan would want us to read them out loud, and I would, I would not like that. I mean, that sounds kind of strange, I mean, to, for me to say something like that, because I like to see myself as an outgoing person, that, "Hey, go ahead, read my stuff," you know. But I'm also that private person that I can only let one person read it at a time.

Sylvia traced the emergence of this fear to negative classroom experiences in elementary school:

> You know, because of the barrier of coming from a Spanish-speaking home to, going to a school and have English. Because I have the accent and stuff—but I didn't get laughed at, it's just that the teachers sometimes would say it in a nice way but I would take it as a negative way, you know. They would try to say it in a nicer way and I would get offended. That's just something I have.

Although Sylvia had initially looked to the small-group sessions as an opportunity to receive friendly, but expert, advice from a quasi-teacher, she eventually found that she preferred going to friends for assistance: "I get a lot of help on writing through my friends. I have friends that help me, and I always say, 'Here, check it for me, please' . . . And then when she would be finished, she'd go, 'Okay, what are you trying to say here?' and she'd help me that way." Sylvia had several friends whom she often approached for help: one who was enrolled in a basic writing class, another in freshman composition, and a third who was majoring in English. She explained that she felt more comfortable with them than with Morgan: "Because, well, because I know the kids, I know the students in my group, but I don't know Morgan that well . . . We've talked on a group basis and stuff about our experiences growing up and stuff, but I still don't have that personal touch."

On the other hand, when I played back taped segments of her work with Morgan, Sylvia seemed to realize that her feelings about the groups were somewhat more mixed than she had first allowed. Sylvia smiled, for instance, as she listened to the group brainstorm papers on stereotyping—a discussion dominated by herself and Morgan, both of them describing what it was like to be accused of "acting white." Morgan did most of the talking at first, but then Sylvia jumped in:

> I remember once, it was so funny to me, because I come from a middle-class background—although we're not white, we still come from the middle class and all. And this family, this guy, he's all, "You're white." I'm all, "No, I'm not" . . . Then he's all, "Why do you try to be, why do you try to act white?" And, well, I'm not, I know who I am and stuff, you know. It was when I was, like, in twelfth grade or something like that. And then he's all, that I was calling him a wetback and stuff, and I'm all, "No, I would never use that against my own race, I would never use it as a negative way. Joking around with friends I would."

Somewhat uncharacteristically, Sylvia had spoken at length in several instances on the tape, her words punctuated only by an occasional "Right" or "Uh huh" from Morgan. Sylvia seemed pleased to listen to her own words played back, but I was also interested in what she thought of Morgan's end of the conversation. Morgan had, after all, both begun and ended the discussion by talking about her own struggle against those who would call her "not black enough," and I asked Sylvia if she felt connected to this, if it helped her reflect upon her own situation. Sylvia responded:

> Well, I see it as kind of similar. We're going, like, we're in the same boat on that. Because when her friends tell her, "You don't act black," to me, what is "acting black"? Because you can dance, or you can sing, or whatever, you know? And when they tell me, "You're not Mexican," what is that? Just because I can't eat hot, spicy stuff, or I can't speak Spanish properly, or whatever? . . . I'm getting her

input, and I'm getting her viewpoint. I mean, she has more experience than I do, and I can learn from her. You know, and how she has accepted it from society, and it hasn't brought her down.

When I asked if the conversation helped her gather ideas for the essay, Sylvia enthusiastically replied, "Yeah! . . . Because I did use some of the ideas that we talked about in my essay . . . it helped out, it really did." Sylvia saw the session as typical of Morgan's teaching style: "Not formal, very informal—not very, but informal. Laid back, almost—she talks about her experiences all the time."

On the other hand, Sylvia found the next tape that I played back to be representative of something that she did not particularly like about Morgan's approach. The group was brainstorming descriptive essays, and although Sylvia volunteered only that she was thinking of writing about her mother, she was in fact mulling over memories of her mother's battle with cancer. Feisty and demanding, Morgan provided questions intended to nudge Sylvia toward greater specificity:

MORGAN: Um, okay, are you, like, thinking of any characteristics you wanna, like, throw out back and forth, that you want to talk about? How would you approach writing about this person?

SYLVIA: *[pause]* Uh, I don't know. *[laughs]*

MORGAN: You're a college student, you *should* know, that's why you're here . . . *[pause, then Sylvia starts to say something]* Any possible approaches?

SYLVIA: Just the way she has influenced me in my life.

MORGAN: What ways has she influenced you? Positive, negative? Let's start from there.

SYLVIA: Both.

MORGAN: Both?

SYLVIA: I mean, mostly positive.

MORGAN: Mostly positive?

SYLVIA: Yeah.

MORGAN: Influenced what about you?

SYLVIA: Um, well, like never to give up.

MORGAN: Okay, so if you put it under *[Sylvia starts to add something, but Morgan continues]*, if you put it under a broader, um, definition, what would you say, never to give up, never to, what would you call that, what she taught you, how she influenced you?

SYLVIA: What would I call it?

MORGAN: Yeah, what did she influence you, what did, what, what did she teach you? If you called it a whole body of things . . . *[pause]* So I guess what I'm driving at, what I'm trying to get to, is like values, morals, beliefs, ambitions.

SYLVIA: Oh, okay.

MORGAN: You know? Okay. So while we're talking, why don't you, uh, make notes about things you could possibly approach about it, not saying that you have to. Let's start, you know, getting that together.

When asked for her response to the session, Sylvia filled in some of what was left unsaid in the rapid-fire exchange of questions and answers:

I did write an essay about my mother, about not giving up. And that to me was of value. I talked about her experience with cancer . . . *[softly]* and, um, how she had cancer twice, and she had just had, uh, my little sister. She had cancer the first time, it was about a year and a half after my sister was born, nearly two, And so, uh, I just saw how the . . . that was the first time, and the second time was about another year and a half, and that's when she got into chemotherapy and radiation and all that. And how the chemicals wore her down, and I would see her come home like a rag doll, almost. And how, one of my cousins was helping her into her bed, and stuff, that was in the beginning of the treatment. And how she had one of her breasts was taken out, and—I mean, just a lot of these things, like her body was taken, and it would bring her down physically, but not mentally. It would bring her up. She would look at us and cry and stuff, but then she would say, "No, I've gotta do it for them, I gotta keep on for them." I admire my mother a lot, I mean.

She said some of this in the paper that she wrote about her mother; why, I asked Sylvia, did she not talk about it in the small groups? She replied:

Because at the time Morgan asked me, and I wasn't ready for this, I wasn't ready for, to be asked all these kind of questions and stuff. And it was just that we were brainstorming, and I was just, that just popped into my head, afterwards . . . it wasn't personal because I talk about that experience a lot. And so . . . in the beginning, when she did have cancer, I would talk about it and I would cry. But I have gotten through that emotional phase. And I mean sometimes I do see her, and I go, "damn," you know, she went through all that, and I cry, but I won't let her see it. But, I don't know, it was okay.

Sylvia had been somewhat offended by Morgan's remark "You're a college student, you *should* know":

I didn't like that comment! I mean, just because you're a college student, and because you're here, doesn't mean you know everything. And it was something that she just threw me off on that one, like a curve ball there, you know. It didn't affect me, it's just that I know I'm a college student, and I know I don't know everything, but what I do know, I can say something about it, whatever.

Morgan approached the group in this insistent manner rather frequently, Sylvia observed. Sometimes, she admitted, the strategy was useful, especially when Morgan would ask questions that had not yet occurred to her—that way, Sylvia explained, "if someone else asks it . . . I can answer it . . . and that's more ideas for my paper."

Still, there was an apparent mismatch between the depth of Sylvia's emotions around this topic and Morgan's insistent approach in the session. When I played the same tape back for Morgan, she commented only that she was "starting to try and talk less," and that she was fairly happy with the response: "When Sylvia said, 'Oh, okay,'" Morgan observed, "it seemed like an 'aha' experience right there." But from Sylvia's point of view, Morgan had missed the mark, interpreting her initial reply of "I don't know" as an expression of insecurity or laziness rather than the plea for time that it in fact was. While Morgan's goals were to provide "collaborative" supports for student learning and to communicate high expectations, both were undermined by the assumptions that she had already made about Sylvia's level of motivation. Her intentions notwithstanding, these assumptions diminished Morgan's curiosity about what Sylvia was trying to say, and pulled at her efforts to provide tactful, appropriate guidance.

Part of being curious about students is to attend to the many ways in which they announce their need for privacy; Sylvia was, indeed, a private young woman, and it was important that Morgan not interpret her occasional guardedness as a personal rebuff or evidence of unresponsiveness. At the same time, however, Sylvia was extremely eager to talk about many aspects of her background, and noted again and again how much she enjoyed our conversations. Had Morgan only been encouraged to ask, I suspect that she, too, would have been provided some useful insights into the subtleties of Sylvia's background and current struggles with writing.

## Notes

1. Although Sylvia qualified as an EOP student on the basis of her parents' income, the family's real estate holdings rendered her ineligible for financial aid. Sylvia received academic counseling from DPU's EOP office, but she was the only focal student not receiving financial aid.

2. A study conducted by Lily Wong Fillmore (1991) suggests that such language loss and ensuing social disruption may be a quite common phenomenon among young children who are taught at school in a language other than that spoken at home. ▪

## Collaborative Activity 8.3

In small groups, consider the conflicts/tensions between Sylvia's home and school cultures. How would you characterize the differing goals, values, and beliefs in these two scenes? Examine the significance of the rhetorical interactions or situations in these scenes: Sylvia's interactions with family, friends, members of organizations, visiting high school students, classmates, her peer instructor (Morgan) and her writing teacher (Williams). What do these interactions reveal about the differing scenes of communication and about Sylvia's roles within these scenes? Be prepared to share your responses with the class.

### Writing Activity 8.5

Think back on your own most recent writing/language experiences before coming to college—whether in high school, in a community college, in your home, or in the workplace—and write a page in which you describe your own transition from these scenes to the university scene. Which college classes have been an easy transition, and which more difficult? Why? Focus on your introduction to the differing expectations of the college scene, particularly the expectations for communicating in this scene—speaking, listening, reading, and writing.

While the scene of the writing course, as the profile of Sylvia shows us, is made up of various participants with diverse backgrounds and levels of preparation, there are shared goals within this scene and goals it shares with the larger college or university scene. As a smaller scene, a port of entry, located on the border of the larger scene of the university, the first-year writing course tries to teach you how to make essential academic writing choices, the kinds of choices that are expected and valued throughout the university. Of course, the specific mission and goals of a writing course will depend, among other things, on the kind of institution you are in. Nevertheless, its specific goals and approaches often take place within a shared larger scene of writing instruction.

You might not be aware that, on a national level, writing programs share objectives for writing instruction. The National Council of Writing Program Administrators (WPA)—a group of college faculty who direct writing programs and oversee the teaching of first-year writing courses—has developed a statement describing the skills and knowledge that all students should possess by the end of first-year writing. They have created these objectives with much input from writing instructors and writing program directors at universities and colleges across the country. The example below, "WPA Outcomes Statement for First-Year Composition," describes the common knowledge, skills, and attitudes that first-year writing programs at postsecondary institutions across the United States seek to cultivate.

### WPA Outcomes Statement for First-Year Composition

## RHETORICAL KNOWLEDGE

By the end of first-year composition, students should

- Focus on a purpose
- Respond to the needs of different audiences

- Respond appropriately to different kinds of rhetorical situations
- Use conventions of format and structure appropriate to the rhetorical situation
- Adopt appropriate voice, tone, and level of formality
- Understand how genres shape reading and writing
- Write in several genres

## CRITICAL THINKING, READING, AND WRITING

By the end of first-year composition, students should

- Use writing and reading for inquiry, learning, thinking, and communicating
- Understand a writing assignment as a series of tasks, including finding, evaluating, analyzing, and synthesizing appropriate primary and secondary sources
- Integrate their own ideas with those of others
- Understand the relationships among language, knowledge, and power

## PROCESSES

By the end of first-year composition, students should

- Be aware that it usually takes multiple drafts to create and complete a successful text
- Develop flexible strategies for generating, revising, editing, and proofreading
- Understand writing as an open process that permits writers to use later invention and rethinking to revise their work
- Understand the collaborative and social aspects of writing processes
- Learn to critique their own and others' works
- Learn to balance the advantages of relying on others with the responsibility of doing their part
- Use a variety of technologies to address a range of audiences

## KNOWLEDGE OF CONVENTIONS

By the end of first-year composition, students should

- Learn common formats for different kinds of texts
- Develop knowledge of genre conventions ranging from structure and paragraphing to tone and mechanics

- Practice appropriate means of documenting their work
- Control such surface features as syntax, grammar, punctuation, and spelling.

---

## Writing Activity 8.6

Write a paragraph in which you define your own criteria for effective writing. What assumptions, for example, do you have about what constitutes effective writing? What do you aim to achieve when you write? What do you think you should be learning in your writing course? Then compare your criteria (1) to the objectives in the example above, (2) to Sylvia's description of the "basic ingredients of an essay," and (3) to the criteria your teacher and your writing course have identified (via the syllabus, assignments, class discussions, etc.).

---

## Collaborative Activity 8.4

Examine the WPA objectives in the example above in light of the scene of the writing course and the college and university scene (You might want to refer to your institution's mission statement, which you analyzed in Writing Activity 8.1, p. 285). How do the WPA objectives reveal the scene of writing courses? For example, do they reflect the role of the writing course as a kind of passport to the university? How do they reveal the scene of the college or university? Do the objectives seem to reflect the university's emphasis on the pursuit, production, and exchange of knowledge? Prepare to share your discoveries with other groups.

---

When college writing instructors collaborated to frame the objectives above, they attached a warning that writing is an extremely complex process and that the objectives for writing courses cannot be taught in reduced or simple ways. The next section will examine how these shared objectives of writing instruction are carried out within the multiple situations and complex and varied rhetorical interactions of the writing class scene.

## The Situations of Writing Courses

The writing class scene consists of a number of situations or rhetorical interactions. Many take place in a particular setting—the classroom space—with participants (teachers and students) pursuing the common subject of writing, with the shared purpose of learning to communicate more effectively. Seeking to develop rhetorical knowledge that will be useful for different purposes and audiences, writing teachers ask students to participate in a variety of rhetorical situations, whether working in groups with other students to discuss a reading, conferring with a teacher over paper topic ideas, reading/responding to papers in a peer review workshop, or participating in the sharing of ideas in large-class discussions. In fact, to carry out the objectives of the writing course noted in the WPA Outcomes Statement, most classroom situations require active student participation, dialogue, and hands-on practice writing and communicating. Some of the rhetorical interactions—such as critical reading and conferencing—might take place outside the physical classroom, but they are nonetheless aspects of the scene of the writing course.

## READING IN WRITING COURSES

Because first-year writing courses emphasize critical thinking, reading, and writing, they require that you do more than absorb and memorize material. *In writing courses, teachers ask students to interact with readings as well as with classmates and the teacher.* Academic readers inquire into the material, raise questions about it, and critically examine it—to stake out claims or positions and actively apply and construct knowledge, developing new frameworks of understanding.

One way to actively engage in learning is through **active reading**. The act of reading a text is not just an act of passively passing your eyes over the text but rather an active creation of the meaning of that text. You create meaning through the connections you make as a reader, and these connections depend on the expectations you bring to the texts as well as the questions you ask of it. Reading for your college writing course (and most other college courses) typically requires such a deliberate, engaged, and critical stance. *As an academic reader, you are expected not only to appreciate what you are reading, but also to take a position in relation to it—to examine its argument, to become aware of its assumptions, to imagine counterarguments and evidence.* In short, reading in your writing course means reading from the perspective of a writer, someone who is looking to engage the reading for ideas to apply or expand or even challenge in one's own writing. As an active reader, you should imagine yourself in *critical dialogue* with the text you are reading. Box 8.2 highlights some strategies for critical reading.

Educator Paulo Freire clarifies this active, critical engagement in learning by comparing teaching and learning to banking. The "banking" concept of education envisions students as passive "receptacles" that teachers/ bank clerks "deposit" information into; meanwhile students passively receive, file, and store the deposits. While the scenes of some of your college courses will

## Box 8.2   *Strategies for Critical Reading*

### 1. Previewing

Before closely reading the text, begin by quickly familiarizing yourself with it, looking for clues about the scene and about where to start. Scan the text for its visual and textual features—the title, author, place and date of publication, and any headings, references, introductory notes, prefaces, abstracts, or graphics that might help you guess what type of text it is. Since particular genres encourage particular ways of reading, you can search genres for clues about the situation and scene for communicating with writers. The following questions will help you to look for signals about where to start with your reading:

- What is the genre of the text I'm about to read? What are my expectations going into the text?
- What is my purpose for reading? What reading strategies best fit my purpose?
- What clues can I learn about the situation and scene from the title, the author, place of publication, date of publication, editorial notes, blurbs, abstracts, prefaces, or introductions?
- Based on a quick scan of the textual features, what guesses can I make regarding the writer's purpose and the role designated for the reader?
- Do I have any previous knowledge of the subject, and how will this affect my reading?
- How will my values, assumptions, attitudes, and beliefs influence my reading?

### 2. Annotating

**Annotating,** the process of making notes and comments in the margins of your text as you read, is a way of entering into an active conversation with the text you are reading. Annotation helps you to read more accurately, think critically about what you read, and retain what you read. You can talk back to the writer, question points that are unclear and comment on areas of agreement and disagreement. Annotation includes marking a text, either by bracketing information, highlighting or underlining, and may include the following marginal annotations:

- *Comments* on the passage ("This is confusing" or "I'm not convinced by this argument")                          *(continued on next page)*

*(continued from previous page)*

- *Evaluations* of the validity of points ("This source is biased" or "These numbers do not add up")
- *Questions* either asking for clarification ("What does this mean?") or challenging claims ("What is the significance of this statistic?")
- *Definitions* of terms or unknown words
- *Paraphrases* or restatements of difficult passages in your own words

### 3. Analyzing

Another method of active reading is **analyzing** a text, which means identifying its components and examining how these components—the writer's purpose, use of evidence, and word choice—work together to create meaning. To read effectively and analytically, you should consider the connections among a number of factors: the scene, the occasion that motivates the response, the controlling purpose, the writer's image or persona, the role you are invited to play as reader, and the textual conventions that help you and the writer play out your roles in the scene. By analyzing a text, you gain a critical perspective into how the text works to create meaning.

### 4. Rereading

When faced with an unfamiliar genre or challenging text, or when required to respond to a text, you will need to read it more than once. Reading critically and actively means *rereading* a text because, when you return to a text a second or third time, you often see what you overlooked the first time. Multiple readings also allow you to critically read and "reposition" yourself—to read from new perspectives and to consider the subject from your positioning in various scenes.

require their share of passively receiving information (through lectures) and filing and storing this information (through memorization), the scene of a writing course requires that you be challenged through what Freire describes as "problem posing" education. In a model of education as problem posing, teachers and students enter into dialogue with one another and with texts, with students cast in the role of "critical coinvestigators." As coinvestigators, students are called upon to critically examine material and to explore connections between their own perspectives and the course content. Instead of passively receiving knowledge, students actively construct knowledge by locating meaning in their observations and interpretations and by being actively engaged in their own learning.

## DISCUSSION IN WRITING COURSES

Rather than a traditional lecture class, you are probably finding that your writing class tends to be defined more as a workshop, with situations that call for interaction, whether through class discussion, group work exchanges, or in-class writing activities. A common situation in the writing class scene is class discussion, where students and teachers are constantly posing problems and asking questions, in addition to sharing diverse viewpoints necessary for critical reflection. You may find it beneficial to pay close attention during class discussions to the teacher's questions and discussion-leading devices, which can reveal his or her assumptions or expectations. How the teacher leads the class discussion and topics/questions that he or she raises may be particularly revealing about what issues the teacher finds important. In addition, listening to the varied perspectives of the class can give you critical insight into a topic or reading as you consider perspectives that you otherwise might not have considered.

## PEER REVIEW IN WRITING COURSES

One of the most important rhetorical interactions in the writing classroom is between student writers who give feedback on each other's writing, often referred to as **peer review** or *peer evaluation*. Such peer review models the collaborative nature of college and university knowledge making that we discussed earlier. Students, working either in pairs or small groups, are able to get immediate feedback on their drafts in progress and to address a real audience as they discuss their drafts face-to-face with their readers. Because peer evaluation gives writers a chance to get feedback on their drafts from someone who does not have the power of a grade over them, this situation makes for a more open and productive exchange of opinion. As a peer reviewer, it is important to exercise your critical reading and thinking skills. While you should refrain from negatively criticizing your classmate's writing, you should be willing to critique it—to respond as an interested and engaged reader who has questions, suggestions, and useful feedback to give to the writer (see the sample peer review in the following section, "The Genres of Writing Courses").

**Collaborative Activity 8.5**

Returning to the excerpt "Sylvia" reprinted earlier, examine Sylvia's interactions with her peer tutor (Morgan). What is the nature of these interactions? Which of the peer tutor strategies do you find effective and which do you find ineffective? To improve these peer review exchanges, what advice would you give Sylvia on her role as writer? What advice would you give to Morgan on her role as peer reviewer? In your small group, come up with a list of guidelines for writers and peer reviewers in the writing class situation that will make these interactions more productive. Your instructor may choose to compile these guidelines so that you can refer to them when you do your own peer reviews.

**Writing Activity 8.7**

One of the complaints of Sylvia's writing teacher is that Sylvia's writing lacks liveliness and vivid detail. However, Sylvia is unsure of how to offer "sufficient support" in her papers. After examining the excerpt from Sylvia's essay on stereotypes, write a paragraph addressed to Sylvia that gives advice on how she might provide the detail her teacher is asking for. Make concrete suggestions. How would you respond to Sylvia's explanation for her difficulty with writing, which she attributes to her "troubled linguistic background"?

# The Genres of Writing Courses

Of all of the various situations and rhetorical interactions within the writing classroom, one might argue that the actual practice of writing is most significant and most influential in shaping the workshop atmosphere of the writing class scene. A popular credo of writing teachers is that "Writers learn to write by writing." First and foremost, writing classes are concerned with the subject of writing and with the shared objective of writing processes, defined in the WPA Outcomes Statement as the development of "multiple drafts to create and complete a successful text" and the use of "flexible strategies for generating, revising, editing, and proofreading." Because these processes of writing repeat themselves in writing classes, from writing assignment to assignment and from writer to writer, there are various genres that correspond to the repeated processes of writing— inventing, drafting, and revising. For instance, to respond to the situation of inventing or generating ideas, students often use the genres of freewriting, brainstorming, or clustering, which are defined as follows:

- **Freewriting:** writing continuously without stopping, leaving yourself free to discover what you think about something without editing or censoring. Typically, a writer begins with a topic, perhaps just a word or a question, and begins writing whatever comes out on that topic without stopping.

- **Brainstorming:** listing (either individually or collaboratively) as many ideas as you can think of on a topic as quickly as you can, without stopping to reread, reflect, or censor any of the things that come to mind. The basic difference between freewriting and brainstorming is the difference between connected prose and a list. You may pause while brainstorming, unlike freewriting, but do not stop to reread or reflect.

- **Clustering:** visually depicting the relationship between ideas by writing in the center of a blank page a word or phrase that captures the heart of what you are trying to write about, drawing a circle around that word, then writing down anything you think of to do with that topic anywhere on the page. When one word prompts other ideas, circle it and draw lines from that word to the other words it prompts. What you end up with is something that looks a bit like a spider web, with circles and lines linking other circles, something like an octopus with many tentacles.

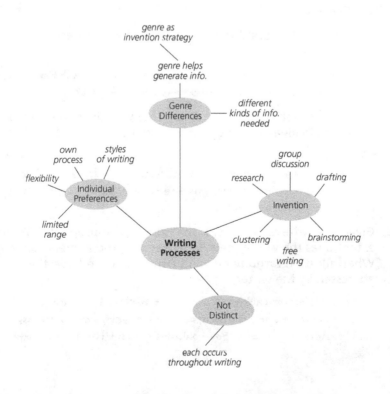

## Collaborative Activity 8.6

What other repeated rhetorical strategies or genres have you employed when generating ideas for a paper? In groups, make a list of additional genres for generating ideas, and write out a brief definition of each. How do you choose when to use which genres? Share your list with the rest of the class, and be prepared to discuss how situation and scene may play a part in your choice of genres for invention.

While these invention genres respond to the situation of generating ideas, the drafting stage often results in different situations, such as interactions between students and their classmates, who give feedback on works in progress. These repeated interactions between peers or peer reviews have led to a patterning of questions and responses, the genre of the peer review sheet. An example of this genre, based on a paper a student wrote arguing against the closing of her hometown theater, appears in the example below.

### Draft Workshop: Response Sheet

**Writer:** Sarah Lee
**Peer Evaluator:** Bob Evans

1. What strengths does this paper have? What is especially interesting or effective?

   You know the issue very well and you stay focused on it throughout your paper. Your personal experience is very effective.

2. State the writer's controlling idea. How well does the draft focus on this main idea? Any suggestions for improvement?

   The controlling idea is the argument that Lafayette needs to join together to save the local theater. I would develop more of your reasons why, maybe address why the town does not support the theater and why they should.

3. Given the writer's purpose, is the audience appropriate? To what extent does the writer seem to be keeping the audience in mind? What questions/arguments might the audience have that aren't addressed by the writer?

   Audience is appropriate—you may want to shift the focus a little more to those who pay for its upkeep (taxpayers, local businesspeople and leaders in the town). You could talk about the $$ a theater brings to the community/town and how much more attractive the town is to outsiders with this source of entertainment available.

4. What additional evidence—examples, details, illustrations or textual support (facts, statistics, quotations)—might strengthen the paper and support the claims being made? Where is more of the writer's own commentary, argumentation or analysis needed (as opposed to sources)?

I think you could add quotes from locals affected by the potential closing—maybe one from a teen, a child, adult, historians, etc. You could even do a survey to see how the town as a whole (or a sampling) feels about losing the theater. This way you could gain more support. You need stronger reasons than just pure entertainment—talk about sentimental/historical value more and quality of life issues?

5. Comment on the organization of the draft. How logical and unified is it? Suggestions? Is the format and genre appropriate given the audience and scene for writing? Make suggestions.

Organization is good; consistent throughout; moves the argument along logically. You may want to include a solution at the end.

6. Comment on voice and tone. Are they appropriate to audience and purpose and to the larger scene of writing?

You may want to redirect voice to be stronger and challenging. Ask residents why don't they support local business? don't they want places of entertainment? Challenge them to act!

7. What two main things should the writer focus on as he/she revises the paper?

—more concrete reasons for supporting the theater

—more citizens' voices

---

## Writing Activity 8.8

Collect peer review sheets from your writing class (perhaps drawing on those you have received or written for your peers), and respond to the following questions regarding what this genre reveals about the classroom situation and scene. What assumptions about writing does the genre reveal? What roles for readers (peer reviewers) and writers does the genre encourage or discourage? What actions does the genre make possible, and what actions does it make difficult?

---

Reread the WPA Outcomes Statement, and then describe how the genre of the peer review sheet reflects the writing course objectives outlined within the statement. Which of the objectives does the peer review sheet seem to be responding to most?

---

While the peer review sheet is a genre frequently used by students as they respond to each other's drafts, instructors have their own typical ways of commenting on and evaluating student papers. For instance, teachers often use the genre of marginal comments, similar to the marginal annotations that we defined in our discussion of critical reading. These notes typically ask questions of clarification, note points of interest, or highlight areas of confusion. Marginal comments are meant to provide a template of sorts for one reader's active response in the process of reading. Finally, teachers may make summary comments or end comments that highlight strengths of the paper and suggest possible ways to revise. These comments often correspond to particular marginal comments made throughout the text and synthesize these individual comments into overall strategies for revision.

While there are multiple genres that enable participants in the writing classroom to respond to various situations—whether generating ideas for writing, drafting, reading/responding to drafts, or evaluating writing—the most important genres are those that you will compose in response to writing assignments. Chapter 9 closely examine three genres that are commonly taught and practiced in the writing classroom scene: the *analysis paper*, the *argument paper* and the *researched position paper*. Since taking the time to understand a genre is an effective way to begin writing it, the following chapters will explore how knowledge of specific writing classroom genres can help writers decide the most effective way of negotiating the writing process and deciding on the most effective rhetorical strategies. We hope to show you that as you encounter different situations as a writer within academic scenes—whether writing a report for history, filling out a scholarship application, or writing a letter to the editor of your student newspaper—you can use your genre knowledge to determine how to act effectively within these scenes of communication.

# Writing Projects

## Writing Project 8.1

Observe the scene of a class you are taking. Drawing on Box 1.2: Guidelines for Observing and Describing Scenes (pp. 44–45), describe the scene, the interactions within the scene, and the genres used to carry out the class objectives. Then use these data to explain how this particular classroom scene both fits the academic scene at large (you may want to refer to Writing Activity 8.1 (p. 285), which asked you to examine your institution's mission statement) and has qualities of its own. Present your findings as a guide that helps college students who are entering this course develop a better idea of what this scene is, how it functions, and how they are expected to act within it.

## Writing Project 8.2

Write a letter to your high school English teacher or to the school board explaining how your high school courses did/did not prepare you for this particular writing course. You might consider the goals and expectations of the courses, criteria for evaluation, types of assignments, types of texts (both those you read and write), use of class time, your role in the classroom, your relationship to your instructor and peers, etc.

## Writing Project 8.3

Choose and then compose a genre that would effectively respond to the following situation: Explain to a group of high school students what to expect from their college writing course, and give them advice on how to prepare. You might consider the goals and expectations of the course, criteria for evaluation, types of assignments, types of texts (both those you read and write), use of class time, your role in the classroom, your relationship to your instructor and peers, etc. While this clarifies your purpose, participants, and subject, it is up to you define the setting (college fair day or a school Web site, for example) and to formulate an appropriate response—a letter, flyer, pamphlet, PowerPoint presentation, Web site, etc.—to this situation.

## Writing Project 8.4

Write a critique of a genre that is used in an academic scene, and address it to your classmates and instructor for this course. The genre may be from your writing class (peer review sheet, journal) or from another course, or it may function within the larger academic scene—the syllabus, textbook, or application form (loan, scholarship, financial aid, housing).

After identifying the patterns and underlying assumptions of the genre, evaluate the possibilities and limitations of this genre in the writing course scene. You will want to draw on the Questions for Critiquing Genre in Box 7.1 (p. 229), as well as refer to the sample critiques in that chapter. Make sure to state and then develop a **claim** that evaluates some aspect of the genre's effects. Then support your claim with **evidence** taken from the genre. In the process of developing your claim, keep in mind that you will not only need to describe the effects a genre has, but also to evaluate the strengths and/or limitations of these effects. Your claim is the point you want to make about the genre, and your evidence is the features of the genre you will use to demonstrate your point. You might wish to review the discussion of claims, pp. 301–302.

## Writing Project 8.5

Study what electronic genres are commonly used in academic scenes at your college or university. For example, many courses now use a class organizing technology like Blackboard or Course in a Box that include genres of discussion boards, announcements, course documents, and so on. Many courses set up a discussion list for the class. Some teachers create Web sites for their students. Select an electronic academic genre, collect multiple examples of the genre, and use Box 2.1 (pp. 93–94) to help you analyze how the genre reflects and reveals its academic situation and scenes. Your analysis, directed at an audience of your writing class (students and instructor), should explore what the rhetorical interactions reveal about this online scene.

## Writing Project 8.6

Reread the "Sylvia" excerpt and compare Sylvia's transition into college to your transition into college. Once you have examined the similarities and differences in your experiences, write an essay in which you make a claim about what accounts for any similarities and differences, and then support that claim with evidence from your and Sylvia's experiences.

# Writing Analyses and Arguments

# 9

In this chapter, we will focus on two genres commonly taught and practiced in college writing courses: The analysis paper and the argument paper. We will begin our inquiry into the writing course and its scene of writing by comparing the analysis paper to another genre you might already be familiar with, the five-paragraph theme. The chapter then moves into a discussion of the situations that call for analysis papers. Using a sample student paper, we describe what analysis is and how to perform it. Then we invite you to read and analyze a professional example. In the second half of the chapter, we guide you through a detailed analysis of the generic features first of analysis papers and then of argument papers. We will help you to identify the different patterns in each genre, to interpret what these patterns mean, and to develop strategies for using that knowledge to make more effective choices as you write analysis and argument papers. At the end of the chapter, we include several samples of student analysis and argument papers.

## The Five-Paragraph Theme versus the Analysis Paper

If your experience in high school was similar to that of many students, then you may have learned to write a genre sometimes called the "five-paragraph theme." For those of you who did not learn it, the **five-paragraph theme** has a set structure of five paragraphs for which it is named:

An introductory paragraph, which contains a thesis

Three body paragraphs, each of which contains one supporting idea and evidence

A concluding paragraph, which summarizes the three supporting ideas and then restates the thesis

Central to the five-paragraph theme is the thesis, the **controlling idea** of a paper, which often takes the form of a three-part structure that matches the theme's organization: For example, "There are three reasons for x: First reason, second reason, third reason."

One of the primary purposes for using the five-paragraph theme is to provide a ready-made organizational structure that adapts to a variety of writing situations in high school. The genre is also easy for teachers to read, allowing them to give students more practice in writing because the teachers can assess a high number of themes in a relatively short amount of time. While the five-paragraph theme thus proves quite useful for many situations in high school scenes, few if any college situations call for a five-paragraph theme. Essay examination might use a five-paragraph structure, but in college this genre requires a level of analysis and complexity that the five-paragraph theme is not meant to handle.

Although the exact shape it takes and the way it gets communicated differ from scene to scene and genre to genre, analysis as a mode of inquiry is valued in many genres across various academic scenes of writing, including writing courses. In college-level writing courses, the analysis paper does resemble the five-paragraph theme in some of its generic features. Both genres revolve around a thesis or controlling idea; both use evidence to develop and support that idea; both include introductions, bodies, and conclusions. As a different genre, though, coming from a different scene and situation, *the analysis paper in college-level writing courses also challenges you to build on your previously learned genres in important ways.* These include:

- Developing a more complex controlling idea
- Incorporating academically authorized evidence rather than personal opinion
- Organizing from the particular controlling idea, and using more than three self-contained supporting paragraphs
- Using more complex transitions to lead readers through that structure
- Analyzing as well as providing evidence

We will discuss each of these in more detail, and we will show you an example of a text written by a first-year student who had some difficulty moving from the five-paragraph theme to the analysis paper. If you have learned in the past to write the five-paragraph theme—perhaps even come to depend on the genre—you may need to keep reminding yourself that it is *not* a genre that will work well in most college writing situations and that the analysis paper has different generic features.

**Writing Activity 9.1**

If you learned to write the five-paragraph theme (or something similar to it), explore the extent to which it has been helpful to you and how it has limited you. If you have not learned the five-paragraph theme, consider the "tricks" you have come to depend on in writing (for example, a pattern for writing introductions or conclusions or a way of organizing certain kinds of papers). Using the Guidelines for Critiquing Genres, Box 7.1 (p. 229), examine how these patterns, like all generic expectations, both make things easier for you and sometimes constrain what you want to do.

# The Scene and Situation of Analysis Papers

Following the pattern we have established in this book and outlined in Box 2.1 (pp. 93–94), we will take you through this genre so important to writing classes and other academic scenes—in short, we will analyze analysis papers.

## PARTICIPANTS, SETTING, AND SUBJECT

Since writing courses are one of the places analysis papers are written, and we described the scene of writing courses in Chapter 5, you already know much about the scene of this genre. You already know, too, much of the situation of the analysis paper, for it inhabits the same setting and involves the same participants as other writing class genres. The writer has the double role not only of author with a claim to make but also of student with learning to demonstrate. The usual readers of analysis papers, teachers and classmates, will similarly read the genre not only to learn from the analysis but also to evaluate how well the analysis paper has been written.

The subjects of analysis papers can range widely, including anything susceptible to analysis. Some common subjects and purposes of analysis papers include:

- To observe a text, activity, or event and to explain what it means and how and why it works
- To take an idea and use it to clarify and understand a concept or phenomenon
- To consider the relationship and consequences of one text, activity, or event on another
- To uncover the implicit assumptions of a text, an argument, a concept, etc.

■ To identify an inconsistency in a text, activity, or event and to explain and explore its implications

For example, an analysis paper might examine how rhetorical appeals operate in a Web page, might use the concept of scene to understand a local organization, might compare the arguments of two articles in a debate, might explore the assumptions underlying the notion of individualism, or might explain apparently conflicting practices in a professional site. In short, analysis papers take as their subjects anything that merits analytic attention.

## THE OBJECTIVES OF ANALYSIS

Analysis is at the heart of analysis papers, of course; it is what gives the genre its name. The place of writing classes as ports of entry helps explain the purpose of the analysis paper, for a major objective of this genre is to teach students about the kinds of analysis expected in the college and university scene. In the writing class analysis is also a major *purpose* of the situation of the analysis paper, for teachers and students use it to demonstrate students' ability to analyze and to write about that analysis.

The ability to analyze is one of the most important skills one can develop in college because analysis in its various forms is central to critical academic inquiry. Essentially, analysis involves taking something apart to understand it—the reverse of **synthesis,** or putting things together. Analysis examines how things work, why they do what they do, what they mean, and what effects they have. To analyze something is not just about taking it apart to see how it works; it is also about trying to understand how it can be improved and changed. Most important of all, analysis requires us to take a critical, more detached observational stance, one in which we withhold judgment and personal opinion as much as possible so that we can get at the internal workings and possible meanings of our object of study.

As a college student, you will be asked to write genres involving analysis in many of your courses. In a literature course, you might be asked to analyze how characters in a novel differ; in psychology, you might be asked to analyze how gender affects interpersonal relationships; in economics, you might be asked to analyze the effect of increased interest rates on the economy; in history, you might be asked to analyze how the cold war changed the balance of power in the world; and in biology, you might be asked to analyze why hatchery salmon are threatening wild salmon. Exactly how you perform these analyses will depend on the conventions and expectations of each disciplinary scene and genre. But generally speaking, in all these instances your challenge as a writer is to critically observe your subject, to take it apart and examine its workings, to read what others have said about it, and then to develop some claim or idea that helps us understand it better.

Although our emphasis in this part of the book is on academic genres, analysis is not something that only academics do only in academic scenes. We analyze all the time in order to function in the world. When we enter a scene of a party, to return to our example in Chapter 1, we analyze it in order to decide how we should act: We take it apart by looking at how people are dressed, what music is playing, what food is served, how people are communicating, etc. Then we put these elements (the clothing, music, food, style of communicating) back together in order to draw a conclusion about what these different elements mean for how we should act. This conclusion that we construct becomes the **claim** we are making about this situation. If we are later asked why we formulated this claim, we could point to the **evidence** (the clothing, music, food, style of communicating) to **support** the claim.

By and large, analysis papers in writing courses operate from a similar premise. After you have analyzed your subject and established a claim (your central conclusion or argument about the subject) that helps explain it in some way, your challenge as a writer is to support and develop that claim with evidence, evidence that will convince your readers that your observation and explanation are justified and significant. The relationship *between* the claim and evidence used to support that claim is central to the analysis paper. But this relationship is not as obvious as it may seem at first. It involves more than just compiling evidence to support a claim. That is, to write an effective analysis paper, you cannot simply string together a series of examples and facts and assume that your readers will connect these pieces back to your claim. As a writer, it is up to *you* to make the meaningful connection for your readers. *You are expected to analyze how your evidence relates to and supports your claim.*

Analysis involves making explicit the assumptions that connect your evidence to your claim. For example, imagine your first day at a new job. Based on your observations of this workplace scene, you come to the conclusion that it is a relaxed work environment. To support this claim, you cite examples from your observations such as the informal dress of your coworkers, the shared jokes and laughter among the staff, and the flexible hours. These facts are your evidence. As someone making this claim, though, you are expected to ask yourself why you connect that evidence to that claim, to make explicit your assumptions: "So what?" So what that the employees dress informally? So what that they laugh and share jokes? So what that the hours are flexible? How and why does this evidence support your claim that this is a relaxed work environment?

To answer these questions, you need to unpack some of the assumptions that connect your evidence to your claim. For example, one of your unstated assumptions is that laughter among coworkers helps to create a relaxed atmosphere. By making that assumption explicit—that is, by show-ing how and why the evidence relates to the claim (how and why laughter creates a relaxed work environment)—you are analyzing your evidence in ways that begin to **make meaning** for your readers.

Of course, the above example is fairly obvious. It will not always be as simple to identify and analyze how your evidence relates to your claims. We will show you more complicated examples later in this chapter. But even in this fairly straightforward example, we can see the basic relationship of the analysis paper:

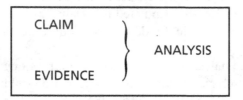

This relationship is a major part of what sets the analysis paper apart from the five-paragraph theme. In the discussion of the student paper, taken from an introductory writing course, that follows Writing Activity 9.2, we will exem-plify analysis and illustrate the challenges some first-year students experience when they are asked to make the transition from five-paragraph themes to col-lege-level analysis papers. We will show how you can advance past the simple association typical of the five-paragraph theme.

## Writing Activity 9.2

Think about a recent scene you observed or situation you participated in where you were called on to analyze an activity, event, process or object—to break some-thing down and to understand how it works and why (it doesn't have to be a situation that led to a written analysis). What was the scene of your analysis? Iden-tify the situation of the analysis—the subject, participants, purposes, and setting. What evidence did you rely on for your analysis? What conclusions did you draw from your analysis, and how did your evidence support these conclusions?

## MOVING FROM THE FIVE-PARAGRAPH THEME TO THE ANALYSIS PAPER

The following student paper begins to meet the challenges of college-level analysis papers but remains a bit limited by its adherence to the five-para-graph theme. Since the five-paragraph theme genre does not lend itself to the kind of analysis expected in college writing courses, the writer of this paper struggles to fully analyze the subject matter.

The writing assignment for this sample paper asks students to analyze two reviews of the same movie that were published in different magazines. Here is part of what the instructor specified in the assignment:

> The primary goal of your essay is to evaluate how well the two reviewers communicated the necessary information to their respective audiences, given the fixed form of a movie or television review.

This assignment calls for an analysis paper. It asks students to take two reviews and analyze how each communicates its information to its intended audience. To do this, students will need to take the reviews apart and examine how each one works in its specific magazine and for its target audience. Then the students will be expected to develop a claim based on this analysis and support it with evidence. Here is one student's paper in response to the assignment.

---

1

The motion picture Terms of Endearment is a comical movie with an unexpected somber ending. The film follows the relationship between a mother and a daughter and the men in their lives. A review of the movie was written in Time and Films in Review. They are two different reviews for two types of audience. Time magazine is geared toward a general audience, while Films in Review is intended for readers who are interested in the movie industry.

Kenneth L. Geist, the author of the review in Films in Review, and Richard Schickel, the author of the review in Time, take different approaches to the review of the movie Terms of Endearment. Half of Geist's review contained information about James L. Brooks, the director of the movie. The other half of the review was about the main characters. Schickel's review dealt mainly with the plot and the characters.

Both authors discuss the plot, but write about it differently. Geist felt that the movie was "a constantly surprising comedy which chronicles the thirty-year relationship of a

2

mother and a daughter and their wayward men." He uses difficult vocabulary intended for a well-educated reader. For example, Geist writes, "Alone and fearful of reaching fifty, Aurora surrenders to her bibulous and lecherous neighbor, Garrett, a former Astronaut, whom she had previously disdained as uncouth." When discussing the story, Geist gave away too much to the reader. He stated that Emma became infected with cancer and eventually died. When Schickel explained the same part in the story, he did not completely give the story away. Instead of saying that Emma has cancer, he refers to it as "Emma's illness." He never states that she dies.

Both Geist and Schickel discussed the director of the movie. Geist went more into depth about James Brooks than Schickel. Geist talked about what a wonderful and talented director Brooks is. He conveys this when he writes, "Brooks, the creator of such memorable television series as the <u>Mary Tyler Moore Show</u>, <u>Lou Grant</u>, and <u>Taxi</u>, has demolished Hollywood's scornful notion that t.v. craftsmen are below the salt of feature filmmakers." He also talks about Brook's gift as a screenwriter. Almost the entire article written by Geist was about Brooks. Only a small portion discussed the characters and the storyline. Schickel wrote very little about Brooks. He only talks about him in one paragraph, while Geist's main focus was Brooks. In Schickel's section on Brooks, he goes into Brook's view on what the film is about. Schickel wanted the readers to know what Brooks was trying to create.

The reviews are both well-written for their intended audience. They both contain information about the plot, characters, and the director. The review in <u>Films in Review</u> should be read if the reader has already viewed the movie and is interested in knowing about the director. Schickel's review should be read by anyone interested in the movie. He wrote an exceptional review which covered the movie well

> 3
>
> without giving the entire story away. Geist gave a lot of interesting facts about Brooks. He wrote a complete review of Brooks, but he gave away the surprise of the movie by revealing too much of the plot. Both reviews are worth reading. The one the reader chooses depends on if he or she is interested in finding out about the movie or the director.

This paper is a good example of the successes and difficulties students face when they begin writing analysis papers. The student has apparently done a fine job of analyzing the two reviews, taking them apart to examine how each differs from the other. The student also seems aware that the two reviews differ because of where they appear and for whom they are written, an awareness that is exactly what the assignment called for. But when the student writes the paper, the student runs into some difficulties, some of which are due to an overreliance on the five-paragraph theme. By doing our own analysis of this student's paper, below, we will identify these difficulties and suggest ways for you to overcome them. A closer look at the paper will further clarify the **inquiry method** of analysis, which is the primary purpose for learning analysis papers.

Here again is the introduction:

> The motion picture <u>Terms of Endearment</u> is a comical movie with an unexpected somber ending. The film follows the relationship between a mother and a daughter and the men in their lives. A review of the movie was written in <u>Time</u> and <u>Films in Review</u>. They are two different reviews for two types of audience. <u>Time</u> magazine is geared toward a general audience, while <u>Films in Review</u> is intended for readers who are interested in the movie industry.

The writer provides a fairly helpful introduction that gives a little bit of background for the movie and the two reviews. But, as you may have noticed, the introduction does not really explain why we are reading this paper, or why we should care about the analysis that follows. It just jumps in and takes the reader by surprise. More appropriately to the five-paragraph theme genre, the claim presented here is a fairly weak listing of points or statement of fact and fails to reflect the purpose of the analysis paper genre: To explain what these differences mean and to explore their implications.

While the introduction does make a statement about how the two reviews differ, it does not ask the **"So what?" question** that is critical to analysis papers: So what that "*Time* magazine is geared toward a general audience, while *Films in Review* is intended for readers who are interested in the movie industry?" A thoughtful reader might respond to this sentence by saying, "it's nice to know that *Time* magazine is geared toward a general audience, while *Films in Review* is intended for readers who are interested in the movie industry, but what does that have to do with this assignment?" After all, the assignment did not ask students to compare the audiences of different magazines; it asked students to compare reviews in two different magazines. By asking the *So what* question, however, the writer might be able to state a better claim, one that is more analytical and that the rest of the paper can support, perhaps something like:

---

**Claim:** Because *Time* magazine is geared toward a general audience, while *Films in Review* is intended for readers who are interested in the movie industry, the two reviews of *Terms of Endearment* address the movie differently.

---

Although it could still be more specific, this new claim, unlike the original, does more than just describe what is fairly obvious. It adds a level of complexity because now the writer has to connect the audiences and the reviews.

Let us now look more closely at the first supporting paragraph:

> Kenneth L. Geist, the author of the review in <u>Films in Review</u>, and Richard Schickel, the author of the review in <u>Time</u>, take different approaches to the review of the movie

> <u>Terms of Endearment</u>. Half of Geist's review contained infor-
> mation about James L. Brooks, the director of the movie. The
> other half of the review was about the main characters.
> Schickel's review dealt mainly with the plot and the characters.

This is perhaps the weakest paragraph in the paper, but it also has a great
deal of potential. In it, the writer tries to support the claim that both movie
reviewers take different approaches in their reviews. As evidence, the writer
cites *Films in Review*'s focus on the director and *Time*'s focus on the plot and
characters. This is interesting evidence. But once again, the question is "So
what?" So what that the reviewers take different approaches? So what that
one focuses on the director while the other focuses on the plot and characters? Here the writer seems to be relying on the reader to make some pretty
important connections, connections that are central to the paper's analysis.

Part of the difficulty here is that the writer never establishes a strong
enough claim in the introduction. Without having something to prove, the
evidence just sits there. The evidence needs a claim to connect back to so
that it can be analyzed. If we use our new revised claim and the already
existing evidence, the two would look something like this:

---

**Claim:** Because *Time* magazine is geared toward a general audience,
while *Films in Review* is intended for readers who are interested in
the movie industry, the two reviews of *Terms of Endearment* address
the movie differently.

**Evidence:** The *Time* review focuses on plot and characters, while the
*Films in Review* review focuses on the director.

---

Something is still missing, though. We still do not know how and why this evidence relates to and supports the claim. This is where analysis comes in. The
writer needs to make more *explicit* the assumptions that underscore the connection between the claim and evidence. *How* does the evidence support the
claim? Such analysis, when added to the claim and evidence, might look
something like this:

**Claim:** Because *Time* magazine is geared toward a general audience, while *Films in Review* is intended for readers who are interested in the movie industry, the two reviews of *Terms of Endearment* address the movie differently.

**Evidence:** The *Time* review focuses on plot and characters, while the *Films in Review* review focuses on the director.

**Analysis:** Readers of *Time*, who make up a general audience, want to read the review so they can decide if they should go see the movie, so focusing on the plot and characters will help this general audience learn something about the movie. But for readers of *Films in Review,* who are interested in the movie industry, it is more interesting to find out who made the movie, how he or she made the movie, etc. So the fact that the *Time* review discusses the plot and characters while *Films in Review* discusses the director reflects how each review is geared toward a different audience.

Notice how the analysis we have added adds meaning to the evidence by making it *relevant* to the writer's claim. It does not rely on the reader to make the connection.

Now let us look at one more supporting paragraph from the sample paper:

> Both authors discuss the plot, but write about it differently. Geist felt that the movie was "a constantly surprising comedy which chronicles the thirty-year relationship of a mother and a daughter and their wayward men." He uses difficult vocabulary intended for a well-educated reader. For example, Geist writes, "Alone and fearful of reaching fifty, Aurora surrenders to her bibulous and lecherous neighbor, Garrett, a former Astronaut, whom she had previously disdained as uncouth." When discussing the story, Geist gave away too much to the reader. He stated that Emma became infected with cancer and eventually died. When Schickel explained the same part in the story, he did not completely give the story away. Instead of saying that Emma has cancer, he refers to it as "Emma's illness." He never states that she dies.

This paragraph provides more good evidence to support the claim that the two reviews differ because of their audiences. It shows the results of the research the student has done on the two reviews and cites it effectively. And importantly, the writer begins to address the "So what?" question. Notice, for example, how the writer analyzes the first piece of evidence:

---

**Evidence:** For example, Geist writes, "Alone and fearful of reaching fifty, Aurora surrenders to her bibulous and lecherous neighbor, Garrett, a former Astronaut, whom she had previously disdained as uncouth."

**So what?**

**Analysis:** He uses difficult vocabulary intended for a well-educated reader.

---

By explaining how the difficult vocabulary in the Geist review is geared toward the more educated reader of *Films in Review*, the writer relates the evidence back to the main claim, which is that each review reflects its target audience.

The analysis is not sustained in the rest of the paragraph, however. Immediately following the first piece of evidence, the writer provides two more examples to show the difference between the reviews:

---

**Evidence:** When discussing the story, Geist gave away too much to the reader. He stated that Emma became infected with cancer and eventually died.

**Evidence:** When Schickel explained the same part in the story, he did not completely give the story away. Instead of saying that Emma has cancer, he refers to it as "Emma's illness." He never states that she dies.

---

Here, we return to the "So what?" question. Why do we, as readers, need to know this? How do these two pieces of evidence relate to the paper's main claim?

## Writing Activity 9.3

As a writer, what would you do with these two pieces of evidence? How would you address the "So what?" question? Write up your own analysis to show how you would relate the evidence to the paper's main claim.

Finally, let us take a look at the sample paper's concluding paragraph:

---

The reviews are both well-written for their intended audience. They both contain information about the plot, characters, and the director. The review in <u>Films in Review</u> should be read if the reader has already viewed the movie and is interested in knowing about the director. Schickel's review should be read by anyone interested in the movie. He wrote an exceptional review which covered the movie well without giving the entire story away. Geist gave a lot of interesting facts about Brooks. He wrote a complete review of Brooks, but he gave away the surprise of the movie by revealing too much of the plot. Both reviews are worth reading. The one the reader chooses depends on if he or she is interested in finding out about the movie or the director.

---

In this conclusion, the writer goes beyond the typical five-paragraph theme by doing more than just restating the points of each paragraph. But the conclusion does not suit the analysis paper well because the writer loses sight of the paper's focus. The writer shifts from analysis to *evaluation,* summarizing the evidence and recommending who should read which review and why. The text would have been more successful as an analysis paper if the focus had stayed on the analysis itself, explaining the meaning of the analysis, its "So what?" For example, the writer could ask: "Okay, now that I have demonstrated that these two reviews differ in their approach to the movie because of their different audiences, what does this mean in the bigger picture? What is the result or consequence of doing the kind of analysis I just did?" *Speculating on the consequences, considering the implications, or explaining the significance of one's claim is a more effective way of concluding an analysis paper because it helps readers better understand the broader relevance of the paper they just finished reading.*

Rewrite the conclusion to the sample paper above. Consider how you might more effectively keep the focus on the analysis itself. Write a conclusion that speculates on the consequences, implications, or significance of the claim the paper makes.

Our analysis of the movie reviews paper has, we hope, given you a better understanding of what analysis involves and provided some ideas about how to build on what you already know about writing. Your previous knowledge of the five-paragraph theme, with its thesis statement, creation of subpoints, and need for supporting detail, can help you adjust to the purposes of the analysis paper, with its claim, evidence, and analysis of how the claim and evidence are connected. As you move into courses in other disciplines, you will of course have to learn different notions of analysis, ones more specifically suited to the kinds of claims and evidence writers make in those scenes. Learning the analysis paper in your writing course can help you adapt to the analysis required in those scenes.

To provide you with a further example of analysis, we have included below a piece written by Rosina Lippi-Green and published in her 1997 book *English with an Accent: Language, Ideology, and Discrimination in the United States.* Although a scholarly chapter rather than an analysis paper, Lippi-Green's text demonstrates effective analysis, connecting claims to evidence and never forgetting the "So what." As you read, notice how Lippi-Green goes about supporting her overall claim that the language of Disney films perpetuates stereotypes. You might want to annotate the text (see Box 8.2: Strategies for Critical Reading, pp. 287–288), underlining the main claims and highlighting the evidence used to support those claims. You might also want to briefly summarize Lippi-Green's analysis of evidence as it relates to the claim and ask questions where you have them in the margins of the text.

■  ■  ■

# Teaching Children How to Discriminate
## What we learn from the Big Bad Wolf

Rosina Lippi-Green

All official institutions of language are repeating machines: school, sports, advertising, popular songs, news, all continually repeat the same structure, the same meaning, often the same words: the stereotype is a political fact, the major figure of ideology.

—Roland Barthes, *The Pleasure of the Text* (1975)

In 1933, while the US was in the depths of a severe depression, Walt Disney's animators created a short cartoon which would make an $88,000 profit in the first two years of its release (Grant 1993: 56). Perhaps this figure is not so surprising, given the statistics of the time: by 1930 there were some 20,000 motion-picture theaters in business, serving 90 million customers weekly (Emery and Emery 1992: 265). Thus the first filming of *Three Little Pigs*, a familiar story with a message of hard work in the face of adversity, was widely seen. The theme of good triumphing over evil was clearly a timely and popular one, and it is one that has not gone out of favor: this cartoon is still shown with regularity, in part or whole, on Disney's cable television channel.

One of the topics which is often discussed in relation to this particular Disney animated short is a scene included in the original release, in which the wolf—in yet another attempt to fool the pigs into opening the door to him—dresses as a Jewish peddler (Grant 1993, Kaufman 1988, Precker 1993b). He has a hook nose, wears sidelocks and a dark broad-rimmed hat similar to one worn by some Orthodox Jews, carries his wares before him, and contrives a Yiddish accent.[1] Kaufman recounts that it wasn't until the film's re-release in 1948, fourteen years later, that Disney reanimated the scene in which the Wolf appears as a Jew. This step was taken in response to communications from the Hays Office, which brought the issue of Jewish sensibilities to Disney's attention.[2] Grant reports that Disney later admitted that the original scene was in bad taste (1993: 54); nevertheless, only the offending visual representation was changed, and much later (at a date never specified clearly), "in case the Yiddish dialect of the original scene might itself be found offensive, the dialogue was changed as well. Now the Wolf spoke in a standard 'dumb' cartoon voice" (Kaufman 1988: 43–44). Even when the wolf no longer appeared Jewish, he spoke with a Yiddish accent, thus maintaining the underlying message based in anti-Semitism and fear of the other: a link between the evil intentions of the wolf and things Jewish. Grant also relates that the newer animation and dialogue still leaned on more general stereotypes and fears: "the disguised wolf no longer has Hebraic tones or mannerisms, instead saying: 'I'm the Fuller brushman. I workin' me way through college.' The syntax alone belies that statement" (1993: 54).

Sixty years later, a similar controversy would arise over the portrayal of characters in Disney's *Aladdin*, a movie set in a mythical Arabic kingdom. An offending line of dialogue in an opening song, "Where they cut off your ear if they don't like your face / It's barbaric, but hey, it's home," was partially changed in response to complaints from the American Arab Anti-Discrimination Committee (AAADC), but as the representative of the AAADC pointed out, the accents of the characters remained as originally filmed. The representative particularly objected to the fact that the good guys—Aladdin, Princess Jasmine and her father—talk like Americans, while all the other Arab characters have heavy accents. This pounds home the message that people with a foreign accent are bad.

(Precker 1993a)[3]

Is there truth to this supposition? What are children to take away from the Big Bad Wolf, and from brutal Arabian palace guards? Is it significant that they see bad guys who sound a certain way, look a certain way, and come from a certain part of town or of the world? Is this a part of how children learn to assign values on the basis of variation in language linked to race, ethnicity, and homeland? To make this point, it would first be necessary to demonstrate regular patterns which are available to children on a day-to-day basis, for as Silverstein (1992) asserts, "we are faced first-off with indexical facts, facts of observed/experienced social practices, the systematicity of which is our central problem: *are* they systematic? if so, *how*?" (322).

This chapter is about the sociolinguistic aspects of the systematic construction of dominance and subordinance in animated films aimed at children.

It is first observably true that somehow, children learn not only how to use variation in their own language, but also how to interpret social variation in the language of others. They do this with or without exposure to television and film, but in the current day, few children grow up without this exposure. The 1995 *World Almanac* reports that 98 percent of all US households, or some 94.2 million homes, have television sets; of these, 79 percent own video cassette recorders and 63 percent subscribe to basic cable. As seen in Figures 1 and 2, when children are not in front of the television set, they are avid consumers of the products of the movie industry; in 1992 over 15 million seats were occupied by children under the age of 2; those between 6 and 11 double this number.

For better or worse, the television and film industries have become a major avenue of contact to the world outside our homes and communities. For many, especially for children, it is the only view they have of people of other races or national origins.

In traditions passed down over hundreds of years from the stage and theater, film uses language variation and accent to draw character quickly, building on established preconceived notions associated with specific regional loyalties, ethnic, racial, or economic alliances. This shortcut to characterization means that certain traits need not be laboriously demonstrated by means of a character's actions and an examination of motive. It also means that these characterizations are culture- and period-bound; in this, films have much in common with fiction, and the representation of our cultures and our selves is equally worthy of study.

It must be noted at the outset that it is not my intention to condemn out of hand all use of abstraction in entertainment film, or even particularly in cartoons.

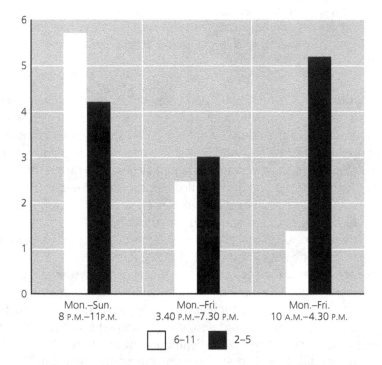

*Figure 1*   Average hours per week children watch television, by time period and two age groups
*Source:* 1995 *World Almanac and Book of Facts*

Some stereotyping may be inevitable. Whether or not all stereotyping has negative repercussions is a matter of interpretation; here I hope to show that while the practice is sometimes mild and no obvious or direct harm follows from it, there are always repercussions. For that reason alone, it would be good to be more generally aware of the way stereotypes function in film directed at children.

## Talking the Talk

Any actor necessarily brings to a role his or her own native language. In many cases, the variety of English is irrelevant to the characterization and can be left alone. Often, however, the director or actor will target a particular social, regional, or foreign accent of English, perhaps because it is intrinsic to the role and cannot be sacrificed. US audiences may or may not suspend disbelief when Robin Hood speaks with a California accent, but it would be harder to cast someone with an upper-class British accent as any of the recent US presidents and not do serious harm to audience expectations and reception.

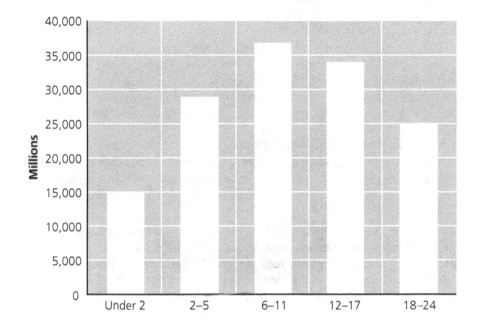

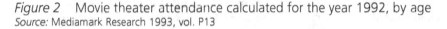

*Figure 2*    Movie theater attendance calculated for the year 1992, by age
*Source:* Mediamark Research 1993, vol. P13

In a similar way, non-native speakers of English who come to the US to make films necessarily bring their L2 accents to their work. This accent may restrict the roles they can play, or they may have roles written or rewritten to suit the immutable nature of their accents (Arnold Schwarzenegger, Gérard Depardieu, Sophia Loren, and Greta Garbo provide examples). Actors undergo accent training of various kinds in an attempt to teach them to imitate what they need for a particular role, although we have seen that even with expensive and careful tutoring not all actors are equally capable of this task, even in the limited way it is asked of them during filming.

What is particularly relevant and interesting in this context, however, is the way that actors *attempt* to manipulate language as a tool in the construction of character, whether or not they are successful. Educational programs for the training of actors for stage and screen often include classes on speech, dialogue, and the contrivance of accent. If it is possible to fool some of the people some of the time, it is still necessary to learn the skill behind this trick.

The materials used in these courses are interesting in and of themselves, because the approach often includes not just the mechanics and technicalities of one particular regional or foreign accent, but also issues of content and approach.

> Dialect actors must avoid going so far with certain speech traits that they end up creating ethnic or linguistic stereotypes . . . language or dialect background does not dictate character actions. Characters with accents must have the same range of choices available to them as characters whose speech is identical to yours.
>
> (Karshner and Stern 1990: Preface)

This is an enlightened and realistic position, certainly. Other materials prepared for actors are not always so even-handed, as seen in *Foreign Dialects: A manual for actors, directors and writers* (Herman and Herman 1943), a volume still in print:

> The Cockney Dialect: . . . The typical Cockney is often a brash little fellow. He is an inveterate heckler, and some of his favorite victims are the soap-box orators in Hyde Park. His speech is usually nasalized, possibly because of adenoid trouble which is quite prevalent in the British Isles. Often, his dialect is delivered in a whine . . . there is always a slovenliness to the pronunciation.
>
> (19)

> The Swedish Dialect: . . . the Swedes are usually more light-hearted than their Scandinavian cousins, more interested in the joys of living and eating. The Norwegians, on the other hand, are likely to be more solid and serious. The Swede likes conviviality, and the Norwegian solitary, lonely contemplation.
>
> (295)

> The Polish Dialect: . . . [Poles] are religious—especially the women—and devoutly Catholic. The Pole is industrious and will not shy from the hardest labor in the steel mills, foundries, and other heavy-duty jobs. He is a pleasure-loving person and it is this quality that leads him into the extremes of conviviality. He is not what may be called a thinking man . . . he is slow to thought, slow to speech, and slow to action.
>
> (351)

Sometimes, the contrivance of accent appears a logical and reasonable dramatic strategy. Often stories about people who come to the US from other countries lean hard on accent to establish the origin of the character (Al Pacino's Cuban-accented English in *Scarface;* Nick Nolte's Italian-accented English in *Lorenzo's Oil* or Marlon Brando's in *The Godfather;* the range of attempted Swedish accents in *I Remember Mama*). For films set in the southern US, actors are often coached long and hard on the acquisition of a second variety of US English (Vivien Leigh in *Gone with the Wind*); sometimes the attempt is not made at all (Clark Gable, Leslie Howard, and other men in the same movie).

Perhaps most interesting, a director often requires actors to use accents as a signal that the action and dialogue would not be taking place in English. Thus, in a Nazi concentration camp in *Schindler's List,* the commanding officer (Ralph Fiennes, who is British) speaks English with a contrived German accent to alert viewers to the fact that he would, in fact, be speaking German. There is a long list of filmed stories in which dialogue would not logically be taking place in English. Such films include *Schindler's List* (German and Polish, as well as other eastern European languages), *Papillon, Dangerous Liaisons, Impromptu,* and *Gigi* (French), *Diary of Anne Frank* (Dutch), *The Good Earth* (Chinese), *Fiddler on the Roof* (Yiddish, Russian), *All Quiet on the Western Front* (German, French), *Dr. Zhivago* and *Gorki Park* (Russian), *Kiss of the Spider Woman* (Spanish), *The Unbearable Lightness of Being* (Czech, French). Here accent becomes a signal of place and context rather than a means to quickly convey character. In such a case, it would make most logical sense to have *all* actors contrive the same French or Russian or Chinese accent.[4]

Rarely, however, is this policy consistent. In most movies, live action or animated, where accent is used as a cue to place, only some characters will speak with a contrived accent. Many possible reasons for this come to mind: Perhaps this is because not all actors are equally capable of targeting the required accent, or of temporarily disguising their own. Perhaps the director prefers no accents to partial or unbelievable ones. Or perhaps, in some cases, accent is used as a shortcut for those roles where stereotype serves as a shortcut to characterization. Actors contrive accents primarily as a characterization tool, although there is sometimes supplementary motivation in establishing the setting of the story. Below, I will consider exactly when certain accents are contrived, and perhaps more important, when mainstream US English (MUSE) is considered acceptable, or even necessary. To do this, we will consider one body of animated film in detail.

## Animated Film

In animated film, even more so than is the case with live-action entertainment, language is used as a quick way to build character and reaffirm stereotype:

> precisely because of their assumed innocence and innocuousness, their inherent ability—even obligation—to defy all conventions of realistic representation, animated cartoons offer up a fascinating zone with which to examine how a dominant culture constructs its subordinates. As non-photographic application of photographic medium, they are freed from the basic cinematic expectation that they convey an "impression of reality." . . . The function and essence of cartoons is in fact the reverse: the impression of irreality, of intangible and imaginary worlds in chaotic, disruptive, subversive collision.
>
> (Burton 1992: 23–24)

There are patterns in the way we project pictures and images of ourselves and others which are available to anyone who watches and listens carefully. A study of accents in animated cartoons over time is likely to reveal the way linguistic stereotypes mirror the evolution of national fears: Japanese and German characters in cartoons during the Second World War (Popeye meets the "oh so solly" Japanese fleet), Russian spy characters in children's cartoons in the 1950s and 1960s (Natasha and Boris meet Rocky and Bullwinkle, or "beeeg trrrouble forrr moose and squirrrrrel"), Arabian characters in the era of hostilities with Iran and Iraq. In the following discussion of systematic patterns found in one specific set of children's animated film, the hypothesis is a simple one: animated films entertain, but they are also a way to teach children to associate specific characteristics and life styles with specific social groups, by means of language variation.[5] To test this hypothesis, 371 characters in all of the available Disney full-length animated films were analyzed.

## Disney Feature Films

On the surface it is quite obvious that Disney films present young children with a range of social and linguistic stereotypes, from *Lady and the Tramp*'s cheerful, musical Italian chefs to *Treasure of the Lost Lamp*'s stingy, Scottish-accented McScrooge. In order to look more systematically at the way Disney films employ accent and dialect to draw character and stereotypes, it was necessary to analyze all released versions of full-length animated Disney films available.[6]

This body of animated films was chosen because the Disney Corporation is the largest producer of such films, and they are perhaps the most highly marketed and advertised of the field (Disney total advertising budget for 1992 was $524.6 million, some significant portion of which was spent directly on feature

*Table 1*   **The Disney films**

| | | | |
|---|---|---|---|
| 1938 | *Snow White* | 1963 | *The Sword in the Stone* |
| 1940 | *Pinocchio* | 1967 | *The Jungle Book* |
| 1941 | *Dumbo* | 1970 | *The Aristocats* |
| 1941 | *The Reluctant Dragon* | 1977 | *The Rescuers* |
| 1942 | *Bambi* | 1981 | *The Fox and the Hound* |
| 1950 | *Cinderella* | 1986 | *The Great Mouse Detective* |
| 1951 | *Alice in Wonderland* | 1989 | *The Little Mermaid* |
| 1952 | *Robin Hood* | 1990 | *Treasure of the Lost Lamp* |
| 1953 | *Peter Pan* | 1990 | *The Rescuers Down Under* |
| 1955 | *Lady and the Tramp* | 1991 | *Beauty and the Beast* |
| 1958 | *Sleeping Beauty* | 1992 | *Aladdin* |
| 1961 | *101 Dalmatians* | 1994 | *The Lion King* |

and animated films). Here I consider only full-length feature films (generally between one and a half to two hours in length) and specifically exclude short features, cartoons, and compilations of shorts grouped together for thematic reasons. Only fully animated films were included in the study, excluding those that combine live-action sequences with animation (*Song of the South, Three Caballeros*). Animated film created for an adult audience (the wartime film *Victory through Air Power* is one example) were also omitted. All characters with speaking roles of more than single-word utterances were included in the analysis.

A total of twenty-four films were viewed multiple times.[7] Each of the 371 characters was analyzed for a variety of language and characterization variables. The detailed linguistic description for each character consisted of a mix of phonetic transcription, quotes of typical syntactic structures, and marked lexical items. In cases where an actor is clearly contriving an accent, a decision was made as to what language variety was most likely intended to be portrayed. That is, a poorly imitated British (or other foreign) accent was still counted as such for the creators and (most) viewers. For example, in *Aladdin,* one of the minor characters, a thief, speaks primarily mainstream American, but also has some trilled *r*'s—definitely not a feature normally associated with American English. This character's accent was still classified as mainstream American, however, since only one atypical feature appeared in his phonology. Another character whose speech exhibits features from two or more dialects is Cogsworth, the butler/clock *in Beauty and the Beast.* He speaks with a contrived British accent in which some American features crop up unpredictably; thus, though it is not an accurate imitation of a middle- or upper-class British dialect, for the purposes of this study it must be classified as such.

After a brief consideration of the findings of the quantitative analysis more generally, I will concentrate on three aspects of language use in Disney films. These are the representation of African Americans; the way that certain groups are represented (particularly lovers and mothers); and finally, using French accents as a case study, the way that even positive stereotyping can be negative and limiting.

## The whole mouse and nothing but the mouse

Of the 371 characters with speaking roles in the twenty-four movies examined, 259 or 69.8 percent are male. Female characters make up the other just over 30 percent. A look at the way female and male characters are deployed, overall, indicates that within the proportions established, they are equally distributed as major and minor characters. Female characters are almost never shown at work outside the home and family; where they do show up, they are mothers and

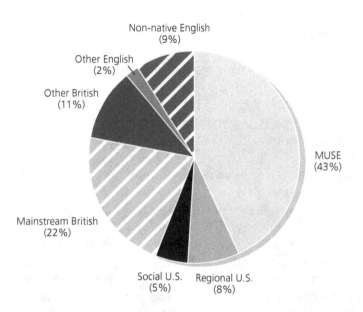

*Figure 3* 371 Disney animated characters by language variety used

princesses, devoted or (rarely) rebellious daughters. When they are at work female characters are waitresses, nurses, nannies, or housekeepers. Men, conversely, are doctors, waiters, advisors to kings, thieves, hunters, servants, detectives, and pilots.

It is certainly and demonstrably the case that the universe shown to young children in these films is one with a clear division between the sexes in terms of life style and life choices. Traditional views of the woman's role in the family are strongly underwritten, and in Disney films, whether they are filmed in 1938 or 1994, the female characters see, or come to accept, their first and most important role in life as that of wife and mother. What does an examination of language use have to add to this observation? What do characters, male and female, speak?

For the most part (43.1 percent) they speak a variety of US English which is not stigmatized in social or regional terms, what has been called MUSE throughout this study. Another 13.9 percent speak varieties of US English which are southern, or urban, or which are associated with particular racial, ethnic, or economic groups. Mainstream varieties of British English are spoken by 21.8 percent (Figure 3).

While 91 of the total 371 characters occur in roles where they would not logically be speaking English, there are only 34 characters who speak English with a foreign accent. The tendency to use foreign accents to convey the setting of the story is confirmed by these distributions; there are twice as many

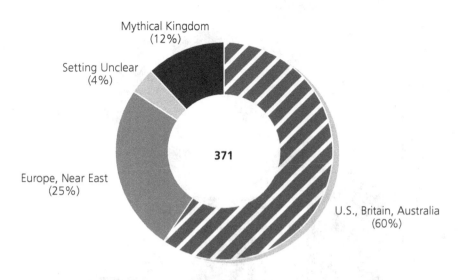

Mythical Kingdom
(12%)

Setting Unclear
(4%)

Europe, Near East
(25%)

U.S., Britain, Australia
(60%)

371

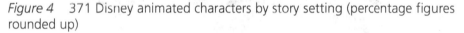

*Figure 4*  371 Disney animated characters by story setting (percentage figures rounded up)

characters with foreign-accented English in stories set in places like France and Italy.

*The Lion King,* set in Africa, is certainly a case of a story in which the logical language would not be English. This is acknowledged, indirectly, in the names of the characters, many of which are derived from Swahili. The good-natured but dumb warthog is called Pumbaa, or *simpleton;* Shenzi, the name of the leader of the hyena pack, means *uncouth.* However, the only character who actually uses traces of Swahili and a contrived Swahili accent is Rafiki (Swahili, *friend*), the wise and eccentric baboon who fulfills the role of spiritual guide.

Figure 3 indicates that some 90 percent of all the characters speak English natively, with an American or British English accent. However, Figure 4 makes it clear that 60 percent of all the characters appear in stories set in English-speaking countries; thus, a significant number of English-speaking characters appear in stories set abroad (sometimes these are "Americans abroad" as in Donald Duck in search of treasure; sometimes these are characters who are not logically English speaking, given their role and the story, as in all the characters in *Aladdin*). In Figure 5 three *language settings* are considered: stories set in English-speaking lands, those set in non-English-speaking countries, and finally, those set in mythical kingdoms where it would be difficult to make an argument for one language or another as primary (*The Little Mermaid,* for example, at times seems to be in a Mediterranean setting). Since a contrived foreign accent is often used to signal that the typical or logical language of the setting

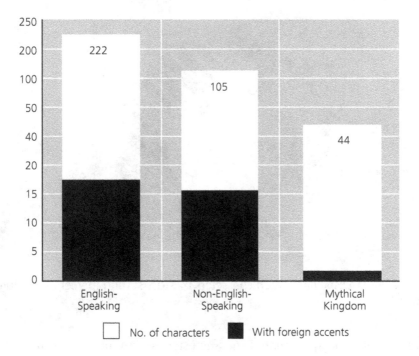

*Figure 5*   371 Disney animated characters by language spoken in the country in which the story is set, and the number of characters with foreign-accented English

would not be English, it is not surprising to see that the highest percentage of characters with foreign-accented English occurs in the second type of language setting. But it is also significant that even more characters with foreign accents appear in stories set in the US and England.

The breakdown of characters by their language variety becomes interesting when we examine that variety in relationship to the motivations and actions of the character's role. Disney films rely heavily on common themes of good and evil, and with very few exceptions they depend also on happy endings. Characters with unambiguously positive roles constitute 49.9 percent of the total; those who are clearly bad or even evil, only 19.4 percent. The remainder are divided between characters who change significantly in the course of the story (always from bad to good) and those characters whose roles are too small and fleeting for such a judgment to be made (86, or 23.2 percent of the total), as seen in Table 2.

Female characters are more likely to show positive motivations and actions (Figure 6). Unlike male characters who sometimes are bad and then become good, bad females show no character development.

*Table 2*    **371 Disney animated characters by major language group and evaluation of character's actions and motivations[8]**

|  | Motivations | | | | |
|---|---|---|---|---|---|
|  | Positive | Negative | Mixed | Unclear | Total % |
| US | 122 | 33 | 11 | 42 | 208 56.1 |
| British | 53 | 28 | 11 | 37 | 129 34.8 |
| Foreign | 10 | 11 | 6 | 7 | 34 9.2 |
| Total | 185 | 72 | 28 | 86 | 371 |
| % | 49.9 | 19.4 | 7.5 | 23.2 | 100.0 |

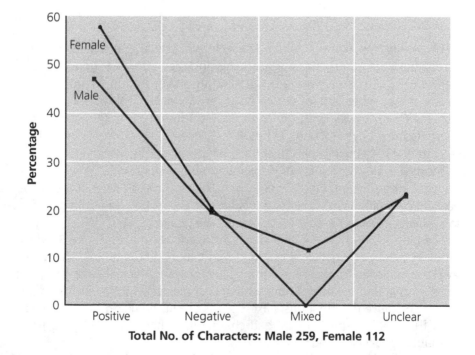

**Total No. of Characters: Male 259, Female 112**

*Figure 6*    371 Disney animated characters by gender and evaluation of actions and motivations

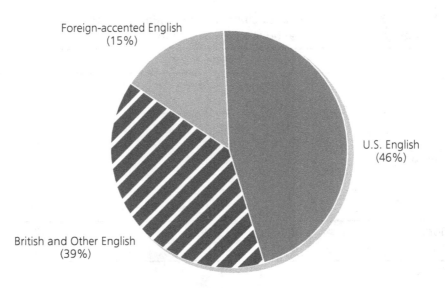

*Figure 7*   72 Disney animated characters with negative motivations and actions, by major language group

The pie chart in Figure 7 would first seem to indicate that there is no rela-tionship between non-native English accents and the portrayal of good and evil. There are 72 characters who are truly bad, in major and minor roles. They include the poacher and would-be child-murderer Percival McLeach in *The Rescuers Down Under* with his contrived southwestern accent and idiom ("purty feather, boy!" "I whupped ya'll!" "Home, home on the range, where the critters 'r ta-id up in chains"), and the whip-and-cleaver wielding Stromboli of *Pinocchio,* with his threats of dismemberment, incredible rages, and florid, contrived Italian accent. Of these evil 72, however, a full 85 percent are native speakers of English; almost half are speakers of US English. Bad guys with for-eign accents account for only 15 percent of the whole.

Taken in context, however, the issue is more complicated. In Figure 8, which compares positive, negative, and mixed motivations (the marginal characters have been removed for the sake of this discussion) by major language groups, it becomes clear that the overall representation of persons with foreign accents is far more negative than that of speakers of US or British English. About 20 per-cent of US English speakers are bad characters, while about 40 percent of non-native speakers of English are evil.

Additional interesting patterns come forward when we examine the representation of specific languages linked to national origin, race, or characterization.

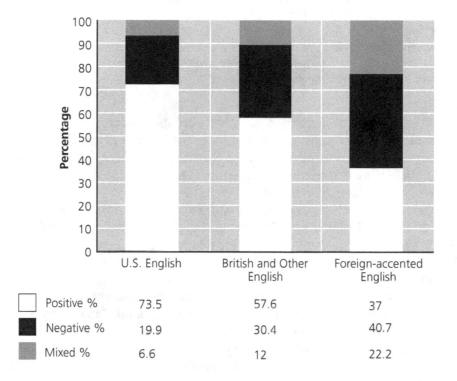

| | U.S. English | British and Other English | Foreign-accented English |
|---|---|---|---|
| Positive % | 73.5 | 57.6 | 37 |
| Negative % | 19.9 | 30.4 | 40.7 |
| Mixed % | 6.6 | 12 | 22.2 |

*Figure 8*   285 Disney animated characters of positive, negative, or mixed motivations and actions, by major language group

## Beasts and beauties

With the 1967 release of *The Jungle Book,* the relationship between voice, language, and characterization entered a new realm in Disney film. This was the first feature in which actors were cast on the basis of voice recognition. Actors and musicians who had already established a personality and reputation with the movie-going public were drawn, quite literally, into the animation and storytelling process. This strategy was not greeted with enthusiasm by all film critics:

> Animating full-bodied, expressive characters is what men like Thomas, Kahl, Johnston and Lounsberry do best. Other artists provide a handsome backdrop and add dazzling animation effects. But breathing heart and soul into a film is not so easily accomplished. *The Jungle Book* lacked this quality, and substituted for it a gallery of characters whose strongest identity was with the stars who

provided their voices. The animators enjoyed working with people like George Sanders, Louis Prima, and Phil Harris, and incorporated elements of their personalities into the animated characters. Audiences naturally responded, so the animators felt justified in continuing this practice. "It is much simpler and more realistic than creating a character and then searching for the right voice," [producer] Reitherman contended.

(Maltin 1987: 74–75)

This additional complication to the use of accent and dialect in the building of character and stereotype is relevant to a discussion of the representation of African Americans by means of language in Disney films.

Especially in more recent years, Disney has engaged African American actors to provide the voices of major characters in their animated films. Sometimes these actors speak MUSE, as is the case with James Earl Jones speaking the role of the father in *The Lion King*. Sometimes they fluctuate between MUSE and AAVE, drawing on rhythmic and lexical items for dramatic and comic effect. This is the case with Whoopi Goldberg's performance as one of the evil hyenas, also in *The Lion King*. Sometimes these actors seem to be using their own variety of English with little embellishment, as was the case when Pearl Bailey spoke the part of Big Mama in *The Fox and the Hound*. Table 3 gives an overview of all the characters in these films who use, to a greater or lesser extent, AAVE. Additional AAVE-speaking characters seem to have flitted in and out of the abduction scene in *The Jungle Book;* however, they were not included in the analysis because the speaking roles were too small to be sure of the variety of English used. It needs to be stated quite clearly that this list does not represent the sum total of all African Americans who had speaking roles in the movies examined, but only those who chose or who were directed to use AAVE for a particular part.

While the 161 MUSE speakers appear in proportions of 43.1 percent humanoid, 54.4 percent animal and 2.5 percent inanimate creatures (such as the talking teapot in *Beauty and the Beast*), all AAVE-speaking characters appear in animal rather than humanoid form. Given the low overall number of AAVE speakers, however, it is hard to draw any inferences from that fact. The issue is further complicated in that every character with a southern accent appears in animal rather than humanoid form. Further examination of unambiguously positive and negative characters indicates that a full 43.4 percent of 90 characters in human form show negative actions and motivations while only 18.6 percent of the 156 animal characters are negative.

Perhaps more disturbing than the issue of human versus animal form is the way in the world which is cast so clearly for those African Americans who are speakers of AAVE. The stereotypes are intact: the male characters seem to be unemployed or show no purpose in life beyond the making of music and pleas-

*Table 3*  **Disney animated characters who use AAVE part or all of the time**

| Name | Actor (where credits available) | Humanoid or animal | Film | Role evaluation | Typical language of setting |
|---|---|---|---|---|---|
| Dandy | Cliff Edwards | crow | *Dumbo* | Mixed | English |
| Fat | Jim Carmichael | crow | | Mixed | English |
| Glasses | Hall Johnson Choir | crow | | Mixed | English |
| Preacher | | crow | | Mixed | English |
| Straw Hat | | crow | | Mixed | English |
| King Louie | Louis Prima | primate | *Jungle Book* | Mixed | Hindi* |
| Big Mama | Pearl Bailey | owl | *Fox and Hound* | Positive | English |
| Scat | Scatman Crothers | cat | *Aristocats* | Mixed | French |
| Shenzi | Whoopi Goldberg | hyena | *Lion King* | Negative | Swahili* |

*The category "typical language" is based on the country in which the story is set. Most of the movies are set in the US, thus the typical language is English. *The Jungle Book* is set in India, and *The Lion King* in Africa. The typical languages of these stories could be any one of many native languages spoken in those places; I have chosen one of the many possible languages in such cases.

ing themselves, and this is as true for the crows in *Dumbo* as it is for the orang-utan King Louie and his crew of primate subjects in *The Jungle Book*. Much has been made of King Louie and his manipulation of the only human being in this story; singing in the scat-style made popular by African American musicians, he convinces his audience that he has one goal in life, and that is to be the one thing he is not: a human being, a man. African American males who are not linguistically assimilated to the sociolinguistic norms of a middle and colorless United States are allowed very few possibilities in life, but they are allowed to want those things they don't have and can't be.

The two female characters are also controversial, but for very different reasons. Pearl Bailey's Big Mama must be seen as a stereotype of the loving, nurturing mammy, but one with a mind of her own. Whoopi Goldberg, who voices the part of one of the hyenas in *The Lion King,* slips in and out of AAVE for comic and dramatic effect. It must be noted that she is the only African American actor to do so in this film, a film which included—for Disney—an unusually high number of African Americans. We never hear AAVE from James Earl Jones as the King. None of the characters, whether they speak MUSE or AAVE, show any clear connection to things African, with the exception of the wise baboon, Rafiki, who occupies a special but peripheral role in the film's story.

In general, children who have little or no contact with African Americans are exposed to a fragmented and distorted view of what it means to be black, based on characterizations which rest primarily on negative stereotype linked directly to language difference.

## Lovers and mothers

Romance is a major plot device in many of Disney's animated films. Of the twenty-four stories examined here, thirteen depend in part or whole on the development of a relationship between a male and a female character which has not to do with friendship, but with love and mate selection. Those characters who are young and in potential search of a mate or love interest provide some of the most interesting material in these films overall. There has been much commentary in the popular press on the physical portrayal of young men and women in extreme and unrealistic terms, for both sexes. Doe-eyed heroines with tiny waists and heroes with bulging necks and overly muscular thighs have been roundly criticized, with little effect. There is little or no discussion of the *language* spoken by lovers, however.[9]

In spite of the setting of the story or the individual's ethnicity, lovers speak mainstream varieties of US or British English (Table 4), with some interesting

*Table 4*   **Lovers and potential lovers in Disney animated films**

| Language variety | Film | Male | Female |
|---|---|---|---|
| Mainstream US | *Beauty and the Beast* | Gaston | (no mate) |
| | | The Beast | Belle |
| | *Rescuers* | Bernard | — |
| | *Rescuers Down Under* | Bernard | — |
| | *Cinderella* | Prince Charming | Cinderella |
| | *Sleeping Beauty* | Prince Philip | Aurora |
| | *Little Mermaid* | Prince Erik | Ariel |
| | *Snow White* | Prince | Snow White |
| | *Lion King* | Simba | Nala |
| | *Lady and the Tramp* | — | Lady |
| Socially marked US | *Lady and the Tramp* | Jock | — |
| | *Aristocats* | O'Malley | — |
| Non-US English | *Robin Hood* | Robin Hood | Maid Marion |
| | *Rescuers Down Under* | Jake | (no mate) |
| | *101 Dalmatians* | Pongo | Perdita |
| | | Roger Radcliff | Anita Radcliff |
| Foreign-accented English | *Rescuers* | — | Miss Bianca |
| | *Rescuers Down Under* | — | Miss Bianca |
| | *Aristocats* | — | Duchess |

exceptions. Of the male characters in Table 4, only two can be said to be logically and certainly speakers of US English: Bernard, who appears twice (*The
Rescuers* and *The Rescuers Down Under*), and Jock (*Lady and the Tramp*). All
the other characters would be speakers of British or Australian English, or of
languages other than English. The languages of the four princes (from
*Cindrella, Snow White, Sleeping Beauty,* and *The Little Mermaid*) are debatable:
the Disney version never specifies where these magical kingdoms are located
(whether in the country of the story's origin or elsewhere).

Two of the male romantic leads speak socially marked varieties of US English:
in *The Aristocats,* O'Malley (voiced by Phil Harris, a popular entertainer and
singer of his day and cast on the power of voice recognition) does nothing to
change or disguise his own English, which is rich in those characteristics which
are often thought of as "working class" (simplified consonant clusters, double-
negative constructions, and other stigmatized phonological and grammatical
features). This is also the case with Jock from *Lady and the Tramp.* Both of these
characters are prototypical rough lovers, men with an edge who need the care
and attention of good women to settle them, and both are rewarded with such
mates—females who speak non-stigmatized varieties—because they prove
themselves worthy. There are no male romantic leads with foreign accents.

There is even less variation among the female romantic leads. There are no
rough, working-class equivalents of O'Malley and Jock. In fact, of the seven
females who speak MUSE, only one is an unambiguous case of a character who
would logically speak US English: Lady of *Lady and the Tramp.* The use of a typical or logical language for the part and background of the character is clearly
less important in this case than a consistent portrayal of an ideal lover and
potential mate which stresses the lack of "otherness."

However, there are two female characters (one of whom occurs in two
movies, *The Rescuers* and *The Rescuers Down Under*) with foreign accents,
but they are both voiced by the same woman, Eva Gabor. The Gabor sisters
were widely known and recognized in US culture in the 1950s and 1960s for
their glamor and demanding behavior in many highly publicized affairs with
rich men. They were recognizable on the basis of their Hungarian accents,
and they brought with them a set of associations about sexually aware and
available females that resulted in typecasting. The roles that Eva Gabor voiced
for Disney were thus of elegant, demanding, and desirable females, and
could be seen not so much as characters with foreign accents as one of the
Gabor sisters in full costume. Perhaps Disney's hope that the public would
associate the character on the screen with the public image of the actress
voicing the part overrode more logical considerations. It was noted by at least
one critic, however, that it made little sense to have the character of *The
Aristocats'* Duchess, a pure-bred Persian cat living in France, speaking with a
Hungarian accent.

*Table 5*   **The language of mothers and fathers in Disney animated films**

| Language | Mothers | Fathers |
|---|---|---|
| MUSE | 15 | 8 |
| Socially marked US | 0 | 0 |
| Regionally marked US | 0 | 1 |
| Mainstream British | 2 | 8 |
| Socially or regionally marked British or other English | 2 | 4 |
| Foreign-accented English | 1 | 1 |

To be truly sexually attractive and available in a Disney film, a character must not only look the idealized part, but he or she must also sound white and middle-class American or British.

In a similar way, mothers and fathers are most likely to have mainstream accents of US or British English, again with some interesting exceptions. As seen in Table 5, only two of these characters speak English with a foreign accent, although what would follow logically from the story setting is that eleven of these mothers and fathers would not be native speakers of English. Another thirteen characters appear in stories where the logical language might or might not be English. This applies particularly to the retelling of fairy tales in magical kingdoms (*Cinderella, Sleeping Beauty, The Little Mermaid*).[10] The two foreign accents which are evident are Gepetto's (contrived) Italian-accented English in *Pinocchio,* and once again Eva Gabor as the glamorous Duchess in *The Aristocats.* The only US-English-speaking father character with an accent which might be stigmatized is Gramps of *The Rescuers,* who is part of a larger group of stereotypical southerners with contrived accents.

Eva Gabor's voicing of the Duchess is the only instance in any of the movies where a mother takes on a romantic lead. Otherwise, in Disney movies parenthood and romance do not intersect. However, there are a great number of single-parent families overall. Of the twenty mothers, nine are widows or become widows in the course of the story, or have no husband in evidence; five are step- or substitute mothers and are unmarried; and in two cases the question of paternity is never raised, perhaps because it could not be answered in a way Disney considered suitable for children's entertainment. This is the case in *The Aristocats,* but more particularly in *The Lion King,* where Mufasa is the undisputed dominant male of his pride, and would thereby have fathered both Simba and Nala, who grow into adulthood and become mates. The fathers, in a similar way, are often widowers or simply without wives: this is the case for eleven of the twenty-two.

There are few married couples with major roles in any film. Mr. and Mrs. Darling make only small appearances in *Peter Pan,* which is also the case for the mother and father in *Lady and the Tramp* and for Colonel Hardy and his wife Winifred in *The Jungle Book.*

Perhaps most interesting is the fact that mothers who speak non-US varieties of English have a little more latitude in social and regional variation in their language. This may be because the non-mainstream varieties of British English are not poorly thought of by US English speakers, who do not distinguish, for the most part, between stigmatized varieties of British English (Geordie, Midlands, Cockney, etc.) and those with more social currency.

Lovers in Disney films marry, and sometimes at a very tender age. But young or middle-aged married couples with growing families are seldom if ever seen. And while young lovers are presented in idealized form both physically and linguistically, in later life stages these same kinds of characters are not quite so narrowly drawn. The picture of motherhood portrayed in these animated films excludes careers and work outside family and home, and clings very closely to language varieties associated with middle-class norms and values. When seen at all, mothers are presented without a hint of ethnicity, regional affiliation, color, or economics. Fathers, often comic or droll characters, have in their language (as in work, preoccupations and interests) a wider set of choices available to them.

### Francophilia Limited

It is not hard to elicit stereotypes of the French, because this is not a national origin group which is seen in negative terms. Because there are good—or neutral—things to say, it is perhaps easier to say them:

> despite, or possibly because of, their civilized natures, the French people retain a childish eagerness for fun and frivolity as well as for knowledge. There is an impishness about many of them which is captivating. They are curious, like most children, and this curiosity leads them into experimenting with such things as piquant sauces for food . . . it can be said of the French . . . that when they are good, they are very, very good—but when they are bad, they are—Apaches.
>
> (Herman and Herman 1943: 143)

Aside from the clearly racist final comment which has to do not with the French, but with a Native American tribe, this view of the nation is not overtly negative. It is condescending, certainly, and narrow, but it does not call France a nation of idiots or a kingdom of evil (as the Herman and Herman volume does not hesitate to do in other cases).

There are two films which are set directly in France: *The Aristocats* and *Beauty and the Beast,* with a total of thirty-eight characters appearing in both stories. There is a wide range of characterizations, excessively evil and good,

*Table 6*    **Characters with French-accented English in Disney animated films**

| Setting | Character | Role | Film |
|---------|-----------|------|------|
| France | Lumiere | maitre d', steward | *Beauty and the Beast* |
|  | Stove | chef |  |
|  | Cherie | chambermaid |  |
|  | Unnamed | milkman | *Aristocats* |
|  | Unnamed | chef |  |
| Elsewhere | Louis | chef | *Little Mermaid* |
|  | Unnamed | waiter | *Rescuers* |

moody, generous, silly, drunken. Male characters include lawyers, aristocrats, barkeepers, vagabonds, inventors, booksellers, hunters, and servants. *Beauty and the Beast* takes place in an active, busy rural village; *The Aristocats* primarily in Paris. There are children and old people, lovers and villains. Of all these thirty-eight very diverse characters, all of whom would logically be speaking French, there are a total of five who indicate this by contriving a French-accented English. In other films, two additional characters appear with French accents, as seen in Table 6.

Of these seven characters, one is female (Cherie, a feather duster), and her primary purpose seems to be as a romantic foil for the character Lumiere; her only line, having been pursued behind the draperies by him, is "Oh no! I've been burnt by you before!" There are other beautiful and charming women and girls in *Beauty and the Beast,* but none of them are coquettish, and none of them have French accents. The subtle but unmistakable message is quite a simple one: there may logically be thirty-eight characters before us who are French, but the truly French, the prototypical French, are those persons associated with food preparation or presentation, or those with a special talent for lighthearted sexual bantering. If a personality is established at all, there are two basic personality types available to them: irascible (the chef in *The Little Mermaid,* and his counterpart in *The Aristocats*); and the sensual rascal.

Is this a terrible picture to give children? After all, there are no truly "French"—linguistically, culturally, truly French—characters who are criminal, who threaten children, who are lazy or conniving. But there are also no French who are surgeons, rock singers, who teach school or drive a cab, or who are elderly. Rich people and aristocrats, in France or elsewhere, speak with British accents no matter what their logical language. The domain of life experience for things French is as narrow, if not as overtly negative, as that for AAVE speakers.

The cultural stereotypes for specific national origin groups are perpetuated in a systematic way in these stories created for, and viewed primarily by, children.

## *Summary*

Close examination of the distributions indicates that these animated films provide material which links language varieties associated with specific national origins, ethnicities, and races with social norms and characteristics in non-factual and sometimes overtly discriminatory ways. Characters with strongly positive actions and motivations are overwhelmingly speakers of socially mainstream varieties of English. Conversely, characters with strongly negative actions and motivations often speak varieties of English linked to specific geographical regions and marginalized social groups. Perhaps even more importantly, those characters who have the widest variety of life choices and possibilities available to them are male, and they are speakers of MUSE or a non-stigmatized variety of British English. These characters may be heroes or villains, human or animal, attractive or unattractive. For females, on the other hand, and for those who mark their alliance to other cultures and places in terms of language, the world is demonstrably a smaller place. The more "negatives" a character has to deal with (gender, color, stigmatized language, less favorable national origin) the smaller the world. Even when stereotyping is not overtly negative, it is confining and misleading.

## That's Entertainment

Disney films are not the only way in which we perpetuate stereotypes on the basis of language. The manipulation of language variety and accent to draw character is an old tool, but it is seldom a completely benign one. Stereotyping is prevalent in television programming and movies: situation comedies (*Beverley Hillbillies, I Love Lucy, Sanford and Son, All in the Family, Molly Goldberg, American Girl, Ma and Pa Kettle, Green Acres, Andy Griffith*) in particular provide numerous examples, which need to be examined more closely.

Language and accent as symbols of greater social conflict are also found in serious dramatic efforts, on television and film. The 1993 film *Falling Down* provides a disturbing example. In that film, a middle-class worker portrayed as beleaguered by inner-city life loses his temper with an irascible convenience-store clerk; the episode begins when the protagonist asks the price of an item. The following is from the script:

> *The proprietor, a middle-aged ASIAN, reads a Korean newspaper . . . the Asian has a heavy accent . . .*
>
> ASIAN: eighdy fie sen.
> D-FENS: What?
> ASIAN: eighdy fie sen.

> D-FENS: I can't understand you . . . I'm not paying eighty-five cents for a stinking soda. I'll give you a quarter. You give me seventy "fie" cents back for the phone . . . What is a fie? There's a "V" in the word. Fie-vuh. Don't they have "v's" in China?
>
> ASIAN: Not Chinese, I am Korean.
>
> D-FENS: Whatever. What differences does that make? You come over here and take my money and you don't even have the grace to learn to speak my language . . .
>
> (Smith 1992: 7–8)

Here, accent becomes a very convenient and fast way to draw on a whole series of very emotional social issues, and all of them in a spirit of conflict, from immigration and the rights and responsibilities thereof, to greater issues of dominance and subservience, race and economics. The scene is very believable; many have had or observed such exchanges. The protagonist, clearly a man on the edge of socially acceptable behavior, is also portrayed as someone pushed to that edge by the pressures of inner-city life. He is overtly cruel and condescending and racist; but, somehow, he is also seen as not completely wrong.

In this film, a foreign accent becomes the signal of what has gone wrong with us as a nation, and his dismay and his anger, while excessive, are cast as understandable. From Charlie Chan to this owner of a corner store, our understanding of Asians—all Asians—has been reduced to a series of simple images. They are inscrutable, hard-working, ambitious, intelligent but unintelligible people, and they make us uncomfortable.

Even films which are made specifically for the purpose of illuminating and exploring racial and other kinds of social injustice are not free of the very subtle effects of standard language ideology. A close examination of Spielberg's *Schindler's List* (1993) shows a great deal of consistency in the use of accent: "The accents of individuals reflect their position in World War II Poland. That is, German characters are given—by and large—German accents, and Jewish characters generally possess Yiddish accents" (Goldstein 1995: 1). Even here, however, the suppression of variation for some characters has been noted, this time falling along lines not of color or religion, but of gender. In an initial exploration, Goldstein found that the more sexually available and attractive a female character was, the less distinctive her accent.

> Following this pattern, the German women who were wives and mistresses— and therefore the most sexually available women in the movie—did not have strong German accents [while] the older and less attractive Jewish women had heavier and thicker Yiddish accents . . . linguistic accent seems to be part of what is deemed attractive about [some] women.
>
> (1995: 6)

These patterns held true for males as well: conservative Jews had stronger Yiddish accents; the worst of the prison guards, brutish Nazis, had the heaviest German accents (ibid.). It seems that even the highest standards in film making cannot be free of the social construction of language. And perhaps there is nothing that can or should be done about this process in its subtlest form. It is, after all, part of the social behavior which is of interest to art as the representation of the human condition.

What children learn from the entertainment industry is to be comfortable with *same* and to be wary about *other,* and that language is a prime and ready diagnostic for this division between what is approachable and what is best left alone. For adults, those childhood lessons are reviewed daily.

## *Notes*

1. "Ethnic stereotypes were, of course, not uncommon in films of the early Thirties, and were usually essayed in a free-wheeling spirit of fun, with no malice intended. By the time the film was reissued in 1948 . . . social attitudes had changed considerably" (1988: 43). Kaufman's construction of the original caricature (Jews as wily and untrustworthy business people) as harmless is one which it is hard to take on good faith, given the general climate of anti-Semitism prevalent in Europe and the US in the 1930s.

2. In 1930, the Motion Picture Producers and Distributors of America (MPPDA) created a self-regulatory code of ethics. The office charged with this duty was put under the direction of Will H. Hays, and went into effect on July 1, 1934. The Hays Office outlined general standards of good taste and specifically forbade certain elements in film. The code specified that "no picture shall be produced which will lower the standards of those who see it. Hence the sympathy of the audience should never be thrown to the side of crime, wrong-doing, evil or sin." The specific regulations included "Revenge in modern times shall not be justified"; "Methods of crime shall not be explicitly presented"; "The sanctity of the institution of marriage and the home shall be upheld"; "Miscegenation (interracial sexual relationships) is forbidden." The Code specifically addressed the inadvisability of caricaturing national-origin groups or portraying them in offensive ways.

    In 1968 a rating system was put into effect, and the Code was no longer used.

3. Other interviews with AAADC representatives were further reported in the same paper:

    > Although they are Arabs, Aladdin and Princess Jasmine, the heroes, talk like Americans. Merchants, soldiers and other ordinary Arabs have thick foreign accents. "This teaches a horrible lesson," says [the representative]. "Maybe they can't redub it now, but we asked them to please be sure there is no accent discrimination in the foreign-language versions."

    > (Precker 1993b)

4. Sometimes a cast is a combination of those who must contrive the accent and those who are native speakers of the language in question, and bring that L2 accent to their performance, as was the case with *Gigi.*

5. It might be argued that many aspects of animated films are actually aimed at the adults who watch films with children, and that the children themselves are less likely to comprehend the stereotypes. The small body of studies in this area indicates that while children's attitudes toward particular language varieties are not fully developed until adolescence, they do begin forming as early as age 5 (Rosenthal 1974, Day 1980). Giles *et al.* (1983) found that significant changes occurred between the ages of 7 and 10 in children's attitudes toward different language varieties.

6. The first round of analysis was conducted as a graduate-level seminar project in social dialectology. The students who contributed to the analysis at that stage were Carlson Arnett, Jennifer Dailey-O'Cain, Rita Simpson, and Matthew Varley. The results of that project were presented as a poster at the 1994 "New Ways of Analyzing Variation" conference at Stanford University. The data presented here represents a second viewing of all films originally studied as well as the addition of three films not included in the original study: *The Lion King, The Aristocats,* and *Snow White.*

7. In the pilot study, each participant watched at least four films, although most had seen more than these initial four. To aid in the consistency of language characterization as well as coding for other

variables, three films were viewed and coded as a group. Subsequently, I reviewed all films and checked the original coding.

8. Standard tests of correlation of the relationship of a character's nationality to his or her motivation (positive, negative, mixed) were shown to be highly significant at levels better than .001.

9. Characters of an age to pursue a partner who do *not* do so in the story line are usually portrayed as awkward, fat, or ugly (examples include the stepsisters in *Cinderella,* the witch-like Cruella de Ville in *101 Dalmatians,* LaFou in *Beauty and the Beast*).

10. Other cases were also ambiguous. Whether Colonel Hardy and his wife Winifred, the military elephants in *The Jungle Book,* are logically speakers of an Indian language or of English could be debated. The same problem applies to this determination for the Indian Chief in *Peter Pan.*

### Works Consulted

Burton, J. (1992) "Don (Juanito) duck and the imperial-patriarchal unconscious: Disney studios, the good neighbor policy, and the packaging of Latin America." *Nationalisms and Sexualities.* A. Parker, M. Russo, D. Sommer, *et al.,* eds. New York: Routledge: 21–41.

Day, R. (1980) "The development of linguistic attitudes and preferences." *TESOL Quarterly* 14: 27–37.

Emery, M. and E. Emery (1992) *The Press and America: An interpretive history of the mass media.* Englewood Cliffs, NJ: Prentice-Hall.

Fairclough, N., C. Harrison, C. Creber, *et al.* (1983) "Developmental and contextual aspects of children's language attitudes." *Language and Communication* 3(2): 141–146.

Goldstein, E. (1995) "Analysis: accent in Spielberg's *Schindler's List.*" Unpublished ms.

Grant, J. (1993) *Encyclopedia of Walt Disney's Animated Characters.* New York: Hyperion.

Herman, L. and M. S. Herman (1943) *Foreign Dialects: A manual for actors, directors and writers.* New York: Theatre Arts Books.

Karshner, R. and D. A. Stern (1990) *Dialect Monologues.* Toluca Lake, CA: Dramaline Publications.

Kaufman, J. B. (1988). "Three little pigs—big little picture." *American Cinematographer* (November): 38–44.

Maltin, L. (1973) *The Disney Films.* New York: Crown.

——— (1987) *Of Mice and Magic: A history of American animated cartoons.* 2nd revised edition. New York: Plume Books.

Precker, M. (1993a) "This Aladdin is rated PC." *Dallas Morning News.* October 2. Dallas: 5c.

——— (1993b) "Animated debate." *Dallas Morning News.* July 12. Dallas: 1c.

Rosenthal, A (1974) "The magic boxes: preschool children's attitudes toward Black and Standard English." *Florida Foreign Language Reporter* 12: 55–62, 92–93.

Silverstein, M. (1992) "The uses and utility of ideology: some reflections." *Pragmatics* 2(3): 311–324.

Smith, E. R. (1992) *Falling Down.* Script revision dated March 17, 1992. Film (1993) directed by J. Schumacher. Arnold Kopelson Productions in association with Warner Bros. Inc.

### Collaborative Activity 9.1

Working with your group, identify three claims that Lippi-Green makes and some of the evidence she uses to support each claim. Then locate passages in the text where she offers analysis, showing the assumptions behind her linking of the evidence to the claim. Be sure to keep your notes, since you may return to this chapter for a later writing assignment.

**Writing Activity 9.5**

Lippi-Green's analysis relies heavily on visual rhetoric or the visual presentation of ideas. Notice how she includes charts, graphs, and tables to illustrate and extend her points. Notice, too, how those visual elements are integrated into the text. Does she refer to them in the body of her chapter? Does she give them captions or labels? Discuss how those visual elements help Lippi-Green support her claims and help her readers understand her analysis. What are the effects of using graphic illustrations and visuals to present evidence? What claims do they reinforce? What concepts or relationships do they clarify? How do they build credibility or ethos?

# Generic Features of the Analysis Paper

With some understanding of the scene and situation of the analysis paper, including its defining purpose of teaching and practicing analysis, we now turn to *describing* the patterns in the generic features of analysis papers. As you may have had a chance to discover for yourself in doing your own genre analysis in Chapter 2, performing such an analysis of the analysis paper can help us understand not just what the expected features are but why they are what they are—how the features of the genre function in and what they can tell us about the scene of the writing course. Such a critical knowledge of conventions and their underlying assumptions will enable you to write analysis papers more effectively and confidently because you will be more informed about the choices you can make.

Compared to genres such as the resumé, the brochure, the lab report, the complaint letter, and the obituary, the analysis paper is a more flexible genre. Although certain assumptions and expectations exist, writers have more room to maneuver within them. This flexibility is why we ask you to remember that the rhetorical patterns and strategies we are about to describe are not meant to *prescribe* how you should write an analysis paper. We will in turn consider

- Content
- Rhetorical Appeals
- Structure
- Format
- Sentences
- Words

## Content

Whatever the writing assignment—to uncover the assumptions of a text, or to take an idea and use it to explore another concept, or to explain what a text, activity, or event means and how it works—writers of analysis papers will typically establish a claim that is central to the paper and develop it with evidence and analysis which explains how the evidence relates to the claim. Indeed, what can be called the "content" of the analysis paper *is* its analysis of the subject. More specifically, the content consists of the idea that the writer has formulated about his or her given subject, an idea that he or she has developed into an issue or problem that can be addressed and supported. As such, the most typical and significant move writers of analysis papers make is to turn the results of their observations and analysis into an issue/problem that becomes the paper's claim. That is, *they turn their study of a subject into an interpretation of the subject.* The introductory section of analysis papers, usually one or two paragraphs, tends to be devoted to making this move toward the claim.

Because they know that they will eventually have to construct a claim based on that subject—one that uncovers some of its assumptions, explains its meaning, and/or examines how it works—writers select subjects that lend themselves to analysis. For example, consider a claim such as "The HBO series *The Sopranos* has attracted a great deal of criticism from some Italian-American groups recently because of its negative stereotypes." While interesting, this claim is ultimately not analyzable. It just states a fact that does not require analysis to examine its meaning. A more appropriate claim would present an idea about *The Sopranos* that requires evidence and analysis to support it:

---

*The Sopranos* exploits negative stereotypes of Italian Americans as gangsters.

---

While this claim is more analyzable, requiring the writer to examine how *The Sopranos* exploits stereotypes, it still needs to stand up to the "So what?" question writers are expected to ask themselves in analysis papers. So what that *The Sopranos* does this? Why is the writer making this claim? A more effective claim, based on the "So what?" question, might be the following:

---

**Claim:** By exploiting negative stereotypes of Italian Americans as gangsters, the highly acclaimed HBO series *The Sopranos* contributes to the perpetuation of this stereotype.

---

With this claim, the writer not only has something to analyze (to uncover how the show exploits stereotypes), but also has a reason for performing the analysis (to show how such stereotyping leads to further stereotyping). The content of an analysis paper, then, concentrates on a subject that lends itself to analysis, develops a controlling idea that makes a central claim about that subject, and uses analysis to support that claim with evidence.

### Collaborative Activity 9.2

After reading the sample analysis papers, decide with your group what the controlling idea (central claim) of each paper is. Then assess how effective that claim is for an analysis paper. What makes the subject analyzable? How well does the claim lead to analysis of the supporting evidence? How well does it pass the "So what?" test?

## RHETORICAL APPEALS

Nor surprisingly, since they are grounded in the logical process of analysis, analysis papers rely heavily on *logos* (the appeal to logic and reasoning) over *pathos* (the appeal to emotion) and *ethos* (the appeal to the writer's credibility). By presenting evidence and making logical points, analysis papers appeal to the readers' reasoning rather than to their emotions or the writer's character. To reinforce this emphasis on the subject, on the logic and the evidence, *writers of analysis papers work toward projecting an image of themselves, an ethos, of a rational person who is examining the evidence objectively.* They take an observational, distant stance in relation to the evidence. They tend to stand back and engage it objectively. Although personal testimony can be used as evidence in some cases, generally writers of analysis papers rely on a critical examination of observed facts such as, for example, what politicians actually say, what advertisements actually contain, and how a certain event coincided with another. There is little room in the body of analysis papers, therefore, for writers to engage in making value judgments or recommendations. Writers withhold such evaluations in order to examine how something works, what it means, and why.

Withholding evaluation does not mean, however, that writers of analysis papers do not have a stake in the analysis. In fact, the writer's presence is most evident in analysis papers when he or she tries to make use of the evidence, examine its meaning, and comment on its relevance. In this way, the writer takes an *active* position, directing the readers' attention to aspects of the evidence that he or she wants them to notice. In some cases, writers will simply write: "Notice how this ad uses the color red to create an atmosphere of seduction." Writers will also guide readers to their point of view in less direct ways:

1. Announcing what the evidence means ("This quote is an excerpt from a letter written in response to a debate over illegal immigration, and exemplifies the Democrats' use of discourse to gain sympathy toward illegal immigration.")

2. Breaking the evidence down into parts that reflect the writer's claim ("The next aspect is that of the woman's posture.")

3. Explaining the meaning of the evidence ("So, in this advertisement Skyy Vodka has used the desire for sex and high status to make their product seem like it will improve people's lives." and "Hence, the sentence assumes more than one meaning. Literally, it instructs the student to avoid interfering with the work of others in the class. The syntax of the sentence also suggests . . . .")

Personal opinion and judgment can also be inferred indirectly from the writer's word choice. Phrases such as "the child's authority is sacrificed" and "the daunting presence of the principal" carry the force of the writer's opinion and appeal subtly to the reader's emotions. So while logos appears to dominate the analysis paper, subtle appeals to emotion and a credible ethos that treats judgments as facts contribute to the effectiveness of the paper.

## Collaborative Activity 9.3

In small groups, examine the sample analysis papers, and assess how each balances logos, pathos, and ethos. In addition to seeing the emphasis on logos, find places where the writers appeal to readers' emotions, where they reveal their judgments, and where they establish their credibility. How well does each writer use the three appeals, given the expectations for analysis papers? Critique the emphasis on logos in these papers. Would any of them be improved by greater use of emotional appeals or by the personal experience of the writers? If so, how?

## STRUCTURE

In keeping with this logical emphasis, analysis papers are structured around a controlling idea that is a central claim and use an introduction-body-conclusion general structure. In general, analysis papers use

1. Introductions to assert their claims

2. Body paragraphs to develop and support those claims with evidence

3. Conclusions to reassert their claims and open out to new implications or extensions of the controlling idea

In terms of structure, then, the analysis paper appears to be organized by sections rather than paragraphs. Unlike the five-paragraph essay, which is paragraph driven, with each paragraph made up of its own self-contained subclaim and support, *the analysis paper is organized by sections, each of which may contain more than one paragraph that works toward developing the central claim.* The introductory and concluding sections may contain more than one paragraph that accomplishes their goals, and the body of the paper is divided into multiple sections (each consisting of one or more paragraphs), with each section trying to accomplish its own goal within the larger structure of the paper.

This typical structure for academic papers suits its academic scene, of course, while still allowing flexibility to suit the wide range of subjects that analysis papers may treat. More specific organizational patterns vary from one paper to the next, as the central claim shifts. Yet the organization of an effective analysis paper will always reflect not some predetermined order (like five paragraphs, or compare ABABAB) but rather an order that makes sense for the logic of the analysis. The unique organization comes from *the unique logic of the central claim.*

## The Introduction

Introductions of analysis papers move from the subject being studied to the claim being asserted. They set up the central claim that will constitute the controlling idea. Writers use different strategies to make this move in their introductions. Very often, they will begin with an opening sentence that makes a general observation about the subject, something such as: "Psychology is defined as the study of the mind"; "People's prejudices are often used to sell products, and many times these prejudices involve women"; and "Throughout the history of the United States, immigration has played a major role in the country's population growth." These opening sentences serve to transport the reader into the "world" of the paper and its subject of study. They also help set up the background that often follows, which adds more information about the observations. For example, the observation regarding prejudice is followed by more specific examples of how advertisers use prejudice to sell products; in addition, the observation regarding immigration in the United States is followed by a brief discussion of what immigration is and how Democrats and Republicans treat it. By helping to frame each paper, these introductory backgrounds not only set up the claim that follows, but they also give readers the impression that they are walking into the context of the claim, almost as if they are discovering the claim for themselves.

Typically, the next move that writers make in the introductory section involves establishing and defining some kind of issue or problem that their claim will address and develop. In analysis papers, the background information not only creates a context for the analysis but also sanctions it. That is, writers frequently use the background information to justify the analysis they are about to perform. For example, in the sample analysis paper about women in advertising, the writer uses the background information (which describes how advertisers use gender prejudices to sell products) to justify and make possible the analysis of various advertisements. The resulting claim is:

---

**Claim:** This combination of status and sex can be powerful, and companies know how to use these ideas to their full advantage to sell their product.

---

The rest of the paper explains how. In this example, the writer uses the introduction to create a context that establishes the authority and the opportunity for her analysis. That analysis becomes the claim that her paper will develop and support.

The rhetorical pattern of introductions thus typically looks something like this:

1. Provide background on the subject

2. Use that background to justify/authorize the analysis

3. Establish a claim based on that analysis

This pattern shows how writers of analysis papers use introductions to create the conditions in which their analyses take place, conditions that not only position their analyses, but also make their analyses possible. Rhetorically, writers often move through this pattern by first describing their subject in seemingly straightforward ways and then using that description to sanction their analysis based on that description. For instance, notice how the writer of the following excerpt uses the introduction to move rhetorically from describing the more obvious functions of grade school, using simple declarative sentences, to establishing a claim that analyzes the less obvious functions of grade school:

---

Grade school is a place children go to be taught the most basic skills for living a normal, happy life. Children will learn multiplication, division, cursive writing, spelling, and reading all in a normalized environment. They will also learn how to interact with others, listen attentively, and speak with confidence. . . . **Beneath all of this educational prepping lies a complex structure of surveillance, control, and centralized authority. A vast system of educational control has been laid out for children to enter into at a very young age.**

---

The sentences in bold represent the paper's central claim and controlling idea, which analyzes how grade school is a system of surveillance and control. In this case, the writer uses the subordinating clause "Beneath all of this educational prepping" to shift from the more obvious background description to the less obvious workings of grade school. Rhetorically, the writer uses this clause to literally uncover the workings of her subject. In the remainder of the paper, the writer analyzes this central claim.

### The Body: Developing and Supporting Claims with Evidence

What is commonly referred to as the "body" of an analysis paper contains the set of paragraphs in which writers develop and support their central claim (what constitutes the controlling idea in analysis papers) in an order that makes sense for that particular claim. Typically, writers develop their idea by breaking down the central claim into its constituent parts. For example, in the immigration paper we discussed earlier, the writer's central claim is as follows:

---

**Claim:** In their attempts to gain public support, both Republicans and Democrats use language techniques to shape public opinion about illegal immigration.

---

As the claim suggests, the writer will be analyzing how politicians use language to affect public opinion. In the body paragraphs that follow the introduction, the writer breaks down this central claim into two parts, one that focuses on Republicans and one that focuses on Democrats. Here are the two resulting subclaims:

---

**Subclaim A:** In their attempt to gain public support, Republicans use language techniques to dehumanize illegal immigrants as well as blame them for economic difficulties.

**Subclaim B:** In contrast, Democrats tend to hold a more sympathetic view towards illegal immigration, as demonstrated in their language.

---

In this case, the writer separates the two subclaims and devotes two paragraphs to supporting each, so that the organization looks like this:

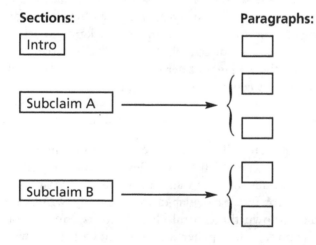

Precisely how many subclaims a writer uses, how he or she organizes them, and how many paragraphs he or she devotes to each one will depend on the demands of the central claim, on the nature of the evidence, and on the writer's strategy. (For example, it would have been just as strategically feasible for the above writer to combine subclaims A and B and devote each supporting paragraph to comparing how Republicans and Democrats talk about immigration.) Whatever organizational strategy a writer chooses, the pattern of development in analysis papers involves unfolding the central claim into its constituent parts, organizing them in some kind of order, and then supporting these parts with evidence and analysis.

The body sections present the evidence, analyze it, and guide the reader through its complexities. The typical pattern of development in analysis papers follows the analytical arrangement we described earlier:

1. The writer first sets up the piece of evidence with some brief background information that describes its context and often also explains its relevance

2. Then the writer presents the actual evidence in as much detail as possible by describing it, summarizing it, quoting from it, and so on

3. The evidence is then followed by analysis, in which the writer extracts the most relevant aspects of the evidence, explains and clarifies it, and then connects the evidence back to the claim it is trying to support

Here is how this pattern works itself out in the immigration paper:

---

**Subclaim:** In their attempt to gain public support, Republicans use language techniques to dehumanize illegal immigrants as well as blame them for economic difficulties.

**Evidence:** The governor of California, Pete Wilson, is one of the strongest voices in the drive to stop illegal immigration. He states: "While our educated citizens find themselves without work, illegal aliens are continuously entering the country, taking jobs, which our brothers and sisters rightfully deserve."

**Analysis:** Notice in this quote that Wilson dehumanizes illegal immigrants, making them seem subordinate to U.S. citizens. By using the word "alien," Wilson paints the picture of grotesque, scary beings in the minds of his readers. . . .

---

As you can see from this pattern, after establishing the first subclaim, the writer introduces the evidence by contextualizing it, letting readers know who Pete Wilson is. Then the writer quotes directly from Wilson, a Republican, using Wilson's own words as evidence. After that, the writer begins to analyze the evidence by pulling from it the relevant parts and explaining them in such a way that they will relate back to and support the subclaim. Such a pattern of claim-evidence-analysis is typical of analysis papers, but the pattern can unfold in various ways. For example, some writers choose to compile an entire paragraph's worth of evidence and then analyze that evidence in a separate paragraph, while other writers opt to begin with the analysis and then turn to the evidence as proof. A prescribed way of unfolding this pattern does not exist; how writers do that depends on their subject, readers, and other factors related to their specific context and strategy.

## Writing Activity 9.6

Outline the structure of one of the sample analysis papers. Use whatever numbering system works for you, but write out in sentences the paper's central claim and the subclaims in order. Under one of the subclaims, note how the writer moves between subclaim, evidence, and analysis, as we did in our analysis of the immigration essay's pattern.

### *The Conclusion*

In the final section of the analysis paper, the conclusion (which can be one or more paragraphs long), the writer typically employs what is sometimes referred to as a "closing to open" strategy. Writers will often close the paper by reiterating their subclaims and showing how, when they are reconnected, they prove the central claim. In this way, they create the impression that the paper has come full circle, that the analysis has been synthesized. They also typically return to the question of "So what?" and extend the significance of their claim. Writers will sometimes consider the implications and consequences of their analysis and how it might be relevant in a larger sense to the lives of readers. Yet another concluding strategy involves writers qualifying their own conclusions by pointing out some shortcomings in their analysis that will need to be addressed in future research. (An effective analysis paper is not—indeed cannot be—the final word on a subject. So do not be afraid to expose some of your paper's shortcomings in your conclusion. Indeed, by acknowledging the paper's shortcomings, writers anticipate and, in an important sense, diffuse their readers' potential concerns.) In some cases, writers will also conclude by calling for further analysis, in so doing asking readers to apply what they have just read to other subjects and once again pointing out the significance of both their subject and their claim.

**Collaborative Activity 9.4**

Compare the ways the sample analysis papers introduce or conclude their papers. First, describe how each moves among the rhetorical parts we describe above. Then evaluate which ones your group finds most effective, and explain why. If your group does not like any of the introductions and conclusions especially well, explain the special challenges of introductions and conclusions and consider the ways the generic conventions may be limiting what writers believe they can do in those sections.

## FORMAT

Analysis papers use formats common to academic papers: Typed, double-spaced, each page numbered, paragraphs indented, with a title and a heading indicating the writer's name, course number, and date. Some teachers specify other format requirements. Such formatting marks the paper as an academic one, suitable to the scene of a classroom and indicative of the role of the submitting student and the evaluating teacher. It also indicates the relative uniformity expected of academic assignments, with plain white paper, black ink, and a serious font. Because the types of assignments, subjects analyzed, and nature of the central claims can be so varied, the length of analysis papers varies widely.

An essential part of the analysis paper's format is the nature and use of transitions, the signals to the reader of the logical move being made from one part of the paper to the next. Writers of analysis papers use transitions as the rhetorical glue that holds the sections together and guides the reader through them. Because analysis papers in writing courses generally do not rely on subheadings in their formatting (as other academic genres such as lab reports do), the use of transitions becomes critical in guiding readers through the stages of analysis. Since the logic of the analysis is the basis for the structure, transitions in analysis papers typically explain the logical connection between parts. These logical connections are usually relatively complex; as a result, transitions in analysis papers tend to require sentences to explain the link, not just the simple transitional words like *however* (simple contrast) or *next* or *first* (simple continuation) that five-paragraph themes rely on.

Writers also use transitions to introduce evidence throughout the body. Evidence loses some of its force if it is just presented as one piece of evidence after another. The use of transitions enables the writer to explain the relevance of the evidence before it is presented, so that readers know what they are about to encounter. Some strategies used to introduce evidence include:

- Contextualizing it ("This example is an excerpt from . . .")
- Drawing attention to it ("Notice how this example . . .")
- Announcing what it means ("The following is a good example of how . . .")
- Breaking the evidence into parts ("Another aspect of the example that is telling is . . .")

Introducing evidence creates the "pointing out" effect that is so common to analysis papers.

The writer uses transitions to keep the reader's attention focused on the evidence as well as to justify further analysis. As such, transitions are one of the key ways that writers can communicate their perspectives to readers in analysis papers, where the focus is not so much on the readers as it is on the subject under scrutiny. Writers seek subtle ways to "talk" to the reader while remaining focused on the subject, as in this example: "The meaning of this sentence may seem obvious [i.e., to you the reader]. However, the language of the sentence requires closer scrutiny for true clarity." As illustrated in this example and the ones above, writers of analysis papers use transitions as signposts to direct readers from one section of the paper to another as well as to focus readers' attention on certain evidence.

## Writing Activity 9.7

Examine the format of the sample analysis papers. What characteristics do they share in terms of layout and appearance? Next, examine three paragraphs from one of the sample papers, and explain how the writer uses transitions to guide the reader through the stages of analysis. Look for transitional words and signposts—signals for logical connections or for pointing out evidence—and explain the effect of these transitions on the reader. Finally, indicate places where stronger transitions are needed and provide examples of what those transitions might look like.

## SENTENCES

The sentences in analysis papers reflect the emphasis on *logos* and the complex relationships of analysis. Sentence structures tend to include more complex sentences, ones that show logical relationships among assertions ("By realizing that the creation of this perfect world is in fact unreal, the consumer can become more aware of the intent of the advertising and its effects on the society." or "The company is counting on men assuming that since women like Skyy Vodka, then men who drink Skyy Vodka will attract the right sort of people, and the people around a man will either raise or lower his status."). Sentences also tend to be **declarative,** assertions of facts and the ways things are ("The American culture is incredibly diverse." or "Both Democrats and Republicans use discourse to gain support."). The more distanced, observational stance of analysis papers is reflected rhetorically in these declarative assertions, as it is in the tendency to rely on forms of the verb *be (am, is, are, was, were, being, been)*. Sentences structured around *be* verbs assert a static existence, that this is just the way things are ("There are strict rules concerning the proper use of these comments, rather like the proper format for writing a letter." or "Authority is prevalent in every aspect of grade school." or "The Skyy Vodka ad is a good example of this combination of sex and status being used to draw men into believing that a product will put excitement into their everyday lives."). Writers of analysis papers tend to present evidence as objectively as possible in order to give the impression that they are showing what is already there, although perhaps what is there is hidden from view.

## WORDS

Writers of analysis papers typically employ objective tone and distanced voice through the words they choose. Along with the use of the word *be,* the words seem to give the impression of pointing out what the writers are observing. Sentences such as the following are used strategically to create this "pointing out" impression with words like *another, typical, many have, example* ("Another interesting usage of syntax by programmers is . . ." or "A typical example of this language is contained in the following sentence." or "Many schools have turned to cameras for an extended version of surveillance." or "This ad is probably the best example of the idea that women are presented as possessions.").

To maintain their credibility, writers will often use qualifying words to modulate their claims and signal their careful presence. For example, writers will typically add qualifying words such as *seems, usually, can be seen as, in many ways,* or *may also*. Such qualifiers let the writer indicate that the analysis is not the absolute final word on the subject but is rather an idea which, while based on solid evidence and inquiry, is nonetheless subject to disagreement. Rhetorically, writers use such qualifications to protect against overgeneralizations and to establish their credibility as careful thinkers.

Examine one paragraph from one of the sample analysis papers for the types of sentences and words used. Can you list examples of declarative sentences, complex ones, ones using a form of *be* as a verb, words that are pointers, abstract, and qualifiers? How would you characterize the kinds of words and sentences the writer uses? How well do these achieve the desired tone or effect?

## Interpreting the Generic Expectations of the Analysis Paper

What we have just described are some general patterns commonly found in analysis papers. Writers, of course, employ multiple variations on these patterns, so any attempt to devise strict directions based on these patterns will be doomed to fail. Yet the patterns and expectations are clear enough to enable us to move to the next step of genre analysis: Interpreting what these patterns reveal about the situation and scene of the analysis paper. What do the generic features we just described tell us about the scene of writing (the writing course) in which the analysis paper is used? What assumptions underscore these features? And how can we identify some of these assumptions so that we can eventually use them to make more informed writing choices?

In analyzing the generic patterns of analysis papers, we are basically engaged in the same activity that writers of analysis papers are engaged in—trying to establish and develop a claim based on the evidence we have identified. We have collected the evidence about analysis papers, and now we have to ask ourselves, "So what?" What does this evidence mean?

As it turns out, just as with most analysis papers, a number of legitimate claims can be developed based on the patterns we have found in analysis papers. For example, we could claim that the patterns reveal how the analysis paper positions the writer as a critical observer. Similarly, we could claim that the purpose of analysis papers is to engage or focus on a subject more than a reader, so that the reader takes on the role of onlooker. Or we could be a bit more cynical and claim that the analysis paper breeds a kind of passivity in which writers and readers interpret how things work and why, instead of acting on them, using them, or trying to change them. There are, of course, other claims we could make as well, each of which we would be able to support with evidence we identified in our genre description. For our genre analysis here, we will focus on the claim that the analysis paper encourages an observational stance or attitude, one that is generally highly valued in academic inquiry. Such a stance focuses attention on the subject under study rather than on the reader or writer. In writing analysis papers, students are invited to participate in a form of inquiry that inducts them into the habits of mind that are common across the university: That habit of mind includes a critical sensibility that seeks to complicate what may appear simple and obvious, an unwillingness to accept things as they appear, and a desire to uncover the assumptions behind how things work and why.

To support this claim, we turn to the evidence we have gathered from the genre itself. The most obvious way in which writers of analysis papers establish an observational stance involves the way they approach and present their subject. We noticed this in the introductions, where writers begin analysis papers by describing their subject in fairly objective ways—defining what it is and/or providing some background about it. Rhetorically, the gesture here is one of placing the subject of study before the writer's and readers' eyes—and so presenting it for examination. Words like *notice* and *this example shows* create a pointing out effect that positions the writer at a critical distance from the subject so that he or she can analyze it objectively. The emphasis on logos makes it seem as though the logic is making the case rather than the writer, just as the logical transitions lead the reader through the reasoning as though it is inevitable. When the writer establishes the claim in an analysis paper, it thus seems as if the claim emerged out of the subject of study and logic itself rather than what is actually the case—that the writer has constructed the claim.

To end our analysis, we might restate and then extend our claim's implications. By privileging such an observational stance, analysis papers reflect the academic scene's valuing of the subject of study over the writer or reader. While resumés focus on the writer and argument papers focus on the reader, analysis papers encourage the writer to act as though the *subject* is all that matters. Just as the Patient Medical History Form encouraged doctors to focus on physical symptoms to the exclusion of the emotional, analysis papers encourage students to focus on the logical to the exclusion of the emotional or personal. The genre of the analysis paper also follows a fairly linear, Western form of logic (claim/evidence/analysis) and instills in students the distanced, impersonal, critical habits of mind valued by the college and university scene.

## Writing Activity 9.9

Now that you have identified the patterns and underlying assumptions of the genre of analysis papers, examine the strengths *and possible limitations* of this genre. Drawing on the Questions for Critiquing Genres in Box 7.1 (p. 229), adapt the questions to the genre of analysis papers and determine what you see as the effects of the genre, including its strengths and weaknesses.

Drawing in part on your findings in the Writing Activity above, discuss in groups what other claims one might make on the basis of our analysis of the analysis paper. You might consider one of the alternatives we presented on page 350 or one of your own. How would you use the evidence to support that claim?

# Questions to Guide Writing Analysis Papers

Now that you have a better understanding of what analysis papers typically do and how they reflect and reveal the scene of the writing course in which they are used, how can you turn that understanding into practice? In Box 9.1, we help you apply that genre knowledge to your own writing.

# Analyzing the Argument Paper

Our purpose in describing the analysis paper in such detail, from its generic features to interpreting these features, is not just to teach you how to write better analysis papers, though of course we hope more effective writing is one result. We also wanted to model for you how to analyze an academic genre so that you could analyze other academic genres as you encounter them. For you to practice doing such analysis yourself, we next will invite you to work with your classmates to perform your own analysis of another commonly used genre in writing courses, the argument paper. Knowledge of this genre will further expand your familiarity with your writing course's scene of writing as well as reinforce your developing skills as a genre analyst and writer.

## Box 9.1    *Questions for Writing Analysis Papers*

### Inventing

1. In what way does my writing assignment call for an analysis paper? What appears to be the instructor's purpose in making this assignment? What specifically about analysis am I being asked to learn or practice? What am I being asked to analyze? How am I being asked to analyze it?

2. What subjects might I choose that would lend themselves to analysis? What do I already know about the subjects I might analyze? What thoughts do I already have about the meaning of the subject and the claims I might want to make?

3. What kinds of information do I need to gather to provide evidence for my analysis? Where will I find the information I need for my analysis (library research, Internet research, interviewing people)?

4. Am I finding something I consider important or interesting? Am I working toward a claim that matters to me?

### Drafting

1. How does the assignment direct my drafting? Will I be working alone or collaboratively? Has the assignment specified stages of drafting, so that I will need to have sections ready to submit to my instructor at specified dates? Do I need to have a draft ready for peer review at a particular time?

2. What central claim will I be making in this paper to serve as my controlling idea? What has my analysis led me to understand? Is it one all my evidence links to? Does it answer the "So what?" question?

3. How should I structure my paper? How shall I introduce and conclude my paper? How shall I organize the body?

*Introductory Section:*

- How should I describe my subject?
- What can I say about the subject that will make it worthy of analysis?
- How can I move from my subject to my claim about the subject?

*(continued on next page)*

*Body Section:*

- What are the components of my central claim, the parts that I need to demonstrate?
- What subpoints have I developed that support my central claim?
- In what order should I arrange those subpoints? What organization follows from my central claim?

*Concluding Section:*

- In what ways has the evidence I have analyzed fulfilled the promise I made in my claim? How can I bring the parts of my analysis back together again?
- How can I extend my claim? Are there any parts of the analysis that are not accounted for by my claim? If so, what are these? Is there evidence in my analysis that leads me to qualify my original claim? What is it? What are the implications of my analysis? What does it mean in the larger scheme of things? Does it ask us to rethink some of our assumptions? Does it challenge us to change the way we think and act?

4. How can I appeal to my readers' reasoning? What do my readers already know about this subject? What do I need to write to sound credible, like a rational mind objectively explaining the subject?

5. As I draft, am I using complex transitions to link the evidence to analysis and the analysis to my central claim? Am I guiding my readers through the organization with transitions? Am I remembering to introduce, present, and analyze the evidence? Am I explaining how the evidence relates to my claim?

6. Now that I see how my analysis is connecting to my central claim, do I need to reconsider my central claim? Am I having to force the evidence to support it, or is my evidence supporting subpoints that fit comfortably with my central claim? Do I agree with what I'm claiming? Am I saying what I wanted to say?

## Revising

1. What am I trying to accomplish as I revise this draft? Does the goal that the draft tries to achieve fit with the general goals of analysis papers? How well does my draft meet the goals I was trying to achieve—the goals promised in the introduction and the central claim?

*(continued on next page)*

2. What do readers expect from analysis papers? Has my draft met these expectations? Is it logical and based in reasoning and analysis? Do I seem rational and credible? How well have I guided readers through my reasoning so they see the connections I'm making between evidence and claim? Which reader expectations have been met and which have not?

3. In what ways does my draft seem like other analysis papers, and in what ways does it seem different? Review the description of the genre's features on pages 337–349: Does the draft follow the pattern described for content, structure, format, sentences, and words? If not, have I deliberately varied from those expectations, either to respond to something specific about my task or to resist the genre's expectations?

4. What additional evidence would be helpful to support my claim? How can I get that evidence? What else do I still need to add to my draft?

5. Does my organization of the body make sense for my central claim? Do parts need to be expanded? Deleted? Moved around to fit together more logically?

6. Have I used sentences and words that seem distanced and objective? Have I qualified my statements appropriately?

7. Have I edited the last version carefully for the conventions of Standardized Edited English, including grammar, usage, punctuation, and spelling? Have I cited any sources I used according to the citation system my instructor specified?

8. Have I formatted my text appropriately, using complex transitions, typing it neatly, adding a title and heading? Do my paragraphs look like an appropriate length to be well developed, or should I combine some paragraphs?

## READING THE SCENE AND SITUATION OF ARGUMENT PAPERS

Like analysis papers, argument papers reflect the goals and assumptions of writing courses. Remember that one objective of writing courses is to prepare students for writing in other academic scenes; many of the genres in writing courses thus are designed to teach skills that are valued in the college and university. Not surprisingly for the scene, then, one of the assumptions behind the argument paper is that argumentation, like analysis, is a rhetorical skill that applies in a variety of contexts. While the argument paper may appear most specifically in writing courses, the skills of argumentation on which it is based—clearly stating a claim and supporting that claim with logical and convincing reasons that are appropriate to a given audience—extend beyond the writing course. In fact, in one way or another, most academic genres require writers to construct and develop arguments.

In academic scenes, particularly the scene of the writing course, arguments often take the shape of what we are calling "argument papers," but they also often appear as problem-solution papers, proposals, letters to authorities, or editorials. Editorials are also common, of course, in journalism courses; in business courses, arguments may take the form of a recommendation report, a genre in which writers recommend a course of action such as "Why small businesses should invest in advertising." In public and workplace scenes, argument genres include complaint letters, letters to the editor, letters of application, resumés, and proposals. Complaint letters, for instance, work to convince a given audience to refund a defective product while resumés work to convince an employer that the job applicant is the right person for an advertised position. Exactly how arguments take shape and why they are used depend on the scene of writing and the genre.

Analysis papers and argument papers share many aspects of the writing course situation: Common settings (classrooms), participants (teachers and students), and even in some ways the same subjects (issues, texts, events, people). Their purposes, however, are distinctly different. As we discussed in the last sections, analysis papers involve making claims about their subject of study, with writers trying to arrive at a better understanding of their subject through analysis (for example, how the television show *The Sopranos* exploits negative stereotypes). Argument papers also involve analysis of a subject, but their goal extends beyond understanding the subject. *In an argument paper, the writer takes a stand in relation to the subject* (like why viewers should boycott the television show *The Sopranos*) and may use analysis to clarify or support the claim or to explain the link between the claim and evidence. For example, when writing an argument that the residence hall should adopt a more flexible visitation policy, the writer would need to analyze the advantages and disadvantages of the policy and explain each part of the proposed policy and how it is workable. *In argument papers, analysis is not the end but rather the means to an end, which usually involves trying to convince readers of something.*

While the subjects of argument papers can range widely and cover any issue that is debatable or controversial, the subjects and purposes of argument papers tend to be reader-focused, as reflected in the following purposes of argument papers:

- To convince readers of an issue of concern
- To propose that readers should/should not do X or issue a call for action
- To argue that a problem exists and the writer/reader needs to solve it
- To illustrate to readers how one event/issue brings about another
- To evaluate an issue/problem and persuade readers to accept those evaluations
- To establish criteria and to argue that X meets or does not meet the criteria

Although the primary purpose of arguments is always to convince someone of something, different argument genres have distinct purposes. For example, a letter to an authority typically aims to convince the authority to take some action: For the chancellor of the university to support construction of a new laboratory building, for a representative to vote for a specific bill, for a local business owner to hire more students. An *academic* argument paper seeks not to convince someone to do something (the intention to gain a high grade always simmers beneath the surface, but that goal is achieved by achieving the more explicit purposes of the assignment). Rather, an academic argument paper seeks to convince the reader that the writer's position is sound, credible, a reasonable position based on an interpretation of the evidence. Not only your teacher but also your classmate readers need to be persuaded that you have considered the issues carefully and honestly and that your position reflects a logical and complex understanding of the topic.

## Writing Activity 9.10

Compare the argument papers with the various argument genres that we have studied in previous chapters: Editorials (Chapter 1), complaint letters (Chapter 2). You might also want to look ahead to the argument genres in later chapters, such as the letter of application and resumé, proposals, and reports or the letters to the editor and editorials. After examining these argument genres, write 2 to 3 paragraphs in which you explore how these different genres respond to different situations (subjects, purposes, settings, and readers). What role does scene (the writing course scene vs. scenes outside the writing course) play in shaping these differing argument genres?

## ROGERIAN AND CLASSICAL ARGUMENT

Part of persuading your readers in all arguments involves addressing "opposing arguments," finding ways to deal with the positions that other people take that might not agree with your own. How you deal with others' positions depends in many ways on the readers and purposes in your particular argument (for example, are you trying to persuade someone to change his or her mind or just to consider an issue not yet recognized?). It also depends on your view of how people are persuaded.

Two common approaches to argument reflect two different perspectives on how to persuade people. One perspective, based in classical rhetoric and a tradition of classical argumentation, treats opposing arguments as things to be countered, dismissed, proven false, or minimized. Another perspective, based in part in a therapy developed by the psychologist Carl Rogers, treats opposing arguments as sources for common ground, as things to be set beside the writer's position in order to find where the two positions can overlap or where a third position can be found that permits both arguments to persist.

**Classical argumentation,** the basis for much academic writing, derives from ancient rhetorical studies of the art of persuasion. *Based mostly on deductive reasoning, the argument begins with a direct statement of the claim (controlling idea), followed by reasons and evidence to support the claim. In order to explore an argument from various angles, the writer then takes opposing views into account and identifies probable counterarguments*—positions directly opposed to the claim. For example, if you want to argue that school uniforms should be mandatory in your local high school, you might follow this claim with reasons that support this assertion: The reduction of peer pressure and social stigmatization, an increased sense of community, and a safer and more productive learning environment. Following a classical argumentation approach, you would also think through opposing arguments and reservations, and would anticipate probable objections, such as concerns about increased conformity and the loss of individual expression. Particularly if you are aiming your argument at readers who are uninformed or undecided on your issue, the classical approach—focusing on arguments both for and against—is an effective strategy.

*In Rogerian argument, writers seek to understand what others believe in order to find places where opposing positions can agree.* One position need not be defeated in order for the other position to win, to use the war metaphor so common in discussions of argument. And people need not change their basic beliefs in order to find points of agreement from which to build a common understanding. Suppose, for example, that you want city commissioners to permit a homeless shelter, while neighbors of the proposed shelter want commissioners to deny the permit. Working to understand the neighbors' concerns might enable you to share their view, to see that the shelter needs to be operated in such a way as not to disrupt the neighborhood. Your argument to the commission might then include not only the reasons a homeless shelter is needed, or even the desirability of that particular location; it might also and more effectively include the ways the shelter can be established to direct homeless traffic away from the neighborhood, to increase security at the shelter, and to disband if it proves harmful to its surroundings after a trial period. If the neighbors also adopt a Rogerian perspective and attempt to understand your position, they might argue more effectively not only that the shelter might harm the neighborhood but also that a shelter could be established in another location to serve that needy population. In both cases, acknowledging the legitimacy of the others' arguments leads not to defeating the others but to finding positions that can meet the beliefs, values, and goals of all sides.

This Rogerian view of argument seems especially appropriate in situations where the participants need to cooperate or where solutions must serve multiple interested parties. Even issues that are firmly entrenched into opposing sides—issues like abortion, capital punishment, or gun control—might be moveable only through Rogerian approaches to find common ground: The common concern over the welfare of mothers and children, for example, or the common desire to keep our society both safe and free.

Some believe that all arguments should take Rogerian approaches in order to build a kinder, gentler argument. Others believe that Rogerian argument is less effective in situations where altering your position might weaken it too much, where encompassing the concerns of others might mean encompassing beliefs or values that you do not wish to support even in minor ways, or where the opposing arguments are weak and do not merit inclusion. Some also believe that people are best persuaded through clear opposition of viewpoints, through strong contestation that demonstrates that one position is superior to another. This more traditional view of argument, as we discussed earlier, often takes the form of a classical argument structure, one that argues its points through defeating the points of its opponents. Opposing arguments are countered through proving the opposing position either false, misguided, or unimportant.

Not surprisingly, these two approaches to argument (Rogerian and classical) often appear in different argument genres. More likely to use Rogerian argument are problem-solution papers and proposals that appeal to a shared vision or common set of values in order to convince readers to implement the solution or adopt the proposal; editorials and argument papers that appeal to a wider range of potentially uninformed or undecided readers more commonly use classical argument. Either can appear in any argument genre, however, for these approaches reflect just as much the beliefs of the writer as they do the expectations of the situation. Some people tend to argue to defeat, while others tend to argue to negotiate. If you can gain an understanding of and facility in both Rogerian and classical argument, you will be the most flexible and most likely to be able to adapt to different situations.

## Writing Activity 9.11

Do you tend to favor either Rogerian or classical argument? Does one approach tend to convince you more than another? Can you think of a time when you changed your mind, or when you were able to change someone else's mind? Which argument approach was used then?

## Collaborative Activity 9.6

In small groups, generate a list of campus problems or issues of concern at your institution. Then choose one issue from the list, and construct a claim that is arguable. Decide who would be the most appropriate audience to hear your claim, and then sketch out (in outline form) two approaches to the argument: (1) the classical argument approach (including reasons to support your argument and refutations of opposing arguments) and (2) the Rogerian approach (identifying common ground and areas of agreement). Based on your topic and audience, which approach seems more effective? Why?

## Collaborative Activity 9.7

As a class, discuss with your instructor his or her objectives in using argument papers in a writing course. (If your teacher prefers that you learn how to write another argument genre and provides a different set of samples of that genre, you can conduct all of the Collaborative Activities in this section on an argument genre other than the argument paper.) Using Box 1.2: Guidelines for Observing and Describing Scenes (pp. 44–45), as well as the questions on situation from Box 2.1: Guidelines for Analyzing a Genre (pp. 93–94), first work in small groups to decide what questions you should ask the class and instructor in order to better understand the scene and situation of argument papers. Then conduct your discussion as a class, assigning individuals in your group the tasks of asking questions and recording answers. After the discussion, reflect on what you learned about argument papers; then synthesize and compile these reflections into a guide sheet or "tip" sheet (your teacher may choose to compile these into one set of guidelines).

To help you build on your knowledge of analysis and apply it to argument papers, we now invite you to conduct your own genre analysis of argument papers. We include several samples of argument papers, all written by students in first-year writing courses. Working with your classmates, use these samples to work through your analysis. Along the way, you will have an opportunity to identify patterns in the genre, to interpret what these patterns mean, and to develop strategies for using that knowledge to make more effective writing choices when you write argument papers.

# Describing Generic Features of Argument Papers

With some understanding of the scene and situation of argument papers, the next step in trying to gain a more critical understanding of the genre involves identifying and describing its generic features. What follows is an explanation of the features that you will examine in greater detail when you perform your analysis of the argument paper, along with a few hints to get you started.

## CONTENT

Similar to an analysis paper, the content of an argument paper revolves around a central claim—an argument that the writer has formulated about his or her subject. The claim stakes out the writer's position on the subject and generates the direction and content of the argument. For example, a **causal claim**, such as "Violent behavior in children is caused by the violence they encounter through playing video games," will likely begin by providing examples of violent themes and images in video games and will then go on to examine the cause/effect relationship among these themes and images and violent behavior in children. Claims may also be **evaluative**, based on values, beliefs, or personal judgment. For example, the claim that "*The Godfather*" is the most accomplished film about mob life ever made" is a claim that makes a value judgment. Typically, evaluative arguments will go on to define specific criteria by which to develop and support this claim. Finally, some claims may make **recommendations** and may convince the readers to carry out a solution to a problem, change or adopt a policy, or take a particular action. A claim based on a recommendation, such as "The minimum wage is too low and needs to be raised," indicates the direction and content of the argument, which will go on to define the problem caused by minimum wage falling behind cost of living and then define a solution and specific plan for enacting the solution, as well as providing justification for the solution.

To argue any of the above claims successfully, you will need to develop the body of the argument with convincing evidence and reasons. One popular method for developing arguments is the **Toulmin method.** The twentieth-century British philosopher Stephen Toulmin wrote a treatise on argumentation entitled *The Uses of Argument* (1958) that describes a method for evaluating the reasonableness of arguments. Toulmin's approach, based on a courtroom model, has been modified to apply to writing arguments as well as analyzing them. According to this approach, all arguments consist of (1) a claim that is controversial or debatable, (2) reasons to support or justify the claim, (3) evidence and data (personal experience, anecdotes, facts, authorities) to support the reasons, and (4) warrants—analyses or assumptions that link the evidence and support to the claim. The following example illustrates this method of developing arguments:

---

*Claim:* Schools should reduce the size of classes.

*Reason:* Students benefit from more one-on-one interaction with teachers.

*Evidence:* Studies link individualized attention to better grades and performance on standardized tests.

*Warrants:* Better grades and performance on standardized tests are things we should strive for.

---

In this case, the **warrant**—the value, belief, or principle that the audience has to hold if the soundness of the argument is to be accepted or *warranted*—is that grades and standardized tests are accurate markers of student learning and hence anything that can help us improve performances in these areas should be supported. Another possible warrant might be that one-on-one interaction between teacher and student is indeed beneficial to learning—another assumption of the above argument. If this link is not assumed, the writer may need to provide additional analysis and explanation that establishes the validity of this warrant and makes this connection.

As you examine the argument, concentrate on the subjects that lend themselves to argument and examine the central claim made about that subject and the use of reasons, evidence, warrants, and analysis to support the claim. You might consider to what extent the type of claim dictates the direction and content of the argument.

## RHETORICAL APPEALS

Whichever approach you take toward others' positions, you will argue most effectively by appealing to your readers' interests and concerns through *logos*, *pathos*, and *ethos*. Arguments use all three types of appeals, although they may emphasize one type over the others. You may find that argument papers in writing courses depend heavily on logos, on the reason and logic that best supports the writer's position. The persuasiveness of the writer's position may also depend on ethos—the credibility, authority, and trustworthiness of the writer. And since many arguments are based on values or beliefs, arguments also heavily rely on pathos or appeals to the audience's values, beliefs, and emotions. Effective arguments convince readers through a combination of logic, emotion, and the credibility of the writer. As you read the sample argument papers, examine the use of appeals, and consider whether certain types of claims lead to an emphasis on a particular appeal.

## STRUCTURE

While the structure of argument papers will depend upon your purpose, audience, approach (classical or Rogerian), and the nature of your claim (causal, evaluative, or recommendation), many academic papers follow the classical argument form or some variation of this. Classical rhetorician Aristotle came up with a four-part structure for argument consisting of an introduction, statement of the claim, proof of the claim, and conclusion, and this was later modified into a six-part structure:

1. Introduction—an attention-grabber or memorable scene

2. Background/explanation of the issue

3. Statement of the claim (the thesis or controlling idea)

4. Presentation of the reasons to support the claim

5. Summary of and refutation of opposing views

6. Conclusion (summary or call to action)

As you examine the sample papers, notice how they either follow or modify this structure. Consider how differing claims dictate different structures.

## FORMAT

Similar to the analysis paper, the argument paper functions for the writing course scene and uses the same format common to academic papers: Neatly typed, double-spaced, each page numbered, paragraphs indented, with a title and a heading indicating the writer's name, course number, and date. You may want to consult our previous discussion in this chapter of the analysis paper format and consider whether or not the discussion of transitions applies to the argument paper as well. As you read the sample papers, you might also consider how various features of layout and format of the paper could make the information more accessible and improve readability.

## SENTENCES AND WORDS

When trying to convince readers through your use of language, paying close attention to your construction of sentences and choice of words is crucial. To create a serious and credible ethos, most writers of argument papers will adopt a fairly formal style with sentences that are longer and more complex. In addition, to appeal to emotion, writers will often use descriptive language or words that carry a powerful emotional impact. However, to maintain ethos, it is important to avoid using words that might manipulate readers through their powerful emotional overtones or through slanted or biased language. For example, an argument on abortion that refers to "baby killing" may risk alienating readers, as would an argument for pay equity among men and women that refers to "feminazis" or an argument supporting drilling for oil in the Alaskan Wildlife Refuge that refers to "environmental wackos." Such emotionally laden terms often defeat the purpose of reasoned and logical argument. As you read the sample argument papers, consider the use of words that seem especially powerful and persuasive as well as any that seem to detract from the argument or from the writer's credibility.

## Collaborative Activity 9.8

Take a close look at the sample argument papers we have included. Then, using the questions outlined in step 3 of Box 2.1: Guidelines for Analyzing Genres (p. 94), describe the features we have been discussing in more detail. If your teacher does not assign another approach, to make the process more manageable we suggest the class divide the work and compile results:

1. Divide the class into six groups.
2. Assign each group one of the types of features in Box 2.1—content, rhetorical appeals, structure, format, sentences, and diction.
3. Have each group work through the sample argument papers, studying the type of feature assigned. They should look for similarities across all the papers. For example, the group working on content, using the questions in Box 2.1, seeks patterns in what kinds of content is included and excluded, what kinds of examples and evidence are used, and how the content is treated in all the papers.
4. Ask each group to report their results to the class as a whole, either in written or oral form. Since features can overlap, be sure to allow members of other groups to contribute their insights into the patterns they see.

## Writing Activity 9.12

Since you will all later need the information about generic patterns of the argument paper, write your own record of the patterns of generic features that the class discovers. You might wish to create a list of features, a brief manual that compiles lists and examples from the sample papers, or a discussion of the features like the one we provided for analysis papers. You might also want to incorporate some of the information about the scene and situation of argument papers that you gathered in Collaborative Activity 9.7 (pp. 360–361).

# Interpreting Generic Expectations of Argument Papers

To construct some ideas about what the patterns you discovered mean, we suggest that you again work with classmates to develop multiple interpretations. Working in the same groups that described the patterns, or the method your teacher assigned you instead, work through the questions outlined in step 4 of Box 2.1: Guidelines for Analyzing Genres (p. 94). Analyze what the patterns you have just described mean. In general, you are seeking answers to the following questions:

- What do the patterns tell us about the scenes of the writing course or college and university in which they are used?
- What do they reveal about the situation of the argument paper, including the assumptions and expectations of the people who use them?

Remember, your goal in performing this kind of analysis is to uncover the underlying assumptions of the patterns and to develop a claim based on them. The patterns themselves thus become the subject of your analysis. They are the evidence you will use to support your claim. Therefore, look carefully at these patterns as you try to answer the questions in step 4 of Box 2.1.

After your group has worked its way through those questions, discuss what claims your group might make about the situation or scene of the argument paper. Select your strongest claims to present to the class as a whole, and discuss as a class what evidence supports each of the claims. You might wish to compare your claims to the claim we made regarding the analysis paper in the section, "Interpreting the Generic Expectations of the Analysis Paper" (p. 350). Keep in mind that such analyses are always open to multiple interpretations, not one right or best answer. Your goal is to understand as much as you can about the argument paper by exploring as many possible interpretations as the evidence supports.

## Writing Activity 9.13

Select a claim about the argument paper that you find most promising or interesting, either one presented to the class or one of your own devising. What sort of insight does it reveal into the purpose and meaning of the genre? After developing your claim, explain how the evidence (the patterns your class identified in the argument paper) supports your claim.

## Collaborative Activity 9.9

In small groups, trade the claims about the argument paper that you worked with in Writing Activity 9.13, and evaluate those claims. Drawing on the questions for critiquing genres in Box 7.1 (p. 229), formulate at least three new claims about the limitations and possibilities of the genre of the argument paper and how it succeeds and fails as a genre.

# Writing within the Generic Expectations of Argument Papers

Now that you have read the scene, situation, and features of the argument paper genre, you can better understand the choices you can make as a writer of argument. Think not only about what you would need to write in order to meet reader expectations but also about where you found variation in the genre—where you might make different choices in order to achieve different purposes or to challenge the genre. In general, as you turn to writing the genre, you want to discover answers to the following questions about inventing, drafting, and revising argument papers:

- Based on what I know about the argument paper, what strategies should I employ during the invention stage? What kind of subject should I seek? How should I approach my subject? What kind of controlling idea should I develop? What kind of research should I do? What kind of stance should I take in relation to it?

- What drafting strategies should I use? That is, what choices should I be making as I work to persuade my reader? What appeals should I emphasize? How should I be organizing the introductory section, the body section, and the concluding section? What are some typical strategies I could use to present evidence? What should my paper be sounding like?

- What revising strategies would be most appropriate for me to use? That is, how should I target my revisions? What expectations do I need to make sure I have met?

Asking yourself such questions based on your knowledge of the genre will enable you to make more informed and effective choices as a writer of argument papers in your writing course.

## Writing Activity 9.14

Make a list of the questions you need to ask as you write an argument paper. You might wish to use Box 9.1: Questions for Writing Analysis Papers (pp. 353–355) as a guide to how to apply the general questions to what you have learned about the argument paper.

## Collaborative Activity 9.10

Compare with your classmates your questions for writing argument papers. Work to compile one set of questions that contains the best of all your lists. Be prepared to share your compiled set of questions with the class.

We will work with you to analyze one other academic genre common to many writing courses, the researched position paper, a form of argument paper. With the understanding of these three academic genres—the analysis paper, argument paper, and researched position paper—you should be well prepared to write effectively in your writing course. You should also have learned how to apply genre analysis in academic scenes so that you can encounter any academic situation in the future, read its scene and generic features, and make writing choices effective for that situation.

# Index

Note: Information presented in tables and figures is denoted by *t* or *f.*